Oracle Press™

Oracle Database
10g SQL

ORACLE®   *Oracle Press*™

Oracle Database 10g SQL

Jason Price

McGraw-Hill/Osborne

New York   Chicago   San Francisco
Lisbon   London   Madrid   Mexico City   Milan
New Delhi   San Juan   Seoul   Singapore   Sydney   Toronto

The **McGraw·Hill** Companies

McGraw-Hill/Osborne
2100 Powell Street, 10th Floor
Emeryville, California 94608
U.S.A.

To arrange bulk purchase discounts for sales promotions, premiums, or fund-raisers, please contact **McGraw-Hill**/Osborne at the above address. For information on translations or book distributors outside the U.S.A., please see the International Contact Information page immediately following the index of this book.

Oracle Database 10*g* SQL

1234567890 FGR FGR 01987654

ISBN 0-07-222981-0

Publisher
   Brandon A. Nordin

Vice President & Associate Publisher
   Scott Rogers

Acquisitions Editor
   Lisa McClain

Project Editors
   Lisa Wolters-Broder, Mark Karmendy

Acquisitions Coordinator
   Athena Honore

Technical Editor
   Ron Hardman

Copy Editor
   Lunaea Weatherstone

Proofreader
   Claire Splan

Indexer
   Valerie Robbins

Composition
   Apollo Publishing Services, Tara A. Davis

Illustrators
   Kathleen Edwards, Melinda Lytle, Michael Mueller

Series Design
   Jani Beckwith, Peter F. Hancik

Cover Series Design
   Sarah F. Hinks

This book was composed with Corel VENTURA™ Publisher.

This book is dedicated to my family.
Even though you're far away,
you are still in my heart.

About the Author

Jason Price is a freelance consultant and former product manager of Oracle Corporation. He has contributed to many of Oracle's products, including the database, the application server, and several of the CRM applications. Jason is an Oracle Certified Database Administrator and Application Developer, and has more than 10 years of experience in the software industry. Jason has written many books on Oracle, Java, and .NET. Jason holds a Bachelor of Science degree (with honors) in physics from the University of Bristol, England.

Contents at a Glance

Contents

ix

Acknowledgments

Thanks to the wonderful people at McGraw-Hill/Osborne, including Lisa McClain, Athena Honore, and Lisa Wolters-Broder. Thanks also to Ron Hardman for his thorough technical review, and to Geoff Lee at Oracle for reviewing the book and acting as the Oracle sponsor.

Introduction

Today's database management systems implement a standard language known as *Structured Query Language*, or SQL. Among other things, SQL allows you to retrieve, add, update, and delete information in a database. SQL is a standard language recognized by the American National Standards Institute (ANSI), and you can use SQL to access an Oracle, SQL Server, DB2, or MySQL database. In this book, you'll learn how to truly master SQL, and you'll find a wealth of practical examples. You can also get all the scripts and programs featured in this book online (see the later section "Retrieving the Examples" for details).

With this book, you will

- Master standard SQL, as well as the extensions developed by Oracle Corporation for use with the specific features of the Oracle database.

- Explore PL/SQL (Procedural Language/SQL), which is built on top of SQL and enables you to write programs that contain SQL statements.

- Use SQL*Plus to execute SQL statements, scripts, and reports; SQL*Plus is a tool that allows you to interact with the database.

- Execute queries, inserts, updates, and deletes against a database.

- Create database tables, sequences, indexes, views, and users.

- Perform transactions containing multiple SQL statements.

- Define database object types and create object tables to handle advanced data.

- Use large objects to store up to 128 terabytes of character and binary data, and pointers to external files.

- Perform complex calculations using analytic functions.

- Use all the very latest Oracle10*g* features, such as the `BINARY_FLOAT` and `BINARY_DOUBLE` types, the `MODEL` clause, and the extensions to large objects and collections.

- Learn about database security.

- Implement high-performance tuning techniques to make your SQL statements really fly.

- Learn the basics of running SQL using Java through JDBC.

This book contains 16 chapters and one appendix.

Chapter 1: Introduction

In this chapter, you'll learn about relational databases, be introduced to SQL, see a few simple queries, use SQL*Plus to execute queries, and briefly see PL/SQL.

Chapter 2: Retrieving Information from Database Tables

You'll explore how to retrieve information from one or more database tables using SELECT statements, use arithmetic expressions to perform calculations, filter rows using a WHERE clause, and sort the rows retrieved from a table.

Chapter 3: Using Simple Functions

In this chapter, you'll learn about some of the Oracle database's built-in functions. A function accepts zero or more input parameters and returns an output parameter. Functions allow you to do things like compute averages and square roots of numbers.

Chapter 4: Storing and Processing Dates and Times

You'll learn how the Oracle database processes and stores dates and times, collectively known as datetimes. You'll also learn about timestamps that allow you to store a specific date and time, and time intervals that allow you to store a length of time.

Chapter 5: Using SQL*Plus

In this chapter, you'll use SQL*Plus to view a table's structure, edit a SQL statement, save and run scripts, format column output, define and use variables, and create reports.

Chapter 6: Subqueries

You'll learn how to place a SELECT statement within an outer SQL statement. The inner SELECT statement is known as a subquery. You'll learn about the different types of subqueries, and see how subqueries allow you to build up very complex statements from simple components.

Chapter 7: Advanced Queries

In this chapter, you'll learn how to perform queries containing advanced operators and functions such as: set operators that combine rows returned by multiple queries, the TRANSLATE() function to convert characters in one string to characters in another string, the DECODE() function to search a set of values for a certain value, the CASE expression to perform if-then-else logic, and the ROLLUP and CUBE clauses to return rows containing subtotals. You'll learn about the analytic functions that enable you to perform complex calculations such as finding the top-selling product type for each month, the top salespersons, and so on. You'll see how to perform queries against data that is organized into a hierarchy. Finally, you'll explore the new Oracle10g MODEL clause to perform inter-row calculations.

Chapter 8: Changing Table Contents

You'll learn how to add, modify, and remove rows using the INSERT, UPDATE, and DELETE statements, and how to make the results of your transactions permanent using the COMMIT statement or undo their results entirely using the ROLLBACK statement. You'll also learn how an Oracle database can process multiple transactions at the same time.

Chapter 9: Database Security

In this chapter, you'll learn about database users and see how privileges are used to enable users to perform specific tasks in the database.

Chapter 10: Creating Tables, Sequences, Indexes, and Views

You'll learn about tables and sequences, which generate a series of numbers, and indexes, which act like an index in a book and allow you quick access to rows. You'll also learn about views, which are predefined queries on one or more tables. Among other benefits, views allow you to hide complexity from a user, and implement another layer of security by only allowing a view to access a limited set of data in the tables.

Chapter 11: Introducing PL/SQL Programming

In this chapter, you'll explore PL/SQL, which is built on top of SQL and enables you to write stored programs in the database that contain SQL statements. PL/SQL is a third-generation language and contains standard programming constructs.

Chapter 12: Database Objects

You'll learn how to create database object types, which may contain attributes and methods. You'll use object types to define column objects and object tables, and see how to manipulate objects using SQL and PL/SQL.

Chapter 13: Collections

In this chapter, you'll learn how to create collection types, which may contain multiple elements. You'll use collection types to define columns in tables, and see how to manipulate collections using SQL and PL/SQL.

Chapter 14: Large Objects

You'll learn about large objects, which can be used to store up to 128 terabytes of character and binary data or point to an external file. You'll also learn about the older LONG types which are still supported in Oracle10*g* for backwards compatibility.

Chapter 15: Running SQL Using Java

In this chapter, you'll learn the basics of running SQL using Java through the Java Database Connectivity (JDBC) applications programming interface, which is the glue that allows a Java program to access a database.

Chapter 16: High Performance SQL Tuning

In this final chapter, you'll see SQL tuning tips that you can use to shorten the length of time your queries take to execute. You'll also learn about the Oracle optimizer and examine how to pass hints to the optimizer.

Appendix: Oracle Data Types

This appendix shows the data types available in Oracle SQL and PL/SQL.

Intended Audience

This book is suitable for the following readers:

- Developers who need to write SQL and PL/SQL

- Database administrators who need in-depth knowledge of SQL

- Business users who need to write SQL queries to get information from their organization's database

- Technical managers or consultants who need an introduction to SQL and PL/SQL

No prior knowledge of the Oracle database, SQL, or PL/SQL is assumed: you can find everything you need to know to become a master in this book.

Retrieving the Examples

All the SQL scripts, programs, and other files used in this book can be downloaded from the Oracle Press website at www.OraclePressBooks.com. The files are contained in a zip file. Once you've downloaded the zip file, you open it using WinZip and select the Extract option from the Actions menu. This will create a directory named `sql_book` that contains the following three subdirectories:

- **SQL**   Contains the SQL scripts used throughout the book, including scripts to create and populate the example database tables

- **sample_files**   Contains the sample files used in Chapter 14

- **Java**   Contains the Java programs used in Chapter 15

Have fun, and I hope you enjoy this book!

CHAPTER
1

Introduction

In this chapter, you will

- Learn about relational databases.

- Be introduced to the Structured Query Language (SQL), which is used to access a database.

- Use SQL*Plus, Oracle's interactive text-based tool for running SQL statements.

- Briefly see PL/SQL, Oracle's procedural programming language built around SQL. PL/SQL allows you to develop programs that are stored in the database.

Let's plunge in and consider what a relational database is.

What Is a Relational Database?

The concept of a relational database is not new. It was originally developed back in 1970 by Dr. E.F. Codd. He laid down the theory of relational databases in his seminal paper entitled "A Relational Model of Data for Large Shared Data Banks" published in *Communications of the ACM* (Association for Computing Machinery), Vol. 13, No. 6, June 1970.

The basic concepts of a relational database are fairly easy to understand. A *relational database* is a collection of related information that has been organized into structures known as *tables*. Each table contains *rows* that are further organized into *columns*. These tables are stored in the database in structures known as *schemas*, which are areas where database users may store their tables. Each user may also choose to grant permissions to other users to access their tables.

Most of us are familiar with data being stored in tables—stock prices and train timetables are sometimes organized into tables. An example used in one of the schemas in this book is a table that records customer information for a hypothetical store. Part of this table consists of columns containing the customer's first name, last name, date of birth (dob), and phone number:

```
first_name last_name  dob          phone
---------- ---------- -----------  -----------
John       Brown      01-JAN-1965  800-555-1211
Cynthia    Green      05-FEB-1968  800-555-1212
Steve      White      16-MAR-1971  800-555-1213
Gail       Black                   800-555-1214
Doreen     Blue       20-MAY-1970
```

This table could be stored in a variety of forms: a piece of paper in a filing cabinet or ledger or in the file system of a computer, for example. An important point to note is that the *information* that makes up a database (in the form of tables) is different from the system used to access that information. The system used to access a database is known as a *database management system*.

In the case of a database consisting of pieces of paper, the database management system might be a set of alphabetically indexed cards in a filing cabinet. For a database accessed using a computer, the database management system is the software that manages the files stored in the file system of the computer. The Oracle database is one such piece of software; other examples include SQL Server, DB2, and MySQL.

Of course, every database must have some way to get data in and out of it, preferably using a common language understood by all databases. Today's database management systems implement a standard language known as *Structured Query Language*, or SQL. Among other things, SQL allows you to retrieve, add, update, and delete information in a database.

Introducing the Structured Query Language (SQL)

Structured Query Language (SQL) is the standard language designed to access relational databases. SQL is pronounced either as the word "sequel" or as the letters "S-Q-L." (I prefer "sequel" as it's quicker to say.)

SQL is based on the groundbreaking work of Dr. E.F. Codd, with the first implementation of SQL being developed by IBM in the mid-1970s. IBM was conducting a research project known as System R, and SQL was born from that project. Later in 1979, a company then known as Relational Software Inc. (known today as Oracle Corporation) released the first commercial version of SQL. SQL is now fully standardized and recognized by the American National Standards Institute (ANSI). You can use SQL to access an Oracle, SQL Server, DB2, or MySQL database.

SQL uses a simple syntax that is easy to learn and use. You'll see some simple examples of its use in this chapter. There are five types of SQL statements, outlined in the following list:

- **Query statements**   Allow you to retrieve rows stored in database tables. You write a query using the SQL SELECT statement.

- **Data Manipulation Language (DML) statements**   Allow you to modify the contents of tables. There are three DML statements:

  - **INSERT**   Allows you to add rows to a table.

  - **UPDATE**   Allows you to change a row.

  - **DELETE**   Allows you to remove rows.

- **Data Definition Language (DDL) statements**   Allow you to define the data structures, such as tables, that make up a database. There are five basic types of DDL statements:

  - **CREATE**   Allows you to create a database structure. For example, CREATE TABLE is used to create a table; another example is CREATE USER, which is used to create a database user.

  - **ALTER**   Allows you to modify a database structure. For example, ALTER TABLE is used to modify a table.

  - **DROP**   Allows you to remove a database structure. For example, DROP TABLE is used to remove a table.

  - **RENAME**   Allows you to change the name of a table.

  - **TRUNCATE**   Allows you to delete the entire contents of a table.

- **Transaction Control (TC) statements** Allow you to permanently record the changes made to the rows stored in a table or undo those changes. There are three TC statements:

  - `COMMIT` Allows you to permanently record changes made to rows.

  - `ROLLBACK` Allows you to undo changes made to rows.

  - `SAVEPOINT` Allows you to set a "savepoint" to which you can roll back changes made to rows.

- **Data Control Language (DCL) statements** Allow you to change the permissions on database structures. There are two DCL statements:

  - `GRANT` Allows you to give another user access to your database structures, such as tables.

  - `REVOKE` Allows you to prevent another user from accessing to your database structures, such as tables.

There are many ways to run SQL statements and get results back from the database, some of which include programs written using Oracle Forms and Reports. SQL statements may also be embedded within programs written in other languages, such as Oracle's Pro*C, which allows you to add SQL statements to a C program. You can also add SQL statements to a Java program though JDBC; for more details see my book *Oracle9i JDBC Programming* (Oracle Press, 2002).

Oracle also has a tool called SQL*Plus that allows you to enter SQL statements using the keyboard or to supply a file that contains SQL statements and run those statements. SQL*Plus enables you to conduct a "conversation" with the database because you can enter SQL statements and view the results returned by the database. You'll be introduced to SQL*Plus in the next section.

Using SQL*Plus

There are two versions of SQL*Plus: the Windows version and the command-line version. You may use the command-line version of SQL*Plus with any operating system on which the Oracle database runs. If you're at all familiar with the Oracle database, chances are that you're already familiar with SQL*Plus. If you're not, don't worry: you'll learn how to use SQL*Plus in this book.

In the next two sections, you'll learn how to start each version of SQL*Plus, beginning with the Windows version. After you've learned how to start SQL*Plus, you'll see how to run a query against the database.

Starting the Windows Version of SQL*Plus

If you are using Windows, you may start SQL*Plus by clicking Start and selecting Programs | Oracle | Application Development | SQL*Plus. Figure 1-1 shows the Log On dialog box for SQL*Plus running on Windows. Enter **scott** for the user name and **tiger** for the password (scott is an example user that is contained in most Oracle databases). The host string is used to tell SQL*Plus where the database is running. If you are running the database on your own computer, you'll typically leave the host string blank—this causes SQL*Plus to attempt to connect to a database on the same machine on which SQL*Plus is running. If the database isn't running on your machine, you should speak with your database administrator (DBA). Click OK to continue.

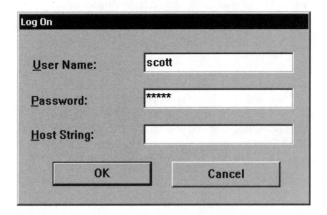

FIGURE 1-1. *The SQL*Plus Log On dialog box*

NOTE
If you can't log on using "scott" and "tiger," speak with your DBA.
They'll be able to provide you with a user_name, password, *and*
host_string *for the purposes of this example.*

After you've clicked OK and successfully logged on to the database, you'll see the SQL*Plus window through which you can interact with the database. Figure 1-2 shows the SQL*Plus window.

Starting the Command-Line Version of SQL*Plus

To start the command-line version of SQL*Plus, you may use the sqlplus command. The full syntax for the sqlplus command is

```
sqlplus [user_name[/password[@host_string]]]
```

where

- *user_name* specifies the name of the database user
- *password* specifies the password for the database user
- *host_string* specifies the database you want to connect to

The following are examples of issuing the `sqlplus` command:

```
sqlplus scott/tiger
sqlplus scott/tiger@orcl
```

NOTE
*If you are using SQL*Plus with the Windows operating system, the Oracle installer automatically adds SQL*Plus to your path. If you are using a non-Windows operating system, you must either be in the same directory as the SQL*Plus program to run it or, better still, have added the program to your path. If you need help with that, talk to your system administrator.*

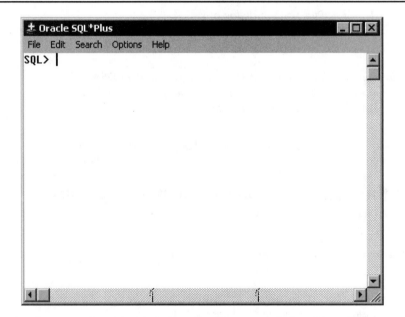

FIGURE 1-2. *The SQL*Plus window*

Performing a SELECT Statement Using SQL*Plus

Once you're logged on to the database using SQL*Plus, try entering the following SELECT statement that returns the current date from the database:

```
SELECT SYSDATE FROM dual;
```

SYSDATE is a built-in Oracle function that returns the current date, and the dual table is a built-in table that contains a single row. You can use the dual table to perform simple queries whose results are not retrieved from a specific table.

NOTE
*SQL statements directly entered into SQL*Plus are terminated using a semicolon character (;).*

Figure 1-3 shows the results of this SELECT statement in SQL*Plus running on Windows. As you can see from the previous figure, the result of the query displays the current date from the database.

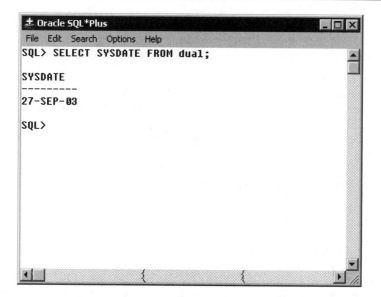

FIGURE 1-3. *Executing a SQL SELECT statement using SQL*Plus*

You can edit your last SQL statement in SQL*Plus by entering EDIT. This is useful when you make a mistake or you want to make a change to your SQL statement. In Windows, when you enter EDIT you are taken to the Notepad application; you then use Notepad to edit your SQL statement. When you exit Notepad and save your statement, the statement is passed to SQL*Plus where you can re-execute it.

NOTE
*You'll learn more about editing SQL statements using SQL*Plus in Chapter 5.*

The SQL*Plus Worksheet

You can also enter SQL statements using the SQL*Plus worksheet, which has an improved user interface. If you are using Windows, you can start SQL*Plus by clicking Start and selecting Programs | Oracle | Application Development | SQL*Plus Worksheet. Figure 1-4 shows the SQL*Plus Worksheet window once you've logged on to the database. If you have SQL*Plus Worksheet installed, go ahead and log on to the database as the scott user, enter the SELECT SYSDATE FROM dual, query, and select Execute from the Worksheet menu.

TIP
You can also execute a statement by clicking the Execute button (it has a lightning bolt on it). You can also press F5 on your keyboard to execute a statement.

Figure 1-4 shows the result of running the query that retrieves the current date. Notice that the top part of the window shows the SQL statement executed and the lower part shows the result of the executed statement.

In the next section, you'll learn how to create a fictional store database schema.

Creating the Store Schema

Most of the examples in this book will use an example database schema that will be used to hold information about the customers, inventory, and sales of a simple store. This example store sells items such as books, videos, DVDs, and CDs. This schema will be named store, the definition of which is contained in the SQL*Plus script store_schema.sql, which is contained in the Zip file you can download from this book's web site. The store_schema.sql script contains the DDL and DML statements to create the store schema. Once you've obtained the script, you may run it using SQL*Plus or have your DBA run it for you. You'll now learn how to run the store_schema.sql script.

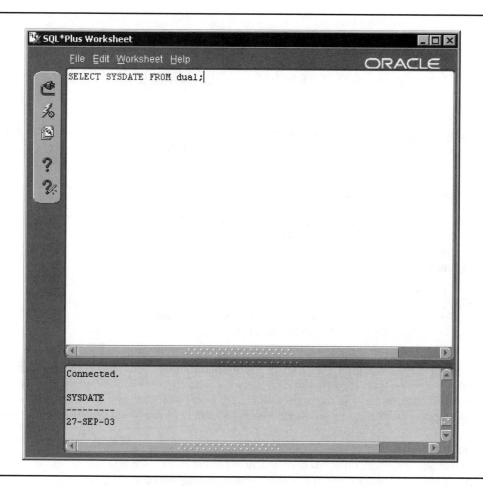

FIGURE 1-4. *Executing a SQL SELECT statement using the SQL*Plus worksheet*

Running the SQL*Plus Script to Create the Store Schema
Perform the following steps:

1. Open the `store_schema.sql` script using an editor and change the password for the `system` user if necessary. The `system` user has privileges to create new users and tables, among other items, and has a default password of `manager`. If that is not the correct password for the `system` user, ask your DBA for the correct password (or just have your DBA run the script for you).

2. Start the SQL*Plus tool.

3. Run the `store_schema.sql` script from within SQL*Plus using the @ command.

The @ command has the following syntax:

```
directory_path\store_schema.sql
```

where *directory_path* is the directory and path where your `store_schema.sql` script is stored.
For example, if the script is stored in a directory named SQL on the C partition of your Windows file system, then you would enter

```
@C:\SQL\store_schema.sql
```

If you're using Unix (or Linux), and you saved the script in a directory named SQL on your tmp file system, for example, you would enter

```
@/tmp/SQL/store_schema.sql
```

NOTE
Windows uses backslash characters (\) in directory paths, whereas Unix and Linux use forward slash characters (/).

When the `store_schema.sql` script has finished running, you'll be connected as the `store` user. If you want to, open the `store_schema.sql` script using a text editor like Windows Notepad and examine the statements contained in it. Don't worry too much about the details of the statements contained in this file—you'll learn the details as you progress through this book.

NOTE
*To end SQL*Plus, you enter **EXIT**. To reconnect to the `store` schema in SQL*Plus, you enter **store** as the user name with a password of **store_password**. While you're connected to the database, SQL*Plus maintains a database session for you. When you disconnect from the database, your session is ended. You can disconnect from the database and keep SQL*Plus running by entering **DISCONNECT**. You can then reconnect to a database by entering **CONNECT**.*

Data Definition Language (DDL) Statements Used to Create the Store Schema

As mentioned earlier, *Data Definition Language* (DDL) statements are used to create users and tables, plus many other types of structures in the database. In this section, you'll learn how to use DDL statements to create the database user and tables for the `store` schema.

NOTE
The SQL statements you'll see in the rest of this chapter are the same as those contained in the store_schema.sql *script. You don't have to type the statements in yourself, just run the* store_schema.sql *script as described earlier.*

The following sections describe how to create a database user, followed by the commonly used data types used in the Oracle database, and finally the various tables used for the hypothetical store.

Creating a Database User

To create a user in the database, you use the CREATE USER statement. The simplified syntax for the CREATE USER statement is as follows:

```
CREATE USER user_name IDENTIFIED BY password;
```

where

- user_name specifies the name you assign to your database user
- password specifies the password for your database user

For example, the following CREATE USER statement creates the store user with a password of store_password:

```
CREATE USER store IDENTIFIED BY store_password;
```

Next, if you want the user to be able to work in the database, the user must be granted the necessary *permissions* to do that work. In the case of store, the user must be able to log on to the database (which requires the connect permission) and create items like database tables (which requires the resource permission). Permissions are granted by a privileged user (the DBA, for example) using the GRANT statement.

The following example grants the connect and resource permissions to store:

```
GRANT connect, resource TO store;
```

Once a user has been created, the database tables and other database objects can be created in the associated schema for that user. For most of the examples in this book, I've chosen to implement a simple store; these tables will be created in the schema of store. Before I get into the details of the tables required for the store, you need to understand a little bit about the commonly used Oracle database types that are used to define the database columns.

Understanding the Common Oracle Database Types

There are many types that may be used to handle data in an Oracle database. Some of the commonly used types are shown in Table 1-1.

Oracle Type	Meaning
CHAR(*length*)	Stores strings of a fixed length. The *length* parameter specifies the length of the string. If a string of a smaller length is stored, it is padded with spaces at the end. For example, CHAR(2) may be used to store a fixed length string of two characters; if C is stored using this definition, then a single space is added at the end. CA would be stored as is with no padding.
VARCHAR2(*length*)	Stores strings of a variable length. The *length* parameter specifies the maximum length of the string. For example, VARCHAR2(20) may be used to store a string of up to 20 characters in length. No padding is used at the end of a smaller string.
DATE	Stores dates and times. The DATE type stores the century, all four digits of a year, the month, the day, the hour (in 24-hour format), the minute, and the second. The DATE type may be used to store dates and times between January 1, 4712 B.C. and December 31, 4712 A.D.
INTEGER	Stores integer numbers. An integer number doesn't contain a floating point: it is a whole number, such as 1, 10, and 115, for example.
NUMBER(*precision*, *scale*)	Stores floating point numbers, but may also be used to store integer numbers. *precision* is the maximum number of digits (in front of and behind a decimal point, if used) that may be used for the number. The maximum precision supported by the Oracle database is 38. *scale* is the maximum number of digits to the right of a decimal point (if used). If neither *precision* nor *scale* is specified, any number may be stored up to a precision of 38 digits. Numbers that exceed the *precision* are rejected by the database.
BINARY_FLOAT	New for Oracle10*g*. Stores a single precision 32-bit floating point number. You'll learn more about BINARY_FLOAT later in the section "The New Oracle10*g* BINARY_FLOAT and BINARY_DOUBLE Types."
BINARY_DOUBLE	New for Oracle10*g*. Stores a double precision 64-bit floating point number. You'll learn more about BINARY_DOUBLE later in the section "The New Oracle10*g* BINARY_FLOAT and BINARY_DOUBLE Types."

TABLE 1-1. *Commonly Used Oracle Data Types*

You can see all the data types in Appendix A. The following table illustrates a few examples of how numbers of type `NUMBER` are stored in the database:

Format	Number Supplied	Number Stored
NUMBER	1234.567	1234.567
NUMBER(6, 2)	123.4567	123.46
NUMBER(6, 2)	12345.67	Number exceeds the specified precision and is rejected by the database.

Examining the Store Tables

In this section, you'll learn how the tables for the `store` schema are created. The `store` schema will hold the details of the hypothetical store. Some of the information held in the store schema includes

- Customer details
- Types of products sold
- Product details
- A history of the products purchased by the customers
- Employees of the store
- Salary grades

The following tables will be used to store this information:

- **customers** Stores customer details
- **product_types** Stores the types of products stocked by the store
- **products** Stores product details
- **purchases** Stores which products were purchased by which customers
- **employees** Stores the employee details
- **salary_grades** Stores the salary grade details

NOTE
The `store_schema.sql` script creates other tables and database items not mentioned in the previous list. You'll learn about these items in later chapters.

In the next sections, you'll see the details of some of the `store` tables, and you'll see the `CREATE TABLE` statements included in the `store_schema.sql` script that creates these tables.

The customers Table   The `customers` table is used to store the details of the customers of the hypothetical store. The following items are to be stored in this table for each one of the store's customers:

- First name

- Last name

- Date of birth (dob)

- Phone number

Each of these items requires a column in the `customers` table, which is created by the `store_schema.sql` script using the following `CREATE TABLE` statement:

```
CREATE TABLE customers (
  customer_id INTEGER
    CONSTRAINT customers_pk PRIMARY KEY,
  first_name VARCHAR2(10) NOT NULL,
  last_name VARCHAR2(10) NOT NULL,
  dob DATE,
  phone VARCHAR2(12)
);
```

As you can see, the `customers` table contains five columns, one for each item in the previous list, and an extra column named `customer_id`. The following list contains the details of each of these columns:

- **`customer_id`**   Stores a unique integer for each row in the table. Each table should have one or more columns that uniquely identifies each row in the table and is known as that table's *primary key*. The `CONSTRAINT` clause for the `customer_id` column indicates that this is the table's primary key. A `CONSTRAINT` clause is used to restrict the values stored in a table or column and, for the `customer_id` column, the `PRIMARY KEY` keywords indicate that the `customer_id` column must contain a unique number for each row. You can also attach an optional name to a constraint, which must immediately follow the `CONSTRAINT` keyword—in this case, the name of the constraint is `customers_pk`. When a row is added to the `customers` table, a unique value for the `customer_id` column must be given, and the Oracle database will prevent you from adding a row with the same primary key value. If you try to do so, you will get an error from the database.

- **`first_name`**   Stores the first name of the customer. You'll notice the use of the `NOT NULL` constraint for the `first_name` column—this means that a value must be supplied for `first_name`. If no constraint is specified, a column uses the default constraint of `NULL` and allows the column to remain empty.

- **`last_name`**   Stores the last name of the customer. This column is `NOT NULL`, and therefore you must supply a value.

■ **dob** Stores the date of birth for the customer. Notice that a NOT NULL constraint is not specified for this column, therefore the default NULL is assumed, and a value is optional.

■ **phone** Stores the phone number of the customer. This is an optional value.

The store_schema.sql script populates the customers table with the following rows:

```
customer_id first_name last_name  dob       phone
----------- ---------- ---------- --------- -----------
          1 John       Brown      01-JAN-65 800-555-1211
          2 Cynthia    Green      05-FEB-68 800-555-1212
          3 Steve      White      16-MAR-71 800-555-1213
          4 Gail       Black                800-555-1214
          5 Doreen     Blue       20-MAY-70
```

Notice that customer #4's date of birth is null, as is customer #5's phone number.

You can see the rows in the customers table for yourself by executing the following SELECT statement using SQL*Plus:

```
SELECT * FROM customers;
```

The asterisk (*) indicates you want to retrieve all the columns from the customers table.

The product_types Table   The product_types table is used to store the names of the product types that may be stocked by the store. This table is created by the store_schema.sql script using the following CREATE TABLE statement:

```
CREATE TABLE product_types (
  product_type_id INTEGER
    CONSTRAINT product_types_pk PRIMARY KEY,
  name VARCHAR2(10) NOT NULL
);
```

The product_types table contains the following two columns:

■ **product_type_id** Uniquely identifies each row in the table; the product_type_id column is the primary key for this table. Each row in the product_types table must have a unique integer value for the product_type_id column.

■ **name** Contains the product type name. It is a NOT NULL column, and therefore a value must be supplied.

The store_schema.sql script populates this table with the following rows:

```
product_type_id name
--------------- ----------
              1 Book
              2 Video
              3 DVD
              4 CD
              5 Magazine
```

This defines the product types for the store. Each product stocked by the store may be of one of these types.

You can see the rows in the `product_types` table for yourself by executing the following `SELECT` statement using SQL*Plus:

```
SELECT * FROM product_types;
```

The products Table   The `products` table is used to store detailed information about the products sold. The following pieces of information are to be stored for each product:

- Product type

- Name

- Description

- Price

The `store_schema.sql` script creates the products table using the following `CREATE TABLE` statement:

```
CREATE TABLE products (
   product_id INTEGER
     CONSTRAINT products_pk PRIMARY KEY,
   product_type_id INTEGER
     CONSTRAINT products_fk_product_types
     REFERENCES product_types(product_type_id),
   name VARCHAR2(30) NOT NULL,
   description VARCHAR2(50),
   price NUMBER(5, 2)
);
```

The columns in this table are as follows:

- **`product_id`**   Uniquely identifies each row in the table. This column is the primary key of the table.

- **`product_type_id`**   Associates each product with a product type. This column is a reference to the `product_type_id` column in the `product_types` table and is known as a *foreign key* because it references a column in another table. The table containing the foreign key (the `products` table) is known as the *detail* or *child* table, and the table that is referenced (the `product_types` table) is known as the *master* or *parent* table. When you add a new product, you should also associate that product with a type by supplying the product type ID number in the `product_type_id` column. This type of relationship is known as a *master-detail* or *parent-child* relationship.

- **`name`**   Stores the product name, which must be specified as the name column is NOT NULL.

- **`description`**   Stores an optional description of the product.

- **price**   Stores an optional price for a product. This column is defined as NUMBER(5, 2) — the precision is 5, and therefore a maximum of 5 digits may be supplied for this number. The scale is 2, and so 2 of those maximum 5 digits may be to the right of the decimal point.

The following is a subset of the rows that are stored in the products table, populated by the store_schema.sql script:

```
product_id     product_type_id name          description      price
----------     --------------- ------------  ------------     ----------
         1                   1 Modern        A                    19.95
                               Science       description
                                             of modern
                                             science

         2                   1 Chemistry     Introduction            30
                                             to Chemistry

         3                   2 Supernova     A star               25.99
                                             explodes

         4                   2 Tank War      Action movie         13.95
                                             about a
                                             future war
```

The first row in the products table has a product_type_id of 1, which means that this product represents a book. The product_type_id value comes from the product_types table, which uses a product_type_id value of 1 to represent books. The second row also represents a book, but the third and fourth rows represent videos.

You can see all the rows in the products table for yourself by executing the following SELECT statement using SQL*Plus:

```
SELECT * FROM products;
```

The purchases Table   The purchases table stores the purchases made by a customer. For each purchase made by a customer, the following information is to be stored:

- Product ID
- Customer ID
- Number of units of the product purchased by the customer

The store_schema.sql script uses the following CREATE TABLE statement to create the purchases table:

```
CREATE TABLE purchases (
  product_id INTEGER
    CONSTRAINT purchases_fk_products
    REFERENCES products(product_id),
```

```
customer_id INTEGER
  CONSTRAINT purchases_fk_customers
  REFERENCES customers(customer_id),
quantity INTEGER NOT NULL,
CONSTRAINT purchases_pk PRIMARY KEY (product_id, customer_id)
);
```

The columns in this table are as follows:

- **product_id** Stores the ID of the product that was purchased. This must match a value in the product_id column for a row in the products table.

- **customer_id** Stores the ID of a customer who made the purchase. This must match a value in the customer_id column for a row in the customers table.

- **quantity** Stores the number of units of the product that were purchased.

The purchases table has a constraint named purchases_pk that spans multiple columns in the table. The purchases_pk constraint is also a PRIMARY KEY constraint and specifies that the table's primary key consists of two columns: product_id and customer_id. The combination of the two values in these columns must be unique for each row in the table.

The following is a subset of the rows that are stored in the purchases table, populated by the store_schema.sql script:

product_id	customer_id	quantity
1	1	1
2	1	3
1	4	1
2	2	1
1	3	1

As you can see, the combination of the values in the product_id and customer_id columns is unique for each row.

The employees Table   The employees table stores the details of the employees of the store. The following information is to be stored:

- Employee ID

- If applicable, the employee ID of the employee's manager

- First name

- Last name

- Title

- Salary

The `store_schema.sql` script uses the following CREATE TABLE statement to create the employees table:

```
CREATE TABLE employees (
  employee_id INTEGER
    CONSTRAINT employees_pk PRIMARY KEY,
  manager_id INTEGER,
  first_name VARCHAR2(10) NOT NULL,
  last_name  VARCHAR2(10) NOT NULL,
  title      VARCHAR2(20),
  salary     NUMBER(6, 0)
);
```

The `store_schema.sql` script populates this table with the following rows:

employee_id	manager_id	first_name	last_name	title	salary
1		James	Smith	CEO	800000
2	1	Ron	Johnson	Sales Manager	600000
3	2	Fred	Hobbs	Salesperson	150000
4	2	Susan	Jones	Salesperson	500000

The salary_grades Table   The `salary_grades` table stores the different grades of salaries available to employees. The following information is to be stored:

- Salary grade ID
- Low salary boundary for the grade
- High salary boundary for the grade

The `store_schema.sql` script uses the following CREATE TABLE statement to create the salary_grades table:

```
CREATE TABLE salary_grades (
  salary_grade_id INTEGER
    CONSTRAINT salary_grade_pk PRIMARY KEY,
  low_salary  NUMBER(6, 0),
  high_salary NUMBER(6, 0)
);
```

The `store_schema.sql` script populates this table with the following rows:

salary_grade_id	low_salary	high_salary
1	1	250000
2	250001	500000
3	500001	750000
4	750001	999999

Adding, Modifying, and Removing Rows

In this section, you'll learn how to add, modify, and remove rows in database tables. You do that using the SQL INSERT, UPDATE, and DELETE statements, respectively. This section doesn't exhaustively cover all the details of using these statements; you'll learn more about them in Chapter 8.

Adding a Row to a Table

You use the INSERT statement to add new rows to a table. You can specify the following information in an INSERT statement:

- The table into which the row is to be inserted
- A list of columns for which you want to specify column values
- A list of values to store in the specified columns

When inserting a row, you need to supply a value for the primary key and all other columns that are defined as NOT NULL. You don't have to specify values for the other columns if you don't want to—and those columns will be automatically set to null.

You can tell which columns are defined as NOT NULL using the SQL*Plus DESCRIBE command. The following example describes the customers table:

```
SQL> DESCRIBE customers
 Name                                      Null?    Type
 ----------------------------------------- -------- ------------
 CUSTOMER_ID                               NOT NULL NUMBER(38)
 FIRST_NAME                                NOT NULL VARCHAR2(10)
 LAST_NAME                                 NOT NULL VARCHAR2(10)
 DOB                                                DATE
 PHONE                                              VARCHAR2(12)
```

As you can see, the customer_id, first_name, and last_name columns are NOT NULL, meaning that you must supply a value for these columns. The dob and phone columns don't require a value—you could omit the values if you wanted, and they would be automatically set to null.

The following INSERT statement adds a row to the customers table. Notice that the order of values in the VALUES list matches the order in which the columns are specified in the column list. Also notice that the statement has two parts: the column list and the values to be added.

```
SQL> INSERT INTO customers (
  2    customer_id, first_name, last_name, dob, phone
  3  ) VALUES (
  4    6, 'Fred', 'Brown', '01-JAN-1970', '800-555-1215'
  5  );

1 row created.
```

NOTE
*SQL*Plus automatically numbers lines after you hit ENTER at the end
of each line.*

In the previous example, SQL*Plus responds that one row has been created after the INSERT
statement is executed. You can verify this by issuing the following SELECT statement:

```
SQL> SELECT *
  2  FROM customers;

CUSTOMER_ID FIRST_NAME LAST_NAME  DOB        PHONE
----------- ---------- ---------- --------- ------------
          1 John       Brown      01-JAN-65 800-555-1211
          2 Cynthia    Green      05-FEB-68 800-555-1212
          3 Steve      White      16-MAR-71 800-555-1213
          4 Gail       Black                800-555-1214
          5 Doreen     Blue       20-MAY-70
          6 Fred       Brown      01-JAN-70 800-555-1215
```

Notice the new row that has been added to the table.

By default, the Oracle database displays dates in the format DD-MON-YY, where DD is the day
number, MON are the first three characters of the month (in uppercase), and YY are the last two
digits of the year. The database actually stores all four digits for the year, but by default it only
displays the last two digits.

Modifying an Existing Row in a Table

You use the UPDATE statement to change rows in a table. Normally, when you use the UPDATE
statement, you specify the following information:

- The table containing the rows that are to be changed

- A WHERE clause that specifies the rows that are to be changed

- A list of column names, along with their new values, specified using the SET clause

You can change one or more rows using the same UPDATE statement. If more than one
row is specified, the same change will be implemented for all of those rows. The following
statement updates the last_name column to Orange for the row in the customers table
whose customer_id column is 2:

```
SQL> UPDATE customers
  2  SET last_name = 'Orange'
  3  WHERE customer_id = 2;

1 row updated.
```

SQL*Plus confirms that one row was updated.

CAUTION
If you forget to add a WHERE clause, all the rows will be updated. This is typically not the result you want.

Notice that the SET clause is used in the previous UPDATE statement to specify the column and the new value for that column. You can confirm the previous UPDATE statement did indeed change customer #2's last name using the following query:

```
SQL> SELECT *
  2  FROM customers
  3  WHERE customer_id = 2;

CUSTOMER_ID FIRST_NAME LAST_NAME  DOB       PHONE
----------- ---------- ---------- --------- ------------
          2 Cynthia    Orange     05-FEB-68 800-555-1212
```

Removing a Row from a Table

You use the DELETE statement to remove rows from a table. As with the UPDATE statement, you typically use a WHERE clause to limit the rows you wish to delete—if you don't, *all* the rows will be deleted from the table.

The following example uses a DELETE statement to remove the row from the customers table whose customer_id is 2:

```
SQL> DELETE FROM customers
  2  WHERE customer_id = 2;

1 row deleted.
```

SQL*Plus confirms that one row has been deleted.
To undo any changes you make to the database, you use ROLLBACK:

```
SQL> ROLLBACK;

Rollback complete.
```

Go ahead and issue a ROLLBACK to undo any changes you've made so far.

The New Oracle10*g* BINARY_FLOAT and BINARY_DOUBLE Types

Oracle10*g* introduces two new data types: BINARY_FLOAT and BINARY_DOUBLE. BINARY_FLOAT stores a single precision 32-bit floating point number; BINARY_DOUBLE stores a double precision 64-bit floating point number. These new data types are based on the IEEE (Institute for Electrical and Electronic Engineering) standard for binary floating-point arithmetic.

Benefits of BINARY_FLOAT and BINARY_DOUBLE

BINARY_FLOAT and BINARY_DOUBLE are intended to be complementary to the existing NUMBER type. BINARY_FLOAT and BINARY_DOUBLE offer the following benefits over NUMBER:

- **Smaller storage required**   BINARY_FLOAT and BINARY_DOUBLE require 5 and 9 bytes of storage space, whereas NUMBER may use up to 22 bytes.

- **Can represent a greater range of numbers**   BINARY_FLOAT and BINARY_ DOUBLE support numbers much larger and smaller than can be stored in a NUMBER.

- **Operations are typically performed faster**   Operations involving BINARY_FLOAT and BINARY_DOUBLE are typically performed faster than on NUMBER. This is because BINARY_FLOAT and BINARY_DOUBLE operations are typically performed in the hardware, whereas NUMBERs must first be converted using software before operations can be performed.

- **Closed operations**   Arithmetic operations involving BINARY_FLOAT and BINARY_ DOUBLE are closed, which means that either a number or a special value is returned. For example, if you divide a BINARY_FLOAT by another BINARY_FLOAT, a BINARY_ FLOAT is returned.

- **Transparent rounding**   BINARY_FLOAT and BINARY_DOUBLE use binary base-2 to represent a number, whereas NUMBER uses decimal base-10. The base used to represent a number affects how rounding occurs for that number. For example, a decimal floating-point number is rounded to the nearest decimal place, but a binary floating-point number is rounded to the nearest binary place.

TIP
If you are developing a system that involves a lot of numerical computations, you should consider using BINARY_FLOAT and BINARY_DOUBLE to represent your numbers.

Using BINARY_FLOAT and BINARY_DOUBLE in a Table

The following statement creates a table named binary_test that contains a BINARY_FLOAT and BINARY_DOUBLE column:

```
CREATE TABLE binary_test (
  bin_float BINARY_FLOAT,
  bin_double BINARY_DOUBLE
);
```

NOTE
You'll find a script named oracle_10g_examples.sql *in the SQL directory, which creates the* binary_test *table in the* store *schema. The script also performs the* INSERT *statements you'll see in this section. You can run this script if you have access to an Oracle10g database.*

The following example adds a row to the binary_test table:

```
INSERT INTO binary_test (
  bin_float, bin_double
) VALUES (
  39.5f, 15.7d
);
```

Notice you use "f" and "d" to indicate a literal number is a BINARY_FLOAT or a BINARY_DOUBLE.

Special Values

In addition to literal values, you can also use the special values shown in Table 1-2 with a BINARY_FLOAT or BINARY_DOUBLE.

The following example inserts BINARY_FLOAT_INFINITY and BINARY_DOUBLE_INFINITY into the binary_test table:

```
INSERT INTO binary_test (
  bin_float, bin_double
) VALUES (
  BINARY_FLOAT_INFINITY, BINARY_DOUBLE_INFINITY
);
```

Special Value	Description
BINARY_FLOAT_NAN	Not a number (NaN) for BINARY_FLOAT type
BINARY_FLOAT_INFINITY	Infinity (INF) for BINARY_FLOAT type
BINARY_DOUBLE_NAN	Not a number (NaN) for BINARY_DOUBLE type
BINARY_DOUBLE_INFINITY	Infinity (INF) for BINARY_DOUBLE type

TABLE 1-2. *Special Values*

Quitting SQL*Plus

You use the EXIT command to quit from SQL*Plus. On Windows this will terminate SQL*Plus; on Unix and Linux it will terminate SQL*Plus and take you back to the command-line prompt from which you started SQL*Plus. The following example quits SQL*Plus using the EXIT command:

```
SQL> EXIT
```

Introducing Oracle PL/SQL

PL/SQL is Oracle's procedural language that allows you to add programming constructs around SQL. PL/SQL is primarily used for adding procedures and functions to a database to implement business logic. PL/SQL contains standard programming constructs such as the following:

- Blocks
- Variable declarations
- Conditionals
- Loops
- Cursors
- The ability to define procedures and functions

The following CREATE PROCEDURE statement defines a procedure named update_product_price(). The procedure multiplies the price of a product by a factor—the product ID and the factor are passed as parameters to the procedure. If the specified product doesn't exist, the procedure takes no action; otherwise, it updates the product price by the factor.

NOTE
Don't worry too much about the details of the PL/SQL shown in the following listing for now—you'll learn the details as you progress through this book. I just want you to get a feel for PL/SQL at this stage.

```
CREATE OR REPLACE PROCEDURE update_product_price (
  p_product_id IN products.product_id%TYPE,
  p_factor     IN NUMBER
) AS
  product_count INTEGER;
BEGIN
  -- count the number of products with the
  -- supplied product_id (should be 1 if the product exists)
```

```
SELECT COUNT(*)
INTO product_count
FROM products
WHERE product_id = p_product_id;

-- if the product exists (product_count = 1) then
-- update that product's price
IF product_count = 1 THEN
  UPDATE products
  SET price = price * p_factor
  WHERE product_id = p_product_id;
  COMMIT;
END IF;
EXCEPTION
  WHEN OTHERS THEN
    ROLLBACK;
END update_product_price;
/
```

Exceptions are used to handle errors that occur in PL/SQL code. The EXCEPTION block in the previous example performs a ROLLBACK if any exception is thrown in the code.

You'll learn more about PL/SQL in Chapter 11.

Summary

In this chapter, you learned

- That a *relational database* is a collection of related information that has been organized into structures known as *tables*. Each table contains *rows* that are further organized into *columns*. These tables are stored in the database in structures known as *schemas*, which are areas where database users may store their objects (such as tables and procedures).

- That *Structured Query Language* (*SQL*) is the standard language designed to access relational databases.

- That SQL*Plus allows you to enter SQL statements using the keyboard or to supply a file that contains SQL statements and run those statements.

- How to run a script in SQL*Plus that creates the example store schema.

- How to execute simple SQL SELECT, INSERT, UPDATE, and DELETE statements.

- That *PL/SQL* is Oracle's procedural language that allows you to add programming constructs around SQL. PL/SQL is primarily used for adding procedures and functions to a database to implement business logic.

In the next chapter, you'll learn more about retrieving information from database tables.

CHAPTER
2

Retrieving
Information from
Database Tables

In this chapter, you will

- Retrieve information from one or more database tables using SELECT statements.
- Use arithmetic expressions to perform calculations.
- Filter rows to just those you are interested in using a WHERE clause.
- Sort the rows retrieved from a table.

The examples in this section use SQL*Plus and the store schema that you, or your DBA, should already have created in the previous chapter. If you want to follow along with the examples, you should start up SQL*Plus and enter store as the user name along with the password of store_password.

Performing Single Table SELECT Statements

The SELECT statement is used to retrieve information from tables in the database. In its simplest form, you specify the table from which you want to retrieve data, and specify a list of column names to retrieve. The SELECT statement in the following example retrieves the customer_id, first_name, last_name, dob, and phone columns from the customers table:

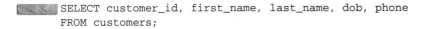

```
SELECT customer_id, first_name, last_name, dob, phone
FROM customers;
```

Immediately after the SELECT keyword, you supply the column names that you want to retrieve; after the FROM keyword, you supply the table name from which the columns are to be retrieved. The SQL statement is ended using a semicolon (;).

NOTE
You don't tell the database management system software exactly how to access the information you want. You just tell it what you want and let the software worry about how to actually get it. More generally, the items that immediately follow the SELECT statement needn't always be columns from a table. They can be any valid expressions, and you will see examples of expressions later in this chapter.

After you press ENTER at the end of the SQL statement, the statement is executed and the results are returned to SQL*Plus for display on the screen as shown in the following output:

```
CUSTOMER_ID FIRST_NAME LAST_NAME  DOB       PHONE
----------- ---------- ---------- --------- ------------
          1 John       Brown      01-JAN-65 800-555-1211
          2 Cynthia    Green      05-FEB-68 800-555-1212
          3 Steve      White      16-MAR-71 800-555-1213
          4 Gail       Black                800-555-1214
          5 Doreen     Blue       20-MAY-70
```

The rows returned by the database are known as a *result set*. As you can see, the Oracle database converts the column names that you specify into their uppercase equivalents. Character and date columns are left-justified; number columns are right-justified. By default, the Oracle database displays dates in the format DD-MON-YY, where DD is the day number, MON is the first three characters of the month (in uppercase), and YY is the last two digits of the year. The database actually stores all four digits for the year, but by default it only displays the last two digits.

NOTE
Your DBA can change the default display format for dates by setting the Oracle database initialization parameter NLS_DATE_FORMAT. You'll learn more about this in Chapter 4.

Although you can specify column names and table names using either lowercase or uppercase, it is better to stick with one style. The examples in this book use uppercase for SQL and Oracle keywords, and lowercase for everything else.

Selecting All Columns from a Table

If you want to select all columns in a table, rather than enumerate each column name in a long list, you can use the asterisk character (*) in your select list. In the following example, the asterisk is used with SELECT to retrieve all columns from the customers table:

```
SELECT *
FROM customers;
```

```
CUSTOMER_ID FIRST_NAME LAST_NAME  DOB       PHONE
----------- ---------- ---------- --------- ------------
          1 John       Brown      01-JAN-65 800-555-1211
          2 Cynthia    Green      05-FEB-68 800-555-1212
          3 Steve      White      16-MAR-71 800-555-1213
          4 Gail       Black                800-555-1214
          5 Doreen     Blue       20-MAY-70
```

As you can see, all the columns in the customers table are displayed.

Understanding Row Identifiers

Each row in an Oracle database has a unique row identifier, or *rowid*, which is used internally by the Oracle database to access the row. A rowid is an 18-digit number that is represented as a base-64 number, and it contains the physical address of a row in an Oracle database. You can view the rowid value for rows in a table by specifying the ROWID column in the select list of a query. The query in the following example retrieves the ROWID and customer_id columns from the customers table:

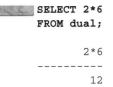

```
SELECT ROWID, customer_id
FROM customers;

ROWID              CUSTOMER_ID
------------------ -----------
AAAF4yAABAAAHeKAAA           1
AAAF4yAABAAAHeKAAB           2
AAAF4yAABAAAHeKAAC           3
AAAF4yAABAAAHeKAAD           4
AAAF4yAABAAAHeKAAE           5
```

Notice the use of base-64 in this output. When you describe a table using the DESCRIBE command, ROWID doesn't appear in the output from the command because it is only used internally by the database. ROWID is known as a *pseudo* column.

Performing Arithmetic

Oracle allows you to perform arithmetic in SQL statements using arithmetic expressions, including addition, subtraction, multiplication, and division. Arithmetic expressions consist of two *operands*—numbers or dates—and an arithmetic *operator*. The four arithmetic operators are shown in the following table.

Operator	Description
+	Addition
–	Subtraction
*	Multiplication
/	Division

The following example shows how to use the multiplication operator (*) to calculate 2 multiplied by 6 (the numbers 2 and 6 are the operands):

```
SELECT 2*6
FROM dual;

       2*6
----------
        12
```

As you can see from this example, the correct result of 12 is displayed. The use of 2*6 in this SQL statement is an example of an *expression*. An expression may contain a combination of columns, literal values, and operators.

The dual Table

You'll notice the use of the `dual` table in the previous example. I mentioned the `dual` table in the previous chapter—`dual` is a table that contains a single row. The following output from the `DESCRIBE` command shows the structure of the `dual` table, along with a `SELECT` statement that selects the row in the `dual` table:

```
DESCRIBE dual;
 Name                                        Null?    Type
 ------------------------------------------- -------- -----------
 DUMMY                                                VARCHAR2(1)

SELECT *
FROM dual;

D
-
X
```

Notice the dual table has one VARCHAR2 column named `dummy`, and contains a single row with the value X.

Using Date Arithmetic

You can use the addition and subtraction operators with dates. You can add a number—representing a number of days—to a date. The following example adds 2 days to July 31, 2003, and displays the resulting date:

```
SELECT TO_DATE('31-JUL-2003') + 2
FROM dual;

TO_DATE(
---------
02-AUG-03
```

NOTE
TO_DATE() is a function that converts a string to a date. You'll learn more about TO_DATE() in Chapter 4.

The next example subtracts two days from August 2, 2003:

```
SELECT TO_DATE('02-AUG-2003') - 2
FROM dual;

TO_DATE('
---------
31-JUL-03
```

You can also subtract one date from another, yielding the number of days between the two dates. The following example subtracts July 31, 2003, from August 2, 2003:

```
SELECT TO_DATE('02-AUG-2003') - TO_DATE('31-JUL-2003')
FROM dual;

TO_DATE('02-AUG-2003')-TO_DATE('31-JUL-2003')
---------------------------------------------
                                            2
```

Using Columns in Arithmetic

Operands do not have to be literal numbers or dates, they may also be columns from a table. In the following example, the `name` and `price` columns are selected from the `products` table; notice that 2 is added to the value in the `price` column using the addition operator (+) to form the expression `price + 2`:

```
SELECT name, price + 2
FROM products;

NAME                              PRICE+2
------------------------------ ----------
Modern Science                      21.95
Chemistry                              32
Supernova                           27.99
Tank War                            15.95
Z Files                             51.99
2412: The Return                    16.95
Space Force 9                       15.49
From Another Planet                 14.99
Classical Music                     12.99
Pop 3                               17.99
Creative Yell                       16.99
My Front Line                       15.49
```

You can also combine more than one operator in an expression. In the following example, the `price` column is multiplied by 3, and then 1 is added to the resulting value:

```
SELECT name, price * 3 + 1
FROM products;

NAME                              PRICE*3+1
------------------------------ ----------
Modern Science                      60.85
Chemistry                              91
Supernova                           78.97
Tank War                            42.85
Z Files                            150.97
2412: The Return                    45.85
Space Force 9                       41.47
From Another Planet                 39.97
```

```
Classical Music                    33.97
Pop 3                              48.97
Creative Yell                      45.97
My Front Line                      41.47
```

The normal rules of arithmetic operator precedence apply in SQL: multiplication and division are performed first, followed by addition and subtraction. If operators of the same precedence are used, they are performed from left to right. For example, if you were to use the following expression: 10*12/3-1, 10 multiplied by 12 would be calculated first, yielding a result of 120; 120 would then be divided by 3, yielding 40; finally, 1 would be subtracted from 40, yielding 39:

```
SELECT 10 * 12 / 3 - 1
FROM dual;

10*12/3-1
----------
        39
```

You can also use parentheses ( ) to specify the order of execution for the operators. For example:

```
SELECT 10 * (12 / 3 - 1)
FROM dual;

10*(12/3-1)
-----------
         30
```

In this example, the parentheses are used to calculate 12/3-1 first, the result of which is then multiplied by 10—yielding 30 as the final answer.

Using Column Aliases

As you've seen, when you select a column from a table, Oracle uses the uppercase version of the column name as the header for the column. For example, when you select the price column, the header in the resulting output is PRICE. When you use an expression, Oracle strips out the spaces, and uses the expression as the header. You aren't limited to using the header generated by Oracle: you can provide your own using an *alias*. In the following example, the expression price * 2 is given the alias DOUBLE_PRICE:

```
SELECT price * 2 DOUBLE_PRICE
FROM products;

DOUBLE_PRICE
------------
        39.9
          60
       51.98
        27.9
       99.98
        29.9
```

```
              26.98
              25.98
              21.98
              31.98
              29.98
              26.98
```

If you want to use spaces and preserve the case of your alias text, you must place the text within double quotation marks (""):

```
SELECT price * 2 "Double Price"
FROM products;

Double Price
------------
        39.9
...
```

You can also use the optional AS keyword before the alias, as shown in the following example:

```
SELECT 10 * (12 / 3 - 1) AS "Computation"
FROM dual;

Computation
-----------
         30
```

Merging Column Output Using Concatenation

You can merge the display of columns using concatenation. This allows you to create more friendly and meaningful output. For example, in the customers table, the first_name and last_name columns contain the customer name. In the previous examples, these columns were selected and displayed independently. Wouldn't it be nice to merge the display of those columns together under one column heading? You can do this using the concatenation operator (||), as shown in the following example:

```
SELECT first_name || ' ' || last_name AS "Customer Name"
FROM customers;

Customer Name
--------------------
John Brown
Cynthia Green
Steve White
Gail Black
Doreen Blue
```

Notice that a space character is concatenated to the first_name column, and then the last_name column is concatenated to the resulting string.

Understanding Null Values

How does a database represent a value that is unknown? The answer is to use a special value, known as a *null value*. A null value is not a blank string—it is a distinct value. A null value means the value for the column is unknown.

When you select a column that contains a null value, you see nothing in that column. You saw this (or rather, didn't see it!) in the earlier examples of selecting rows from the `customers` table: customer #4 has a null value in the `dob` column, and customer #5 has a null value in the `phone` column.

You can also check for null values using the `IS NULL` clause in a `SELECT` statement. In the following example, customer #4 is retrieved based on the fact that the `dob` column is null:

```
SELECT customer_id, first_name, last_name, dob
FROM customers
WHERE dob IS NULL;


CUSTOMER_ID FIRST_NAME LAST_NAME   DOB
----------- ---------- ---------- ---------
          4 Gail       Black
```

Similarly, in the following example, customer #5 is retrieved based on the fact that the `phone` column is null:

```
SELECT customer_id, first_name, last_name, phone
FROM customers
WHERE phone IS NULL;


CUSTOMER_ID FIRST_NAME LAST_NAME   PHONE
----------- ---------- ---------- ------------
          5 Doreen     Blue
```

Since null values don't display anything, how do you tell the difference between a null value and a blank string if you retrieve all the rows? The answer is to use one of Oracle's built-in functions: `NVL()`. `NVL()` allows you to convert a null value into another value—which you can actually read. `NVL()` accepts two parameters: a column (or more generally, any expression that results in a value), and the value that should be substituted if the first parameter is null. In the following example, `NVL()` is used to convert a null value in the `phone` column to the string `Unknown phone number`:

```
SELECT customer_id, first_name, last_name,
NVL(phone, 'Unknown phone number') AS PHONE_NUMBER
FROM customers;


CUSTOMER_ID FIRST_NAME LAST_NAME   PHONE_NUMBER
----------- ---------- ---------- --------------------
          1 John       Brown       800-555-1211
          2 Cynthia    Green       800-555-1212
          3 Steve      White       800-555-1213
          4 Gail       Black       800-555-1214
          5 Doreen     Blue        Unknown phone number
```

In addition to using `NVL()` to convert string columns that contain null values, you can use `NVL()` to convert number columns and date columns. In the following example, `NVL()` is used to convert a null value in the `dob` column to the date `01-JAN-2000`:

```
SELECT customer_id, first_name, last_name,
NVL(dob, '01-JAN-2000') AS DOB
FROM customers;
```

```
CUSTOMER_ID FIRST_NAME LAST_NAME  DOB
----------- ---------- ---------- ---------
          1 John       Brown      01-JAN-65
          2 Cynthia    Green      05-FEB-68
          3 Steve      White      16-MAR-71
          4 Gail       Black      01-JAN-00
          5 Doreen     Blue       20-MAY-70
```

Notice that customer #4's `dob` is now displayed as `01-JAN-00`.

Displaying Distinct Rows

Suppose you were interested in learning which customers actually made purchases of products. You can get that information using the following query, which retrieves the `purchased_by` column from the `purchases` table:

```
SELECT purchased_by
FROM purchases;
```

```
PURCHASED_BY
------------
           1
           1
           4
           2
           3
           2
           3
           4
           3
```

You can then scan the `purchased_by` column from the rows visually to identify each customer who made a purchase. As you can see, it's not easy, because some customers made more than one purchase. If the list were a lot longer and featured more customers, the task would become even more tedious. Wouldn't it be great if you could throw out the duplicate rows that contain the same customer ID? Well, you'll be happy to know that Oracle does indeed have the ability to do that: you can suppress the display of duplicate rows using the `DISTINCT` keyword. In the following example, the `DISTINCT` keyword is used to suppress the duplicate rows from the previous query:

```
SELECT DISTINCT purchased_by
FROM purchases;

PURCHASED_BY
------------
           1
           2
           3
           4
```

From this list, it's easy to see that customers #1, #2, #3, and #4 made purchases; the duplicate rows are suppressed. Next, you'll learn an additional way of limiting the rows retrieved in a query.

Filtering Rows Using the WHERE Clause

You can use the WHERE clause in a SELECT statement to filter the rows returned from the database. This is very important as Oracle has the capacity to store large numbers of rows in a table and you may only be interested in a very small subset of those rows. You place the WHERE clause after the FROM clause:

```
SELECT ...
FROM
WHERE ...;
```

In the following example, the WHERE clause is used to retrieve the row from the customers table that has the value 2 stored in the customer_id column:

```
SELECT *
FROM customers
WHERE customer_id = 2;

CUSTOMER_ID FIRST_NAME LAST_NAME  DOB       PHONE
----------- ---------- ---------- --------- ------------
          2 Cynthia    Green      05-FEB-68 800-555-1212
```

Notice this example uses the equality operator (=) in the WHERE clause. The equality operator is just one of the comparison operators, which you'll learn about next.

Using Comparison Operators

There are many other comparison operators that you can use in a WHERE clause besides the equality operator. The following table lists the comparison operators.

Operator	Description
=	Equal
<> or !=	Not equal
<	Less than
>	Greater than

<=	Less than or equal
>=	Greater than or equal
ANY	Compares one value with *any* value in a list
ALL	Compares one value with *all* values in a list

The following SELECT statement uses the not equal (<>) operator in the WHERE clause to retrieve the rows from the customers table whose customer_id is not equal to 2:

```
SELECT *
FROM customers
WHERE customer_id <> 2;

CUSTOMER_ID FIRST_NAME LAST_NAME  DOB       PHONE
----------- ---------- ---------- --------- ------------
          1 John       Brown      01-JAN-65 800-555-1211
          3 Steve      White      16-MAR-71 800-555-1213
          4 Gail       Black                800-555-1214
          5 Doreen     Blue       20-MAY-70
```

The next example retrieves the customer_id and name columns from the products table where the customer_id column is greater than 8 using the > operator:

```
SELECT customer_id, name
FROM products
WHERE customer_id > 8;

CUSTOMER_ID NAME
----------- ----------------
          9 Classical Music
         10 Pop 3
         11 Creative Yell
         12 My Front Line
```

You use the ANY operator in a WHERE clause to compare a value with *any* of the values in a list. You must place an =, <>, <, >, <=, or >= operator before ANY. The following SELECT statement uses the ANY operator to retrieve rows from the customers table where the value in the customer_id column is greater than any of the values 2, 3, or 4:

```
SELECT *
FROM customers
WHERE customer_id > ANY (2, 3, 4);

CUSTOMER_ID FIRST_NAME LAST_NAME  DOB       PHONE
----------- ---------- ---------- --------- ------------
          5 Doreen     Blue       20-MAY-70
          4 Gail       Black                800-555-1214
          3 Steve      White      16-MAR-71 800-555-1213
```

Notice that customer #3 is included in the results because 3 is greater than 2.

You use the ALL operator in a WHERE clause to compare a value with *all* of the values in a list. You must place an =, <>, <, >, <=, or >= operator before ALL. The following SELECT statement uses the ALL operator to retrieve rows from the customers table where the value in the customer_id column is greater than all of the values 2, 3, and 4:

```
SELECT *
FROM customers
WHERE customer_id > ALL (2, 3, 4);
```

```
CUSTOMER_ID FIRST_NAME LAST_NAME  DOB        PHONE
----------- ---------- ---------- ---------- ------------
          5 Doreen     Blue       20-MAY-70
```

Notice that only customer #5 is returned because 5 is greater than 2, 3, and 4. There are no rows in the customers table with a customer_id greater than 5 and so only one row is returned.

Using the SQL Operators

The SQL operators allow you to limit rows based on pattern matching of strings, lists of values, ranges of values, and null values. The SQL operators are listed in the following table:

Operator	Description
LIKE	Matches patterns in strings
IN	Matches lists of values
BETWEEN	Matches a range of values
IS NULL	Matches null values
IS NAN	New for Oracle10g. Matches the NaN special value, which means "not a number"
IS INFINITE	New for Oracle10g. Matches infinite BINARY_FLOAT and BINARY_DOUBLE values

You can also use the NOT operator to reverse the meaning of LIKE, IN, BETWEEN, and IS NULL:

- NOT LIKE
- NOT IN
- NOT BETWEEN
- IS NOT NULL
- IS NOT NAN
- IS NOT INFINITE

The following sections cover the LIKE, IN, and BETWEEN operators.

Using the LIKE Operator

You use the LIKE operator in a WHERE clause to see if any of the character strings in a text column match a pattern that you specify. You specify patterns using a combination of normal characters and the following two wildcard characters:

- **Underscore character (_)** Matches one character in a specified position
- **Percent character (%)** Matches any number of characters beginning at the specified position

The following SELECT statement uses the LIKE operator with the pattern '_o%' applied to the first_name column of the customers table The underscore character (_) before the o matches any one character in the first position of the column value, and the percent character (%) matches any characters following the o:

```
SELECT *
FROM customers
WHERE first_name LIKE '_o%';

CUSTOMER_ID FIRST_NAME LAST_NAME  DOB       PHONE
----------- ---------- ---------- --------- ------------
          1 John       Brown      01-JAN-65 800-555-1211
          5 Doreen     Blue       20-MAY-70
```

As you can see, two records are retrieved, because the strings John and Doreen both have o as the second character.

The following example uses NOT LIKE to reverse the rows retrieved by the previous query:

```
SELECT *
FROM customers
WHERE first_name NOT LIKE '_o%';

CUSTOMER_ID FIRST_NAME LAST_NAME  DOB       PHONE
----------- ---------- ---------- --------- ------------
          2 Cynthia    Green      05-FEB-68 800-555-1212
          3 Steve      White      16-MAR-71 800-555-1213
          4 Gail       Black                800-555-1214
```

As expected, all rows other than the rows in the previous example are retrieved.

If you need to perform a text match on the actual underscore or percent characters in a string, you can use the ESCAPE option. The following example retrieves the products whose name contains the string a_product:

```
SELECT first_name
FROM customers
WHERE first_name LIKE '%a\_product%' ESCAPE '\';
```

The ESCAPE option specifies that the backslash character precedes any wildcard characters used with the LIKE operator—in this example, the underscore (_) is the wildcard used. The underscore is then used in the text match, rather than being treated as a wildcard character as would otherwise be the case.

Using the IN Operator

You can use the IN operator in a WHERE clause to select only those rows whose column value is in a list that you specify. The following SELECT statement uses the IN operator to retrieve rows from the customers table where the value in the customer_id column is 2, 3, or 5:

```
SELECT *
FROM customers
WHERE customer_id IN (2, 3, 5);
```

```
CUSTOMER_ID FIRST_NAME LAST_NAME  DOB       PHONE
----------- ---------- ---------- --------- ------------
          2 Cynthia    Green      05-FEB-68 800-555-1212
          3 Steve      White      16-MAR-71 800-555-1213
          5 Doreen     Blue       20-MAY-70
```

NOT IN reverses the rows selected by IN—if IN were replaced by NOT IN for the previous example, all rows except those shown above would be retrieved.

CAUTION
NOT IN returns false if a value in the list is null.

The following example shows no rows are returned when NOT IN processes a null in a list of values:

```
SELECT *
FROM customers
WHERE customer_id NOT IN (2, 3, 5, NULL);
```

```
no rows selected
```

Using the BETWEEN Operator

You use the BETWEEN operator in a WHERE clause to select rows whose column value is inclusive within a specified range. The following example uses the BETWEEN operator to retrieve rows from the customers table where the customer_id column is between 1 and 3:

```
SELECT *
FROM customers
WHERE customer_id BETWEEN 1 AND 3;
```

```
CUSTOMER_ID FIRST_NAME LAST_NAME  DOB       PHONE
----------- ---------- ---------- --------- ------------
          1 John       Brown      01-JAN-65 800-555-1211
          2 Cynthia    Green      05-FEB-68 800-555-1212
          3 Steve      White      16-MAR-71 800-555-1213
```

The range specified with the BETWEEN operator is inclusive so the rows where the customer_id column is equal to 1, 2, or 3 are retrieved. As you'd expect, NOT BETWEEN reverses the rows retrieved.

Using the Logical Operators

There are three logical operators that may be used in a WHERE clause. The logical operators allow you to limit rows based on logical conditions. The logical operators are listed in the following table:

Operator	Description
x AND y	Returns true when both x and y are true
x OR y	Returns true when either x or y is true
NOT x	Returns true if x is false, and returns false if x is true

The following example illustrates the use of the AND operator to retrieve rows from the customers table where *both* of the following conditions are met:

- The dob column is greater than January 1, 1970.

- The customer_id column is greater than 3.

```
SELECT *
FROM customers
WHERE dob > '01-JAN-1970'
AND customer_id > 3;

CUSTOMER_ID FIRST_NAME LAST_NAME  DOB        PHONE
----------- ---------- ---------- ---------- ------------
          5 Doreen     Blue       20-MAY-70
```

The following example illustrates the use of the OR operator to retrieve rows from the customers table where *either* of the following conditions is met:

- The dob column is greater than January 1, 1970.

- The customer_id column is greater than 3.

```
SELECT *
FROM customers
WHERE dob > '01-JAN-1970'
OR customer_id > 3;

CUSTOMER_ID FIRST_NAME LAST_NAME  DOB        PHONE
----------- ---------- ---------- ---------- ------------
          3 Steve      White      16-MAR-71  800-555-1213
          4 Gail       Black                 800-555-1214
          5 Doreen     Blue       20-MAY-70
```

You can use the logical operators AND and OR to combine expressions in a WHERE clause.

Understanding Operator Precedence

If you combine AND and OR in the same expression, the AND operator takes precedence over the OR operator (which means it's executed first). The comparison operators take precedence over AND. Of course, you can override these using parentheses.

The following example retrieves rows from the customers table where *either* of the following two conditions is met:

- The dob column is greater than January 1, 1970.

- The customer_id column is less than 2 *and* the phone column has 1211 at the end.

```
SELECT *
FROM customers
WHERE dob > '01-JAN-1970'
OR customer_id < 2
AND phone LIKE '%1211';
```

```
CUSTOMER_ID FIRST_NAME LAST_NAME  DOB       PHONE
----------- ---------- ---------- --------- ------------
          1 John       Brown      01-JAN-65 800-555-1211
          3 Steve      White      16-MAR-71 800-555-1213
          5 Doreen     Blue       20-MAY-70
```

As I mentioned, the AND operator takes precedence over OR, so you can think of the previous query's WHERE clause as follows:

```
dob > '01-JAN-1970' OR (customer_id < 2 AND phone LIKE '%1211')
```

Therefore, customers #1, #3, and #5 are displayed.

Sorting Rows Using the ORDER BY Clause

You use the ORDER BY clause to sort the rows retrieved from the database. The ORDER BY clause may specify one or more columns on which to sort the data and must follow the FROM clause or the WHERE clause (if a WHERE clause is supplied).

The following example uses the ORDER BY clause to sort the last_name column values from the customers table:

```
SELECT *
FROM customers
ORDER BY last_name;
```

```
CUSTOMER_ID FIRST_NAME LAST_NAME  DOB       PHONE
----------- ---------- ---------- --------- ------------
          4 Gail       Black                800-555-1214
          5 Doreen     Blue       20-MAY-70
          1 John       Brown      01-JAN-65 800-555-1211
          2 Cynthia    Green      05-FEB-68 800-555-1212
          3 Steve      White      16-MAR-71 800-555-1213
```

By default, the ORDER BY clause sorts the columns in ascending order (lower values appear first). You can use the DESC keyword to sort the columns in descending order (higher values appear first). You can also use the ASC keyword to explicitly specify an ascending sort—as I mentioned, this is the default, but you can still specify it.

The following example uses the ORDER BY clause to sort the first_name column values from the customers table in ascending order, followed by a sort on the last_name column values in descending order:

```
SELECT *
FROM customers
ORDER BY first_name ASC, last_name DESC;
```

```
CUSTOMER_ID FIRST_NAME LAST_NAME  DOB       PHONE
----------- ---------- ---------- --------- ------------
          2 Cynthia    Green      05-FEB-68 800-555-1212
          5 Doreen     Blue       20-MAY-70
          4 Gail       Black                800-555-1214
          1 John       Brown      01-JAN-65 800-555-1211
          3 Steve      White      16-MAR-71 800-555-1213
```

You can also use a column position number in the ORDER BY clause to indicate which column to sort: 1 means sort by the first column selected, 2 means sort by the second column, and so on. In the following example, column 1 (the customer_id column) is used to sort the rows:

```
SELECT customer_id, first_name, last_name
FROM customers
ORDER BY 1;
```

```
CUSTOMER_ID FIRST_NAME LAST_NAME
----------- ---------- ----------
          1 John       Brown
          2 Cynthia    Green
          3 Steve      White
          4 Gail       Black
          5 Doreen     Blue
```

Because the customer_id column is in position 1, it is the column used in the sort.

Performing SELECT Statements that Use Two Tables

Most database schemas have more than one table, with those tables storing different aspects of an enterprise. For example, the store schema has a number of tables that represent different aspects of the store. Up to now, all the queries involved only one database table from the store. However, you might want to get information from more than one table—for example, you might want to get the name of the product type and display that name along with the name of the actual product itself. In this section, you'll learn how to perform queries that span multiple tables.

Let's consider an example. Assume you want to view the names of the products, along with the name of the product type for each product in the same output. Now, you know that the name of the product is stored in the name column of the products table, and that the name of the product type is stored in the `name` column of the `product_types` table. You also know from the previous chapter that the `products` and `product_types` tables are related to each other via the foreign key column `product_type_id`. Just to refresh your memory, the `product_type_id` column (the foreign key) of the `products` table points to the `product_type_id` column (the primary key) of the `product_types` table.

So, if you select the `name` and `product_type_id` columns from the `products` table for product #1, you have

```
SELECT name, product_type_id
FROM products
WHERE product_id = 1;

NAME                              PRODUCT_TYPE_ID
-----------------------------     ---------------
Modern Science                                  1
```

And if you select the `name` column from the `product_types` table for the product type with a `product_type_id` of 1, you have

```
SELECT name
FROM product_types
WHERE product_type_id = 1;

NAME
----------
Book
```

From this, you know that product #1 is a book. Nothing very complicated so far, but what you really want is to view the product name and the product type name on the same line. How do you do this?

The answer is to join the two tables in the query. To join two tables means that you specify both the tables in the query's `FROM` clause, and then use related columns (a foreign key from one table and the primary key from another table, for example) from each table. You also use an operator—such as the equality operator (=)—in the query's `WHERE` clause.

NOTE

The tables whose columns are used in the join must also be contained in the `FROM` clause of the `SELECT` statement. The columns used in the join are usually related through a foreign key.

So, for the example, the `FROM` clause would be as follows:

```
FROM products, product_types
```

The `WHERE` clause could be as follows:

```
WHERE product_type_id = product_type_id
```

There's a problem with this WHERE clause: both the products and product_types tables contain a column named product_type_id. You must tell the database which tables to use. To do this, you supply the table names before the column names so that the database knows which columns to use: products.product_type_id and product_types.product_type_id. So the WHERE clause becomes

```
WHERE products.product_type_id = product_types.product_type_id
```

There's one more problem before you put your final query together: how do you tell the database you want the name columns from both the product_types and products tables? You can't just select the name column because the database wouldn't know which name column you meant. The answer is to include the table names and columns in the SELECT clause—products.name and product_types.name—so there's no confusion. So the SELECT clause becomes

```
SELECT products.name, product_types.name
```

Let's put everything together into a complete SELECT statement and see the returned rows:

```
SELECT products.name, product_types.name
FROM products, product_types
WHERE products.product_type_id = product_types.product_type_id;
```

NAME	NAME
Modern Science	Book
Chemistry	Book
Supernova	Video
Tank War	Video
Z Files	Video
2412: The Return	Video
Space Force 9	DVD
From Another Planet	DVD
Classical Music	CD
Pop 3	CD
Creative Yell	CD

Perfect! This is exactly what you wanted: the name of the product and the name of the product type. Notice, however, that the product with the name "My Front Line" is missing from this output. The product_type_id for this product row is null, and because of that the row doesn't appear in the output. You'll see how to include this row later in the section "Understanding Outer Joins."

NOTE
The join syntax you've seen in this section uses Oracle's syntax for joins that is based on the American National Standards Institute (ANSI) SQL/86 standard. With the introduction of Oracle9i, the database also implements the ANSI SQL/92 standard syntax for joins and you'll learn this new syntax later in the section "Performing Joins Using the SQL/92 Syntax." You should use the SQL/92 standard in your queries when working with Oracle9i and above, and use SQL/86 queries only when you're using Oracle8i and below.

Supplying Table Aliases

Earlier, in the section "Performing SELECT Statements that Use Two Tables," you saw that one way to qualify columns in queries that involve columns of the same name in different tables is to include the entire table name. The example in the earlier section used the following query:

```
SELECT products.name, product_types.name
FROM products, product_types
WHERE products.product_type_id = product_types.product_type_id;
```

Notice that the products and product_types table names are used in the SELECT and WHERE clauses. Repeating the table names is redundant typing. A better way is to define table aliases to reference the tables in the FROM clause, and then use that alias when referencing the tables elsewhere in the query. For example, let's use the alias p for the products table and pt for the product_types table. The query then becomes

```
SELECT p.name, pt.name
FROM products p, product_types pt
WHERE p.product_type_id = pt.product_type_id;
```

Notice that the alias for each table is specified in the FROM clause after each table name, and that the alias is used with each column reference.

TIP
Table aliases also make your queries more readable, especially when you start writing longer queries referencing many tables.

Cartesian Products

If a join condition is missing, you will end up selecting all rows from one table joined to all the rows in the other table, a situation known as a *Cartesian product*. When this occurs, you may end up with a lot of rows being displayed. For example, assume you had one table containing 50 rows and a second table containing 100 rows. If you select columns from those two tables without a join, you would get 5,000 rows returned. This is because each row from table 1 would be joined to each row in table 2, which would yield a total of 50 multiplied by 100 rows, or 5,000 rows.

The following example shows a subset of the rows from a Cartesian product between the product_types and products tables:

```
SELECT pt.product_type_id, p.product_id FROM
product_types pt, products p;
```

```
PRODUCT_TYPE_ID PRODUCT_ID
--------------- ----------
              1          1
              2          1
              3          1
              4          1
              5          1
              1          2
```

```
           2                 2
           3                 2
           4                 2
           5                 2
           1                 3
. . .
           5                11
           1                12
           2                12
           3                12
           4                12
           5                12

60 rows selected.
```

A total of 60 rows are selected because the product_types and products tables contain 5 and 12 rows, respectively (5 * 12 = 60).

Performing SELECT Statements that Use More than Two Tables

Joins can be used to connect any number of tables. You can use the following formula to calculate the number of joins you will need in your WHERE clause:

Add all the number of tables used in your query, and then subtract 1 from this total.

In the example shown in the previous section, there were two tables used in the query: products and product_types. Therefore, the number of joins required is 1 (=2 - 1), and indeed only one join is used in that example.

Let's consider a more complicated example that will involve four tables and will therefore require three joins. Let's say you want to see the following information:

- The purchases each customer has made

- The customer's first and last name

- The name of the product they purchased

- The name of the product type

In order to view this information, you need to query the customers, purchases, products, and product_types tables, and your joins will need to navigate the foreign key relationships between these tables. The following list shows the required navigation:

1. To get the customer who made the purchase, you join the customers and purchases tables using the customer_id columns from those respective tables.

2. To get the product purchased, you join the products and purchases tables using the product_id columns from those respective tables.

3. To get the product type name for the product, you join the products and product_types tables using the product_type_id columns from those respective tables.

Using this navigation, your query may appear as follows (notice the aliases and joins used in this query):

```
SELECT c.first_name, c.last_name, p.name AS PRODUCT, pt.name AS TYPE
FROM customers c, purchases pr, products p, product_types pt
WHERE c.customer_id = pr.customer_id
AND p.product_id = pr.product_id
AND p.product_type_id = pt.product_type_id;
```

Notice that I've also renamed the heading for the product name to PRODUCT, and renamed the product type name to TYPE. The output of this query is as follows:

```
FIRST_NAME LAST_NAME  PRODUCT                             TYPE
---------- ---------- ----------------------------------- ----------
John       Brown      Modern Science                      Book
Cynthia    Green      Modern Science                      Book
Steve      White      Modern Science                      Book
Gail       Black      Modern Science                      Book
John       Brown      Chemistry                           Book
Cynthia    Green      Chemistry                           Book
Steve      White      Chemistry                           Book
Gail       Black      Chemistry                           Book
Steve      White      Supernova                           Video
```

The two examples you've seen so far use the equality operator (=) in the joins, and because of this, these joins are known as *equijoins*. As you'll see in the next section, the equijoin is not the only join you can use.

Understanding Join Conditions and Join Types

Earlier in this chapter, you saw that a table join consists of a column from a table, an operator, followed by another column. You also saw some simple examples that use joins. In this section, you'll explore join conditions and join types that allow you to create more advanced queries.

There are two types of *join conditions*, which are based on the operator you use in your join:

- **Equijoins**   You use the equality operator (=) in the join. You've already seen examples of equijoins.

- **Non-equijoins**   You use an operator other than equals in the join, such as <, >, BETWEEN, and so on. You'll see examples of non-equijoins shortly.

In addition to the join condition, there are also three different types of joins:

- **Inner joins**   Return a row *only* when the columns in the join contain values that satisfy the join condition. This means that if a row has a null value in one of the columns in the join condition, that row isn't returned. The examples you've seen so far have been inner joins.

- **Outer joins**   Can return a row *even when* one of the columns in the join condition contains a null value.

- **Self joins**   Return rows joined on the same table.

You'll learn about non-equijoins, outer joins, and self joins next.

Understanding Non-equijoins

A non-equijoin uses an operator other than the equality operator in the join. Examples of non-equality operators are not-equal (<>), less than (<), greater than (>), less than or equal to (<=), greater than or equal to (>=), LIKE, IN, and BETWEEN. The following example uses a non-equijoin to retrieve the salary grades for the employees, which is determined using the BETWEEN operator:

```
SELECT e.first_name, e.last_name, e.title, e.salary,
  sg.salary_grade_id
FROM employees e, salary_grades sg
WHERE e.salary BETWEEN sg.low_salary AND sg.high_salary;
```

```
FIRST_NAME LAST_NAME  TITLE                  SALARY SALARY_GRADE_ID
---------- ---------- ------------------ ---------- ---------------
Fred       Hobbs      Salesperson            150000               1
Susan      Jones      Salesperson            500000               2
Ron        Johnson    Sales Manager          600000               3
James      Smith      CEO                    800000               4
```

Understanding Outer Joins

An *outer join* retrieves a row even when one of the columns in the join contains a null value. You perform an outer join by supplying the outer join operator in the join condition; the outer join operator is a plus character in parentheses (+).

Let's take a look at an example. Remember the query earlier that didn't show the "My Front Line" product because its product_type_id is null? You can use an outer join to get that row; notice that the outer join operator (+) is on the opposite side of the product_type_id column in the product table (this is the column that contains the null value):

```
SELECT p.name, pt.name
FROM products p, product_types pt
WHERE p.product_type_id = pt.product_type_id (+);
```

```
NAME                             NAME
------------------------------   ----------
Modern Science                   Book
Chemistry                        Book
Supernova                        Video
Tank War                         Video
Z Files                          Video
2412: The Return                 Video
Space Force 9                    DVD
From Another Planet              DVD
Classical Music                  CD
Pop 3                            CD
Creative Yell                    CD
My Front Line
```

Notice that "My Front Line"—the product with the null product_type_id—is now shown at the end.

NOTE
*You can place the outer join operator on either side of the join
operator, but you always keep it on the opposite side of the column
that contains the null value for which you still want the row.*

The following query returns the same results as the previous one, but notice that the outer join operator is on the left of the equality operator in the join condition:

```
SELECT p.name, pt.name
FROM products p, product_types pt
WHERE pt.product_type_id (+) = p.product_type_id;
```

Left and Right Outer Joins
Outer joins can be split into two types:

- Left outer joins
- Right outer joins

To understand the difference between left and right outer joins, consider the following syntax:

```
SELECT ...
FROM table1, table2
...
```

Assume the tables are to be joined on `table1.column1` and `table2.column2`. Also, assume `table1` contains a row with a null value in `column1`. To perform a left outer join, the `WHERE` clause is

```
WHERE table1.column1 = table2.column2 (+);
```

NOTE
*In a left outer join, the outer join operator is actually on the right
of the equality operator.*

Next, assume `table2` contains a row with a null value in `column2`. To perform a right outer join, you switch the position of the outer join operator to the *left* of the equality operator and the `WHERE` clause becomes

```
WHERE table1.column1 (+) = table2.column2;
```

NOTE
*As you'll see, depending on whether `table1` and `table2` both
contain rows with null values, you get different results depending
on whether you use a left or right outer join.*

Let's take a look at some concrete examples to make left and right outer joins clearer.

An Example of a Left Outer Join   The following example shows the use of a left outer join; notice that the outer join operator appears on the *right* of the equality operator:

```
SELECT p.name, pt.name
FROM products p, product_types pt
WHERE p.product_type_id = pt.product_type_id (+);
```

```
NAME                              NAME
------------------------------    ----------
Modern Science                    Book
Chemistry                         Book
Supernova                         Video
Tank War                          Video
Z Files                           Video
2412: The Return                  Video
Space Force 9                     DVD
From Another Planet               DVD
Classical Music                   CD
Pop 3                             CD
Creative Yell                     CD
My Front Line
```

Notice all the rows from the `products` table are displayed in this example, including the "My Front Line" row that has a null value in the `product_type_id` column.

An Example of a Right Outer Join   The `product_types` table contains a type of product not referenced in the `products` table (magazine); notice this product type at the end of the following listing:

```
SELECT *
FROM product_types;
```

```
PRODUCT_TYPE_ID NAME
--------------- ----------
              1 Book
              2 Video
              3 DVD
              4 CD
              5 Magazine
```

You can see this product type by using a right outer join, as shown in the following example; notice that the outer join operator actually appears on the *left* of the equality operator:

```
SELECT p.name, pt.name
FROM products p, product_types pt
WHERE p.product_type_id (+) = pt.product_type_id;
```

```
NAME                                 NAME
------------------------------       ----------
Modern Science                       Book
Chemistry                            Book
Supernova                            Video
Tank War                             Video
Z Files                              Video
2412: The Return                     Video
Space Force 9                        DVD
From Another Planet                  DVD
Classical Music                      CD
Pop 3                                CD
Creative Yell                        CD
                                     Magazine
```

Limitations on Outer Joins

There are limitations on using outer joins, and you'll learn some of these limitations in this section.

You may only place the outer join operator on one side of the join (not both). If you try to place the outer join operator on both sides you get an error, as shown in the following example:

```
SQL> SELECT p.name, pt.name
  2  FROM products p, product_types pt
  3  WHERE p.product_type_id (+) = pt.product_type_id (+);
WHERE p.product_type_id (+) = pt.product_type_id (+)
                 *
ERROR at line 3:
ORA-01468: a predicate may reference only one outer-joined table
```

You cannot use an outer join condition with the IN operator:

```
SQL> SELECT p.name, pt.name
  2  FROM products p, product_types pt
  3  WHERE p.product_type_id (+) IN (1, 2, 3, 4);
WHERE p.product_type_id (+) IN (1, 2, 3, 4)
                 *
ERROR at line 3:
ORA-01719: outer join operator (+) not allowed in operand of OR or IN
```

You cannot use an outer join condition with another join using the OR operator:

```
SQL> SELECT p.name, pt.name
  2  FROM products p, product_types pt
  3  WHERE p.product_type_id (+) = pt.product_type_id
  4  OR p.product_type_id = 1;
WHERE p.product_type_id (+) = pt.product_type_id
                 *
ERROR at line 3:
ORA-01719: outer join operator (+) not allowed in operand of OR or IN
```

> **NOTE**
> *These are only a few of the limitations when using the outer join operator. For all the limitations, consult Oracle Corporation's SQL Reference manual.*

Understanding Self Joins

A self join is a join made on the same table. To perform a self join, you must use a different table alias to identify each reference of the table used in your query. Let's consider an example. The `store` schema contains a table named `employees` that contains a list of the employees. The `manager_id` column contains the `employee_id` of the manager for the employee (if that employee has a manager). The `employees` table contains the following rows:

```
EMPLOYEE_ID MANAGER_ID FIRST_NAME LAST_NAME  TITLE         SALARY
----------- ---------- ---------- ---------- -----------   --------
          1            James      Smith      CEO           800000
          2          1 Ron        Johnson    Sales Manager 600000
          3          2 Fred       Hobbs      Salesperson   150000
          4          2 Susan      Jones      Salesperson   500000
```

As you can see, James Smith—the CEO—has a null value for the `manager_id`, meaning that he doesn't have a manager (he answers only to the shareholders). Fred Hobbs and Susan Jones both work for Ron Johnson.

You can use a self join to display the names of each employee and their manager. In the following example, the `employees` table is referenced twice, using two aliases `w` and `m`. The `w` alias is used to get the worker name, and the `m` alias is used to get the manager name. The self join is made between `w.manager_id` and `m.employee_id`:

```
SELECT w.first_name || ' ' || w.last_name || ' works for '||
  m.first_name || ' ' || m.last_name
FROM employees w, employees m
WHERE w.manager_id = m.employee_id;

W.FIRST_NAME||''||W.LAST_NAME||'WORKSFOR'||M.FIRST_NA
----------------------------------------------------
Ron Johnson works for James Smith
Fred Hobbs works for Ron Johnson
Susan Jones works for Ron Johnson
```

Since James Smith's `manager_id` is null—he's the CEO—no row is displayed for him.

You can of course perform outer joins in combination with self joins. In the following example, an outer join is used with the self join shown in the previous example so that you can see the row for James Smith. You'll notice the use of the `NVL()` function to provide a string indicating that James Smith works for the shareholders (remember, he's the CEO, so he reports to the shareholders of the company):

```
SELECT w.last_name || ' works for ' ||
  NVL(m.last_name, 'the shareholders')
FROM employees w, employees m
WHERE w.manager_id = m.employee_id;
```

```
W.LAST_NAME||'WORKSFOR'||NVL(M.LAST_N
-------------------------------------
Smith works for the shareholders
Johnson works for Smith
Hobbs works for Johnson
Jones works for Johnson
```

Performing Joins Using the SQL/92 Syntax

The join syntax you've seen so far used Oracle's syntax for joins. Oracle's syntax is based on the ANSI SQL/86 standard. With the introduction of Oracle9*i*, the database also implements the ANSI SQL/92 standard syntax for joins. To make your SQL fully compliant with the new standard, you should use SQL/92 in your queries. In addition, you'll see how using SQL/92 helps you avoid unwanted Cartesian products.

NOTE
You can find out more about the ANSI SQL standards at their web site www.ansi.org and perform a search on SQL.

Performing Inner Joins on Two Tables Using SQL/92

Earlier, you saw the following query that uses the SQL/86 standard for performing an inner join:

```
SELECT p.name, pt.name
FROM products p, product_types pt
WHERE p.product_type_id = pt.product_type_id;
```

SQL/92 introduced the INNER JOIN and ON clauses for performing an inner join. The following example rewrites the previous query using the INNER JOIN and ON clauses:

```
SELECT p.name, pt.name
FROM products p INNER JOIN product_types pt
ON p.product_type_id = pt.product_type_id;
```

You can use non-equijoin operators with the ON clause. Earlier, you saw the following query that uses the SQL/86 standard for performing a non-equijoin:

```
SELECT e.first_name, e.last_name, e.title, e.salary,
  sg.salary_grade_id
FROM employees e, salary_grades sg
WHERE e.salary BETWEEN sg.low_salary AND sg.high_salary;
```

The following example rewrites this query to use the SQL/92 standard:

```
SELECT e.first_name, e.last_name, e.title, e.salary,
  sg.salary_grade_id
FROM employees e INNER JOIN salary_grades sg
ON e.salary BETWEEN sg.low_salary AND sg.high_salary;
```

Simplifying Joins with the USING Keyword

SQL/92 allows you to further simplify the join condition through the USING clause, but only when your query has the following limitations:

- Your query must use an equijoin.

- The columns in your equijoin have the same name.

Most of the joins you'll perform will be equijoins, and if you always use the same name as the primary key for your foreign keys, you'll satisfy the previous limitations.

The previous example used an equijoin on the product_type_id columns in the products and product_types tables, so the query may be rewritten to use the USING clause instead of ON. The following example shows this:

```
SELECT p.name, pt.name
FROM products p INNER JOIN product_types pt
USING (product_type_id);
```

If you wanted to view the product_type_id, you must only provide this column name on its own without a table name or alias in the SELECT clause. For example:

```
SELECT p.name, pt.name, product_type_id
FROM products p INNER JOIN product_types pt
USING (product_type_id);
```

If you tried to provide a table alias with the column, such as p.product_type_id for example, you'll get an error. For example:

```
SQL> SELECT p.name, pt.name, p.product_type_id
  2  FROM products p INNER JOIN product_types pt
  3  USING (product_type_id);
SELECT p.name, pt.name, p.product_type_id
                        *
ERROR at line 1:
ORA-25154: column part of USING clause cannot have qualifier
```

Also, you only use the column name on its own within the USING clause. For example, if you try to specify USING (p.product_type_id) in the previous query instead of USING (product_type_id), you get the following error:

```
SQL> SELECT p.name, pt.name, p.product_type_id
  2  FROM products p INNER JOIN product_types pt
  3  USING (p.product_type_id);
USING (p.product_type_id)
        *
ERROR at line 3:
ORA-01748: only simple column names allowed here
```

CAUTION
Don't use a table name or alias when referencing columns used in a
USING clause. You'll get an error if you do.

Performing Inner Joins on More than Two Tables Using SQL/92

Earlier you saw the following SQL/86 query that retrieves rows from the customers, purchases, products, and product_types tables:

```
SELECT c.first_name, c.last_name, p.name AS PRODUCT, pt.name AS TYPE
FROM customers c, purchases pr, products p, product_types pt
WHERE c.customer_id = pr.customer_id
AND p.product_id = pr.product_id
AND p.product_type_id = pt.product_type_id;
```

The following example rewrites this query using SQL/92; notice how the foreign key relationships are navigated through multiple INNER JOIN and USING clauses:

```
SELECT c.first_name, c.last_name, p.name AS PRODUCT, pt.name AS TYPE
FROM customers c INNER JOIN purchases pr
USING (customer_id)
INNER JOIN products p
USING (product_id)
INNER JOIN product_types pt
USING (product_type_id);
```

Performing Inner Joins on Multiple Columns Using SQL/92

If your join uses more than one column from the two tables, you provide those columns in your ON clause along with the AND operator. For example, let's say you have two tables named table1 and table2 and you want to join these tables using columns named column1 and column2 in both tables. Your query would be

```
SELECT ...
FROM table1 INNER JOIN table2
ON table1.column1 = table2.column1
AND table1.column2 = table2.column2;
```

You can further simplify your query though the USING clause, but only if you're performing an equijoin and the column names are identical. For example, the following query rewrites the previous example with the USING clause:

```
SELECT ...
FROM table1 INNER JOIN table2
USING (column1, column2);
```

Performing Outer Joins Using SQL/92

Earlier you saw how to perform outer joins using the outer join operator (+). SQL/92 uses a different syntax for performing outer joins. Instead of using (+), you specify the type of join in the FROM clause of your SELECT statement using the following syntax:

```
FROM table1 { LEFT | RIGHT | FULL } OUTER JOIN table2
```

where

- table1 and table2 specify the tables that you want to join.
- LEFT specifies you want to perform a left outer join.
- RIGHT specifies you want to perform a right outer join.
- FULL specifies you want to perform a full outer join; a full outer join uses all rows in table1 and table2 including those that have null values in the columns used in the join. You can't directly perform a full outer join using the (+) operator.

You'll see how to perform left, right, and full outer joins using the SQL/92 syntax in the following sections.

Performing Left Outer Joins Using SQL/92

Earlier you saw the following query that performed a left outer join:

```
SELECT p.name, pt.name
FROM products p, product_types pt
WHERE p.product_type_id = pt.product_type_id (+);
```

The next example rewrites this query using the SQL/92 LEFT OUTER JOIN keywords:

```
SELECT p.name, pt.name
FROM products p LEFT OUTER JOIN product_types pt
USING (product_type_id);
```

Performing Right Outer Joins Using SQL/92

Earlier you saw the following query that performed a right outer join:

```
SELECT p.name, pt.name
FROM products p, product_types pt
WHERE p.product_type_id (+) = pt.product_type_id;
```

The next example rewrites this query using the SQL/92 RIGHT OUTER JOIN keywords:

```
SELECT p.name, pt.name
FROM products p RIGHT OUTER JOIN product_types pt
USING (product_type_id);
```

Performing Full Outer Joins Using SQL/92

A full outer join uses all rows in the joined tables including those that have null values in either of the columns used in the join. The following example shows a query that uses the SQL/92 FULL OUTER JOIN keywords:

```
SELECT p.name, pt.name
FROM products p FULL OUTER JOIN product_types pt
USING (product_type_id);
```

```
NAME                                 NAME
------------------------------------ ----------
Chemistry                            Book
Modern Science                       Book
2412: The Return                     Video
Z Files                              Video
Tank War                             Video
Supernova                            Video
From Another Planet                  DVD
Space Force 9                        DVD
Creative Yell                        CD
Pop 3                                CD
Classical Music                      CD
My Front Line
                                     Magazine
```

Notice that both "My Front Line" from the products table and "Magazine" from the product_ types table are displayed.

Performing Self Joins Using SQL/92

The following example uses SQL/86 to perform a self join on the employees table:

```
SELECT w.last_name || ' works for ' || m.last_name
FROM employees w, employees m
WHERE w.manager_id = m.employee_id;
```

The next example rewrites this query to use the SQL/92 INNER JOIN and ON keywords:

```
SELECT w.last_name || ' works for ' || m.last_name
FROM employees w INNER JOIN employees m
ON w.manager_id = m.employee_id;
```

Performing Cross Joins Using SQL/92

Earlier you saw how omitting a join condition between two tables leads to a Cartesian product. By using the SQL/92 join syntax, you avoid inadvertently producing a Cartesian product because you must always provide an ON or USING clause to join the tables. This is a good thing because you usually don't want a Cartesian product.

If you really want a Cartesian product, the SQL/92 standard requires that you explicitly state this in your query using the CROSS JOIN keywords. In the following example, a Cartesian product between the product_types and products tables is generated using the CROSS JOIN keywords:

```
SELECT *
FROM product_types CROSS JOIN products;
```

Summary

In this chapter, you learned

- How to perform single and multiple table SELECT statements.

- How to select all columns from a table using the asterisk (*) in a SELECT statement.

- How a row identifier (rowid) is used internally by the Oracle database to access a row.

- How to perform arithmetic in SQL statements.

- How to use addition and subtraction operators with dates.

- How to reference tables and columns using aliases.

- How to merge column output using the concatenation operator (| |).

- How nulls are used to represent unknown values.

- How to display distinct rows using the DISTINCT operator.

- How to limit retrieval of rows using the WHERE clause.

- How to sort rows using the ORDER BY clause.

- How to perform inner, outer, and self joins using the SQL/86 and SQL/92 syntax. SQL/86 is used by Oracle8*i* and below. SQL/92 is used by Oracle9*i* and above.

In the next chapter, you'll learn how to use functions.

CHAPTER
3

Using Simple
Functions

In this chapter, you'll learn about some of the Oracle database's built-in functions. A function accepts zero or more input parameters and returns an output parameter. There are two main types of functions you can use in an Oracle database:

- **Single row functions**   These operate on one row at a time and return one row of output for each input row. An example single row function is CONCAT(x, y), which appends y to x and returns the resulting string.

- **Aggregate functions**   These operate on multiple rows at the same time and return one row of output. An example aggregate function is AVG(x), which returns the average of x where x may be a column or, more generally, an expression.

You'll learn about single row functions first, followed by aggregate functions. There are also other more complex types of functions that you'll learn about as you progress through this book.

Sometimes you might want to group blocks of rows in a table and get some information on those groups of rows. For example, you might want to get the average price for the different types of products in the products table. In the final section of this chapter, you'll learn how to group blocks of similar rows together, and also see how to use those blocks of rows in aggregate functions.

Using Single Row Functions

You use single row functions when you want to perform an operation on one row at a time and get one row of output for each row. There are five main types of single row functions:

- **Character functions**   Allow you to manipulate strings of characters and return strings or numbers.

- **Numeric functions**   Allow you to perform calculations and return numbers.

- **Conversion functions**   Allow you to convert a value from one data type to another.

- **Date functions**   Allow you to process dates and times.

- **Regular expression functions**   Allow you to use regular expressions when searching data. These functions are new for Oracle Database 10*g*.

You'll learn about character functions first, followed by numeric functions, conversion functions, and regular expression functions.

NOTE
You'll learn about date functions in the next chapter.

Character Functions

These functions accept character input, which may come from a column in a table or, more generally, from any expression. This input is then processed in some way and a result returned. One example function is UPPER(), which converts all the letters in a character string to uppercase and returns the new string. Another example is NVL(), which converts a null value to a value passed to the function. Table 3-1 shows some of the character functions.

Function	Description
ASCII(*x*)	Returns the ASCII value of the character *x*.
CHR(*x*)	Returns the character with the ASCII value of *x*.
CONCAT(*x*, *y*)	Appends *y* to *x* and then returns the resulting string.
INITCAP(*x*)	Converts the initial letter of each word in *x* to uppercase and returns that string.
INSTR(*x*, *find_string* [, *start*] [, *occurrence*])	Searches for *find_string* in *x* and returns the position at which *find_string* occurs. You can supply an optional *start* position to begin the search. Also, you can supply an optional *occurrence* that indicates which occurrence of *find_string* should be returned.
LENGTH(*x*)	Returns the number of characters in *x*.
LOWER(*x*)	Converts the letters in *x* to lowercase and returns that string.
LPAD(*x*, *width* [, *pad_string*])	Pads *x* with spaces to left, to bring the total length of the string up to *width* characters. You can supply an optional *pad_string*, which specifies the string to be repeated to the left of *x* to fill up the padded space.
LTRIM(*x* [, *trim_string*])	Trims characters from the left of *x*. You can supply an optional *trim_string* that specifies the characters to trim; if no *trim_string* is supplied, spaces are trimmed by default.
NANVL(*x*, *value*)	New for Oracle Database 10*g*. Returns *value* if *x* matches the NaN special value (not a number), otherwise *x* is returned.
NVL(*x*, *value*)	Returns *value* if *x* is null; otherwise, *x* is returned.
NVL2(*x*, *value1*, *value2*)	Returns *value1* if *x* is not null; if *x* is null, *value2* is returned.
REPLACE(*x*, *search_string*, *replace_string*)	Searches *x* for *search_string* and replaces it with *replace_string*.
RPAD(*x*, *width* [, *pad_string*])	Same as LPAD(), but with *x* padded to the right.

TABLE 3-1. *Character Functions*

Function	Description
RTRIM(*x* [, *trim_string*])	Same as LTRIM(), but *x* is trimmed from the right.
SOUNDEX(*x*)	Returns a string containing the phonetic representation of *x*. This lets you compare words that are spelled differently, but sound alike in English.
SUBSTR(*x*, *start* [, *length*])	Returns a substring of *x* that begins at the position specified by *start*. An optional *length* for the substring may be supplied.
TRIM([*trim_char* FROM) *x*)	Trims characters from the left and right of *x*. You can supply an optional *trim_char* that specifies the characters to trim; if no *trim_char* is supplied, spaces are trimmed by default.
UPPER(*x*)	Converts the letters in *x* to uppercase and returns that string.

TABLE 3-1. *Character Functions* (continued)

In Table 3-1—and all the syntax definitions that follow—*x* and *y* may represent columns from a table or, more generally, any valid expressions. You'll learn more about some of the functions shown in Table 3-1 in the following sections.

ASCII() and CHR()

You use ASCII(*x*) to get the ASCII value of the character *x*. You use CHR(*x*) to get the character with the ASCII value of *x*.

The following example gets the ASCII value of a, A, z, Z, 0, and 9 using ASCII():

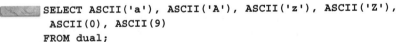

```
SELECT ASCII('a'), ASCII('A'), ASCII('z'), ASCII('Z'),
  ASCII(0), ASCII(9)
FROM dual;

ASCII('A') ASCII('A') ASCII('Z') ASCII('Z')    ASCII(0)    ASCII(9)
---------- ---------- ---------- ---------- ---------- ----------
        97         65        122         90         48         57
```

NOTE
The dual *table is used in this example. As you saw in the previous chapter, the* dual *table contains a single row through which you may perform queries that don't go against a particular table.*

The following example gets the characters with the ASCII value of 97, 65, 122, 90, 48, and 57 using CHR():

```
SELECT CHR(97), CHR(65), CHR(122), CHR(90),
  CHR(48), CHR(57)
FROM dual;

C C C C C C
- - - - - -
a A z Z 0 9
```

Notice the characters returned from CHR() in this example are the same as those passed to ASCII() in the previous example. This shows that CHR() and ASCII() have the opposite effect.

CONCAT()

You use CONCAT(*x*, *y*) to append *y* to *x*. CONCAT() then returns the resulting string.

The following example selects the first_name and last_name columns from the products table, appending last_name to first_name using CONCAT():

```
SELECT CONCAT(first_name, last_name)
FROM customers;

CONCAT(FIRST_NAME,LA
--------------------
JohnBrown
CynthiaGreen
SteveWhite
GailBlack
DoreenBlue
```

NOTE
The CONCAT() function is the same as the | | operator you saw in the previous chapter.

INITCAP()

You use INITCAP(*x*) to convert the initial letter of each word in *x* to uppercase.

The following example selects the product_id and description columns from the products table, and uses INITCAP() to convert the first letter of each word in description to uppercase:

```
SELECT product_id, INITCAP(description)
FROM products
WHERE product_id < 4;

PRODUCT_ID INITCAP(DESCRIPTION)
---------- -----------------------------
         1 A Description Of Modern Science
         2 Introduction To Chemistry
         3 A Star Explodes
```

INSTR()

You use INSTR(*x*, *find_string* [, *start*] [, *occurrence*]) to search for *find_string* in *x*. INSTR() returns the position at which *find_string* occurs. The optional *start* position allows you to specify the position to start the search in *x*. You can also supply an optional *occurrence* that indicates which occurrence of *find_string* should be returned.

The following example selects the name column from the products table and displays the position where the string Science occurs in the name column for product #1:

```
SELECT name, INSTR(name, 'Science')
FROM products
WHERE product_id = 1;

NAME                                INSTR(NAME,'SCIENCE')
-------------------------------     ---------------------
Modern Science                                         8
```

The next example displays the position where the second occurrence of e occurs, starting from the beginning of the product name using INSTR():

```
SELECT name, INSTR(name, 'e', 1, 2)
FROM products
WHERE product_id = 1;

NAME                                INSTR(NAME,'E',1,2)
-------------------------------     -------------------
Modern Science                                       11
```

Notice the second e in Modern Science is the eleventh character.

You can also use dates in character functions. The following example displays the position where the string JAN occurs in dob for customer #1 using INSTR():

```
SELECT customer_id, dob, INSTR(dob, 'JAN')
FROM customers
WHERE customer_id = 1;

CUSTOMER_ID DOB        INSTR(DOB,'JAN')
----------- ---------  ----------------
          1 01-JAN-65                 4
```

LENGTH()

You use LENGTH(*x*) to get the number of characters in *x*. The following example displays the length of the strings in the name column of the products table using LENGTH():

```
SELECT name, LENGTH(name)
FROM products;
```

```
NAME                              LENGTH(NAME)
-----------------------------     ------------
Modern Science                              14
Chemistry                                    9
Supernova                                    9
Tank War                                     8
Z Files                                      7
2412: The Return                            16
Space Force 9                               13
From Another Planet                         19
Classical Music                             15
Pop 3                                        5
Creative Yell                               13
My Front Line                               13
```

The next example displays the total number of characters that make up the product `price` using `LENGTH()`; notice that the decimal point (.) is counted in the number of `price` characters:

```
SELECT price, LENGTH(price)
FROM products
WHERE product_id < 3;

     PRICE LENGTH(PRICE)
---------- -------------
     19.95             5
        30             2
```

LOWER() and UPPER()

You use `LOWER(x)` to convert the letters in *x* to lowercase. Similarly, you use `UPPER(x)` to convert the letters in *x* to uppercase.

The following example selects the `first_name` and `last_name` columns from the `customers` table and converts them to uppercase using the `UPPER()` function, and the strings in the `last_name` column are converted to lowercase using the `LOWER()` function:

```
SELECT UPPER(first_name), LOWER(last_name)
FROM customers;

UPPER(FIRS LOWER(LAST
---------- ----------
JOHN       brown
CYNTHIA    green
STEVE      white
GAIL       black
DOREEN     blue
```

LPAD() and RPAD()

You use LPAD(x, width [, pad_string]) to pad x with spaces to left to bring the total length of the string up to width characters. If a string is supplied in pad_string, this string is repeated to the left to fill up the padded space. The resulting padded string is then returned. Similarly, you use RPAD(x, width [, pad_string]) to pad x with strings to the right.

The following example selects the name and price columns from the products table. The name column is right-padded using RPAD() to a length of 30 characters, with periods filling up the padded space. The price column is left-padded using LPAD() to a length of 8, with the string *+ filling up the padded space.

```
SELECT RPAD(name, 30, '.'), LPAD(price, 8, '*+')
FROM products
WHERE product_id < 4;

RPAD(NAME,30,'.')               LPAD(PRI
------------------------------ --------
Modern Science................ *+*19.95
Chemistry..................... *+*+*+30
Supernova..................... *+*25.99
```

> **NOTE**
> *This example shows that you can use some of the character functions using numbers. Specifically, the price column in the example contains a number and was left padded by LPAD().*

LTRIM(), RTRIM(), and TRIM()

You use LTRIM(x [, trim_string]) to trim characters from the left of x. You can supply an optional trim_string that specifies the characters to trim; if no trim_string is supplied, spaces are trimmed by default. Similarly, you use RTRIM() to trim characters from the right of x. You use TRIM() to trim characters from the left and right of x. For example:

```
SELECT
  LTRIM('   Hello Gail Seymour!'),
  RTRIM('Hi Doreen Oakley!abcabc', 'abc'),
  TRIM('0' FROM '000Hey Steve Button!00000')
FROM dual;

LTRIM('HELLOGAILSEY RTRIM('HIDOREENOA TRIM('0'FROM'000H
-------------------- ----------------- -----------------
Hello Gail Seymour! Hi Doreen Oakley! Hey Steve Button!
```

NVL()

You use NVL() to convert a null to a known value. NVL(x, value) returns value if x is null; otherwise, x is returned.

The following example selects the customer_id and phone columns from the customers table. Null values for the phone column are converted to the string Unknown Phone Number by NVL():

```
SELECT customer_id, NVL(phone, 'Unknown Phone Number')
FROM customers;

CUSTOMER_ID NVL(PHONE,'UNKNOWNPH
----------- --------------------
          1 800-555-1211
          2 800-555-1212
          3 800-555-1213
          4 800-555-1214
          5 Unknown Phone Number
```

NVL2()

NVL2(*x*, *value1*, *value2*) returns *value1* if *x* is not null. If *x* is null, *value2* is returned.

The following example selects the customer_id and phone columns from the customers table. Not null values for the phone column are converted to the string Known and null values are converted to Unknown by NVL2():

```
SELECT customer_id, NVL2(phone, 'Known', 'Unknown')
FROM customers;

CUSTOMER_ID NVL2(PH
----------- -------
          1 Known
          2 Known
          3 Known
          4 Known
          5 Unknown
```

Notice that the phone column values are converted to Known for customers #1 through #4 because the phone column values for those rows are not null. For customer #5 the phone column value is converted to Unknown because the phone column is null for that row.

REPLACE()

You use REPLACE(*x*, *search_string*, *replace_string*) to search *x* for *search_string* and replace it with *replace_string*.

The following example retrieves the name column from the products table for product #1 (whose name is Modern Science) and replaces the string Science with Physics using REPLACE():

```
SELECT REPLACE(name, 'Science', 'Physics')
FROM products
WHERE product_id = 1;

REPLACE(NAME,'SCIENCE','PHYSICS')
-------------------------------------------------
Modern Physics
```

The name for product #1 is Modern Science and so the example returns Modern Physics.

NOTE
REPLACE () doesn't modify the actual row in the database, only the returned row in the result set.

SOUNDEX()

You use SOUNDEX(*x*) to get a string containing the phonetic representation of *x*. This lets you compare words that are spelled differently but sound alike in English.

The following example selects the first_name and last_name columns from the customers table where last_name sounds like whyte using SOUNDEX():

```
SELECT first_name, last_name
FROM customers
WHERE SOUNDEX(last_name) = SOUNDEX('whyte');

FIRST_NAME LAST_NAME
---------- ----------
Steve      White
```

The next example does the same thing as the previous one except the string bloo is passed to SOUNDEX():

```
SELECT first_name, last_name
FROM customers
WHERE SOUNDEX(last_name) = SOUNDEX('bloo');

FIRST_NAME LAST_NAME
---------- ----------
Doreen     Blue
```

SUBSTR()

You use SUBSTR(*x*, *start* [, *length*]) to return a substring of *x* that begins at the position specified by *start*. You can also provide an optional *length* for the substring.

The following example uses SUBSTR() to select a seven-character substring starting at position 2 from the name column of the products table:

```
SELECT SUBSTR(name, 2, 7)
FROM products
WHERE product_id < 4;

SUBSTR(
-------
odern S
hemistr
upernov
```

Using Expressions with Functions

You're not limited to just using columns in functions: you can supply any valid expression that evaluates to a string. The following example uses the SUBSTR() function to select the substring little from the string Mary had a little lamb:

```
SELECT SUBSTR('Mary had a little lamb', 12, 6)
FROM dual;

SUBSTR
------
little
```

Combining Functions

You can use any valid combination of functions in a SQL statement. The following example combines the UPPER() and SUBSTR() functions; notice that the output from SUBSTR() is passed to UPPER():

```
SELECT name, UPPER(SUBSTR(name, 2, 8))
FROM products
WHERE product_id < 4;

NAME                               UPPER(SU
---------------------------------- --------
Modern Science                     ODERN SC
Chemistry                          HEMISTRY
Supernova                          UPERNOVA
```

NOTE
This ability to combine functions is not limited to character functions. Any valid combination of functions will work.

Numeric Functions

You use the numeric functions to perform calculations. These functions accept an input number, which may come from a column in a table or from an expression that evaluates to a number. A calculation is performed with this input and a number is returned. An example of a numeric function is SQRT(), which returns the square root of the input number.

NOTE
Some numeric functions, strictly speaking, don't actually perform a calculation. Some just return some attribute of the input number. For example, SIGN() returns –1 if the input number is negative, 1 if the input number is positive, or zero if the input number is 0.

Table 3-2 shows some of the numeric functions.

Function	Description	Examples
ABS(*x*)	Returns the absolute value of *x*.	ABS(10) = 10 ABS(-10) = 10
ACOS(*x*)	Returns the arccosine of *x*.	ACOS(1) = 0 ACOS(-1) = 3.14159265
ASIN(*x*)	Returns the arcsine of *x*.	ASIN(1) = 1.57079633 ASIN(-1) = -1.5707963
ATAN(*x*)	Returns the arctangent of *x*.	ATAN(1) = .785398163 ATAN(-1) = -.78539816
ATAN2(*x*, *y*)	Returns the arctangent of *x* and *y*.	ATAN2(1, -1) = 2.35619449
BITAND(*x*, *y*)	Returns the result of performing a bitwise AND on *x* and *y*.	BITAND(0, 0) = 0 BITAND(0, 1) = 0 BITAND(1, 0) = 0 BITAND(1, 1) = 1 BITAND(1010, 1100) = 64
COS(*x*)	Returns the cosine of *x*, where *x* is an angle in radians.	COS(90 * 3.1415926) = 1 COS(45 * 3.1415926) = -1
COSH(*x*)	Returns the hyperbolic cosine of *x*.	COSH(3.1415926) = 11.5919527
CEIL(*x*)	Returns the smallest integer greater than or equal to *x*.	CEIL(5.8) = 6 CEIL(-5.2) = -5
EXP(*x*)	Returns the result of the number *e* raised to the power *x*, where *e* is approximately 2.71828183.	EXP(1) = 2.71828183 EXP(2) = 7.3890561
FLOOR(*x*)	Returns the largest integer less than or equal to *x*.	FLOOR(5.8) = 5 FLOOR(-5.2) = -6
LOG(*x*, *y*)	Returns the logarithm, base *x*, of *y*.	LOG(2, 4) = 2 LOG(2, 5) = 2.32192809
LN(*x*)	Returns the natural logarithm of *x*.	LN(2.71828183) = 1
MOD(*x*, *y*)	Returns the remainder when *x* is divided by *y*.	MOD(8, 3) = 2 MOD(8, 4) = 0
POWER(*x*, *y*)	Returns the result of *x* raised to the power *y*.	POWER(2, 1) = 2 POWER(2, 3) = 8

TABLE 3-2. *Numeric Functions*

Function	Description	Examples
ROUND(x [, y])	Returns the result of rounding x an optional y decimal places. If y is omitted, x is rounded to zero decimal places. If y is negative, x is rounded to the left of the decimal point.	ROUND(5.75) = 6 ROUND(5.75, 1) = 5.8 ROUND(5.75, -1) = 10
SIGN(x)	Returns − 1 if x is negative, 1 if x is positive, or 0 if x is zero.	SIGN(-5) = -1 SIGN(5) = 1 SIGN(0) = 0
SIN(x)	Returns the sine of x.	SIN(0) = 0
SINH(x)	Returns the hyperbolic sine of x.	SINH(1) = 1.17520119
SQRT(x)	Returns the square root of x.	SQRT(25) = 5 SQRT(5) = 2.23606798
TAN(x)	Returns the tangent of x.	TAN(0) = 0
TANH(x)	Returns the hyperbolic tangent of x.	TANH(1) = .761594156
TRUNC(x [, y])	Returns the result of truncating x an optional y decimal places. If y is omitted, x is truncated to zero decimal places. If y is negative, x is truncated to the left of the decimal point.	TRUNC(5.75) = 5 TRUNC(5.75, 1) = 5.7 TRUNC(5.75, -1) = 0

TABLE 3-2. *Numeric Functions* (continued)

You'll learn more about some of the functions shown in Table 3-2 in the following sections.

ABS()

You use ABS(x) to get the absolute value of x. The absolute value of a number is that number without any positive or negative sign. The following example displays the absolute value of 10 and − 10:

```
SELECT ABS(10), ABS(-10)
FROM dual;

   ABS(10)    ABS(-10)
---------- ----------
        10          10
```

As you can see, the absolute value of 10 is 10; this is because there is no sign explicitly associated with it. The absolute value of − 10 is 10 because the negative sign is dropped.

Of course, the parameters input to any of the number functions don't have to be literal numbers. The input may also be columns from a table or, more generally, any valid expression. The following example displays the absolute value of subtracting 30 from the `price` column from the `products` table for the first three products:

```
SELECT product_id, price, price - 30, ABS(price - 30)
FROM products
WHERE product_id < 4;
```

```
PRODUCT_ID      PRICE   PRICE-30 ABS(PRICE-30)
---------- ---------- ---------- -------------
         1      19.95     -10.05         10.05
         2         30          0             0
         3      25.99      -4.01          4.01
```

CEIL()

You use `CEIL(x)` to get the smallest integer greater than or equal to x. The following example uses `CEIL()` to display the absolute value of 5.8 and − 5.2, respectively:

```
SELECT CEIL(5.8), CEIL(-5.2)
FROM dual;
```

```
CEIL(5.8) CEIL(-5.2)
---------- ----------
        6         -5
```

The ceiling for 5.8 is 6; this is because 6 is the smallest integer greater than 5.8. The ceiling for − 5.2 is -5; this is because − 5.2 is negative, and the smallest integer greater than this is − 5.

FLOOR()

You use `FLOOR(x)` to get the largest integer less than or equal to x. The following example uses `FLOOR()` to display the absolute value of 5.8 and − 5.2, respectively:

```
SELECT FLOOR(5.8), FLOOR(-5.2)
FROM dual;
```

```
FLOOR(5.8) FLOOR(-5.2)
---------- -----------
        5          -6
```

The floor for 5.8 is 5; this is because 5 is the largest integer less than 5.8. The floor for − 5.2 is − 6; this is because − 5.2 is negative, and the largest integer less than this is –6.

MOD()

You use `MOD(x, y)` to get the remainder when x is divided by y. The following example uses `MOD()` to display the remainder when 8 is divided by 3 and 4, respectively:

```
SELECT MOD(8, 3), MOD(8, 4)
FROM dual;
```

```
MOD(8,3)   MOD(8,4)
---------- ----------
        2          0
```

The remainder when 8 is divided by 3 is 2; this is because 3 goes into 8 twice, leaving 2 left over—the remainder. The remainder when 8 is divided by 4 is 0; this is because 4 goes into 8 twice, leaving nothing left over.

POWER()

You use POWER(x, y) to get the result of x raised to the power y. The following example uses POWER() to display 2 raised to the power 1 and 3, respectively:

```
SELECT POWER(2, 1), POWER(2, 3)
FROM dual;

POWER(2,1) POWER(2,3)
---------- ----------
         2          8
```

When 2 is raised to the power 1, this is equivalent to 2*1, the result is 2; 2 raised to the power 3 is equivalent to 2*2*2, the result of which is 8.

ROUND()

You use ROUND(x, [y]) to get the result of rounding x an optional y decimal places. If y is omitted, x is rounded to zero decimal places. If y is negative, x is rounded to the left of the decimal point.

The following example uses ROUND() to display the result of rounding 5.75 to zero, 1, and − 1 decimal places, respectively:

```
SELECT ROUND(5.75), ROUND(5.75, 1), ROUND(5.75, -1)
FROM dual;

ROUND(5.75) ROUND(5.75,1) ROUND(5.75,-1)
----------- ------------- --------------
          6           5.8             10
```

5.75 rounded to zero decimal places is 6. 5.75 rounded to one decimal place (to the right of the decimal point) is 5.8. 5.75 rounded to one decimal place (to the left of the decimal point, as indicated using a negative sign) is 10.

SIGN()

You use SIGN(x) to get the sign of x. SIGN() returns − 1 if x is negative, 1 if x is positive, or 0 if x is zero. The following example displays the sign of − 5, 5, and 0, respectively:

```
SELECT SIGN(-5), SIGN(5), SIGN(0)
FROM dual;

  SIGN(-5)    SIGN(5)    SIGN(0)
---------- ---------- ----------
        -1          1          0
```

The sign of − 5 is − 1; the sign of 5 is 1; the sign of 0 is 0.

SQRT()

You use SQRT(*x*) to get the square root of *x*. The following example displays the square root of 25 and 5, respectively:

```
SELECT SQRT(25), SQRT(5)
FROM dual;

  SQRT(25)    SQRT(5)
---------- ----------
         5  2.23606798
```

The square root of 25 is 5; the square root of 5 is approximately 2.236.

TRUNC()

You use TRUNC(*x*, [*y*]) to get the result of truncating the number *x* to an optional *y* decimal places. If *y* is omitted, *x* is truncated to zero decimal places. If *y* is negative, *x* is truncated to the left of the decimal point. The following example displays truncating 5.75 to zero, 1, and − 1 decimal places:

```
SELECT TRUNC(5.75), TRUNC(5.75, 1), TRUNC(5.75, -1)
FROM dual;

TRUNC(5.75) TRUNC(5.75,1) TRUNC(5.75,-1)
----------- ------------- --------------
          5           5.7              0
```

As you can see from this example, 5.75 truncated to zero decimal places is 5. 5.75 truncated to one decimal place (to the right of the decimal point) is 5.7. 5.75 truncated to one decimal place (to the left of the decimal point, as indicated using a negative sign) is 0.

Conversion Functions

Sometimes you might want to convert a value from one data type to another. For example, you might want to reformat the price of a product that is stored as a number (1346.95, for example) to string containing dollar signs and commas ($1,346.95). You can use a conversion function to convert a value from one data type to another.

Table 3-3 shows some of the conversion functions.

You'll learn more about the TO_CHAR() and TO_NUMBER() functions in the following sections. You'll learn about some of the other functions in Table 3-3 as you progress through this book.

TO_CHAR()

You use TO_CHAR(*x* [, *format*]) to convert *x* to a string. You can also provide an optional *format* that indicates the format of *x*. The structure *format* depends on whether *x* is a number or date.

Function	Description
`ASCIISTR(x)`	Converts *x* to an ASCII string, where *x* may be a string in any character set.
`BIN_TO_NUM(x)`	Converts *x* to a binary number. Returns a NUMBER.
`CAST(x AS type_name)`	Converts a value in *x* from one data type to another specified in `type_name`.
`CHARTOROWID(x)`	Converts *x* to a ROWID.
`COMPOSE(x)`	Converts *x* to a Unicode string in its fully normalized form in the same character set as *x*. Unicode uses a 2-byte character set and can represent over 65,000 characters; it may also be used to represent non-English characters.
`CONVERT(x, source_char_set, dest_char_set)`	Converts *x* from `source_char_set` to `dest_char_set`.
`DECODE(x, search, result, default)`	Compares *x* with the value in `search`; if equal, `DECODE()` returns `search`, otherwise the value in `default` is returned.
`DECOMPOSE(x)`	Converts *x* to a Unicode string after decomposition in the same character set as *x*.
`HEXTORAW(x)`	Converts the character *x* containing hexadecimal digits (base 16) to a binary number (RAW). This function returns the returns RAW number.
`NUMTODSINTERVAL(x)`	Converts the number *x* to an INTERVAL DAY TO SECOND. You'll learn about date and time interval–related functions in the next chapter.
`NUMTOYMINTERVAL(x)`	Convert the number *x* to an INTERVAL YEAR TO MONTH.
`RAWTOHEX(x)`	Converts the binary number (RAW) *x* to a VARCHAR2 character containing the equivalent hexadecimal number.
`RAWTONHEX(x)`	Converts the binary number (RAW) *x* to an NVARCHAR2 character containing the equivalent hexadecimal number. An NVARCHAR2 is used to store strings in the national character set.
`ROWIDTOCHAR(x)`	Converts the ROWID *x* to a VARCHAR2 character.
`ROWIDTONCHAR(x)`	Converts the ROWID *x* to an NVARCHAR2 character.
`TO_BINARY_DOUBLE(x)`	New for Oracle Database 10g. Converts *x* to a BINARY_DOUBLE.

TABLE 3-3. *Conversion Functions*

Function	Description
TO_BINARY_FLOAT(*x*)	New for Oracle Database 10*g*. Converts *x* to a BINARY_FLOAT.
TO_CHAR(*x* [, *format*])	Converts *x* to a VARCHAR2 string. You can supply an optional *format* that indicates the format of *x*.
TO_CLOB(*x*)	Converts *x* to a character large object (CLOB). A CLOB is used to store large amounts of character data.
TO_DATE(*x* [, *format*])	Converts *x* to a DATE.
TO_DSINTERVAL(*x*)	Convert the string *x* to an INTERVAL DAY TO SECOND.
TO_MULTI_BYTE(*x*)	Converts the single-byte characters in *x* to their corresponding multi-byte characters. The return type is the same as the type for *x*.
TO_NCHAR(*x*)	Converts *x* in the database character set to an NVARCHAR2.
TO_NCLOB(*x*)	Converts *x* to an NCLOB. An NCLOB is used to store large amounts of national language character data.
TO_NUMBER(*x* [, *format*])	Converts *x* to a NUMBER.
TO_SINGLE_BYTE(*x*)	Converts the multi-byte characters in *x* to their corresponding single-byte characters. The return type is the same as the type for *x*.
TO_TIMESTAMP(*x*)	Converts the string *x* to a TIMESTAMP.
TO_TIMESTAMP_TZ(*x*)	Converts the string *x* to a TIMESTAMP WITH TIME ZONE.
TO_YMINTERVAL(*x*)	Converts the string *x* to an INTERVAL YEAR TO MONTH.
TRANSLATE(*x*, *from_string*, *to_string*)	Converts all occurrences of *from_string* in *x* to *to_string*.
UNISTR(*x*)	Converts the characters in *x* to the national language character set (NCHAR).

TABLE 3-3. *Conversion Functions* (continued)

NOTE
You'll learn how to use TO_CHAR() *to convert a number to a string in this section, and see how to convert a date to a string in the next chapter.*

Let's take a look at a couple of simple examples that use TO_CHAR() to convert a number to a string. The following example converts 12345.67 to a string:

```
SELECT TO_CHAR(12345.67)
FROM dual;

TO_CHAR(1
---------
 12345.67
```

The next example uses TO_CHAR() to convert 12345678.90 to a string and specifies this number is to be converted using the format 99,999.99. This results in the string returned by TO_CHAR() having a comma to delimit the thousands:

```
SELECT TO_CHAR(12345.67, '99,999.99')
FROM dual;

TO_CHAR(12
----------
 12,345.67
```

The optional *format* string you may pass to TO_CHAR() has a number of parameters that affect the string returned by TO_CHAR(). Some of these parameters are listed in Table 3-4.

Parameter	Format Examples	Description
9	999	Returns digits in specified positions with leading negative sign if the number is negative.
0	0999 9990	0999: Returns a number with leading zeros. 9990: Returns a number with trailing zeros.
.	999.99	Returns a decimal point in the specified position.
,	9,999	Returns a comma in the specified position.
$	$999	Returns a leading dollar sign.
B	B9.99	If the integer part of a fixed point number is zero, returns spaces for the zeros.
C	C999	Returns the ISO currency symbol in the specified position. The symbol comes from the NLS_ISO_ CURRENCY parameter.
D	9D99	Returns the decimal point symbol in the specified position. The symbol comes from the NLS_NUMERIC_ CHARACTER parameter (default is a period character).
EEEE	9.99EEEE	Returns number using the scientific notation.
FM	FM90.9	Removes leading and trailing spaces from number.

TABLE 3-4.   *Format Parameters*

Parameter	Format Examples	Description
G	9G999	Returns the group separator symbol in the specified position. The symbol comes from the NLS_NUMERIC_CHARACTER parameter.
L	L999	Returns the local currency symbol in the specified position. The symbol comes from the NLS_CURRENCY parameter.
MI	999MI	Returns a negative number with a trailing minus sign. Returns a positive number with a trailing space.
PR	999PR	Returns a negative number in angle brackets (< >). Returns a positive number with leading and trailing spaces.
RN rn	RN rn	Returns number as Roman numerals. RN returns uppercase numerals; rn returns lowercase numerals. Number must be an integer between 1 and 3999.
S	S999 999S	S999: Returns a negative number with a leading negative sign; returns a positive number with a leading positive sign. 999S: Returns a negative number with a trailing negative sign; returns a positive number with a trailing positive sign.
TM	TM	Returns a number using the minimum number of characters. Default is TM9, which returns the number using fixed notation unless the number of characters is greater than 64. If greater than 64, the number is returned using scientific notation.
U	U999	Returns the dual currency symbol (Euro, for example) in the specified position. The symbol comes from the NLS_DUAL_CURRENCY parameter.
V	99V99	Returns number multiplied by 10^x where x is the number of 9 characters after the V. If necessary, the number is rounded.
X	XXXX	Returns the number in hexadecimal. If the number is not an integer, the number is rounded to an integer.

TABLE 3-4. *Format Parameters* (continued)

Let's look at some more examples of converting numbers to strings using TO_CHAR(). The following table shows examples of calling TO_CHAR() along with the output returned from TO_CHAR().

TO_CHAR() Function Call	Output
TO_CHAR(12345.67, '99999.99')	12345.67
TO_CHAR(12345.67, '99,999.99')	12,345.67
TO_CHAR(-12345.67, '99,999.99')	-12,345.67
TO_CHAR(12345.67, '099,999.99')	012,345.67
TO_CHAR(12345.67, '99,999.9900')	12,345.6700
TO_CHAR(12345.67, '$99,999.99')	$12,345.67
TO_CHAR(0.67, 'B9.99')	.67
TO_CHAR(12345.67, 'C99,999.99')	USD12,345.67
TO_CHAR(12345.67, '99999D99')	12345.67
TO_CHAR(12345.67, '99999.99EEEE')	1.23E+04
TO_CHAR(0012345.6700, 'FM99999.99')	12345.67
TO_CHAR(12345.67, '99999G99')	123,46
TO_CHAR(12345.67, 'L99,999.99')	$12,345.67
TO_CHAR(-12345.67, '99,999.99MI')	12,345.67-
TO_CHAR(-12345.67, '99,999.99PR')	<12,345.67>
TO_CHAR(2007, 'RN')	MMVII
TO_CHAR(12345.67, 'TM')	12345.67
TO_CHAR(12345.67, 'U99,999.99')	$12,345.67
TO_CHAR(12345.67, '99999V99')	1234567

TO_CHAR() will return a string of pound characters (#) if you try and format a number that contains too many digits for the format you have provided. For example:

```
SELECT TO_CHAR(12345678.90, '99,999.99')
FROM dual;

TO_CHAR(12
----------
##########
```

Pound characters are returned by TO_CHAR() because the number 12345678.90 has more digits than those allowed in the format string 99,999.99.

You can, of course, use TO_CHAR() to convert columns containing numbers to strings. For example, the following query uses TO_CHAR() to convert the price column of the products table to a string:

```
SELECT product_id, 'The price of this product is' ||
  TO_CHAR(price, '$99.99')
FROM products
WHERE product_id < 5;

PRODUCT_ID 'THEPRICEOFTHISPRODUCTIS'||TO_CHAR(
---------- ----------------------------------
         1 The price of this product is $19.95
         2 The price of this product is $30.00
         3 The price of this product is $25.99
         4 The price of this product is $13.95
```

TO_NUMBER()

You use TO_NUMBER(*x* [, *format*]) to convert *x* to a number. You can provide an optional *format* string to indicate the format of *x*. Your *format* string may use the same parameters as those listed earlier in Table 3-4.

The following example converts the string 970.13 to a number using TO_NUMBER():

```
SELECT TO_NUMBER('970.13')
FROM dual;

TO_NUMBER('970.13')
-------------------
             970.13
```

The next example converts the string 970.13 to a number using TO_NUMBER() and then adds 25.5 to that number:

```
SELECT TO_NUMBER('970.13') + 25.5
FROM dual;

TO_NUMBER('970.13')+25.5
------------------------
                  995.63
```

The next example converts the string -$12,345.67 to a number, passing the format string $99,999.99 to TO_NUMBER():

```
SELECT TO_NUMBER('-$12,345.67', '$99,999.99')
FROM dual;
```

```
TO_NUMBER('-$12,345.67','$99,999.99')
-----------------------------------
                           -12345.67
```

Regular Expression Functions

In this section, you'll learn about regular expression functions, which extend the search capabilities for strings and allow you to search for a specified set of characters or pattern of characters.

A regular expression is a pattern you use to match against a string. For example, let's say you have the following series of years:

```
1965
1968
1971
1970
```

Say you want to get the years between 1965 and 1968 inclusive. You can do that using the following regular expression:

```
^196[5-8]$
```

The regular expression contains a number of *metacharacters*. In this example, ^, [5-8], and $ are the metacharacters. ^ matches the beginning position of a string; [5-8] matches characters between 5 and 8; $ matches the end position of a string. Therefore ^196 matches a string that begins with 196, and [5-8]$ matches a string that ends with 5, 6, 7, or 8. So ^196[5-8]$ matches 1965, 1966, 1967, and 1968, which is the required result.

In the next example, assume you have the following string that contains a quote from Shakespeare's *Romeo and Juliet*:

```
But, soft! What light through yonder window breaks?
```

Let's say you want to get the substring light. You can do this by applying the following regular expression to the quote string:

```
l[[:alpha:]]{4}
```

In this example, [[:alpha:]] and {4} are the metacharacters. [[:alpha:]] matches an alphanumeric character A-Z and a-z; {4} repeats the previous match four times. When l, [[:alpha:]], and {4} are combined, they match a sequence of five letters starting with l. Therefore, when the regular expression l[[:alpha:]]{4} is applied to the string, the substring light is matched.

Table 3-5 lists some of the metacharacters you can use in a regular expression, along with their meaning and a simple example of their use.

Metacharacters	Meaning	Examples
\	Indicates that the match character is a special character, a literal, or a backreference. (A backreference repeats the previous match.)	\n matches the newline character \\ matches \ \(matches (\) matches)
^	Matches the position at the start of the string.	^A matches A if A is the first character in the string.
$	Matches the position at the end of the string.	$B matches B if B is the last character in the string.
*	Matches the preceding character zero or more times.	ba*rk matches brk, bark, baark, and so on.
+	Matches the preceding character one or more times.	ba+rk matches bark, baark, and so on, but not brk.
?	Matches the preceding character zero or one time.	ba?rk matches brk and bark only.
{n}	Matches a character exactly n times, where n is an integer.	hob{2}it matches hobbit.
{n,m}	Matches a character at least n times and at most m times, where n and m are both integers.	hob{2,3}it matches hobbit and hobbbit only.
.	Matches any single character except null.	hob.it matches hobait, hobbit, and so on.
(pattern)	A subexpression that matches the specified pattern. You use subexpressions to build up complex regular expressions. You can access the individual matches, known as captures, from this type of subexpression.	anatom(y|ies) matches anatomy and anatomies.
x|y	Matches x or y, where x and y are one or more characters.	war|peace matches war or peace.
[abc]	Matches any of the enclosed characters.	[ab]bc matches abc and bbc.

TABLE 3-5.   *Regular Expression Metacharacters*

Metacharacters	Meaning	Examples
[a-z]	Matches any character in the specified range.	[a-c]bc matches abc, bbc, and cbc.
[: :]	Specifies a character class and matches any character in that class.	[:alphanum:] matches alphanumeric characters 0-9, A-Z, and a-z. [:alpha:] matches alphabetic characters A-Z and a-z. [:blank:] matches space or tab. [:digit:] matches digits 0-9. [:graph:] matches non-blank characters. [:lower:] matches lowercase alphabetic characters a-z. [:print:] is similar to [:graph:] except [:print:] includes the space character. [:punct:] matches punctuation characters .,"', and so on. [:space:] matches all whitespace characters. [:upper:] matches all uppercase alphabetic characters A-Z. [:xdigit:] matches characters permissible in a hexadecimal number 0-9, A-F, and a-f.
[..]	Matches one collation element, like a multicharacter element.	No example.
[==]	Specifies equivalence classes.	No example.
\n	This is a backreference to an earlier capture, where n is a positive integer.	(.)\1 matches two consecutive identical characters. The (.) captures any single character except null, and the \1 repeats the capture, matching the same character again, therefore matching two consecutive identical characters.

TABLE 3-5. *Regular Expression Metacharacters* (continued)

Table 3-6 shows the regular expression functions available in Oracle Database 10*g*. You'll learn more about the regular expression functions in the following sections.

Function	Description
REGEXP_LIKE(x, pattern [, match_option])	Returns true when the source x matches the regular expression pattern. You can change the default matching using match_option, which may be set to: • 'c', which specifies case sensitive matching (default) • 'i', which specifies case insensitive matching • 'n', which allows you to use the match-any-character operator • 'm', which treats x as multiple line
REGEXP_INSTR(x, pattern [, start [, occurrence [, return_option [, match_option]]]])	Searches for pattern in x and returns the position at which pattern occurs. You can supply an optional: • start position to begin the search. • occurrence that indicates which occurrence of pattern_exp should be returned. • return_option that indicates what integer to return. 0 specifies the integer to return is the position of the first character in x; non-zero specifies the integer to return is the position of the character in x after the occurrence. • match_option to change the default matching.
REGEXP_REPLACE(x, pattern [, replace_string [, start [, occurrence [, match_option]]]])	Searches x for pattern and replaces it with replace_string. The other options have the same meaning as those shown earlier.
REGEXP_SUBSTR(x, pattern [, start [, occurrence [, match_option]]])	Returns a substring of x that matches pattern, which begins at the position specified by start. The other options have the same meaning as those shown earlier.

TABLE 3-6. *Regular Expression Functions*

REGEXP_LIKE()

You use REGEXP_LIKE(x, pattern [, match_option]) to search x for the regular expression pattern. You can provide an optional match_option string to indicate the default matching.

The following example retrieves customers whose date of birth is between 1965 and 1968 using REGEXP_LIKE():

```
SELECT customer_id, first_name, last_name, dob
FROM customers
WHERE REGEXP_LIKE(TO_CHAR(dob, 'YYYY'), '^196[5-8]$');
```

```
CUSTOMER_ID FIRST_NAME LAST_NAME  DOB
----------- ---------- ---------- ---------
          1 John       Brown      01-JAN-65
          2 Cynthia    Green      05-FEB-68
```

The next example retrieves customers whose first name starts with J or j. Notice the regular expression passed to REGEXP_LIKE() is ^j and the match option is i, which indicates case insensitive matching and so ^j matches J or j:

```
SELECT customer_id, first_name, last_name, dob
FROM customers
WHERE REGEXP_LIKE(first_name, '^j', 'i');
```

```
CUSTOMER_ID FIRST_NAME LAST_NAME  DOB
----------- ---------- ---------- ---------
          1 John       Brown      01-JAN-65
```

REGEXP_INSTR()

You use REGEXP_INSTR(x, pattern [, start [, occurrence [, return_option [, match_option]]]]) to search for pattern in x; REGEXP_INSTR() returns the position at which pattern occurs. The position starts at number 1.

The following example returns the position that matches the regular expression l[[:alpha:]]{4} using REGEXP_INSTR():

```
SELECT
  REGEXP_INSTR('But, soft! What light through yonder window breaks?',
  'l[[:alpha:]]{4}') AS result
FROM dual;
```

```
    RESULT
----------
        17
```

Notice 17 is returned, which is the position of the l in light.

The next example returns the position of the second occurrence that matches the regular expression s[[:alpha:]]{3} starting at position 1:

```
SELECT
  REGEXP_INSTR('But, soft! What light through yonder window softly breaks?',
  's[[:alpha:]]{3}', 1, 2) AS result
FROM dual;
```

```
    RESULT
----------
        45
```

The next example returns the position of the second occurrence that matches the letter o starting at position 10 using `REGEXP_INSTR()`:

```
SELECT
  REGEXP_INSTR('But, soft! What light through yonder window breaks?',
  'o', 10, 2) AS result
FROM dual;

    RESULT
----------
        32
```

REGEXP_REPLACE()

You use `REGEXP_REPLACE(x, pattern [, replace_string [, start [, occurrence [, match_option]]]])` to search *x* for *pattern* and replace it with *replace_string*.

The following example replaces the substring that matches the regular expression `l[[:alpha:]]{4}` with the string sound using `REGEXP_REPLACE()`:

```
SELECT
  REGEXP_REPLACE('But, soft! What light through yonder window breaks?',
  'l[[:alpha:]]{4}', 'sound') AS result
FROM dual;

RESULT
--------------------------------------------------
But, soft! What sound through yonder window breaks?
```

Notice light has been replaced by sound.

REGEXP_SUBSTR()

You use `REGEXP_SUBSTR(x, pattern [, start [, occurrence [, match_option]]])` to get a substring of *x* that matches *pattern*, which begins at the position specified by *start*.

The following example returns the substring that matches the regular expression `l[[:alpha:]]{4}` using `REGEXP_SUBSTR()`:

```
SELECT
  REGEXP_SUBSTR('But, soft! What light through yonder window breaks?',
  'l[[:alpha:]]{4}') AS result
FROM dual;

RESUL
-----
light
```

Using Aggregate Functions

The functions you've seen up to now operate on a single row at a time and return one row of output for each input row. In this section, you'll learn how about aggregate functions, which operate on a group of rows at the same time and return one row of output for each group of rows. Examples of when you want to use an aggregate function include computing the average price of a product and finding the maximum price of a product.

NOTE
Aggregate functions are also known as group *functions because they operate on groups of rows.*

The aggregate functions are mainly numerical, and you typically use them to return a value based on a set of values contained in columns of rows. As you'll see shortly, some of the aggregate functions allow you to perform sophisticated statistical computations. Table 3-7 lists some of the aggregate functions. These functions all return a NUMBER.

Here are some points to remember when using aggregate functions:

■ You can use the COUNT(), MAX(), and MIN() functions with numbers, strings, and datetimes.

■ Null values are ignored by aggregate functions. This is because a null value indicates the value is unknown and is therefore not applicable to the aggregate function's calculation.

■ You can use the DISTINCT keyword with an aggregate function to exclude duplicate entries from the aggregate function's calculation.

You'll learn more about some of the aggregate functions shown in Table 3-7 in the following sections.

Function	Description
AVG(x)	Returns the average value of x.
COUNT(x)	Returns the number of rows returned by a query involving x.
MAX(x)	Returns the maximum value of x.
MEDIAN(x)	Returns the median value of x.
MIN(x)	Returns the minimum value of x.
STDDEV(x)	Returns the standard deviation of x.
SUM(x)	Returns the sum of x.
VARIANCE(x)	Returns the variance of x.

TABLE 3-7.   *Aggregate Functions*

AVG()

You use AVG (*x*) to get the average value of *x*. The following example gets the average price of the products; notice that the price column from the products table is passed to the AVG () function:

```
SELECT AVG(price)
FROM products;

AVG(PRICE)
----------
19.7308333
```

You can use the aggregate functions with any valid expression. For example, the following query passes the expression price + 2 to AVG (); this adds 2 to each row's price column value and then returns the average of those values.

```
SELECT AVG(price + 2)
FROM products;

AVG(PRICE)
----------
21.7308333
```

You can use the DISTINCT keyword to exclude identical values from a group computation. For example, the following query uses the DISTICT keyword to exclude identical values in the price column when computing the average using AVG ():

```
SELECT AVG(DISTINCT price)
FROM products;

AVG(DISTINCTPRICE)
------------------
        20.2981818
```

Notice the average in this example value is slightly different from the average shown in the first example of this section, which didn't include the DISTINCT keyword. The average values are different because the price column contains two values that are the same: 13.49 for products #7 and #12. The price column value for product #12 is considered a duplicate and is excluded from the computation performed by AVG ()—and this results in the average being different.

COUNT()

You use COUNT (*x*) to get the number of rows returned by a query. The following example gets the number of rows in the products table using COUNT ():

```
SELECT COUNT(product_id)
FROM products;

COUNT(PRODUCT_ID)
-----------------
```

12

TIP
*You should avoid using the asterisk (*) with the COUNT () function
as it may take longer for COUNT () to return the result. Instead, you
should use a column in the table or use the ROWID column. As you
saw in the previous chapter, the ROWID column contains the internal
location of the row in the Oracle database.*

The following example passes ROWID to COUNT() and gets the number of rows in the
products table:

```
SELECT COUNT(ROWID)
FROM products;

COUNT(ROWID)
------------
          12
```

MAX() and MIN()

You use MAX(x) and MIN(x) to get the maximum and minimum values for x. The following
example displays the maximum and minimum values of the price column from the products
table using MAX() and MIN():

```
SELECT MAX(price), MIN(price)
FROM products;

MAX(PRICE) MIN(PRICE)
---------- ----------
     49.99      10.99
```

You may use MAX() and MIN() with any type, including strings and dates. When you use
MAX() with strings, the strings are ordered alphabetically with the "maximum" string being at
the bottom of a list and the "minimum" string being at the top of the list. For example, the string
Albert would appear before Zeb in such a list. The following example gets the maximum and
minimum name strings from the products table using MAX() and MIN():

```
SELECT MAX(name), MIN(name)
FROM products;

MAX(NAME)                       MIN(NAME)
------------------------------  ------------------------------
Z Files                         2412: The Return
```

In the case of dates, the "maximum" date occurs at the latest point, and the "minimum"
date at the earliest point. The next example displays the maximum and minimum dob from the
customers table using MAX() and MIN():

```
SELECT MAX(dob), MIN(dob)
FROM customers;
```

```
MAX(DOB)  MIN(DOB)
--------- ---------
16-MAR-71 01-JAN-65
```

STDDEV()

You use STDDEV(*x*) to get the standard deviation of *x*. Standard deviation is a statistical function, and is defined as being the square root of the variance (you'll learn about variance shortly).

The following example displays the standard deviation of the price column values from the products table using STDDEV():

```
SELECT STDDEV(price)
FROM products;

STDDEV(PRICE)
-------------
   11.0896303
```

SUM()

SUM(*x*) adds all the values in *x* and returns the total. The following example displays the sum of the price column from the products table using SUM():

```
SELECT SUM(price)
FROM products;

SUM(PRICE)
----------
    236.77
```

VARIANCE()

You use VARIANCE(*x*) to get the variance of *x*. Variance is a statistical function and is defined as the spread or variation of a group of numbers in a sample, equal to the square of the standard deviation.

The following example gets the variance of the price column values from the products table using VARIANCE():

```
SELECT VARIANCE(price)
FROM products;

VARIANCE(PRICE)
---------------
     122.979899
```

Grouping Rows

Sometimes you might want to group blocks of rows in a table and get some information on those groups of rows. For example, you might want to get the average price for the different types of products in the products table. I'll show you how to do this the hard way, then I'll show you the easy way that involves using the GROUP BY clause to group similar rows together.

To do it the hard way, you limit the rows passed to the AVG() function using a WHERE clause. For example, the following query gets the average price for books from the products table (books have a product_type_id of 1):

```
SELECT AVG(price)
FROM products
WHERE product_type_id = 1;

AVG(PRICE)
----------
    24.975
```

To get the average price for the other types of products, you would need to perform additional queries with different values for the product_type_id in the WHERE clause. This is all very labor intensive! You'll be glad to know there's an easier way to do this through the use of the GROUP BY clause.

Using the GROUP BY Clause to Group Rows

You use the GROUP BY clause to group rows into blocks with a common column value. For example, the following query groups the rows from the products table into blocks with the same product_type_id:

```
SELECT product_type_id
FROM products
GROUP BY product_type_id;

PRODUCT_TYPE_ID
---------------
              1
              2
              3
              4
```

Notice there's one returned row in the result set for each block of rows with the same product_type_id. For example, there's one row for products with a product_type_id of 1, another for products with a product_type_id of 2, and so on. There are actually two rows in the products table with a product_type_id of 1, and four rows with a product_type_id of 2. These rows are grouped together into separate blocks, one block for each product_type_id. The first block contains two rows, the second contains four rows, and so on.

Using Multiple Columns in a Group

You can specify multiple columns in a GROUP BY clause. For example, the following query includes the product_id and customer_id columns from the purchases table in a GROUP BY clause:

```
SELECT product_id, customer_id
FROM purchases
GROUP BY product_id, customer_id;

PRODUCT_ID CUSTOMER_ID
---------- -----------
         1           1
         1           2
         1           3
         1           4
         2           1
         2           2
         2           3
         2           4
         3           3
```

Using Groups of Rows with Aggregate Functions

You can use blocks of rows to an aggregate function. The aggregate function performs its computation on the group of rows in each block and returns one value per block. For example, to get the average price for the different types of products in the products table, you:

- Use the GROUP BY clause to group rows into blocks with the same product_type_id.

- Use the AVG() function to get the average price for each block containing a group of rows.

The following query shows the use of the GROUP BY clause and AVG() function:

```
SELECT product_type_id, AVG(price)
FROM products
GROUP BY product_type_id;

PRODUCT_TYPE_ID AVG(PRICE)
--------------- ----------
              1     24.975
              2      26.22
              3      13.24
              4      13.99
                    13.49
```

Notice there are five rows in this output, with each row corresponding to one or more rows in the products table grouped together with the same product_type_id column value. There are two rows in the products table with a product_type_id of 1. These two rows have been grouped together and passed to the AVG() function in the previous query. AVG() computes and returns the average price for the two rows, which is 24.975 as shown in the first row of the previous result set. Similarly, there are four rows with a product_type_id of 2, with an average price of 26.22 as shown in the second row of the result set.

Notice the last row of output has a null value for the product_type_id. This final group consists of the single row with the null product_type_id at the end of the products table. If there was another row in the products table with a null product_type_id, that row would also be placed in the final group. That row's price column value would have also been used in the average computation.

You can use any of the aggregate functions with the GROUP BY clause. For example, the following query gets the number of rows in each product_type_id group using the COUNT() function:

```
SELECT product_type_id, COUNT(product_id)
FROM products
GROUP BY product_type_id;
```

```
PRODUCT_TYPE_ID COUNT(PRODUCT_ID)
--------------- -----------------
              1                 2
              2                 4
              3                 2
              4                 3
                                1
```

Notice I used the product_id column in the COUNT() function in this query, rather than product_type_id. This is because product_type_id is null for product #12, and would be ignored by the COUNT() function, as shown in the following example, which displays 0 for COUNT(product_type_id) in the last row of the result set:

```
SELECT product_type_id, COUNT(product_type_id)
FROM products
GROUP BY product_type_id;
```

```
PRODUCT_TYPE_ID COUNT(PRODUCT_TYPE_ID)
--------------- ----------------------
              1                      2
              2                      4
              3                      2
              4                      3
                                     0
```

Using the ORDER BY Clause to Sort Groups

By default, GROUP BY sorts the rows in ascending order based on the values in the group column. For example, in the previous query the rows were sorted on the product_type_id column. You can change the column used in the sort using the ORDER BY clause, which you saw in the previous chapter. For example, the following query sorts the output using ORDER BY COUNT (product_type_id):

```
SELECT product_type_id, COUNT(product_type_id)
FROM products
GROUP BY product_type_id
ORDER BY COUNT(product_type_id);
```

```
PRODUCT_TYPE_ID COUNT(PRODUCT_TYPE_ID)
--------------- ----------------------
                                     0
              1                      2
              3                      2
              4                      3
              2                      4
```

One point to note is that you don't have to include the columns used in the GROUP BY clause in your SELECT clause. For example, the following query is the same as the previous example except product_type_id is omitted from the SELECT clause:

```
SELECT COUNT(product_id)
FROM products
GROUP BY product_type_id
ORDER BY COUNT(price);
```

```
COUNT(PRODUCT_ID)
-----------------
                1
                2
                2
                3
                4
```

Incorrect Usage of Aggregate Function Calls

When your query contains an aggregate function—and selects columns not placed within an aggregate function—those columns must be placed in a GROUP BY clause. If you forget to do this, you'll get the following error: ORA-00937: not a single-group group function. For example, the following query selects the product_type_id column and AVG(price) but omits a GROUP BY clause for product_type_id:

```
SQL> SELECT product_type_id, AVG(price)
  2  FROM products;
SELECT product_type_id, AVG(price)
       *
ERROR at line 1:
ORA-00937: not a single-group group function
```

The error occurs because the database doesn't know what to do with the product_type_id column in the result set. Think about it: the query attempts to use the AVG() aggregate function that operates on multiple rows, but the query also attempts to get the product_type_id column values for each individual row. You can't have both at the same time. You must provide a GROUP BY clause to tell the database to group multiple rows with the same product_type_id column value together. The database will then pass those groups of rows to the AVG() function.

CAUTION
When your query contains an aggregate function—and selects
columns not placed within an aggregate function—those columns
must be placed in a GROUP BY *clause.*

Also, you cannot use an aggregate function to limit rows in a WHERE clause. If you try to do so you will get the following error: ORA-00934: group function is not allowed here. For example:

```
SQL> SELECT product_type_id, AVG(price)
  2  FROM products
  3  WHERE AVG(price) > 20
  4  GROUP BY product_type_id;
WHERE AVG(price) > 20
      *
ERROR at line 3:
ORA-00934: group function is not allowed here
```

The error occurs because you may only use the WHERE clause to filter *individual* rows—and not *groups* of rows. To filter groups of rows you use the HAVING clause, which you'll learn about in the next section.

Using the HAVING Clause to Filter Groups of Rows

You use the HAVING clause to filter groups of rows. You place the HAVING clause after your GROUP BY clause:

```
SELECT ...
FROM ...
WHERE
GROUP BY ...
HAVING ...
ORDER BY ...;
```

NOTE
GROUP BY *can be used without* HAVING, *but* HAVING *must be used*
in conjunction with GROUP BY.

Let's take a look at an example. Say you want to view the types of products that have an average price greater than $20. To do this, you

■ Use the GROUP BY clause to group rows into blocks with the same product_type_id.

■ Use the HAVING clause to limit the returned results to those groups that have an average price greater than $20.

The following query shows the use of these GROUP BY and HAVING clauses:

```
SELECT product_type_id, AVG(price)
FROM products
GROUP BY product_type_id
HAVING AVG(price) > 20;

PRODUCT_TYPE_ID AVG(PRICE)
--------------- ----------
              1     24.975
              2      26.22
```

As you can see, only the groups of rows having an average price greater than $20 are displayed.

Using the WHERE and GROUP BY Clauses Together

You can use the WHERE and GROUP BY clauses together in the same query. When you do this, the WHERE clause first filters the rows returned, then the remaining rows are grouped into blocks by the GROUP BY clause. For example, the following query uses

■ A WHERE clause to filter the rows from the products table to those whose price is less than $15

■ A GROUP BY clause to group the remaining rows by the product_type_id column

```
SELECT product_type_id, AVG(price)
FROM products
WHERE price < 15
GROUP BY product_type_id;

PRODUCT_TYPE_ID AVG(PRICE)
--------------- ----------
              2      14.45
              3      13.24
              4      12.99
                     13.49
```

Using the WHERE, GROUP BY, and HAVING Clauses Together

You can use the WHERE, GROUP BY, and HAVING clauses together in the same query. When you do this, the WHERE clause first filters the rows, then the remaining rows are grouped into blocks by the GROUP BY clause, and finally the row groups are filtered by the HAVING clause. For example, the following query uses

■ A WHERE clause to filter the rows from the products table to those whose price is less than $15

- A GROUP BY clause to group the remaining rows by the `product_type_id` column

- A HAVING clause to filter the row groups to those whose average price is greater than $13

```
SELECT product_type_id, AVG(price)
FROM products
WHERE price < 15
GROUP BY product_type_id
HAVING AVG(price) > 13;

PRODUCT_TYPE_ID AVG(PRICE)
--------------- ----------
              2      14.45
              3      13.24
                     13.49
```

Compare these results with the previous example. Notice that the group of rows with the `product_type_id` of 4 is filtered out. That's because the group of rows has an average price less than $13.

The final example adds an ORDER BY clause to the previous example to order the results by the average price:

```
SELECT product_type_id, AVG(price)
FROM products
WHERE price < 15
GROUP BY product_type_id
HAVING AVG(price) > 13
ORDER BY AVG(price);

PRODUCT_TYPE_ID AVG(PRICE)
--------------- ----------
              3      13.24
                     13.49
              2      14.45
```

Summary

In this chapter, you learned that

- The Oracle database has two main groups of functions: single row functions and aggregate functions.

- Single row functions operate on one row at a time and return one row of output for each input row. There are five main types of single row functions: character functions, numeric functions, conversion functions, date functions, and regular expression functions.

■ Aggregate functions operate on multiple rows at the same time and return one row of output.

■ Blocks of rows may be grouped together using the GROUP BY clause.

■ Groups of rows may be filtered using the HAVING clause.

In the next chapter, you'll learn about dates and times.

CHAPTER
4

Storing and
Processing
Dates and Times

In this chapter, you will

- Process and store a specific date and time, collectively known as a *datetime*. An example of a datetime is 7:15:30 PM on October 10, 2005. You store a datetime using the DATE type. The DATE type stores the century, all four digits of a year, the month, the day, the hour (in 24-hour format), the minute, and the second.

- Use *timestamps*, which allow you to store a specific date and time. A timestamp stores the century, all four digits of a year, the month, the day, the hour (in 24-hour format), the minute, and the second. The advantages of a timestamp over a DATE are that a timestamp can store a fractional second, and a timestamp can store a time zone.

- Use time *intervals*, which allow you to store a length of time. An example time interval is 1 year 3 months.

Let's plunge in and see some simple examples of storing and retrieving dates using the DATE type.

Simple Examples of Storing and Retrieving Dates

By default, you can supply a date with the format DD-MON-YYYY to the database, where:

- DD is a two-digit day such as 05

- MON is the first three letters of the month such as FEB

- YYYY is a four-digit year such as 1968

Let's take a look at an example of adding a row to the customers table, which contains a DATE column named dob. The following INSERT statement adds a row to the customers table, setting the dob column to 05-FEB-1968:

```
INSERT INTO customers (
    customer_id, first_name, last_name, dob, phone
) VALUES (
    6, 'Fred', 'Brown', '05-FEB-1968', '800-555-1215'
);
```

You can also use the DATE keyword to supply a date literal to the database. Your date must use the ANSI standard date format YYYY-MM-DD, where:

- YYYY is a four-digit year

- MM is a two-digit month from 1 to 12

- DD is a two-digit day

TIP
*ANSI standard dates have the advantage that your INSERT statement
could potentially run against non-Oracle databases.*

For example, to specify a date of October 25, 1972, you use DATE '1972-10-25'. The
following INSERT statement adds a row to the customers table, supplying DATE '1972-10-25'
to the dob column:

```
INSERT INTO customers (
  customer_id, first_name, last_name, dob, phone
) VALUES (
  7, 'Steve', 'Purple', DATE '1972-10-25', '800-555-1215'
);
```

By default, the database outputs dates in the format DD-MON-YY, where YY are the last two
digits of the year. For example, the following query retrieves rows from the customers table
and then performs a ROLLBACK to undo the results of the INSERT statements; notice the two-
digit years in the dob column returned by the query:

```
SELECT *
FROM customers;
```

CUSTOMER_ID	FIRST_NAME	LAST_NAME	DOB	PHONE
1	John	Brown	01-JAN-65	800-555-1211
2	Cynthia	Green	05-FEB-68	800-555-1212
3	Steve	White	16-MAR-71	800-555-1213
4	Gail	Black		800-555-1214
5	Doreen	Blue	20-MAY-70	
6	Fred	Brown	05-FEB-68	800-555-1215
7	Steve	Purple	25-OCT-72	800-555-1215

```
ROLLBACK;
```

Customer #4's dob is null and is therefore blank in the previous output.

NOTE
*If you actually ran the two INSERT statements shown earlier using
SQL*Plus, make sure you undo the changes by executing the ROLLBACK
statement. That way, you'll keep the database in its initial state, and
the output from your queries will match mine. If you forget to roll back,
you can remove your new rows using DELETE, or you can simply
rerun the store_schema.sql script.*

In this section, you saw some simple examples of using dates that use default formats. You'll
learn how to provide your own date formats in the following section and see how to convert
datetimes from one type to another.

Converting Datetimes Using TO_CHAR() and TO DATE()

Oracle has functions that enable you to convert a value in one data type to another. You saw some of these functions in the previous chapter. In this section, you'll see how to use TO_CHAR() and TO_DATE() to convert between strings and datetimes. Table 4-1 summarizes the TO_CHAR() and TO_DATE() functions.

Let's start off by examining how you use TO_CHAR() to convert a datetime to a string. Later, you'll see how to use TO_DATE() to convert a string to a DATE.

Using TO_CHAR() to Convert a Datetime to a String

You can use TO_CHAR(x [, *format*]) to convert the datetime x to a string. You can also provide an optional *format* that indicates the format of x. An example format is MONTH DD, YYYY, where:

- ■ MONTH is the full name of the month in uppercase such as JANUARY

- ■ DD is the two-digit day

- ■ YYYY is the four-digit year

The following example uses TO_CHAR() to convert the dob column from the customers table to a string with the format MONTH DD, YYYY:

```
SELECT customer_id, TO_CHAR(dob, 'MONTH DD, YYYY')
FROM customers;

CUSTOMER_ID TO_CHAR(DOB,'MONTH
----------- ------------------
          1 JANUARY   01, 1965
          2 FEBRUARY  05, 1968
          3 MARCH     16, 1971
          4
          5 MAY       20, 1970
```

Function	Description
TO_CHAR(x [, *format*])	Converts the number or datetime x to a string. You can also supply an optional *format* for x. You saw how to use TO_CHAR() to convert a number to a string in the previous chapter.
TO_DATE(x [, *format*])	Converts the string x to a DATE.

TABLE 4-1. *TO_CHAR() and TO_DATE() Conversion Functions*

The next example gets the current date and time from the database using the SYSDATE function and converts it to a string using TO_CHAR() with the format MONTH DD, YYYY, HH24:MI:SS. The time portion of this format indicates that the hours are in 24-hour format, along with the minutes and seconds.

```
SELECT TO_CHAR(SYSDATE, 'MONTH DD, YYYY, HH24:MI:SS')
FROM dual;

TO_CHAR(SYSDATE, 'MONTHDD,YYY
---------------------------
OCTOBER   21, 2003, 19:32:36
```

When you use TO_CHAR() to convert a datetime to a string, the format string has a number of parameters that affect the returned string. Some of these parameters are listed in Table 4-2.

Aspect	Parameter	Description	Example
Century	CC	Two-digit century.	21
	SCC	Two-digit century with a negative sign (–) for B.C.	–10
Quarter	Q	One-digit quarter of the year.	1
Year	YYYY	All four digits of the year.	2006
	IYYY	All four digits of the ISO year.	2006
	RRRR	All four digits of the rounded year, which depends on the current year. See the section "How Oracle Interprets Two-Digit Years" for details.	2006
	SYYYY	All four digits of the year with a negative sign (–) for B.C.	–1001
	Y,YYY	All four digits of the year with a comma.	2,006
	YYY	Last three digits of the year.	006
	IYY	Last three digits of the ISO year.	006
	YY	Last two digits of the year.	06
	IY	Last two digits of the ISO year.	06
	RR	Last two digits of the rounded year, which depends on the current year. See the section "How Oracle Interprets Two-Digit Years" for details.	06

TABLE 4-2. *Datetime Formatting Parameters*

Aspect	Parameter	Description	Example
	Y	Last digit of the year.	6
	I	Last digit of the ISO year.	6
	YEAR	Name of the year in uppercase.	TWO THOUSAND-SIX
	Year	Name of the year with the first letter in uppercase.	Two Thousand-Six
Month	MM	Two-digit month of the year.	01
	MONTH	Full name of the month in uppercase, right-padded with spaces to a total length of nine characters.	JANUARY
	Month	Full name of the month with first letter in uppercase, right-padded with spaces to a total length of nine characters.	January
	MON	First three letters of the name of the month in uppercase.	JAN
	Mon	First three letters of the name of the month with the first letter in uppercase.	Jan
	RM	Roman numeral month.	The Roman numeral month for the fourth month (April) is IV.
Week	WW	Two-digit week of the year.	02
	IW	Two-digit ISO week of the year.	02
	W	One-digit week of the month.	2
Day	DDD	Three-digit day of the year.	103
	DD	Two-digit day of the month.	31
	D	One-digit day of the week.	5
	DAY	Full name of the day in uppercase.	SATURDAY
	Day	Full name of the day with the first letter in uppercase.	Saturday
	DY	First three letters of the name of the day in uppercase.	SAT
	Dy	First three letters of the name of the day with the first letter in uppercase.	Sat

TABLE 4-2. *Datetime Formatting Parameters* (continued)

Aspect	Parameter	Description	Example
	J	Julian day—the number of days that have passed since January 1, 4713 B.C.	2439892
Hour	HH24	Two-digit hour in 24-hour format.	23
	HH	Two-digit hour in 12-hour format.	11
Minute	MI	Two-digit minute.	57
Second	SS	Two-digit second.	45
	FF[1..9]	Fractional seconds with an optional number of digits to the right of the decimal point. Only applies timestamps, which you'll learn about later in the section "Using Timestamps."	When dealing with 0.123456789 seconds, FF3 would round to 0.123.
	SSSSS	Number of seconds past 12 A.M.	46748
	MS	Millisecond (millionths of a second).	100
	CS	Centisecond (hundredths of a second).	10
Separators	-/,.;: "text"	Characters that allow you to separate the aspects of a date and time. You can supply freeform text in quotes as a separator.	When dealing with the date December 13, 1969, DD-MM-YYYY would produce 12-13-1969 and DD/MM/YYYY would produce 12/13/1969
Suffixes	AM or PM	AM or PM as appropriate.	AM
	A.M. or P.M.	A.M. or P.M. as appropriate.	P.M.
	AD or BC	AD or BC as appropriate.	AD
	A.D. or B.C.	A.D. or B.C. as appropriate.	B.C.
	TH	Suffix to a number. You can make the suffix uppercase by specifying the numeric format in uppercase and vice versa for lowercase.	When dealing with a day number of 28, ddTH would produce 28th and DDTH would produce 28TH

TABLE 4-2. *Datetime Formatting Parameters* (continued)

Aspect	Parameter	Description	Example
	SP	Number is spelled out.	When dealing with a day number of 28, DDSP would produce TWENTY-EIGHT and ddSP would produce twenty-eight
	SPTH	Combination of TH and SP.	When dealing with a day number of 28, DDSPTH would produce TWENTY-EIGHTH and ddSPTH would produce twenty-eighth
Era	EE	Full era name for Japanese Imperial, ROC Official, and Thai Buddha calendars.	No example
	E	Abbreviated era name.	No example
Time zones	TZH	Time zone hour. You'll learn about time zones later in the section "Understanding Time Zones."	12
	TZM	Time zone minute.	30
	TZR	Time zone region.	PST
	TZD	Time zone with daylight savings information.	No example

TABLE 4-2. *Datetime Formatting Parameters* (continued)

The following table shows examples of strings to format the date February 5, 1968, along with the string returned from a call to TO_CHAR().

Format String	Returned String
MONTH DD, YYYY	FEBRUARY 05, 1968
MM/DD/YYYY	02/05/1968
MM-DD-YYYY	02-05-1968
DD/MM/YYYY	05/02/1968
DAY MON, YY AD	MONDAY FEB, 68 AD
DDSPTH "of" MONTH, YEAR A.D.	FIFTH of FEBRUARY, NINETEEN SIXTY-EIGHT A.D.

Format String	Returned String
CC, SCC	20, 20
Q	1
YYYY, IYYY, RRRR, SYYYY, Y,YYY, YYY, IYY, YY, IY, RR, Y, I, YEAR, Year	1968, 1968, 1968, 1968, 1,968, 968, 968, 68, 68, 68, 8, 8, NINETEEN SIXTY-EIGHT, Nineteen Sixty-Eight
MM, MONTH, Month, MON, Mon, RM	02, FEBRUARY , February , FEB, Feb, II
WW, IW, W	06, 06, 1
DDD, DD, DAY, Day, DY, Dy, J	036, 05, MONDAY , Monday , MON, Mon, 2439892
ddTH, DDTH, ddSP, DDSP, DDSPTH	05th, 05TH, five, FIVE, FIFTH

You can see the results shown in this table by calling TO_CHAR() in a query. The following query converts February 5, 1968, to a string with the format MONTH DD, YYYY:

```
SELECT TO_CHAR(TO_DATE('05-FEB-1968'), 'MONTH DD, YYYY')
FROM dual;

TO_CHAR(TO_DATE('0
------------------
FEBRUARY  05, 1968
```

NOTE
The TO_DATE() *function converts a string to a datetime. You'll learn more about the* TO_DATE() *function shortly.*

The following table shows examples of strings to format the time 19:32:36 (32 minutes and 36 seconds past 7 P.M.)—along with the output that would be returned from a call to TO_CHAR() with that time and format string.

Format String	Returned String
HH24:MI:SS	19:32:36
HH.MI.SS AM	7.32.36 PM

Using TO_DATE() to Convert a String to a Datetime

You can use TO_DATE(x [, *format*]) to convert the x string to a datetime. You can provide an optional *format* string to indicate the format of x. If you omit *format*, your date can be in the default format DD-MON-YYYY or DD-MON-YY.

NOTE
*The NLS_DATE_FORMAT database parameter specifies the default
date format. As you'll learn later in the section "Setting the Default
Date Format," you can change the setting of NLS_DATE_FORMAT.*

The following example uses TO_DATE() to convert the strings 04-JUL-2006 and 04-JUL-
06 to the date July 4, 2006; notice the final date is displayed in the default format of DD-MON-YY:

```
SELECT TO_DATE('04-JUL-2006'), TO_DATE('04-JUL-06')
FROM dual;

TO_DATE(' TO_DATE('
--------- ---------
04-JUL-06 04-JUL-06
```

Specifying a Datetime Format

As mentioned, you can supply an optional format for your datetime to TO_DATE(). You use the
same format parameters as those defined previously in Table 4-2. The following example uses
TO_DATE() to convert the string July 4, 2006 to a date, passing the format string MONTH DD,
YYYY to TO_DATE():

```
SELECT TO_DATE('July 4, 2006', 'MONTH DD, YYYY')
FROM dual;

TO_DATE('
---------
04-JUL-06
```

The next example passes the format string MM.DD.YY to TO_DATE() and converts the string
7.4.06 to the date July 4, 2006; again, the final date is displayed in the default format DD-MON-YY:

```
SELECT TO_DATE('7.4.06', 'MM.DD.YY')
FROM dual;

TO_DATE('
---------
04-JUL-06
```

Specifying Times

You can, of course, specify a time with a datetime. If you don't supply a time with a datetime, the
time part of your datetime defaults to 12:00:00 A.M. You can supply the format for a time using the
various formats shown earlier in Table 4-3. One example time format is HH24:MI:SS, where:

- HH24 is a two-digit hour in 24-hour format from 00 to 23.

- MI is a two-digit minute from 00 to 59.

- SS is a two-digit second from 00 to 59.

An example of a time that uses the `HH24:MI:SS` format is 19:32:36. A full example datetime that uses this time is

```
05-FEB-1968 19:32:36
```

with the format for this datetime being

```
DD-MON-YYYY HH24:MI:SS
```

The following `TO_DATE()` call shows the use of this datetime format and value:

```
TO_DATE('05-FEB-1968 19:32:36', 'DD-MON-YYYY HH24:MI:SS')
```

The datetime returned by `TO_DATE()` in the previous example is used in the following `INSERT` statement that adds a row to the `customers` table. Notice the `dob` column for the new row is set to the datetime returned by `TO_DATE()`:

```
INSERT INTO customers (
    customer_id, first_name, last_name,
    dob,
    phone
) VALUES (
    6, 'Fred', 'Brown',
    TO_DATE('05-FEB-1968 19:32:36', 'DD-MON-YYYY HH24:MI:SS'),
    '800-555-1215'
);
```

You use `TO_CHAR()` to view the time part of a datetime. For example, the following query retrieves the rows from the `customers` table and uses `TO_CHAR()` to convert the `dob` column values; notice customer #6 has the time previously set in the `INSERT`:

```
SELECT customer_id, TO_CHAR(dob, 'DD-MON-YYYY HH24:MI:SS')
FROM customers;

CUSTOMER_ID TO_CHAR(DOB,'DD-MON-
----------- --------------------
          1 01-JAN-1965 00:00:00
          2 05-FEB-1968 00:00:00
          3 16-MAR-1971 00:00:00
          4
          5 20-MAY-1970 00:00:00
          6 05-FEB-1968 19:32:36

ROLLBACK;
```

Notice the time for the `dob` column for customers #1, #2, #3, and #5 is set to 00:00:00 (12 A.M.). This is the default time substituted by the database when you don't provide a time in a datetime.

> **NOTE**
> *If you actually ran the earlier INSERT statement in SQL*Plus, make*
> *sure you undo the change using ROLLBACK.*

Combining TO_CHAR() and TO_DATE() Calls

You can combine TO_CHAR() and TO_DATE() calls. This allows you to supply and view datetimes in different formats. For example, the following query combines TO_CHAR() and TO_DATE() to view just the time part of a datetime; notice that the output from TO_DATE() is passed to TO_CHAR():

```
SELECT TO_CHAR(TO_DATE('05-FEB-1968 19:32:36',
  'DD-MON-YYYY HH24:MI:SS'), 'HH24:MI:SS')
FROM dual;

TO_CHAR(
--------
19:32:36
```

Setting the Default Date Format

The default date format is specified in the NLS_DATE_FORMAT database parameter. Your DBA can change the setting of NLS_DATE_FORMAT by setting this parameter's value in the database's init.ora or spfile.ora file, which is read when the database is started. Your DBA can also set NLS_DATE_FORMAT using an ALTER SYSTEM command.

You can also set the NLS_DATE_FORMAT parameter for your own session using SQL*Plus. You do this using ALTER SESSION.

> **NOTE**
> *A session is started when you connect to a database and is ended*
> *when you disconnect.*

For example, the following ALTER SESSION statement sets NLS_DATE_FORMAT to MONTH-DD-YYYY using SQL*Plus:

```
SQL> ALTER SESSION SET NLS_DATE_FORMAT = 'MONTH-DD-YYYY';

Session altered
```

You can see the use of this new date format in the output from the following query that retrieves the dob column for customer #1:

```
SELECT dob
FROM customers
WHERE customer_id = 1;

DOB
-----------------
JANUARY  -01-1965
```

You may also use the new date format when inserting a row in the database. For example, the following INSERT statement adds a new row to the customers table. Notice the use of the format MONTH-DD-YYYY when supplying the dob column's value:

```
INSERT INTO customers (
  customer_id, first_name, last_name, dob, phone
) VALUES (
  6, 'Fred', 'Brown', 'MARCH-15-1970', '800-555-1215'
);
```

If you then disconnect from the database and connect again as the store user, you'll find that the date format is back to the default. That's because any changes you make using the ALTER SESSION statement only last for that particular session: when you disconnect, you lose the change.

How Oracle Interprets Two-Digit Years

The Oracle database stores all four digits of the year, but if you only supply two digits Oracle will interpret the century depending on whether the YY or RR format is being used.

TIP
I recommend you always specify all four digits of the year when supplying a date to an Oracle database. That way, you won't get confused as to which year you mean.

Let's take a look at the YY format first, followed by the RR format.

Using the YY Format

If your date format uses YY for the year and you supply the two digits of a year, the century for your year is assumed to be the same as the present century currently set on your database server. Therefore, *the first two digits of your supplied year are set to the first two digits of the present year.* For example, if your supplied year is 15 and the present year is 2006, your supplied year is set to 2015. Also, 75 is set to 2075.

NOTE
If you use the YYYY format but only supply a two-digit date, your date is interpreted using the YY format.

Let's take a look at a query that uses the YY format when interpreting the years 15 and 75. In the following example, notice that the input dates 15 and 75 are passed to TO_DATE(), whose output is passed to TO_CHAR(), which converts the dates to a string with the format DD-MON-YYYY. (I use YYYY so you can see all four digits of the year returned by TO_DATE().)

```
SELECT
  TO_CHAR(TO_DATE('04-JUL-15', 'DD-MON-YY'), 'DD-MON-YYYY'),
  TO_CHAR(TO_DATE('04-JUL-75', 'DD-MON-YY'), 'DD-MON-YYYY')
FROM dual;
```

```
TO_CHAR(TO_ TO_CHAR(TO_
----------- -----------
04-JUL-2015 04-JUL-2075
```

As expected, 15 and 75 are interpreted as 2015 and 2075.

Using the RR Format

If your date format is RR and you supply the last two digits of a year, the first two digits of your year are determined using the two-digit year you supply (your *supplied year*) and the last two digits of the present date on your database server (the *present year*). The rules used to determine the century of your supplied year are as follows:

- **Rule 1** If your supplied year is between 00 and 49 and the present year is between 00 and 49, the century is the same as the present century. Therefore, *the first two digits of your supplied year are set to the first two digits of the present year.* For example, if your supplied year is 15 and the present year is 2005, your supplied year is set to 2015.

- **Rule 2** If your supplied year is between 50 and 99 and the present year is between 00 and 49, the century is the present century minus 1. Therefore, *the first two digits of your supplied year are set to the present year's first two digits minus 1.* For example, if your supplied year is 75 and the present year is 2005, your supplied year is set to 1975.

- **Rule 3** If your supplied year is between 00 and 49 and the present year is between 50 and 99, the century is the present century plus 1. Therefore, *the first two digits of your supplied year are set to the present year's first two digits plus 1.* For example, if your supplied year is 15 and the present year is 2075, your supplied year is set to 2115.

- **Rule 4** If your supplied year is between 50 and 99 and the present year is between 50 and 99, the century is the same as the present century. Therefore, *the first two digits of your supplied year are set to the first two digits of the present year.* For example, if your supplied year is 55 and the present year is 2075, your supplied year is set to 2055.

Table 4-3 summarizes these results.

NOTE
If you use the RRRR format but only supply a two-digit date, your date is interpreted using the RR format.

Let's take a look at a query that uses the RR format when interpreting the years 15 and 75. For the following example, you should assume the present year is 2005.

```
SELECT
    TO_CHAR(TO_DATE('04-JUL-15', 'DD-MON-RR'), 'DD-MON-YYYY'),
    TO_CHAR(TO_DATE('04-JUL-75', 'DD-MON-RR'), 'DD-MON-YYYY')
FROM dual;

TO_CHAR(TO_ TO_CHAR(TO_
----------- -----------
04-JUL-2015 04-JUL-1975
```

		Two-Digit Supplied Year	
		00-49	**50-99**
Last Two Digits of Present Year	**00-49**	Rule 1: First two digits of supplied year are set to first two digits of present year	Rule 2: First two digits of supplied year are set to present year's first two digits minus 1
	50-99	Rule 3: First two digits of supplied year are set to present year's first two digits plus 1	Rule 4: First two digits of supplied year are set to first two digits of present year

TABLE 4-3. *How Two-Digit Years Are Interpreted*

As expected from rules 1 and 2, 15 and 75 are interpreted as 2015 and 1975. For the next example, you should assume the present year is 2075.

```
SELECT
  TO_CHAR(TO_DATE('04-JUL-15', 'DD-MON-RR'), 'DD-MON-YYYY'),
  TO_CHAR(TO_DATE('04-JUL-55', 'DD-MON-RR'), 'DD-MON-YYYY')
FROM dual;

TO_CHAR(TO_ TO_CHAR(TO_
----------- -----------
04-JUL-2115 04-JUL-2055
```

As expected from rules 3 and 4, 15 and 75 are interpreted as 2115 and 2055.

Using Datetime Functions

You use the datetime functions to get or process datetimes and timestamps (you'll learn about timestamps later in this chapter). Table 4-4 shows some of the datetime functions. In this table, x represents a datetime or a timestamp.

You'll learn more about the functions shown in Table 4-4 in the following sections.

Function	Description
ADD_MONTHS(*x*, *y*)	Returns the result of adding *y* months to *x*. If *y* is negative, *y* months are subtracted from *x*.
LAST_DAY(*x*)	Returns the last day of the month that contains *x*.
MONTHS_BETWEEN(*x*, *y*)	Returns the number of months between *x* and *y*. If *x* appears before *y* on the calendar, the number returned is positive, otherwise the number is negative.
NEXT_DAY(*x*, *day*)	Returns the datetime of the next day following *x*; *day* is specified as a literal string—SATURDAY, for example.
ROUND(*x* [, *unit*])	Rounds *x*. By default, *x* is rounded to the beginning of the nearest day. You may supply an optional *unit* string to indicate the rounding unit. For example, YYYY rounds *x* to the first day of the nearest year.
SYSDATE()	Returns the current datetime set for the operating system on which the database resides.
TRUNC(*x* [, *unit*])	Truncates *x*. By default, *x* is truncated to the beginning of the day. You may supply an optional *unit* string that indicates the truncating unit. For example, MM truncates *x* to the first day of the month.

TABLE 4-4. *Datetime Functions*

ADD_MONTHS()

You use ADD_MONTHS(*x*, *y*) to get the result of adding *y* months to *x*. If *y* is negative, *y* months are subtracted from *x*. The following example adds 13 months to January 1, 2005:

```
SELECT ADD_MONTHS('01-JAN-2005', 13)
FROM dual;

ADD_MONTH
---------
01-FEB-06
```

The following example subtracts 13 months from the January 1, 2005; notice that −13 months are "added" to this date using ADD_MONTHS():

```
SELECT ADD_MONTHS('01-JAN-2005', -13)
FROM dual;

ADD_MONTH
---------
01-DEC-03
```

You can provide a time and date to the ADD_MONTHS() function. For example, the following query adds two months to the datetime 7:15:26 PM on January 1, 2005:

```
SELECT ADD_MONTHS(TO_DATE('01-JAN-2005 19:15:26',
  'DD-MON-YYYY HH24:MI:SS'), 2)
FROM dual;

ADD_MONTH
---------
01-MAR-05
```

The next query rewrites the previous example to convert the returned datetime from ADD_MONTHS() to a string using to TO_CHAR() with the format DD-MON-YYYY HH24:MI:SS:

```
SELECT TO_CHAR(ADD_MONTHS(TO_DATE('01-JAN-2005 19:15:26',
  'DD-MON-YYYY HH24:MI:SS'), 2), 'DD-MON-YYYY HH24:MI:SS')
FROM dual;

TO_CHAR(ADD_MONTHS(T
--------------------
01-MAR-2005 19:15:26
```

NOTE
You can provide a time and date to any of the functions shown earlier in Table 4-4.

LAST_DAY()

You use LAST_DAY(x) to get the date of the last day of the month that contains x. The following example displays the last date in January 2005:

```
SELECT LAST_DAY('01-JAN-2005')
FROM dual;

LAST_DAY(
---------
31-JAN-05
```

MONTHS_BETWEEN()

You use MONTHS_BETWEEN(x, y) to get the number of months between x and y. If x occurs before y in the calendar, the number returned by MONTHS_BETWEEN() is negative.

NOTE
The ordering of the dates in your call to the MONTHS_BETWEEN() function is important: the later date must appear first if you want the result as a positive number.

The following example displays the number of months between May 25, 2005, and January 15, 2005. Notice that since the later date (May 25, 2005) appears first, the result returned is a positive number:

```
SELECT MONTHS_BETWEEN('25-MAY-2005', '15-JAN-2005')
FROM dual;

MONTHS_BETWEEN('25-MAY-2005','15-JAN-2005')
-------------------------------------------
                                  4.32258065
```

The next example reverses the same dates in the call to the MONTHS_BETWEEN() function, and therefore the returned result is a negative number of months:

```
SELECT MONTHS_BETWEEN('15-JAN-2005', '25-MAY-2005')
FROM dual;

MONTHS_BETWEEN('15-JAN-2005','25-MAY-2005')
-------------------------------------------
                                  -4.3225806
```

NEXT_DAY()

You use NEXT_DAY(x, day) to get the date of the next day following x; you specify day as a literal string, such as SATURDAY.

The following example displays the date of the next Saturday after January 1, 2005:

```
SELECT NEXT_DAY('01-JAN-2005', 'SATURDAY')
FROM dual;

NEXT_DAY(
---------
08-JAN-05
```

ROUND()

You use ROUND(x [, $unit$]) to round x. By default, x is rounded to the beginning of the nearest day. If you supply an optional $unit$ string, x is rounded to that unit; for example, YYYY rounds x to the first day of the nearest year. You can use many of the parameters shown earlier in Table 4-2 to round a datetime.

The following example uses ROUND() to round October 25, 2005, up to the first day in the nearest year, which is January 1, 2006. Notice that the date is specified as 25-OCT-2005 and is contained within a call to the function TO_DATE() function:

```
SELECT ROUND(TO_DATE('25-OCT-2005'), 'YYYY')
FROM dual;

ROUND(TO_
---------
01-JAN-06
```

The next example rounds May 25, 2005, to the first day in the nearest month, which is June 1, 2005, because May 25 is closer to the beginning of June than it is to the beginning of May:

```
SELECT ROUND(TO_DATE('25-MAY-2005'), 'MM')
FROM dual;

ROUND(TO_
---------
01-JUN-05
```

The next example rounds 7:45:26 P.M. on May 25, 2005, to the nearest hour, which is 8:00 P.M.:

```
SELECT TO_CHAR(ROUND(TO_DATE('25-MAY-2005 19:45:26',
  'DD-MON-YYYY HH24:MI:SS'), 'HH24'), 'DD-MON-YYYY HH24:MI:SS')
FROM dual;

TO_CHAR(ROUND(TO_DAT
--------------------
25-MAY-2005 20:00:00
```

SYSDATE()

You use SYSDATE() to get the current datetime set in the operating system on which the database resides. In the following example, notice that the parentheses are omitted from the function call. This is because the SYSDATE() function accepts no parameters.

```
SELECT SYSDATE
FROM dual;

SYSDATE
---------
21-OCT-03
```

TRUNC()

You use TRUNC(x [, unit]) to truncate x. By default, x is truncated to the beginning of the day. If you supply an optional unit string, x is truncated to that unit; for example, MM truncates x to the first day in the month. You can use many of the parameters shown earlier in Table 4-2 to truncate a datetime.

The following example uses TRUNC() to truncate May 25, 2005, to the first day in the year, which is January 1, 2005:

```
SELECT TRUNC(TO_DATE('25-MAY-2005'), 'YYYY')
FROM dual;

TRUNC(TO_
---------
01-JAN-05
```

The next example truncates May 25, 2005, to the first day in the month, which is May 1, 2005:

```
SELECT TRUNC(TO_DATE('25-MAY-2005'), 'MM')
FROM dual;

TRUNC(TO_
---------
01-MAY-05
```

The next example truncates 7:45:26 P.M. on May 25, 2005, to the hour, which is 7:00 P.M.:

```
SELECT TO_CHAR(TRUNC(TO_DATE('25-MAY-2005 19:45:26',
 'DD-MON-YYYY HH24:MI:SS'), 'HH24'), 'DD-MON-YYYY HH24:MI:SS')
FROM dual;

TO_CHAR(TRUNC(TO_DAT
--------------------
25-MAY-2005 19:00:00
```

Understanding Time Zones

The Oracle9*i* database introduced the ability to use different time zones. A time zone is an offset from the time in Greenwich, England. The time in Greenwich was once known as Greenwich Mean Time (GMT), but is now known as Coordinated Universal Time (UTC, which comes from the French initials for the words). You specify a time zone using either an offset from UTC or the name of the region. When you specify an offset, you use HH:MI prefixed with a plus or minus sign:

 +|-HH:MI

where

- + or – indicates an increase or decrease for the offset from UTC
- HH:MI indicates the time zone hour and minute for the offset

NOTE
The time zone hour and minute use the format parameters TZH and TZR shown earlier in Table 4-2.

The following examples show offsets of –7 hours behind UTC and +2 hours 15 minutes ahead of UTC:

```
-07:00
+02:15
```

You may also specify a time zone using the name of a region. For example, PST indicates Pacific Standard Time, which is seven hours behind UTC. EST indicates Eastern Standard Time, which is four hours behind UTC.

NOTE
The time zone region uses the format parameter TZR *shown earlier in Table 4-2.*

Time Zone–Related Functions

There are a number of functions that are related to time zones; these functions are shown in Table 4-5.

You'll learn more about the functions shown in Table 4-5 in the following sections.

The Database Time Zone and Session Time Zone

If you're working for a large worldwide organization, the database you access may be located in a different time zone than your local time zone. The time zone for the database is known as the *database time zone,* and the time zone set for your database session is known as the *session time zone.* You'll learn about the database and session time zones in the following sections.

The Database Time Zone

The database time zone is controlled using the TIME_ZONE database parameter. Your DBA can change the setting of the TIME_ZONE parameter in the database's init.ora or spfile.ora file. You can get the database time zone using the DBTIMEZONE() function:

```
SELECT DBTIMEZONE
FROM dual;

DBTIME
------
-05:00
```

Function	Description
CURRENT_DATE()	Returns the current date in the local time zone set for the database session.
DBTIMEZONE()	Returns the time zone for the database.

NEW_TIME(
  x,
  time_zone1,
  time_zone2
)
	Converts x from time_zone1 to time_zone2 and returns the new datetime.

SESSIONTIMEZONE()	Returns the time zone for the database session.
TZ_OFFSET(time_zone)	Returns the offset for time_zone in hours and minutes.

TABLE 4-5. *Time Zone–Related Functions*

The Session Time Zone

By default, your session time zone is the same as the database time zone. You can change your session time zone using the ALTER SESSION statement to set the TIME_ZONE parameter. For example, the following ALTER SESSION statement sets the local time zone to Pacific Standard Time (PST):

```
ALTER SESSION SET TIME_ZONE = 'PST';
```

NOTE
Setting the session time zone doesn't change the database time zone.

You can get your session time zone using the SESSIONTIMEZONE() function:

```
SELECT SESSIONTIMEZONE
FROM dual;

SESSIONTIMEZONE
---------------
PST
```

Getting the Current Date in the Session Time Zone

Earlier, you saw how the SYSDATE() function is used to get the date set for the operating system where the database resides. This gives you the date in the database time zone. You can get the date in your session time zone using the CURRENT_DATE() function. For example:

```
SELECT CURRENT_DATE
FROM dual;

CURRENT_D
---------
06-OCT-03
```

Obtaining Time Zone Offsets

You can get the time zone offset hours using the TZ_OFFSET() function, passing the time zone region name to TZ_OFFSET(). For example, the following query uses TZ_OFFSET() to get the time zone offset hours for PST, which is –7 hours:

```
SELECT TZ_OFFSET('PST')
FROM dual;

TZ_OFFS
-------
-07:00
```

Obtaining Time Zone Names

You can obtain all the time zone names by selecting all the rows from v$timezone_names. To query v$timezone_names you should first connect to the database as the system user. The following query shows some of the rows from v$timezone_names:

```
SELECT *
FROM v$timezone_names;

TZNAME              TZABBREV
------------------- --------
Africa/Cairo          LMT
Africa/Cairo          EET
Africa/Cairo          EEST
Africa/Tripoli        LMT
Africa/Tripoli        CET
Africa/Tripoli        CEST
Africa/Tripoli        EET
America/Adak          LMT
```

You may use any of the TZABBREV column values as your time zone setting.

Converting a Datetime from One Time Zone to Another

You use the NEW_TIME() function to convert a datetime from one time zone to another. For example, the following query uses NEW_TIME() to convert 7:45 P.M. on May 13, 2006, from PST to EST:

```
SELECT TO_CHAR(NEW_TIME(TO_DATE('25-MAY-2006 19:45',
  'DD-MON-YYYY HH24:MI'), 'PST', 'EST'), 'DD-MON-YYYY HH24:MI')
FROM dual;

TO_CHAR(NEW_TIME(
-----------------
25-MAY-2006 22:45
```

EST is three hours ahead of PST, and therefore three hours are added to 7:45 P.M. to give 10:45 P.M.—or 22:45 in 24-hour format.

Using Timestamps

The Oracle9*i* database introduced the ability to store timestamps. A timestamp stores the century, all four digits of a year, the month, the day, the hour (in 24-hour format), the minute, and the second. The advantages of a timestamp over a DATE are

- A timestamp can store a fractional second.

- A timestamp can store a time zone.

Let's examine the timestamp types.

Using the Timestamp Types

There are three timestamp types, which are shown in Table 4-6.
You'll learn how to use these timestamp types in the following sections.

Type	Description

`TIMESTAMP [`
`(seconds_precision)`
`]`
	Stores the century, all four digits of a year, the month, the day, the hour (in 24-hour format), the minute, and the second. You can specify an optional precision for the seconds by supplying `seconds_precision`, which can be an integer from 0 to 9. The default is 6; which means you can store up to 6 digits to the right of the decimal point for your second. If you try to add a row with more digits in your fractional second than your `TIMESTAMP` can store, your fraction is rounded.

`TIMESTAMP [`
`(seconds_precision)`
`] WITH TIME ZONE`
	Extends `TIMESTAMP` to store a time zone.

`TIMESTAMP [`
`(seconds_precision)`
`] WITH LOCAL TIME ZONE`
	Extends `TIMESTAMP` to convert a supplied datetime to the local time zone set for the database. The process of conversion is known as *normalizing* the datetime.

TABLE 4-6. *Timestamp Types*

Using the TIMESTAMP Type

As with the other types, you can use the `TIMESTAMP` type to define a column in a table. The following statement creates a table named `purchases_with_timestamp` that stores customer purchases. This table contains a `TIMESTAMP` column named `made_on` to record when a purchase was made:

```
CREATE TABLE purchases_with_timestamp (
    product_id INTEGER REFERENCES products(product_id),
    customer_id INTEGER REFERENCES customers(customer_id),
    made_on TIMESTAMP(4)
);
```

NOTE
The purchases_with_timestamp table is created and populated with rows by the store_schema.sql script. You'll see other tables in the rest of this chapter that are also created by the script, so you don't need to type in the CREATE TABLE statements.

Notice I've provided a precision of 4 for the `TIMESTAMP` in the `made_on` column. This means up to four digits may be stored to the right of the decimal point for the second.

To keep things simple, I haven't bothered defining a primary key for the `purchases_with_timestamp` table. In your own tables, you should typically provide a primary key.

To supply a TIMESTAMP literal value to the database, you use the TIMESTAMP keyword along with a datetime in the following format:

```
TIMESTAMP 'YYYY-MM-DD HH24:MI:SS.SSSSSSSSS'
```

Notice there are nine S characters after the decimal point, which means you can supply up to nine digits for the fractional second in your literal string.

How many you can actually store in your TIMESTAMP column depends on how many digits you set for storage of fractional seconds when the column was defined. For example, you can store up to four digits to the made_on column of the purchases_with_timestamp table. If you tried to add a row with more than four fractional second digits, your fraction is rounded. For example,

```
2005-05-13 07:15:31.123456789
```

would be rounded to

```
2005-05-13 07:15:31.1235
```

The following INSERT statement adds a row to the purchases_with_timestamp table. Notice the use of the TIMESTAMP keyword to supply a datetime literal:

```
INSERT INTO purchases_with_timestamp (
  product_id, customer_id, made_on
) VALUES (
  1, 1, TIMESTAMP '2005-05-13 07:15:31.1234'
);
```

NOTE
You don't need to enter this INSERT statement: it is performed by the store_schema.sql script. That goes for the other INSERT statements you'll see in the rest of this chapter.

The following query retrieves the row:

```
SELECT *
FROM purchases_with_timestamp;

PRODUCT_ID CUSTOMER_ID MADE_ON
---------- ----------- -------------------------
         1           1 13-MAY-05 07.15.31.1234 AM
```

Using the TIMESTAMP WITH TIME ZONE Type
The TIMESTAMP WITH TIME ZONE type extends TIMESTAMP to allow you to store a time zone. The following statement creates a table named purchases_timestamp_with_tz that stores

customer purchases. This table contains a `TIMESTAMP WITH TIME ZONE` column named `made_on` to record when a purchase was made:

```
CREATE TABLE purchases_timestamp_with_tz (
  product_id INTEGER REFERENCES products(product_id),
  customer_id INTEGER REFERENCES customers(customer_id),
  made_on TIMESTAMP(4) WITH TIME ZONE
);
```

To supply a timestamp literal with a time zone to the database, you simply add the time zone to your `TIMESTAMP` clause. For example, the following `TIMESTAMP` clause includes a time zone offset of –07:00:

```
TIMESTAMP '2005-05-13 07:15:31.1234 -07:00'
```

You may also supply a time zone region, as shown in the following example that specifies PST as the time zone:

```
TIMESTAMP '2005-05-13 07:15:31.1234 PST'
```

The following `INSERT` statements add two rows to the `purchases_timestamp_with_tz` table using the two previous `TIMESTAMP` literals to set the `dob` column values for the new rows:

```
INSERT INTO purchases_timestamp_with_tz (
  product_id, customer_id, made_on
) VALUES (
  1, 1, TIMESTAMP '2005-05-13 07:15:31.1234 -07:00'
);

INSERT INTO purchases_timestamp_with_tz (
  product_id, customer_id, made_on
) VALUES (
  1, 2, TIMESTAMP '2005-05-13 07:15:31.1234 PST'
);
```

The following query retrieves the rows:

```
SELECT *
FROM purchases_timestamp_with_tz;

PRODUCT_ID CUSTOMER_ID MADE_ON
---------- ----------- ---------------------------------
         1           1 13-MAY-05 07.15.31.1234 AM -07:00
         1           2 13-MAY-05 07.15.31.1234 AM PST
```

Using the TIMESTAMP WITH LOCAL TIME ZONE Type

The `TIMESTAMP WITH LOCAL TIME ZONE` type extends `TIMESTAMP` to store a timestamp in the local time zone set for your database. When you supply a timestamp for storage in a `TIMESTAMP WITH LOCAL TIME ZONE` column, your timestamp is converted—or *normalized*—

to the time zone set for the database. If you then retrieve the timestamp, it is normalized to the time zone set for your session.

TIP
Using TIMESTAMP WITH LOCAL TIME ZONE *is very useful if your organization has implemented a global system that is accessed throughout the world. This is because the database then stores timestamps in the local time where the database is located, but you still see the timestamp normalized to your own time zone.*

For example, let's say your database time zone is PST (seven hours behind UTC) and you want to store the following timestamp in the database:

```
2005-05-13 07:15:30 EST
```

Because EST is four hours behind UTC, the difference between EST and PST of three hours (7 − 4 = 3) is subtracted from your timestamp to give the following normalized timestamp that is stored in the database:

```
2005-05-13 04:15:30
```

The following statement creates a table named `purchases_with_local_tz` that stores customer purchases. This table contains a TIMESTAMP WITH LOCAL TIME ZONE column named made_on to record when a purchase was made:

```
CREATE TABLE purchases_with_local_tz (
  product_id INTEGER REFERENCES products(product_id),
  customer_id INTEGER REFERENCES customers(customer_id),
  made_on TIMESTAMP(4) WITH LOCAL TIME ZONE
);
```

The following INSERT statement adds a row to the `purchases_with_local_tz` table with the dob column value set to 2005-05-13 07:15:30 EST:

```
INSERT INTO purchases_with_local_tz (
  product_id, customer_id, made_on
) VALUES (
  1, 1, TIMESTAMP '2005-05-13 07:15:30 EST'
);
```

The following query retrieves the row:

```
SELECT *
FROM purchases_with_local_tz;

PRODUCT_ID CUSTOMER_ID MADE_ON
---------- ----------- -------------------------
         1           1 13-MAY-05 04.15.30.0000 AM
```

Notice only the normalized timestamp is stored and no time zone is displayed.

CAUTION
The timestamp will be normalized to your database time zone, so your normalized timestamp may be different.

If you then set the local time zone for your session to EST and repeat the previous query, you'll see the timestamp normalized to EST:

```
ALTER SESSION SET TIME_ZONE = 'EST';

Session altered.

SELECT *
FROM purchases_with_local_tz;

PRODUCT_ID CUSTOMER_ID MADE_ON
---------- ----------- -------------------------
         1           1 13-MAY-05 07.15.30.0000 AM
```

Timestamp-Related Functions

There are a number of functions that allow you to get and process timestamps. These functions are shown in Table 4-7.

You'll learn more about the functions shown in Table 4-7 in the following sections.

CURRENT_TIMESTAMP(), LOCALTIMESTAMP(), and SYSTIMESTAMP()

The following query calls the CURRENT_TIMESTAMP(), LOCALTIMESTAMP(), and SYSTIMESTAMP() functions:

```
SELECT CURRENT_TIMESTAMP, LOCALTIMESTAMP, SYSTIMESTAMP
FROM dual;

CURRENT_TIMESTAMP
-----------------------------------
LOCALTIMESTAMP
-----------------------------------
SYSTIMESTAMP
-----------------------------------
07-OCT-03 10.41.24.000000 AM -07:00
07-OCT-03 10.41.24.000000 AM
07-OCT-03 10.41.24.000000 AM -07:00
```

If you then change your TIME_ZONE to EST and repeat the previous query, you'll get results similar to the following output:

```
ALTER SESSION SET TIME_ZONE = 'EST';

Session altered.

SELECT CURRENT_TIMESTAMP, LOCALTIMESTAMP, SYSTIMESTAMP
```

```
FROM dual;

CURRENT_TIMESTAMP
----------------------------------------------------------------
LOCALTIMESTAMP
----------------------------------------------------------------
SYSTIMESTAMP
----------------------------------------------------------------
07-OCT-03 01.42.30.000001 PM EST
07-OCT-03 01.42.30.000001 PM
07-OCT-03 10.42.30.000001 AM -07:00
```

Notice the changes in the results between this query and the previous example.

Function	Description
CURRENT_TIMESTAMP()	Returns a TIMESTAMP WITH TIME ZONE containing the current session time along with the session time zone.
EXTRACT({ YEAR | MONTH | DAY | HOUR | MINUTE | SECOND } | { TIMEZONE_HOUR | TIMEZONE_MINUTE } | { TIMEZONE_REGION | } TIMEZONE_ABBR } FROM x)	Extracts and returns a year, month, day, hour, minute, second, or time zone from x; x may be one of the timestamp types or a DATE.
FROM_TZ(x, time_zone)	Converts the TIMESTAMP x and time zone specified by time_zone to a TIMESTAMP WITH TIMEZONE.
LOCALTIMESTAMP()	Returns a TIMESTAMP containing the current time in the session time zone.
SYSTIMESTAMP()	Returns a TIMESTAMP WITH TIME ZONE containing the current database time along with the database time zone.
SYS_EXTRACT_UTC(x)	Converts the TIMESTAMP WITH TIMEZONE x to a TIMESTAMP containing the date and time in UTC.
TO_TIMESTAMP(x, [format])	Converts the string x to a TIMESTAMP. You may also specify an optional format for x.
TO_TIMESTAMP_TZ(x, [format])	Converts the string x to a TIMESTAMP WITH TIMEZONE. You may also specify an optional format for x.

TABLE 4-7. *Timestamp-Related Functions*

EXTRACT()

You use EXTRACT() to extract and return a year, month, day, hour, minute, second, or time zone from *x*; *x* may be one of the timestamp types or a DATE. The following example uses EXTRACT() to get the year, month, and day from a DATE returned by TO_DATE():

```
SELECT
    EXTRACT(YEAR FROM TO_DATE('01-JAN-2005 19:15:26',
      'DD-MON-YYYY HH24:MI:SS')) AS YEAR,
    EXTRACT(MONTH FROM TO_DATE('01-JAN-2005 19:15:26',
      'DD-MON-YYYY HH24:MI:SS')) As MONTH,
    EXTRACT(DAY FROM TO_DATE('01-JAN-2005 19:15:26',
      'DD-MON-YYYY HH24:MI:SS')) AS DAY
FROM dual;

      YEAR       MONTH        DAY
---------- ---------- ----------
      2005           1          1
```

The next example uses EXTRACT() to get the hour, minute, and second from a TIMESTAMP returned by TO_TIMESTAMP():

```
SELECT
    EXTRACT(HOUR FROM TO_TIMESTAMP('01-JAN-2005 19:15:26',
      'DD-MON-YYYY HH24:MI:SS')) AS HOUR,
    EXTRACT(MINUTE FROM TO_TIMESTAMP('01-JAN-2005 19:15:26',
      'DD-MON-YYYY HH24:MI:SS')) AS MINUTE,
    EXTRACT(SECOND FROM TO_TIMESTAMP('01-JAN-2005 19:15:26',
      'DD-MON-YYYY HH24:MI:SS')) AS SECOND
FROM dual;

HOUR     MINUTE     SECOND
---------- ---------- ----------
      19         15         26
```

The final example uses EXTRACT() to get the time zone hour, minute, second, region, and region abbreviation from a TIMESTAMP WITH TIMEZONE returned by TO_TIMESTAMP_TZ():

```
SELECT
    EXTRACT(TIMEZONE_HOUR FROM TO_TIMESTAMP_TZ(
      '01-JAN-2005 19:15:26 -7:15', 'DD-MON-YYYY HH24:MI:SS TZH:TZM'))
      AS TZH,
    EXTRACT(TIMEZONE_MINUTE FROM TO_TIMESTAMP_TZ(
      '01-JAN-2005 19:15:26 -7:15', 'DD-MON-YYYY HH24:MI:SS TZH:TZM'))
      AS TZM,
    EXTRACT(TIMEZONE_REGION FROM TO_TIMESTAMP_TZ(
      '01-JAN-2005 19:15:26 PST', 'DD-MON-YYYY HH24:MI:SS TZR'))
      AS TZR,
```

```
EXTRACT(TIMEZONE_ABBR FROM TO_TIMESTAMP_TZ(
   '01-JAN-2005 19:15:26 PST', 'DD-MON-YYYY HH24:MI:SS TZR'))
   AS TZA
FROM dual;


      TZH        TZM TZR              TZA
---------- ---------- ----------- ----------
      -7        -15 PST              PST
```

FROM_TZ()

You use FROM_TZ(x, $time\_zone$) to convert the TIMESTAMP x and time zone specified by $time\_zone$ to a TIMESTAMP WITH TIMEZONE. For example:

```
SELECT FROM_TZ(TIMESTAMP '2005-05-13 07:15:31.1234', 'EST')
FROM dual;

FROM_TZ(TIMESTAMP'2005-05-1307:15:3
-----------------------------------
13-MAY-05 07.15.31.123400000 AM EST
```

Notice the addition of the EST time zone to the supplied TIMESTAMP.

SYS_EXTRACT_UTC()

You use SYS_EXTRACT_UTC(x) to convert the TIMESTAMP WITH TIMEZONE x to a TIMESTAMP containing the date and time in UTC. For example:

```
SELECT
   SYS_EXTRACT_UTC(TIMESTAMP '2005-05-13 19:15:26 PST')
FROM dual;

SYS_EXTRACT_UTC(TIMESTAMP'2005-
-------------------------------
14-MAY-05 02.15.26.000000000 AM
```

PST is seven hours behind UTC, so the example returns a TIMSTAMP seven hours ahead of the supplied TIMESTAMP WITH TIMEZONE that is passed to SYS_EXTRACT_UTC().

TO_TIMESTAMP()

You use TO_TIMESTAMP(x, $format$) to convert the string x (CHAR, VARCHAR2, NCHAR, or NVARCHAR2) to a TIMESTAMP. You may also specify an optional $format$ for x. For example:

```
SELECT TO_TIMESTAMP('2005-05-13 07:15:31.1234',
  'YYYY-MM-DD HH24:MI:SS.FF')
FROM dual;

TO_TIMESTAMP('2005-05-1307:15:3
-------------------------------
13-MAY-05 07.15.31.123400000 AM
```

TO_TIMESTAMP_TZ()

You use TO_TIMESTAMP_TZ(*x*, [*format*]) to convert *x* to a TIMESTAMP WITH TIMEZONE with an optional *format* for *x*. For example, the following query passes the time zone region PST (uses the format TZR) to TO_TIMESTAMP_TZ():

```
SELECT TO_TIMESTAMP_TZ('2005-05-13 07:15:31.1234 PST',
  'YYYY-MM-DD HH24:MI:SS.FF TZR')
FROM dual;

TO_TIMESTAMP_TZ('2005-05-1307:15:31
------------------------------------
13-MAY-05 07.15.31.123400000 AM PST
```

The next example passes a time zone hour and minute of –7:00 (uses the format TZR and TZM) to TO_TIMESTAMP_TZ():

```
SELECT TO_TIMESTAMP_TZ('2005-05-13 07:15:31.1234 -7:00',
  'YYYY-MM-DD HH24:MI:SS.FF TZH:TZM')
FROM dual;

TO_TIMESTAMP_TZ('2005-05-1307:15:31.12
--------------------------------------
13-MAY-05 07.15.31.123400000 AM -07:00
```

Using Time Intervals

The Oracle9*i* database introduced data types that allow you to store time *intervals*. Examples of time intervals include

- 1 year 3 months
- 25 months
- –3 days 5 hours 16 minutes
- 1 day 7 hours
- –56 hours

NOTE
Time intervals are not to be confused with datetimes or timestamps. A datetime or timestamp records a specific date and time (7:32:16 P.M. on October 28, 2006, for example). A time interval records a length of time (1 year 3 months, for example).

In the store example, you might want to offer limited time discounts on products. For example, you might want to allow customers to use a coupon that is valid for a few months, or a special promotion discount that is valid for a few days. You'll see examples that feature coupons and promotions later in this section.

Table 4-8 shows the interval types.

Type	Description
INTERVAL YEAR[(*years_precision*)] TO MONTH	Stores a time interval measured in years and months. You can specify an optional precision for the years by supplying *years_ precision*, which may be an integer from 0 to 9. The default precision is 2, which means you can store two digits for the years in your interval. If you try to add a row with more year digits than your INTERVAL YEAR TO MONTH column can store, you'll get an error. You can store a positive or negative time interval.
INTERVAL DAY[(*days_precision*)] TO SECOND[(*seconds_precision*)]	Stores a time interval measured in days and seconds. You can specify an optional precision for the days by supplying a *days_ precision* integer from 0 to 9 (default is 2). In addition, you can also specify an optional precision for the fractional seconds by supplying a *seconds_precision* integer from 0 to 9 (default is 6). You can store a positive or negative time interval.

TABLE 4-8. *Time Interval Types*

You'll learn how to use the time interval types in the following sections.

Using the INTERVAL YEAR TO MONTH Type

You use the INTERVAL YEAR TO MONTH type to store time intervals measured in years and months. The following statement creates a table named coupons that stores coupon information. The coupons table contains an INTERVAL YEAR TO MONTH column named duration to record the interval of time for which the coupon is valid:

```
CREATE TABLE coupons (
  coupon_id INTEGER CONSTRAINT coupons_pk PRIMARY KEY,
  name VARCHAR2(30) NOT NULL,
  duration INTERVAL YEAR(3) TO MONTH
);
```

Notice I've provided a precision of 3 for the duration column. This means up to three digits may be stored for the year part of the interval.

To supply an INTERVAL YEAR TO MONTH literal value to the database, you use the following simplified syntax:

```
INTERVAL '[+|-][y][-m]' [YEAR[(years_precision)]]] [TO MONTH]
```

where

■ + or – is an optional indicator that specifies whether the time interval is positive or negative (default is positive).

■ *y* is the optional number of years for the interval.

■ *m* is the optional number of months for the interval. If you supply years *and* months, you must include TO MONTH in your literal.

■ *years_precision* is the optional precision for the years (default is 2).

The following table shows some examples of year to month interval literals.

Literal	Description
INTERVAL '1' YEAR	Interval of 1 year
INTERVAL '11' MONTH	Interval of 11 months
INTERVAL '14' MONTH	Interval of 14 months (equivalent to 1 year 2 months)
INTERVAL '1-3' YEAR TO MONTH	Interval of 1 year 3 months
INTERVAL '0-5' YEAR TO MONTH	Interval of 0 years 5 months
INTERVAL '123' YEAR(3) TO MONTH	Interval of 123 years with a precision of 3 digits
INTERVAL '-1-5' YEAR TO MONTH	A negative interval of 1 year 5 months
INTERVAL '1234' YEAR(3)	Invalid interval: 1234 contains four digits and therefore contains one too many digits allowed by the precision of 3 (which allows up to three digits)

The following INSERT statements add rows to the coupons table with the duration column set to some of the valid intervals shown in the previous table:

```
INSERT INTO coupons (coupon_id, name, duration)
VALUES (1, '$1 off Z Files', INTERVAL '1' YEAR);
INSERT INTO coupons (coupon_id, name, duration)
VALUES (2, '$2 off Pop 3', INTERVAL '11' MONTH);
INSERT INTO coupons (coupon_id, name, duration)
VALUES (3, '$3 off Modern Science', INTERVAL '14' MONTH);
INSERT INTO coupons (coupon_id, name, duration)
VALUES (4, '$2 off Tank War', INTERVAL '1-3' YEAR TO MONTH);
INSERT INTO coupons (coupon_id, name, duration)
VALUES (5, '$1 off Chemistry', INTERVAL '0-5' YEAR TO MONTH);
INSERT INTO coupons (coupon_id, name, duration)
VALUES (6, '$2 off Creative Yell', INTERVAL '123' YEAR(3));
```

If you try to add a row with the duration column set to the invalid interval of INTERVAL '1234' YEAR(3), you'll get an error because the precision of the duration column is 3 and is therefore too small. The following INSERT shows the error:

```
SQL> INSERT INTO coupons (coupon_id, name, duration)
  2  VALUES (7, '$1 off Z Files', INTERVAL '1234' YEAR(3));
VALUES (7, '$1 off Z Files', INTERVAL '1234' YEAR(3))
                                       *
ERROR at line 2:
ORA-01873: the leading precision of the interval is too small
```

The following query retrieves the rows from the `coupons` table so you can see the formatting of the `duration` column values:

```
SELECT *
FROM coupons;
```

```
COUPON_ID NAME                          DURATION
---------- ----------------------------- --------
         1 $1 off Z Files                 +001-00
         2 $2 off Pop 3                   +000-11
         3 $3 off Modern Science          +001-02
         4 $2 off Tank War                +001-03
         5 $1 off Chemistry               +000-05
         6 $2 off Creative Yell           +123-00
```

Using the INTERVAL DAY TO SECOND Type

You use the `INTERVAL DAY TO SECOND` type to store time intervals measured in days and seconds. The following statement creates a table named `promotions` that stores promotion information. The promotions table contains an `INTERVAL DAY TO SECOND` column named `duration` to record the interval of time for which the promotion is valid:

```
CREATE TABLE promotions (
  promotion_id INTEGER CONSTRAINT promotions_pk PRIMARY KEY,
  name VARCHAR2(30) NOT NULL,
  duration INTERVAL DAY(3) TO SECOND (4)
);
```

Notice I've provided a precision of 3 for the day and a precision of 4 for the fractional seconds of the `duration` column. This means up to three digits may be stored for the day of the interval and up to four digits to the right of the decimal point for the fractional seconds.

To supply an `INTERVAL DAY TO SECOND` literal value to the database, you use the following simplified syntax:

```
INTERVAL '[+|-][d] [h[:m[:s]]]' [DAY[(days_precision)]])
[TO HOUR | MINUTE | SECOND[(seconds_precision)]]
```

where

- **+** or **–** is an optional indicator that specifies whether the time interval is positive or negative (default is positive).

- *d* is the number of days for the interval.

- *h* is the optional number of hours for the interval; if you supply days and hours, you must include TO HOUR in your literal.

- *m* is the optional number of minutes for the interval; if you supply days and minutes, you must include TO MINUTES in your literal.

- *s* is the optional number of seconds for the interval; if you supply days and seconds you must include TO SECOND in your literal.

■ *days_precision* is the optional precision for the days (default is 2).

■ *seconds_precision* is the optional precision for the fractional seconds (default is 6).

The following table shows some examples of day to second interval literals.

Literal	Description
INTERVAL '3' DAY	Interval of 3 days
INTERVAL '2' HOUR	Interval of 2 hours
INTERVAL '25' MINUTE	Interval of 25 minutes
INTERVAL '45' SECOND	Interval of 45 seconds
INTERVAL '3 2' DAY TO HOUR	Interval of 3 days 2 hours
INTERVAL '3 2:25' DAY TO MINUTE	Interval of 3 days 2 hours 25 minutes
INTERVAL '3 2:25:45' DAY TO SECOND	Interval of 3 days 2 hours 25 minutes 45 seconds
INTERVAL '123 2:25:45.12' DAY(3) TO SECOND(2)	Interval of 123 days 2 hours 25 minutes 45.12 seconds; the precision for days is 3 digits and the precision for the fractional seconds is 2 digits
INTERVAL '3 2:00:45' DAY TO SECOND	Interval of 3 days 2 hours 0 minutes 45 seconds
INTERVAL '-3 2:25:45' DAY TO SECOND	Negative interval of 3 days 2 hours 25 minutes 45 seconds
INTERVAL '1234 2:25:45' DAY(3) TO SECOND	Invalid interval because the number of digits in the days exceeds the specified precision of 3
INTERVAL '123 2:25:45.123' DAY TO SECOND(2)	Invalid interval because the number of digits in the fractional seconds exceeds the specified precision of 2

The following INSERT statements add rows to the promotions table with the duration column values set to some of the valid intervals shown in the previous table:

```
INSERT INTO promotions (promotion_id, name, duration)
VALUES (1, '10% off Z Files', INTERVAL '3' DAY);
INSERT INTO promotions (promotion_id, name, duration)
VALUES (2, '20% off Pop 3', INTERVAL '2' HOUR);
INSERT INTO promotions (promotion_id, name, duration)
VALUES (3, '30% off Modern Science', INTERVAL '25' MINUTE);
INSERT INTO promotions (promotion_id, name, duration)
VALUES (4, '20% off Tank War', INTERVAL '45' SECOND);
INSERT INTO promotions (promotion_id, name, duration)
```

```
VALUES (5, '10% off Chemistry', INTERVAL '3 2:25' DAY TO MINUTE);
INSERT INTO promotions (promotion_id, name, duration)
VALUES (6, '20% off Creative Yell',
 INTERVAL '3 2:25:45' DAY TO SECOND);
INSERT INTO promotions (promotion_id, name, duration)
VALUES (7, '15% off My Front Line',
 INTERVAL '123 2:25:45.12' DAY(3) TO SECOND(2));
```

The following query retrieves the rows from the `promotions` table so you can see the formatting of the `duration` column values:

```
SELECT *
FROM promotions;


PROMOTION_ID NAME                             DURATION
------------ ------------------------------   ------------------
           1 10% off Z Files                  +003 00:00:00.0000
           2 20% off Pop 3                    +000 02:00:00.0000
           3 30% off Modern Science           +000 00:25:00.0000
           4 20% off Tank War                 +000 00:00:45.0000
           5 10% off Chemistry                +003 02:25:00.0000
           6 20% off Creative Yell            +003 02:25:45.0000
           7 15% off My Front Line            +123 02:25:45.1200
```

Time Interval–Related Functions

There are a number of functions that allow you to get and process time intervals; these functions are shown in Table 4-9.

You'll learn more about the functions shown in Table 4-9 in the following sections.

Function	Description
NUMTODSINTERVAL(x, interval_unit)	Converts the number x to an INTERVAL DAY TO SECOND with the interval for x supplied in *interval_unit*, which you may set to DAY, HOUR, MINUTE, or SECOND.
NUMTOYMINTERVAL(x, interval_unit)	Converts the number x to an INTERVAL YEAR TO MONTH with the interval for x supplied in *interval_unit*, which you may set to YEAR or MONTH.
TO_DSINTERVAL(x)	Converts the string x to an INTERVAL DAY TO SECOND.
TO_YMINTERVAL(x)	Converts the string x to an INTERVAL YEAR TO MONTH.

TABLE 4-9.   *Time Interval–Related Functions*

NUMTODSINTERVAL()

You use NUMTODSINTERVAL(*x, interval_unit*) to convert the number *x* to an INTERVAL DAY TO SECOND with the interval for *x* supplied in *interval_unit*. You may set *interval_unit* to DAY, HOUR, MINUTE, or SECOND. For example:

```
SELECT
    NUMTODSINTERVAL(1.5, 'DAY'),
    NUMTODSINTERVAL(3.25, 'HOUR'),
    NUMTODSINTERVAL(5, 'MINUTE'),
    NUMTODSINTERVAL(10.123456789, 'SECOND')
FROM dual;

NUMTODSINTERVAL(1.5,'DAY')
-------------------------------------------
NUMTODSINTERVAL(3.25,'HOUR')
-------------------------------------------
NUMTODSINTERVAL(5,'MINUTE')
-------------------------------------------
NUMTODSINTERVAL(10.123456789,'SECOND')
-------------------------------------------
+000000001 12:00:00.000000000
+000000000 03:15:00.000000000
+000000000 00:05:00.000000000
+000000000 00:00:10.123456789
```

NUMTOYMINTERVAL()

You use NUMTOYMINTERVAL(*x, interval_unit*) to convert the number *x* to an INTERVAL YEAR TO MONTH with the interval for *x* supplied in *interval_unit*. You may set *interval_unit* to YEAR or MONTH. For example:

```
SELECT
    NUMTOYMINTERVAL(1.5, 'YEAR'),
    NUMTOYMINTERVAL(3.25, 'MONTH')
FROM dual;

NUMTOYMINTERVAL(1.5,'YEAR')
--------------------------
NUMTOYMINTERVAL(3.25,'MONTH')
--------------------------
+000000001-06
+000000000-03
```

Summary

In this chapter, you learned that

■ You may store a datetime using the DATE type. The DATE type stores the century, all four digits of a year, the month, the day, the hour (in 24-hour format), the minute, and the second.

- You may use TO_CHAR() and TO_DATE() to convert between strings and dates and times.

- The Oracle database always stores all four digits of a year, and will interpret two-digit years according to a set of rules. The best practice is for you to always supply all four digits of the year so that you don't get confused as to which year you mean.

- You may use functions to get or process dates and times. An example is ADD_ MONTHS(x, y), which returns the result of adding y months to x.

- The Oracle9i database introduced the ability to use different time zones. A time zone is an offset from the time in Greenwich, England. The time in Greenwich was once known as Greenwich Mean Time (GMT), but is now known as Coordinated Universal Time (UTC). You specify a time zone using either an offset from UTC or the name of the region.

- The Oracle9i database introduced the ability to store timestamps. A timestamp stores the century, all four digits of a year, the month, the day, the hour (in 24-hour format), the minute, and the second. The advantages of a timestamp over a DATE are a timestamp can store a fractional second, and a timestamp can store a time zone.

- The Oracle9i database introduced the ability to handle time intervals, which allow you to store a length of time. An example time interval is 1 year 3 months.

In the next chapter, you'll learn about SQL*Plus.

CHAPTER
5

Using SQL*Plus

In this chapter, you will

- View the structure of a table
- Edit a SQL statement
- Save and run scripts containing SQL statements and SQL*Plus commands
- Format column output
- Define and use variables
- Create simple reports

In the last section of this chapter, you'll also learn how to write SQL statements that generate other SQL statements. Let's plunge in and examine how you view the structure of a table.

Viewing the Structure of a Table

You use the DESCRIBE command to view the structure of a table. You can save some typing by shortening the DESCRIBE command to DESC (DESC[RIBE]). Knowing the structure of a table is useful because you can use the information to formulate a SQL statement. For example, you can figure out the columns you want to query in a SELECT statement.

NOTE
*You typically omit the semicolon character (;) when issuing SQL*Plus commands.*

The following example uses the DESCRIBE command to view the structure of the customers table; notice that the semicolon character (;) is omitted from the end of the command:

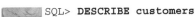

```
SQL> DESCRIBE customers
 Name                     Null?            Type
 --------------------     --------    --------------
 CUSTOMER_ID              NOT NULL        NUMBER(38)
 FIRST_NAME               NOT NULL      VARCHAR2(10)
 LAST_NAME                NOT NULL      VARCHAR2(10)
 DOB                                            DATE
 PHONE                                  VARCHAR2(12)
```

As you can see from this example, the output from the DESCRIBE command has three columns that show the structure of the database table:

- **Name** Lists the names of the columns contained in the table. In the example, you can see the customers table has five columns: customer_id, first_name, last_name, dob, and phone.

■   **Null?**   Indicates whether the column can store null values. If NOT NULL, the column cannot store nulls. If blank, the column can store null values. In the example, you can see the customer_id, first_name, and last_name columns cannot store null values, but the dob and phone columns can store null values.

■   **Type**   Indicates the type of the column. In the example, you can see the type of the customer_id column is NUMBER(38) and the type of the first_name is VARCHAR2(10).

The next example uses the shortened DESC command to view the structure of the products table:

```
SQL> DESC products
Name                        Null?           Type
--------------------        --------        ---------------
PRODUCT_ID                  NOT NULL          NUMBER(38)
PRODUCT_TYPE_ID                               NUMBER(38)
NAME                        NOT NULL        VARCHAR2(30)
DESCRIPTION                                 VARCHAR2(50)
PRICE                                         NUMBER(5,2)
```

Editing SQL Statements

As you may have noticed, it becomes tedious to have to repeatedly type similar SQL statements into SQL*Plus. You will be pleased to know SQL*Plus stores your previous SQL statement in a buffer. You can then edit the lines that make up your SQL statement stored in the buffer. Some of the editing commands are listed in the following table. Notice the optional part of each command indicated using square brackets; for example, you can abbreviate the APPEND command to A.

Command	Description
A[PPEND] text	Appends text to the current line.
C[HANGE] /old/new	Changes the text specified by old to new in the current line.
CL[EAR] BUFF[ER]	Clears all lines from the buffer.
DEL	Deletes the current line.
DEL x	Deletes the line specified by the line number x (line numbers start with 1).
L[IST]	Lists all the lines in the buffer.
L[IST] x	Lists line number x.
R[UN] or /	Runs the statement stored in the buffer. You can also use / to run the statement.
x	Makes the line specified by the line number x the current line.

Let's take a look at some examples of using the SQL*Plus editing commands. First, enter the following SELECT statement into SQL*Plus:

```
SQL> SELECT customer_id, first_name, last_name
  2  FROM customers
  3  WHERE customer_id = 1;
```

SQL*Plus automatically increments and displays the line number when your SQL statement spans more than one line. Make line 1 the current line by entering 1 at the prompt:

```
SQL> 1
  1* SELECT customer_id, first_name, last_name
```

Notice that SQL*Plus displays the current line. Add the dob column to the list of columns to retrieve using the APPEND command:

```
SQL> APPEND , dob
  1* SELECT customer_id, first_name, last_name, dob
```

Next, list all the lines in the buffer using the LIST command:

```
SQL> LIST
  1  SELECT customer_id, first_name, last_name, dob
  2  FROM customers
  3* WHERE customer_id = 1
```

Notice that the current line has been changed to the last line, as indicated by the asterisk character (*). Change the final line to select the customer where the customer_id column is 2 using the CHANGE command. Notice that the line that has been changed is displayed after the command is run:

```
SQL> CHANGE /customer_id = 1/customer_id = 2
  3* WHERE customer_id = 2
```

Finally, execute the query using the RUN command. Notice that the text of the query is repeated before the returned row:

```
SQL> RUN
  1  SELECT customer_id, first_name, last_name, dob
  2  FROM customers
  3* WHERE customer_id = 2

CUSTOMER_ID FIRST_NAME LAST_NAME  DOB
----------- ---------- ---------- ---------
          2 Cynthia    Green      05-FEB-68
```

You can also use a forward slash character (/) to run the SQL statement stored in the buffer. For example:

```
SQL> /

CUSTOMER_ID FIRST_NAME LAST_NAME  DOB
----------- ---------- ---------- ---------
          2 Cynthia    Green      05-FEB-68
```

Saving, Retrieving, and Running Files

SQL*Plus allows you save, retrieve, and run text files containing SQL*Plus commands and SQL statements. You've already seen one example of running a SQL*Plus script: you saw how to run the `store_schema.sql` script file in Chapter 1, which created the `store` schema.

Some of the file commands are listed in the following table.

Command	Description
SAV[E] *filename* [{ REPLACE | APPEND }]	Saves the contents of the SQL*Plus buffer to a file specified by *filename*. You can append the content of the buffer to an existing file using the APPEND option. You can also overwrite an existing file using the REPLACE option.
GET *filename*	Retrieves the contents of the file specified by *filename* into the SQL*Plus buffer.
STA[RT] *filename*	Retrieves the contents of the file specified by *filename* into the SQL*Plus buffer, and then attempts to run the contents of the buffer.
@ *filename*	Same as the START command.
ED[IT]	Copies the contents of the SQL*Plus buffer to a file named `afiedt.buf` and then starts the default editor for the operating system. When you exit the editor, the contents of your edited file are copied to the SQL*Plus buffer.
ED[IT] *filename*	Same as the EDIT command, but you can specify a file to start editing. You specify the file to edit using the *filename* parameter.
SPO[OL] *filename*	Copies the output from SQL*Plus to the file specified by *filename*.
SPO[OL] OFF	Stops the copying of output from SQL*Plus to the file, and closes that file.

Let's take a look at some examples of using these SQL*Plus commands. First, enter the following SQL statement into SQL*Plus:

```
SQL> SELECT customer_id, first_name, last_name
  2  FROM customers
  3  WHERE customer_id = 1;
```

Save the contents of the SQL*Plus buffer to a file named cust_query.sql using the SAVE command:

```
SQL> SAVE cust_query.sql
Created file cust_query.sql
```

NOTE
By default the cust_query.sql file is stored in the bin subdirectory where you installed the Oracle software.

Retrieve the contents of the cust_query.sql file using the GET command:

```
SQL> GET cust_query.sql
  1  SELECT customer_id, first_name, last_name
  2  FROM customers
  3* WHERE customer_id = 1
```

Run the contents of the cust_query.sql file using the START command:

```
SQL> START cust_query.sql

CUSTOMER_ID FIRST_NAME LAST_NAME
----------- ---------- ----------
          1 John       Brown
```

Edit the contents of the SQL*Plus buffer using the EDIT command:

```
SQL> EDIT
```

The EDIT command starts the default editor for your operating system. On Windows the default editor is Notepad, and on Unix or Linux the default editor is vi or emacs. You can set the default editor using the DEFINE command:

```
DEFINE _EDITOR = 'editor'
```

where *editor* is the name of your preferred editor.
For example, the following command sets the default editor to vi:

```
DEFINE _EDITOR = 'vi'
```

Figure 5-1 shows the contents of the SQL*Plus buffer in Notepad. Notice that the SQL statement is terminated using a slash character (/) rather than a semicolon.

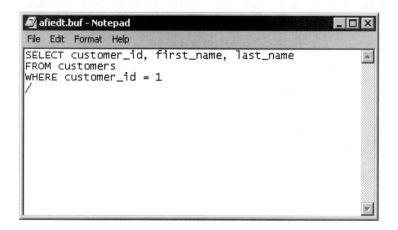

FIGURE 5-1. *Editing the SQL*Plus buffer contents using Notepad*

In your editor, change the WHERE clause to WHERE customer_id = 2 and save and quit from your editor. For example, in Notepad you select File | Exit to quit Notepad; click Yes to save your query when prompted by Notepad. SQL*Plus displays the following output containing your modified query. Notice that the WHERE clause has been changed:

```
Wrote file afiedt.buf

 1   SELECT customer_id, first_name, last_name
 2   FROM customers
 3*  WHERE customer_id = 2
```

Run your modified query using the slash character (/):

```
SQL> /

CUSTOMER_ID FIRST_NAME LAST_NAME
----------- ---------- ----------
          2 Cynthia    Green
```

Next, use the SPOOL command to copy the output from SQL*Plus to a file named cust_results.txt, run your query again, and then turn spooling off by executing SPOOL OFF:

```
SQL> SPOOL cust_results.txt
SQL> /

CUSTOMER_ID FIRST_NAME LAST_NAME
----------- ---------- ----------
          2 Cynthia    Green

SQL> SPOOL OFF
```

Feel free to examine the cust_results.txt file; it will contain the previous output between the slash (/) and SPOOL OFF. By default, this file is stored in the directory where the Oracle software is installed under the bin subdirectory. You can specify the full directory path where you want the file to be written using the SPOOL command by adding a directory path to your filename. For example:

```
SPOOL C:\my_files\spools\cust_results.txt
```

Formatting Columns

You use the COLUMN command to format the display of column headings and column data. The simplified syntax for the COLUMN command is as follows:

```
COL[UMN] {column | alias} [options]
```

where

- *column* specifies the column name.

- *alias* specifies the column alias to be formatted. In Chapter 2 you saw that you can "rename" a column using a column alias; you can then reference your alias in the COLUMN command.

- *options* specifies one or more options to be used to format the column or alias.

There are a number of options you can use with the COLUMN command. The following table shows some of these options.

Option	Description
FOR[MAT] *format*	Sets the format for the display of the column or alias to that specified in the *format* string.
HEA[DING] *heading*	Sets the text for the heading of the column or alias to that specified in the *heading* string.
JUS[TIFY] [{ left | center | right }]	Aligns the column output to the left, center, or right.
WRA[PPED]	Wraps the end of a string onto the next line of output. This option may cause individual words to be split across multiple lines.
WOR[D_WRAPPED]	Similar to the WRAPPED option except that individual words aren't split across two lines.
CLE[AR]	Clears any formatting of columns (sets the formatting back to the default).

The *format* string in the previous table may take a number of formatting parameters. The parameters you specify depend on the data stored in your column:

- If your column contains characters, you can use A*x* to format the characters, where *x* specifies the width for the characters. For example, A12 sets the width to 12 characters.

- If your column contains numbers, you can use any of the number formats shown in Table 3-4 of Chapter 3. For example, $99.99 sets the format to a dollar sign, followed by two digits, the decimal point, and another two digits.

- If your column contains a date, you can use any of the date formats shown in Table 4-2 of Chapter 4. For example, MM-DD-YYYY sets the format to a two-digit month (MM), a two-digit day (DD), and a four-digit year (YYYY).

Let's consider an example. You're going to format the output of a query that retrieves the product_id, name, description, and price columns from the products table. The display requirements, the format strings, and the COLUMN commands are shown in the following table.

Column	Display Requirement	Format	COLUMN Command
product_id	Two digits	99	COLUMN product_id FORMAT 99
name	Thirteen-character word-wrapped strings and change heading to PRODUCT_NAME	A13	COLUMN name HEADING PRODUCT_NAME FORMAT A13 WORD_WRAPPED
description	Thirteen-character word-wrapped strings	A13	COLUMN description FORMAT A13 WORD_WRAPPED
price	Dollar symbol, with two digits to the right of the decimal point and two digits to the left of the decimal point	$99.99	COLUMN price FORMAT $99.99

Enter the following COLUMN commands into SQL*Plus in preparation for executing a query against the products table:

```
SQL> COLUMN product_id FORMAT 99
SQL> COLUMN name HEADING PRODUCT_NAME FORMAT A13 WORD_WRAPPED
SQL> COLUMN description FORMAT A13 WORD_WRAPPED
SQL> COLUMN price FORMAT $99.99
```

Next, run the following query to retrieve some rows from the products table. Notice the formatting of the columns in the output due to the previous COLUMN commands:

```
SQL> SELECT product_id, name, description, price
  2  FROM products
  3  WHERE product_id < 6;
```

```
PRODUCT_ID PRODUCT_NAME  DESCRIPTION      PRICE
---------- ------------- -------------   --------
         1 Modern        A description   $19.95
           Science       of modern
                         science

         2 Chemistry     Introduction    $30.00
                         to Chemistry

         3 Supernova     A star          $25.99
                         explodes

         4 Tank War      Action movie    $13.95

PRODUCT_ID PRODUCT_NAME  DESCRIPTION      PRICE
---------- ------------- -------------   --------
                         about a
                         future war

         5 Z Files       Series on       $49.99
                         mysterious
                         activities
```

This output is readable, but wouldn't it be nice if you could just display the headings once at the top? You can do that by setting the page size.

Setting the Page Size

You set the number of lines in a page using the SET PAGESIZE command. This command sets the number of lines that SQL*Plus considers one "page" of output, after which SQL*Plus will display the headings again.

Set the page size to 100 lines using the following SET PAGESIZE command and run your query again using /:

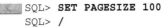
```
SQL> SET PAGESIZE 100
SQL> /

PRODUCT_ID PRODUCT_NAME  DESCRIPTION      PRICE
---------- ------------- -------------   --------
         1 Modern        A description   $19.95
           Science       of modern
                         science

         2 Chemistry     Introduction    $30.00
                         to Chemistry

         3 Supernova     A star          $25.99
                         explodes

         4 Tank War      Action movie    $13.95
                         about a
```

```
              future war

5 Z Files     Series on        $49.99
              mysterious
              activities
```

Notice the headings are only shown once at the top, and the resulting output looks better.

NOTE
The maximum number for the page size is 50,000.

Setting the Line Size

You set the number of characters in a line using the SET LINESIZE command. Set the line size to 50 lines using the following SET LINESIZE command and run the new query shown in the following example:

```
SQL> SET LINESIZE 50
SQL> SELECT * FROM customers;

CUSTOMER_ID FIRST_NAME LAST_NAME  DOB
----------- ---------- ---------- ---------
PHONE
-----------
          1 John       Brown      01-JAN-65
800-555-1211

          2 Cynthia    Green      05-FEB-68
800-555-1212

          3 Steve      White      16-MAR-71
800-555-1213

          4 Gail       Black
800-555-1214

          5 Doreen     Blue       20-MAY-70
```

The lines don't span more than 50 characters.

NOTE
The maximum number for the line size is 32,767.

Clearing Column Formatting

You clear the formatting for a column using the CLEAR option of the COLUMN command. For example, the following COLUMN command clears the formatting for the product_id column:

```
SQL> COLUMN product_id CLEAR
```

You can clear the formatting for all columns using CLEAR COLUMNS. For example:

```
SQL> CLEAR COLUMNS
columns cleared
```

Once you've cleared your columns, the output from queries will use the default format for the columns.

Using Variables

In this section, you'll see how to create variables that may be used in place of actual values in SQL statements. These variables are known as *substitution variables* because they are used as substitutes for values. When you run your SQL statement, you enter values for your variables and those values are then substituted into your SQL statement.

There are two basic types of variables you can use in SQL*Plus:

- **Temporary variables**   A temporary variable is only valid for the SQL statement in which it is used and doesn't persist.

- **Defined variables**   A defined variable persists until you explicitly remove it, redefine it, or exit SQL*Plus.

You'll learn how to use these types of variables in this section.

Why Are Variables Useful?
Variables are useful because you can create scripts that a user who doesn't know SQL can run. Your script would prompt the user to enter the value for a variable and use that value in a SQL statement. Let's take a look at an example.

Suppose you wanted to create a script for a user who doesn't know SQL, but who wants to see the details of a single specified product in the store. To do this, you could hard code the product_id value in the WHERE clause of a SELECT statement and place that SELECT statement in a SQL*Plus script. For example, the following SELECT statement retrieves product #1:

```
SELECT product_id, name, price
FROM products
WHERE product_id = 1;
```

This query works, but it only retrieves that one product. What if you wanted to change the product_id value to retrieve a different row? You could modify the script, but this would be tedious. Wouldn't it be great if you could supply a variable for the product_id column in the WHERE clause when the query is actually run? A variable would enable you to write a general SQL statement that would work for any product, and the user would simply enter the value for that variable.

Temporary Variables

You define a temporary variable using the ampersand character (&) in a SQL statement, followed by the name you want to call your variable. For example, &product_id_var defines a variable named product_id_var.

When you run the following SELECT statement, SQL*Plus prompts you to enter a value for product_id_var and then uses that variable's value in the WHERE clause of the SELECT statement. If you enter the value 2 for product_id_var, the details for product #2 will be displayed.

```
SQL> SELECT product_id, name, price
  2  FROM products
  3  WHERE product_id = &product_id_var;
Enter value for product_id_var: 2
old   3: WHERE product_id = &product_id_var
new   3: WHERE product_id = 2

PRODUCT_ID NAME                                      PRICE
---------- ------------------------------- ----------
         2 Chemistry                                    30
```

Notice SQL*Plus does the following:

1. Prompts you to enter a value for product_id_var.

2. Substitutes the value you entered for product_id_var in the WHERE clause.

SQL*Plus shows you the substitution in the old and new lines in the output, along with the line number in the query where the substitution was performed. In the previous example, you can see that the old and new lines indicate that product_id_var is set to 2 in the WHERE clause of the SELECT statement.

If you rerun the query using the slash character (/), SQL*Plus will ask you to enter a new value for product_id_var. For example:

```
SQL> /
Enter value for product_id_var: 3
old   3: WHERE product_id = &product_id_var
new   3: WHERE product_id = 3

PRODUCT_ID NAME                                      PRICE
---------- ------------------------------- ----------
         3 Supernova                                 25.99
```

Once again, SQL*Plus echoes the old line of the SQL statement (old 3: WHERE product_id = &product_id_var) followed by the new line containing the variable value you entered (new 3: WHERE product_id = 3).

Controlling Output Lines

You may control the output of the old and new lines using the SET VERIFY command. If you
enter SET VERIFY OFF, the old and new lines are suppressed. For example:

```
SQL> SET VERIFY OFF
SQL> /
Enter value for product_id_var: 4

PRODUCT_ID NAME                                     PRICE
---------- ------------------------------ ----------
         4 Tank War                                 13.95
```

To turn the echoing of the lines back on, you enter SET VERIFY ON. For example:

```
SQL> SET VERIFY ON
```

Changing the Variable Definition Character

You can use the SET DEFINE command to specify a character other than ampersand (&) for defining
a variable. The following example shows how to set the variable character to the pound character
(#) using SET DEFINE and shows a new SELECT statement:

```
SQL> SET DEFINE '#'
SQL> SELECT product_id, name, price
  2  FROM products
  3  WHERE product_id = #product_id_var;
Enter value for product_id_var: 5
old   3: WHERE product_id = #product_id_var
new   3: WHERE product_id = 5

PRODUCT_ID NAME                                     PRICE
---------- ------------------------------ ----------
         5 Z Files                                  49.99
```

The next example uses SET DEFINE to change the character back to an ampersand:

```
SQL> SET DEFINE '&'
```

Substituting Table and Column Names Using Variables

You're not limited to using variables to substitute column values: you can also use variables to
substitute the names of tables and columns. For example, the following query defines variables
for you to enter a column name (col_var) or table name (table_var), as well as a column
value (col_val_var):

```
SQL> SELECT name, &col_var
  2  FROM &table_var
  3  WHERE &col_var = &col_val;
Enter value for col_var: product_type_id
old   1: SELECT name, &col_var
new   1: SELECT name, product_type_id
```

```
Enter value for table_var: products
old    2: FROM &table_var
new    2: FROM products
Enter value for col_var: product_type_id
Enter value for col_val: 1
old    3: WHERE &col_var = &col_val
new    3: WHERE product_type_id = 1


NAME                           PRODUCT_TYPE_ID
------------------------------ ---------------
Modern Science                               1
Chemistry                                    1
```

You can avoid having to repeatedly enter a variable by using &&. For example:

```
SELECT name, &&col_var
FROM &table_name
WHERE &&col_var = &col_val;
```

Being able to supply column and table names, as well as variable values, gives you a lot of flexibility in writing interactive queries that another user may run. That user doesn't need to write the SQL: you can simply give them a script and have them enter the variable values for the query.

Defined Variables

You can define a variable prior to using that variable in a SQL statement. You may use these variables multiple times within a SQL statement. A defined variable persists until you explicitly remove it, redefine it, or exit SQL*Plus.

You define a variable using the DEFINE command. When you're finished with your variable, you remove it using UNDEFINE. You'll learn about each of these commands in this section. You'll also learn about the ACCEPT command, which allows you to define a variable and specify a data type for that variable.

You can also define variables in a SQL*Plus script and pass in values to those variables when you run the script. This enables you to write generic reports that any user can run—even if they're unfamiliar with SQL. You'll learn how to create simple reports in the section "Creating Simple Reports."

Defining and Listing Variables Using the DEFINE Command

You use the DEFINE command to both define a new variable and list the currently defined variables. The following example defines a variable named product_id_var and sets its value to 7:

```
SQL> DEFINE product_id_var = 7
```

You can view the definition of a variable using the DEFINE command followed by the name of the variable. The following example displays the definition of product_id_var:

```
SQL> DEFINE product_id_var
DEFINE PRODUCT_ID_VAR          = "7" (CHAR)
```

Notice that `product_id_var` is defined as a CHAR variable.

You can see all your session variables by entering DEFINE on its own line. For example:

```
SQL> DEFINE
...
DEFINE PRODUCT_ID_VAR = "7" (CHAR)
```

You can use a defined variable to specify an element such as a column value in a SQL statement. For example, the following query uses the variable `product_id_var` defined earlier and references its value in the WHERE clause:

```
SQL> SELECT product_id, name, price
  2  FROM products
  3  WHERE product_id = &product_id_var;
old   3: WHERE product_id = &product_id_var
new   3: WHERE product_id = 7

PRODUCT_ID NAME                                PRICE
---------- ------------------------------ ----------
         7 Space Force 9                        13.49
```

Notice that you're not prompted to the value of `product_id_var`; that's because `product_id_var` was set to 7 when the variable was defined earlier.

Defining and Setting Variables Using the ACCEPT Command

The ACCEPT command waits for a user to enter a value for a variable. You can use the ACCEPT command to set an existing variable to a new value, or to define a new variable and initialize it with a value. The ACCEPT command also allows you to specify the data type for your variable. The simplified syntax for the ACCEPT command is as follows:

```
ACCEPT variable_name [type] [FORMAT format] [PROMPT prompt] [HIDE]
```

where

- *variable_name* specifies the name assigned to your variable.

- *type* specifies the data type for your variable. You can use the CHAR, NUMBER, and DATE types. By default, variables are defined using the CHAR type. DATE variables are actually stored as CHAR variables.

- *format* specifies the format used for your variable. Some examples include A15 (15 characters), 9999 (a four-digit number), and DD-MON-YYYY (a date). You can view the number formats in Table 3-4 of Chapter 3; you can view the date formats in Table 4-2 of Chapter 4.

- *prompt* specifies the text displayed by SQL*Plus as a prompt to the user to enter the variable's value.

- HIDE indicates the value entered for the variable is to be hidden. For example, you might want to hide passwords or other sensitive information. Hidden values are displayed using asterisks (*) as you enter the characters.

Let's take a look at some examples of the ACCEPT command. The first example defines a variable named customer_id_var as a two-digit number:

```
SQL> ACCEPT customer_id_var NUMBER FORMAT 99 PROMPT 'Customer id: '
Customer id: 5
```

The next example defines a DATE variable named date_var; the format for this DATE is DD-MON-YYYY:

```
SQL> ACCEPT date_var DATE FORMAT 'DD-MON-YYYY' PROMPT 'Date: '
Date: 12-DEC-2006
```

The next example defines a CHAR variable named password_var; the value entered is hidden using the HIDE option:

```
SQL> ACCEPT password_var CHAR PROMPT 'Password: ' HIDE
Password: *******
```

In Oracle9*i* and below, the value entered appears as a string of asterisk characters (*) to hide the value as you enter it. In Oracle10*i*, nothing is displayed as you type the value.

You can view your variables using the DEFINE command. For example:

```
SQL> DEFINE
...
DEFINE CUSTOMER_ID_VAR =          5 (NUMBER)
DEFINE DATE_VAR        = "12-DEC-2006" (CHAR)
DEFINE PASSWORD_VAR    = "1234567" (CHAR)
```

Notice that date_var is stored as a CHAR.

Removing Variables Using the UNDEFINE Command

You remove variables using the UNDEFINE command. The following example uses UNDEFINE to remove customer_id_var, date_var, and password_var:

```
SQL> UNDEFINE customer_id_var
SQL> UNDEFINE date_var
SQL> UNDEFINE password_var
```

NOTE
*All your variables are removed when you exit SQL*Plus, even if you don't explicitly remove them using the UNDEFINE command.*

Creating Simple Reports

You can use temporary and defined variables in a SQL*Plus script. This allows you to create scripts that prompt the user for entry of variables that can then be used to generate reports. You'll find the SQL*Plus scripts referenced in this section in the Zip file you can download from this book's web site.

TIP
*Bear in mind that SQL*Plus was not specifically designed as a reporting tool. If you have complex reporting requirements, you should use software like Oracle Reports.*

Using Temporary Variables in a Script

The following script `report1.sql` uses a temporary variable named `product_id_var` in the `WHERE` clause of a `SELECT` statement:

```
-- suppress display of the statements and verification messages
SET ECHO OFF
SET VERIFY OFF

SELECT product_id, name, price
FROM products
WHERE product_id = &product_id_var;
```

The `SET ECHO OFF` command stops SQL*Plus from displaying the SQL statements and commands in the script. `SET VERIFY OFF` suppresses display of the verification messages. I put these two commands in to minimize the number of extra lines displayed by SQL*Plus when you run the script.

You can run `report1.sql` in SQL*Plus using the @ command. For example:

```
SQL> @ C:\SQL\report1.sql
Enter value for product_id_var: 2

PRODUCT_ID NAME                                PRICE
---------- ------------------------------ ----------
         2 Chemistry                              30
```

You can give this script to another user and they can run it without them having to know SQL.

Using Defined Variables in a Script

The following script (named `report2.sql`) uses the `ACCEPT` command to define a variable named `product_id_var`:

```
SET ECHO OFF
SET VERIFY OFF

ACCEPT product_id_var NUMBER FORMAT 99 PROMPT 'Enter product id: '
```

```
SELECT product_id, name, price
FROM products
WHERE product_id = &product_id_var;

-- clean up
UNDEFINE product_id_var
```

Notice that a user-friendly prompt is specified for the entry of `product_id_var`, and that `product_id_var` is removed at the end of the script—this makes the script cleaner.

You can run the `report2.sql` script using SQL*Plus:

```
SQL> @ C:\SQL\report2.sql
Enter product id: 4


PRODUCT_ID NAME                                 PRICE
---------- ------------------------------ ----------
         4 Tank War                             13.95
```

Passing a Value to a Variable in a Script

You can pass a value to a variable when you run your script. When you do this, you reference the variable in your script using a number. The following script `report3.sql` shows an example of this; notice the variable is identified using `&1`:

```
SET ECHO OFF
SET VERIFY OFF

SELECT product_id, name, price
FROM products
WHERE product_id = &1;
```

When you run `report3.sql`, you supply the variable's value after the script name. The following example passes the value 3 to `report3.sql`:

```
SQL> @ C:\SQL\report3.sql 3
PRODUCT_ID NAME                                 PRICE
---------- ------------------------------ ----------
         3 Supernova                            25.99
```

You can add any number of parameters, with each value specified on the command line corresponding to the matching number in the file. The first parameter corresponds to `&1`, the second to `&2`, and so on. The following script `report4.sql` shows an example of this:

```
SET ECHO OFF
SET VERIFY OFF

SELECT product_id, product_type_id, name, price
FROM products
```

```
WHERE product_type_id = &1
AND price > &2;
```

The following example run of `report4.sql` shows the addition of two values for &1 and &2, which are set to 1 and 9.99, respectively:

```
SQL> @ C:\SQL\report4.sql 1 9.99
```

```
PRODUCT_ID PRODUCT_TYPE_ID NAME                                    PRICE
---------- --------------- ------------------------------- ----------
         1               1 Modern Science                          19.95
         2               1 Chemistry                                  30
```

Because &1 is set to 1, the `product_type_id` column in the WHERE clause is set to 1. Also, &2 is set to 9.99, so the price column in the WHERE clause is set to 9.99. Therefore, rows with a `product_type_id` of 1 and a `price` greater than 9.99 are displayed.

Adding a Header and Footer

You add a header and footer to your report using the TTITLE and BTITLE commands. The following script `report5.sql` shows this:

```
TTITLE 'Product Report'
BTITLE 'Thanks for running the report'

SET ECHO OFF
SET VERIFY OFF
SET PAGESIZE 30
SET LINESIZE 70
CLEAR COLUMNS
COLUMN product_id HEADING ID FORMAT 99
COLUMN name HEADING 'Product Name' FORMAT A20 WORD_WRAPPED
COLUMN description HEADING Description FORMAT A30 WORD_WRAPPED
COLUMN price HEADING Price FORMAT $99.99

SELECT product_id, name, description, price
FROM products;

CLEAR COLUMNS
```

The following example shows a run of `report5.sql`:

```
SQL> @ C:\SQL\report5.sql
```

```
Fri May 16                                              page    1
                        Product Report

 ID Product Name        Description                      Price
 --- -------------------- ------------------------------ -------
```

```
 1 Modern Science      A description of modern       $19.95
                       science

 2 Chemistry           Introduction to Chemistry     $30.00
 3 Supernova           A star explodes               $25.99
 4 Tank War            Action movie about a future   $13.95
                       war

 5 Z Files             Series on mysterious          $49.99
                       activities

 6 2412: The Return    Aliens return                 $14.95
 7 Space Force 9       Adventures of heroes          $13.49
 8 From Another Planet Alien from another planet     $12.99
                       lands on Earth

 9 Classical Music     The best classical music      $10.99
10 Pop 3               The best popular music        $15.99
11 Creative Yell       Debut album                   $14.99
12 My Front Line       Their greatest hits           $13.49

            Thanks for running the report
```

Computing Subtotals

You can add a subtotal for a column using a combination of the BREAK ON and COMPUTE commands. BREAK ON causes SQL*Plus to break up output based on a change in a column value, and COMPUTE causes SQL*Plus to compute a value for a column.

The following script report6.sql shows how to compute a subtotal for products of the same type:

```
BREAK ON product_type_id
COMPUTE SUM OF price ON product_type_id

SET ECHO OFF
SET VERIFY OFF
SET PAGESIZE 50
SET LINESIZE 70

CLEAR COLUMNS
COLUMN price HEADING Price FORMAT $999.99

SELECT product_type_id, name, price
FROM products
ORDER BY product_type_id;

CLEAR COLUMNS
```

The following example shows a run of `report6.sql`:

```
SQL> @ C:\SQL\report6.sql

PRODUCT_TYPE_ID NAME                                   Price
--------------- ------------------------------ --------
              1 Modern Science                        $19.95
                Chemistry                             $30.00
* * * * * * * * * * * * * * *                        --------
sum                                                   $49.95
              2 Supernova                             $25.99
                Tank War                              $13.95
                Z Files                               $49.99
                2412: The Return                      $14.95
* * * * * * * * * * * * * * *                        --------
sum                                                  $104.88
              3 Space Force 9                         $13.49
                From Another Planet                   $12.99
* * * * * * * * * * * * * * *                        --------
sum                                                   $26.48
              4 Classical Music                       $10.99
                Pop 3                                 $15.99
                Creative Yell                         $14.99
* * * * * * * * * * * * * * *                        --------
sum                                                   $41.97
                My Front Line                         $13.49
* * * * * * * * * * * * * * *                        --------
sum                                                   $13.49
```

Notice that whenever a new value for `product_type_id` is encountered, SQL*Plus breaks up the output and computes a sum for the `price` columns for the rows with the same `product_type_id`. The `product_type_id` value is only shown once for rows with the same `product_type_id`. For example, Modern Science and Chemistry are both books and have a `product_type_id` of 1, and 1 is shown once for Modern Science. The sum of the prices for these two books is $49.95. The other sections of the report contain the sum of the prices for products with different `product_type_id` values.

Automatically Generating SQL Statements

In this last section, I'll briefly show you a technique of writing SQL statements that produce other SQL statements. This is very useful and can save you a lot of typing when writing SQL statements that are similar. One simple example is a SQL statement that produces DROP TABLE statements that remove tables from a database. The following query produces a series of DROP TABLE statements that drop the tables in the `store` schema:

```
SELECT 'DROP TABLE ' || table_name || ';'
FROM user_tables;

'DROPTABLE'||TABLE_NAME||';'
-----------------------------------------
```

```
DROP TABLE COUPONS;
DROP TABLE CUSTOMERS;
DROP TABLE EMPLOYEES;
DROP TABLE PRODUCTS;
DROP TABLE PRODUCT_TYPES;
DROP TABLE PROMOTIONS;
DROP TABLE PURCHASES;
DROP TABLE PURCHASES_TIMESTAMP_WITH_TZ;
DROP TABLE PURCHASES_WITH_LOCAL_TZ;
DROP TABLE PURCHASES_WITH_TIMESTAMP;
DROP TABLE SALARY_GRADES;
```

NOTE
user_tables contains the details of the tables in the user's schema. The table_name column contains names of the tables.

You can spool the generated SQL statements to a file and use them later.

Summary

In this chapter, you learned how to

- View the structure of a table

- Edit a SQL statement

- Save, retrieve, and run files containing SQL and SQL*Plus commands

- Format column output and set the page and line sizes

- Use variables in SQL*Plus

- Create simple reports

- Write SQL statements that generate other SQL statements

In the next chapter, you'll learn how to nest one query within another. The nested query is known as a subquery.

CHAPTER
6

Subqueries

All the queries you've seen so far in this book have contained just one SELECT statement. In this chapter, you will

■ Learn how to place a SELECT statement within an outer SELECT, UPDATE, or DELETE statement. The inner SELECT statement is known as a *subquery.*

■ Learn about the different types of subqueries and see how to use them.

■ See how subqueries allow you to build up very complex statements from simple components.

Types of Subqueries
There are two basic types of subqueries:

■ **Single row subqueries**   Return zero or one row to the outer SQL statement.

■ **Multiple row subqueries**   Return one or more rows to the outer SQL statement.

In addition, there are three subtypes of subqueries that may return single or multiple rows:

■ **Multiple column subqueries**   Return more than one column to the outer SQL statement.

■ **Correlated subqueries**   Reference one or more columns in the outer SQL statement. The subquery is known as a correlated subquery because the subquery is related to the outer SQL statement.

■ **Nested subqueries**   Are placed within another subquery. You can nest subqueries to a depth of 255.

You'll learn about each of these types of subqueries in this chapter, and see how to add subqueries to SELECT, UPDATE, and DELETE statements. Let's plunge in and look at how to write single row subqueries.

Writing Single Row Subqueries
A single row subquery is one that returns zero or one row to the outer SQL statement. As you'll see in this section, you may place a subquery in a WHERE clause, a HAVING clause, or a FROM clause of a SELECT statement. You'll also see some errors you might encounter when issuing subqueries.

Subqueries in a WHERE Clause
You may place a subquery in the WHERE clause of another query. Let's take a look at a very simple example of a query that contains a subquery placed in its WHERE clause; notice the subquery is placed within parentheses (...):

```
SELECT first_name, last_name
FROM customers
WHERE customer_id =
  (SELECT customer_id
   FROM customers
   WHERE last_name = 'Brown');
```

```
FIRST_NAME LAST_NAME
---------- ----------
John       Brown
```

This example retrieves the `first_name` and `last_name` of the row from the `customers` table whose `last_name` is Brown. Let's break this query down and analyze what's going on. The subquery in the WHERE clause is as follows:

```
SELECT customer_id
FROM customers
WHERE last_name = 'Brown';
```

This subquery is executed first (and only once) and returns the `customer_id` for the row whose `last_name` is Brown. The `customer_id` for this row is 1, which is passed to the WHERE clause of the outer query. Therefore, the outer query may be considered to be identical to the following query:

```
SELECT first_name, last_name
FROM customers
WHERE customer_id = 1;
```

Using Other Single Row Operators

The previous example used the equality operator (=) in the WHERE clause. You may also use other comparison operators such as <>, <, >, <=, and >= with a single row subquery. The following example uses > in the outer query's WHERE clause; the subquery uses the AVG() function to get the average price of the products, which is passed to the WHERE clause of the outer query. The final result of the entire query is to get the `product_id`, name, and `price` of products whose price is greater than that average price.

```
SELECT product_id, name, price
FROM products
WHERE price >
  (SELECT AVG(price)
   FROM products);
```

```
PRODUCT_ID NAME                              PRICE
---------- ----------------------------- ----------
         1 Modern Science                    19.95
         2 Chemistry                            30
         3 Supernova                         25.99
         5 Z Files                           49.99
```

Let's break the example down to understand how it works. The following shows the output from the subquery when it's run on its own:

```
SELECT AVG(price)
FROM products;

AVG(PRICE)
----------
19.7308333
```

The value of 19.7308333 is used in the WHERE clause of the outer query shown earlier to get the products whose price is greater than that average.

Subqueries in a HAVING Clause

As you saw in Chapter 3, you use the HAVING clause to filter groups of rows. You may place a subquery in a HAVING clause of an outer query. This allows you to filter groups of rows based on the result returned by your subquery.

The following example uses a subquery in the HAVING clause of the outer query. The example retrieves the product_type_id and the average price for products whose average price is less than the maximum of the average for the groups of the same type product type:

```
SELECT product_type_id, AVG(price)
FROM products
GROUP BY product_type_id
HAVING AVG(price) <
  (SELECT MAX(AVG(price))
   FROM products
   GROUP BY product_type_id);

PRODUCT_TYPE_ID AVG(PRICE)
--------------- ----------
              1     24.975
              3      13.24
              4      13.99
                     13.49
```

Notice the subquery uses AVG() to first compute the average price for each product type. The result returned by AVG() is then passed to MAX(), which returns the maximum of the averages.

Let's break the example down to understand how it works. The following shows the output from the subquery when it is run on its own:

```
SELECT MAX(AVG(price))
FROM products
GROUP BY product_type_id;

MAX(AVG(PRICE))
---------------
          26.22
```

This value of 26.22 is used in the HAVING clause of the outer query shown earlier to filter the group's rows to those having an average price less than 26.22. The following query shows a version of the outer query that retrieves the `product_type_id` and average price of the products grouped by `product_type_id`:

```
SELECT product_type_id, AVG(price)
FROM products
GROUP BY product_type_id;
```

```
PRODUCT_TYPE_ID AVG(PRICE)
--------------- ----------
              1     24.975
              2      26.22
              3      13.24
              4      13.99
                     13.49
```

You can see that that the groups with a `product_type_id` of 1, 3, 4, and null have an average price less than 26.22. As expected, these are the same groups returned by the query containing the subquery at the start of this section.

Subqueries in a FROM Clause (Inline Views)

You may place a subquery in the FROM clause of an outer query. These types of subqueries are also known as *inline views* because the subquery provides data inline with the FROM clause. The following simple example retrieves the products whose `product_id` is less than 3:

```
SELECT product_id
FROM
   (SELECT product_id
    FROM products
    WHERE product_id < 3);
```

```
PRODUCT_ID
----------
         1
         2
```

Notice the subquery returns the rows from the `products` table whose `product_id` is less than 3 to the outer query, which then retrieves and displays those `product_id` values. As far as the FROM clause of the outer query is concerned, the output from the subquery is just another source of data.

The next example is more useful and retrieves the `product_id` and `price` from the `products` table in the outer query, and the subquery retrieves the number of times a product has been purchased:

```
SELECT prds.product_id, price, purchases_data.product_count
FROM products prds,
   (SELECT product_id, COUNT(product_id) product_count
```

```
FROM purchases
   GROUP BY product_id) purchases_data
WHERE prds.product_id = purchases_data.product_id;
```

```
PRODUCT_ID      PRICE PRODUCT_COUNT
---------- ---------- -------------
         1      19.95             4
         2         30             4
         3      25.99             1
```

Notice the subquery retrieves the `product_id` and `COUNT(product_id)` from the `purchases` table and returns them to the outer query. As you can see, the output from subquery is just another source of data to the `FROM` clause of the outer query.

A Couple of Errors You Might Encounter

In this section, you'll see some errors you might encounter. Specifically, you'll see that a single row subquery may return a maximum of one row, and you'll see a subquery may not contain an `ORDER BY` clause.

Single Row Subqueries May Return a Maximum of One Row

If your subquery returns more than one row, you'll get the following error:

ORA-01427: single-row subquery returns more than one row.

For example, the subquery in the following statement attempts to pass multiple rows to the equality operator (=) in the outer query:

```
SQL> SELECT product_id, name
  2  FROM products
  3  WHERE product_id =
  4    (SELECT product_id
  5     FROM products
  6     WHERE name LIKE '%e%');

  (SELECT product_id
   *
ERROR at line 4:
ORA-01427: single-row subquery returns more than one row
```

There are nine rows in the `products` table whose name contains the letter e, and the subquery attempts to pass these rows to the equality operator in the outer query. Since the equality operator can only handle a single row, the query is invalid and an error is returned.

You'll learn how to return multiple rows from a subquery later in the section "Writing Multiple Row Subqueries."

Subqueries May Not Contain an ORDER BY Clause

A subquery may not contain an `ORDER BY` clause. Instead, you must do any ordering in your outer query. For example, the following outer query has an `ORDER BY` clause at the end that sorts on the `product_id` column:

```
SELECT product_id, name, price
FROM products
WHERE price >
  (SELECT AVG(price)
   FROM products)
ORDER BY product_id DESC;

PRODUCT_ID NAME                               PRICE
---------- ------------------------------ ----------
         5 Z Files                            49.99
         3 Supernova                          25.99
         2 Chemistry                             30
         1 Modern Science                     19.95
```

Writing Multiple Row Subqueries

You use a multiple row subquery to return one or more rows to the outer SQL statement. To handle a subquery that returns multiple rows, your outer query may use the IN, ANY, or ALL operator. As you saw in Chapter 2, you can use these operators to check and compare values supplied in a list of literal values. As you'll see in this section, you can also supply this list of values from a subquery.

> **NOTE**
> You can also use the EXISTS operator to check if a value is in a list returned by a correlated subquery, which you'll learn about later in the section "Writing Correlated Subqueries."

Using IN with a Multiple Row Subquery

As you saw in Chapter 2, you use IN to check if a value is in a specified list of values. The list of values may come from the results returned by a subquery. You can also use NOT IN to perform the logical opposite of IN: you use NOT IN to check if a value is not in a specified list of values.

The following simple example uses IN to check if a product_id is in the list of product_id values returned by the subquery; the subquery returns the product_id column values for the products whose name contains the letter e:

```
SELECT product_id, name
FROM products
WHERE product_id IN
  (SELECT product_id
   FROM products
   WHERE name LIKE '%e%');

PRODUCT_ID NAME
---------- -------------------
         1 Modern Science
         2 Chemistry
         3 Supernova
```

```
 5 Z Files
 6 2412: The Return
 7 Space Force 9
 8 From Another Planet
11 Creative Yell
12 My Front Line
```

The next example uses NOT IN to check if a product_id is not in the list of product_id values in the purchases table:

```
SELECT product_id, name
FROM products
WHERE product_id NOT IN
(SELECT product_id
FROM purchases);

PRODUCT_ID NAME
---------- -------------------
         4 Tank War
         5 Z Files
         6 2412: The Return
         7 Space Force 9
         8 From Another Planet
         9 Classical Music
        10 Pop 3
        11 Creative Yell
        12 My Front Line
```

Using ANY with a Multiple Row Subquery

You use the ANY operator to compare a value with any value in a list. You must place an =, <>, <, >, <=, or >= operator before ANY in your query. The following example uses ANY to check if any of the employees has a salary less than any of the lowest salaries in the salary_grades table:

```
SELECT employee_id, last_name
FROM employees
WHERE salary < ANY
  (SELECT low_salary
   FROM salary_grades);

EMPLOYEE_ID LAST_NAME
----------- ----------
          2 Johnson
          3 Hobbs
          4 Jones
```

Using ALL with a Multiple Row Subquery

You use the ALL operator to compare a value with any value in a list. You must place an =, <>, <, >, <=, or >= operator before ALL in your query. The following example uses ALL to check if any of the employees has a salary greater than all of the highest salaries in the salary_grades table:

```
SELECT employee_id, last_name
FROM employees
WHERE salary > ALL
  (SELECT high_salary
   FROM salary_grades);

no rows selected
```

As you can see from this result, no employee has a salary greater than the highest salary. This is probably a good thing, since you don't want an employee earning more than the highest salary!

Writing Multiple Column Subqueries

The subqueries you've seen so far have returned rows containing one column. You're not limited to one column: you can write subqueries that return multiple columns. The following example retrieves the products with lowest price in each product type group:

```
SELECT product_id, product_type_id, name, price
FROM products
WHERE (product_type_id, price) IN
  (SELECT product_type_id, MIN(price)
   FROM products
   GROUP BY product_type_id);

PRODUCT_ID PRODUCT_TYPE_ID NAME                            PRICE
---------- --------------- ------------------------------ ----------
         1               1 Modern Science                  19.95
         4               2 Tank War                        13.95
         8               3 From Another Planet             12.99
         9               4 Classical Music                 10.99
```

Notice the subquery returns the `product_type_id` and the minimum value of the `price` column values. The outer query has a WHERE clause with the two columns `product_type_id` and `price` in parentheses.

Writing Correlated Subqueries

A correlated subquery references one or more columns in the outer query. The subquery is known as a correlated subquery because the subquery is related to the outer query. You typically use a correlated subquery when you need an answer to a question that depends on a value in each row contained in the outer query.

A Correlated Subquery Example

The following correlated subquery retrieves products that have a price greater than the average for their product type:

```
SELECT product_id, product_type_id, name, price
FROM products outer
```

```
WHERE price >
  (SELECT AVG(price)
   FROM products inner
   WHERE inner.product_type_id = outer.product_type_id);
```

```
PRODUCT_ID PRODUCT_TYPE_ID NAME                                 PRICE
---------- --------------- ---------------------------- ----------
         2               1 Chemistry                            30
         5               2 Z Files                           49.99
         7               3 Space Force 9                     13.49
        10               4 Pop 3                             15.99
        11               4 Creative Yell                     14.99
```

Notice I've used the alias `outer` to label the outer query and the alias `inner` for the inner query. The inner and outer parts are correlated using the `product_type_id` column.

In a correlated subquery, each row in the outer query is passed one at a time to the subquery. The subquery reads each row in turn from the outer query and applies it to the subquery until all the rows from the outer query have been processed. The results from the entire query are then returned.

In the previous example, the outer query retrieves each row from the `products` table and passes each row to the inner query. Each row is read by the inner query, which calculates the average price for each product where the `product_type_id` in the inner query is equal to the `product_type_id` in the outer query.

Using EXISTS and NOT EXISTS with a Correlated Subquery

You use the `EXISTS` operator to check for the existence of rows returned by a subquery. Although you can use `EXISTS` with non-correlated subqueries, you'll typically use it with correlated subqueries. `NOT EXISTS` does the logical opposite of `EXISTS`. You use `NOT EXISTS` when you need to check if rows do not exist in the results returned by a subquery.

Using EXISTS with a Correlated Subquery

The following example uses `EXISTS` to retrieve employees who manage other employees:

```
SELECT employee_id, last_name
FROM employees outer
WHERE EXISTS
  (SELECT employee_id
   FROM employees inner
   WHERE inner.manager_id = outer.employee_id);
```

```
EMPLOYEE_ID LAST_NAME
----------- ----------
          1 Smith
          2 Johnson
```

Since `EXISTS` just checks for the existence of rows returned by the subquery, your subquery doesn't have to return a column: you can just return a literal value. This can improve performance of your query. For example, the following query rewrites the previous example with the subquery returning the literal value 1:

```
SELECT employee_id, last_name
FROM employees outer
WHERE EXISTS
  (SELECT 1
   FROM employees inner
   WHERE inner.manager_id = outer.employee_id);


EMPLOYEE_ID LAST_NAME
----------- ----------
          1 Smith
          2 Johnson
```

Using NOT EXISTS with a Correlated Subquery

The following example uses NOT EXISTS to retrieve products that haven't been purchased:

```
SELECT product_id, name
FROM products outer
WHERE NOT EXISTS
  (SELECT 1
   FROM purchases inner
   WHERE inner.product_id = outer.product_id);


PRODUCT_ID NAME
---------- --------------------
         4 Tank War
         5 Z Files
         6 2412: The Return
         7 Space Force 9
         8 From Another Planet
         9 Classical Music
        10 Pop 3
        11 Creative Yell
        12 My Front Line
```

EXISTS and NOT EXISTS Versus IN and NOT IN

Earlier in the section "Using IN with a Multiple Row Subquery," you saw how the IN operator is used to check if a value is contained in a list. EXISTS is different from IN: EXISTS just checks for the existence of rows, whereas IN checks actual values.

TIP
EXISTS typically offers better performance than IN with subqueries. Therefore you should use EXISTS rather than IN wherever possible.

You should be careful when writing queries that use NOT EXISTS or NOT IN. When a list of values contains a null, NOT EXISTS returns true, but NOT IN returns false. Consider the following example that uses NOT EXISTS and retrieves the product types that don't have any products of that type in the products table:

```
SELECT product_type_id, name
FROM product_types outer
WHERE NOT EXISTS
  (SELECT 1
  FROM products inner
  WHERE inner.product_type_id = outer.product_type_id);

PRODUCT_TYPE_ID NAME
--------------- ----------
              5 Magazine
```

Notice one row is returned by this example. The next example rewrites the previous query to use NOT IN; notice no rows are returned:

```
SELECT product_type_id, name
FROM product_types
WHERE product_type_id NOT IN
  (SELECT product_type_id
  FROM products);

no rows selected
```

No rows are returned because the subquery returns a list of product_id values, one of which is null. The product_type_id for product #12 is null. Because of this, the NOT IN operator in the outer query returns false and therefore no rows are returned. You can get around this by using the NVL() function to convert nulls to a value. In the following example, NVL() is used to convert null product_type_id values to 0:

```
SELECT product_type_id, name
FROM product_types
WHERE product_type_id NOT IN
  (SELECT NVL(product_type_id, 0)
  FROM products);

PRODUCT_TYPE_ID NAME
--------------- ----------
              5 Magazine
```

This time the expected row appears.

Writing Nested Subqueries

You can nest subqueries inside other subqueries to a depth of 255. But you should use this technique sparingly; you may find your query performs better using table joins. The following example contains a nested subquery. Notice that it is contained within a subquery, which is itself contained in an outer query:

```
SELECT product_type_id, AVG(price)
FROM products
GROUP BY product_type_id
HAVING AVG(price) <
  (SELECT MAX(AVG(price))
   FROM products
   WHERE product_type_id IN
     (SELECT product_id
      FROM purchases
      WHERE quantity > 1)
   GROUP BY product_type_id);
```

```
PRODUCT_TYPE_ID AVG(PRICE)
--------------- ----------
              1     24.975
              3      13.24
              4      13.99
                     13.49
```

As you can see, this example is quite complex and contains three queries: a nested subquery, a subquery, and the outer query. These query parts are run in that order. Let's break the example down into the three parts and examine the results returned. The nested subquery is as follows:

```
SELECT product_id
FROM purchases
WHERE quantity > 1
```

This subquery returns the `product_id` values for the products that have been purchased more than once. The rows returned by this subquery are

```
PRODUCT_ID
----------
         2
         1
```

The subquery that receives this output is

```
SELECT MAX(AVG(price))
FROM products
WHERE product_type_id IN
  (... output from previous nested subquery ...)
GROUP BY product_type_id
```

This subquery returns the maximum of the averages of the prices for the products returned by the previous nested subquery. The row returned is

```
MAX(AVG(PRICE))
---------------
          26.22
```

This row is returned to the following outer query:

```
SELECT product_type_id, AVG(price)
FROM products
GROUP BY product_type_id
HAVING AVG(price) <
  (... output from previous subquery ...);
```

This query returns the `product_type_id` and average price of products that are less than average returned by the previous subquery. The rows returned are

```
PRODUCT_TYPE_ID AVG(PRICE)
--------------- ----------
              1     24.975
              3      13.24
              4      13.99
                     13.49
```

These are, of course, the rows returned by the complete query shown earlier.

Writing UPDATE and DELETE Statements Containing Subqueries

So far, you've only seen subqueries contained in a `SELECT` statement. As you'll see in this section, you can also use subqueries with `UPDATE` and `DELETE` statements.

Writing an UPDATE Statement Containing a Subquery

In an `UPDATE` statement, you set the new column value equal to the result returned by a single row subquery. For example, the following `UPDATE` statement sets employee #4's salary to the average of the high salary grades returned by a subquery:

```
UPDATE employees
SET salary =
  (SELECT AVG(high_salary)
   FROM salary_grades)
WHERE employee_id = 4;
```

```
1 row updated.
```

This increases employee #4's salary from $500,000 to $625,000 (this is the average of the high salaries from the `salary_grades` table).

NOTE
If you execute the UPDATE statement, remember to execute a ROLLBACK to undo the change.

Writing a DELETE Statement Containing a Subquery

You use the results returned by the subquery in the WHERE clause of your DELETE statement. For example, the following DELETE statement removes the employee whose salary is greater than the average of the high salary grades returned by a subquery:

```
DELETE FROM employees
WHERE salary >
  (SELECT AVG(high_salary)
   FROM salary_grades);
```

```
1 row deleted.
```

This DELETE statement removes employee #1.

NOTE
If you execute the DELETE statement, remember to execute a ROLLBACK to undo the removal of the row.

Summary

In this chapter, you learned that

- A subquery is a query placed within a SELECT, UPDATE, or DELETE statement.

- Single row subqueries return zero or one row.

- Multiple row subqueries return one or more rows.

- Multiple column subqueries return more than one column.

- Correlated subqueries reference one or more columns in the outer SQL statement.

- Nested subqueries are subqueries placed within another subquery.

In the next chapter, you'll learn about advanced queries.

CHAPTER
7

Advanced Queries

In this chapter, you will

- Learn how to use the set operators, which allow you to combine rows returned by two or more queries.

- Use the `TRANSLATE()` function to convert characters in one string to characters in another string based on a set of translation characters.

- Use the `DECODE()` function to search a set of values for a certain value.

- Learn how to use the `CASE` expression to perform if-then-else logic in SQL without having to use PL/SQL. (You'll learn how to use PL/SQL in Chapter 11.)

- Learn how to perform queries against data that is organized into a hierarchy.

- Use the `ROLLUP` clause to return rows containing a subtotal for each group.

- Use the `CUBE` clause to return rows containing a subtotal for all combinations of columns along with a total at the end.

- Learn about the analytic functions that enable you to perform complex calculations such as finding the top-selling product type for each month, the top salespersons, and so on.

- Use the new Oracle Database 10*g* `MODEL` clause to perform inter-row calculations.

Let's plunge in and examine the set operators.

Using the Set Operators

The set operators allow you to combine rows returned by two or more queries. Table 7-1 shows the four set operators.

You must keep in mind the following restriction when using a set operator:

- The number of columns and the column types returned by the queries must match— although the column names may be different.

Operator	Description
`UNION ALL`	Returns all the rows retrieved by the queries, including duplicate rows.
`UNION`	Returns all non-duplicate rows retrieved by the queries.
`INTERSECT`	Returns rows that are retrieved by both queries.
`MINUS`	Returns the remaining rows when the rows retrieved by the second query are subtracted from the rows retrieved by the first query.

TABLE 7-1. *Set Operators*

You'll learn how to use each of the set operators shown in Table 7-1 shortly, but first let's look at the example tables you'll use later in this section.

The Example Tables

You'll see the use of the `products` and `more_products` tables in the following sections. The `products` and `more_products` tables are created by the `store_schema.sql` script as follows:

```
CREATE TABLE products (
  product_id INTEGER
    CONSTRAINT products_pk PRIMARY KEY,
  product_type_id INTEGER
    CONSTRAINT products_fk_product_types
    REFERENCES product_types(product_type_id),
  name VARCHAR2(30) NOT NULL,
  description VARCHAR2(50),
  price NUMBER(5, 2)
);

CREATE TABLE more_products (
  prd_id INTEGER
    CONSTRAINT more_products_pk PRIMARY KEY,
  prd_type_id INTEGER
    CONSTRAINT more_products_fk_product_types
    REFERENCES product_types(product_type_id),
  name VARCHAR2(30) NOT NULL,
  available CHAR(1)
);
```

The `products` table contains the following rows. Note that I've only shown the product ID, product type ID, and name columns because these are the only columns used in the examples. The tables contain other columns just so you can see that the tables don't have to be identical to use the set operators.

```
PRODUCT_ID PRODUCT_TYPE_ID NAME
---------- --------------- -------------------
         1               1 Modern Science
         2               1 Chemistry
         3               2 Supernova
         4               2 Tank War
         5               2 Z Files
         6               2 2412: The Return
         7               3 Space Force 9
         8               3 From Another Planet
         9               4 Classical Music
        10               4 Pop 3
        11               4 Creative Yell
        12                 My Front Line
```

The more_products table contains the following rows:

```
    PRD_ID PRD_TYPE_ID NAME
---------- ----------- --------------
         1           1 Modern Science
         2           1 Chemistry
         3             Supernova
         4           2 Lunar Landing
         5           2 Submarine
```

Using the UNION ALL Operator

The UNION ALL operator returns all the rows retrieved by the queries, including duplicate rows. The following example uses UNION ALL. Notice all the rows from products and more_products are retrieved, including duplicates:

```
SELECT product_id, product_type_id, name
FROM products
UNION ALL
SELECT prd_id, prd_type_id, name
FROM more_products;

PRODUCT_ID PRODUCT_TYPE_ID NAME
---------- --------------- ----------------------------
         1               1 Modern Science
         2               1 Chemistry
         3               2 Supernova
         4               2 Tank War
         5               2 Z Files
         6               2 2412: The Return
         7               3 Space Force 9
         8               3 From Another Planet
         9               4 Classical Music
        10               4 Pop 3
        11               4 Creative Yell
        12                 My Front Line
         1               1 Modern Science
         2               1 Chemistry
         3                 Supernova
         4               2 Lunar Landing
         5               2 Submarine

17 rows selected.
```

You can sort the rows using the ORDER BY clause and the position of the column in the two queries. The following example sorts on the first column:

```
SELECT product_id, product_type_id, name
FROM products
UNION ALL
```

```
SELECT prd_id, prd_type_id, name
FROM more_products
ORDER BY 1;
```

```
PRODUCT_ID PRODUCT_TYPE_ID NAME
---------- --------------- -------------------
         1               1 Modern Science
         1               1 Modern Science
         2               1 Chemistry
         2               1 Chemistry
         3               2 Supernova
         3                 Supernova
         4               2 Tank War
         4               2 Lunar Landing
         5               2 Z Files
         5               2 Submarine
         6               2 2412: The Return
         7               3 Space Force 9
         8               3 From Another Planet
         9               4 Classical Music
        10               4 Pop 3
        11               4 Creative Yell
        12                 My Front Line
```

Using the UNION Operator

The UNION operator returns all non-duplicate rows retrieved by the queries. The following example uses UNION; notice all non-duplicate rows from products and more_products are retrieved:

```
SELECT product_id, product_type_id, name
FROM products
UNION
SELECT prd_id, prd_type_id, name
FROM more_products;
```

```
PRODUCT_ID PRODUCT_TYPE_ID NAME
---------- --------------- -------------------
         1               1 Modern Science
         2               1 Chemistry
         3               2 Supernova
         3                 Supernova
         4               2 Lunar Landing
         4               2 Tank War
         5               2 Submarine
         5               2 Z Files
         6               2 2412: The Return
         7               3 Space Force 9
         8               3 From Another Planet
         9               4 Classical Music
```

```
10              4 Pop 3
11              4 Creative Yell
12                My Front Line
```

15 rows selected.

Using the INTERSECT Operator

The INTERSECT operator returns rows that are retrieved by both queries. The following example uses INTERSECT. Notice only rows that are common to both products and more_products are retrieved:

```
SELECT product_id, product_type_id, name
FROM products
INTERSECT
SELECT prd_id, prd_type_id, name
FROM more_products;

PRODUCT_ID PRODUCT_TYPE_ID NAME
---------- --------------- --------------
         1               1 Modern Science
         2               1 Chemistry
```

Using the MINUS Operator

The MINUS operator returns the remaining rows when the rows retrieved by the second query are subtracted from the rows retrieved by the first query. The following example uses MINUS; notice the rows from more_products are subtracted from products and the remaining rows returned:

```
SELECT product_id, product_type_id, name
FROM products
MINUS
SELECT prd_id, prd_type_id, name
FROM more_products;

PRODUCT_ID PRODUCT_TYPE_ID NAME
---------- --------------- --------------------
         3               2 Supernova
         4               2 Tank War
         5               2 Z Files
         6               2 2412: The Return
         7               3 Space Force 9
         8               3 From Another Planet
         9               4 Classical Music
        10               4 Pop 3
        11               4 Creative Yell
        12                 My Front Line
```

10 rows selected.

Combining Set Operators

You can combine more than two queries with multiple set operators, with the returned results from one operator feeding into the next operator. By default, set operators are evaluated from top to bottom, but you should indicate the order using parentheses in case Oracle Corporation changes the default behavior in future releases.

In the examples in this section, I'll use the following `product_changes` table that is created by the `store_schema.sql` script:

```
CREATE TABLE product_changes (
  product_id INTEGER
    CONSTRAINT prod_changes_pk PRIMARY KEY,
  product_type_id INTEGER
    CONSTRAINT prod_changes_fk_product_types
    REFERENCES product_types(product_type_id),
  name VARCHAR2(30) NOT NULL,
  description VARCHAR2(50),
  price NUMBER(5, 2)
);
```

The following output shows the `product_id`, `product_type_id`, and `name` columns from the `product_changes` table:

```
PRODUCT_ID PRODUCT_TYPE_ID NAME
---------- --------------- --------------
         1               1 Modern Science
         2               1 New Chemistry
         3               1 Supernova
        13               2 Lunar Landing
        14               2 Submarine
        15               2 Airplane
```

The next example performs the following:

- Uses the UNION operator to combine the results from the `products` and `more_products` tables.

- Uses the INTERSECT operator to combine the results from the previous UNION operator with the results from the `product_changes` table.

- Uses parentheses to indicate the order of evaluation, which is the UNION between the `products` and `more_products` tables followed by the INTERSECT.

```
(SELECT product_id, product_type_id, name
FROM products
UNION
SELECT prd_id, prd_type_id, name
FROM more_products)
INTERSECT
```

```
SELECT product_id, product_type_id, name
FROM product_changes;

PRODUCT_ID PRODUCT_TYPE_ID NAME
---------- --------------- ---------------
         1               1 Modern Science
```

The next example changes the parentheses so that the INTERSECT is performed first; notice the different results:

```
SELECT product_id, product_type_id, name
FROM products
UNION
(SELECT prd_id, prd_type_id, name
FROM more_products
INTERSECT
SELECT product_id, product_type_id, name
FROM product_changes);

PRODUCT_ID PRODUCT_TYPE_ID NAME
---------- --------------- -------------------
         1               1 Modern Science
         2               1 Chemistry
         3               2 Supernova
         4               2 Tank War
         5               2 Z Files
         6               2 2412: The Return
         7               3 Space Force 9
         8               3 From Another Planet
         9               4 Classical Music
        10               4 Pop 3
        11               4 Creative Yell
        12                 My Front Line
```

This concludes the discussion of the set operators.

Using the TRANSLATE() Function

You use TRANSLATE(*x, from_string, to_string*) to convert the occurrences of characters in *from_string* found in *x* to corresponding characters in *to_string*. The easiest way to see how TRANSLATE() works is to examine some examples.

The following example uses TRANSLATE() to shift each character in the string SECRET MESSAGE: MEET ME IN THE PARK by four places to the right: A becomes E, B becomes F, and so on:

```
SELECT TRANSLATE('SECRET MESSAGE: MEET ME IN THE PARK',
  'ABCDEFGHIJKLMNOPQRSTUVWXYZ',
  'EFGHIJKLMNOPQRSTUVWXYZABCD') FROM dual;
```

```
TRANSLATE('SECRETMESSAGE:MEETMEINTH
-----------------------------------
WIGVIX QIWWEKI: QIIX QI MR XLI TEVO
```

The next example takes the output of the previous example and shifts the characters four places to the left: E becomes A, F becomes B, and so on:

```
SELECT TRANSLATE('WIGVIX QIWWEKI: QIIX QI MR XLI TEVO',
 'EFGHIJKLMNOPQRSTUVWXYZABCD',
 'ABCDEFGHIJKLMNOPQRSTUVWXYZ') FROM dual;
```

```
TRANSLATE('WIGVIXQIWWEKI:QIIXQIMRXL
----------------------------------
SECRET MESSAGE: MEET ME IN THE PARK
```

You can of course pass column values to TRANSLATE(). The following example passes the name column from the products table to TRANSLATE() and also shifts the lowercase as well as uppercase characters:

```
SELECT product_id, TRANSLATE(name,
 'ABCDEFGHIJKLMNOPQRSTUVWXYZabcdefghijklmnopqrstuvwxyz',
 'EFGHIJKLMNOPQRSTUVWXYZABCDefghijklmnopqrstuvwxyzabcd')
FROM products;
```

```
PRODUCT_ID TRANSLATE(NAME,'ABCDEFGHIJKLMN
---------- ------------------------------
         1 Qshivr Wgmirgi
         2 Gliqmwxvc
         3 Wytivrsze
         4 Xero Aev
         5 D Jmpiw
         6 2412: Xli Vixyvr
         7 Wtegi Jsvgi 9
         8 Jvsq Ersxliv Tperix
         9 Gpewwmgep Qywmg
        10 Tst 3
        11 Gviexmzi Cipp
        12 Qc Jvsrx Pmri
```

You can also use TRANSLATE() to convert numbers. The following example takes the number 12345 and converts 5 to 6, 4 to 7, 3 to 8, 2 to 9, and 1 to 0:

```
SELECT TRANSLATE(12345,
 54321,
 67890) FROM dual;
```

```
TRANS
-----
09876
```

Using the DECODE() Function

You use DECODE(*value*, *search_value*, *result*, *default_value*) to compare *value* with *search_value*. If the values are equal, DECODE() returns *result*, otherwise *default_value* is returned. DECODE() allows you to perform if-then-else logic in SQL without having to use PL/SQL.

The following example illustrates the use of DECODE():

```
SELECT DECODE(1, 1, 2, 3)
FROM dual;

DECODE(1,1,2,3)
---------------
              2
```

In this example, DECODE() returns 2 because 1 is compared to 1 and since they are equal 2 is returned.

The next example uses DECODE() to compare 1 to 2, and since they are not equal 3 is returned:

```
SELECT DECODE(1, 2, 1, 3)
FROM dual;

DECODE(1,2,1,3)
---------------
              3
```

The next example compares the available column in the more_products table. If available equals Y, the string Product is available is returned, otherwise the string Product is not available is returned:

```
SELECT prd_id, available,
  DECODE(available, 'Y', 'Product is available',
    'Product is not available')
FROM more_products;

PRD_ID A DECODE(AVAILABLE,'Y','PR
---------- - -----------------------
         1 Y Product is available
         2 Y Product is available
         3 N Product is not available
         4 N Product is not available
         5 Y Product is available
```

You can pass multiple search and result parameters to DECODE(), as shown in the following example:

```
SELECT product_id, product_type_id,
  DECODE(product_type_id,
    1, 'Book',
    2, 'Video',
```

```
   3, 'DVD',
   4, 'CD',
   'Magazine')
FROM products;
```

```
PRODUCT_ID PRODUCT_TYPE_ID DECODE(P
---------- --------------- --------
         1               1 Book
         2               1 Book
         3               2 Video
         4               2 Video
         5               2 Video
         6               2 Video
         7               3 DVD
         8               3 DVD
         9               4 CD
        10               4 CD
        11               4 CD
        12                 Magazine
```

Notice that if:

- `product_type_id` is 1, `Book` is returned

- `product_type_id` is 2, `Video` is returned

- `product_type_id` is 3, `DVD` is returned

- `product_type_id` is 4, `CD` is returned

- `product_type_id` is any other value, `Magazine` is returned

Using the CASE Expression

You use the `CASE` expression to perform if-then-else logic in SQL without having to use PL/SQL. `CASE` works in a similar manner to `DECODE()`, but you should use `CASE` since it is ANSI-compliant.
There are two types of `CASE` expressions:

- Simple case expressions, which use expressions to determine the returned value

- Searched case expressions, which use conditions to determine the returned value

Using Simple CASE Expressions

Simple `CASE` expressions use expressions to determine the returned value and have the following syntax:

```
CASE search_expression
  WHEN expression1 THEN result1
  WHEN expression2 THEN result2
```

```
    . . .
  WHEN expressionN THEN resultN
  ELSE default_result
END
```

where

- *search_expression* is the expression to be evaluated.

- *expression1, expression2, ..., expressionN* are the expressions to be evaluated against *search_expression*.

- *result1, result2, ..., resultN* are the returned results (one for each possible expression). If *expression1* evaluates to *search_expression*, *result1* is returned, and so on.

- *default_result* is the default result returned when no matching expression is found.

The following example illustrates the use of a simple CASE expression:

```
SELECT product_id, product_type_id,
  CASE product_type_id
  WHEN 1 THEN 'Book'
  WHEN 2 THEN 'Video'
  WHEN 3 THEN 'DVD'
  WHEN 4 THEN 'CD'
  ELSE 'Magazine'
  END
FROM products;

PRODUCT_ID PRODUCT_TYPE_ID CASEPROD
---------- --------------- --------
         1               1 Book
         2               1 Book
         3               2 Video
         4               2 Video
         5               2 Video
         6               2 Video
         7               3 DVD
         8               3 DVD
         9               4 CD
        10               4 CD
        11               4 CD
        12                 Magazine
```

Using Searched CASE Expressions

Searched CASE expressions use conditions to determine the returned value and have the following syntax:

```
CASE
  WHEN condition1 THEN result1
```

```
  WHEN condition2 THEN result2
  ...
  WHEN conditionN THEN resultN
  ELSE default_result
END
```

where

- *condition1, condition2, ..., conditionN* are the expressions to be evaluated.

- *result1, result2, ..., resultN* are the returned results (one for each possible condition). If *condition1* is true, *result1* is returned, and so on.

- *default_result* is the default result returned when no true condition is found.

The following example illustrates the use of a searched CASE expression:

```
SELECT product_id, product_type_id,
  CASE
   WHEN product_type_id = 1 THEN 'Book'
   WHEN product_type_id = 2 THEN 'Video'
   WHEN product_type_id = 3 THEN 'DVD'
   WHEN product_type_id = 4 THEN 'CD'
   ELSE 'Magazine'
  END
FROM products;
```

```
PRODUCT_ID PRODUCT_TYPE_ID CASEPROD
---------- --------------- --------
         1               1 Book
         2               1 Book
         3               2 Video
         4               2 Video
         5               2 Video
         6               2 Video
         7               3 DVD
         8               3 DVD
         9               4 CD
        10               4 CD
        11               4 CD
        12                 Magazine
```

You can use operators in a searched CASE expression, as shown in the following example:

```
SELECT product_id, price,
  CASE
   WHEN price > 15 THEN 'Expensive'
   ELSE 'Cheap'
  END
FROM products;
```

```
PRODUCT_ID      PRICE CASEWHENP
---------- ---------- ---------
         1      19.95 Expensive
         2         30 Expensive
         3      25.99 Expensive
         4      13.95 Cheap
         5      49.99 Expensive
         6      14.95 Cheap
         7      13.49 Cheap
         8      12.99 Cheap
         9      10.99 Cheap
        10      15.99 Expensive
        11      14.99 Cheap
        12      13.49 Cheap
```

Hierarchical Queries

You'll quite often encounter data that is organized into a hierarchy, such as the people who work in a company, a family tree, or the parts that make up an engine. In this section, you'll learn how to perform queries against a table that stores the employees who work for the example store.

The Example Data

You'll see the use of a table named more_employees, which is created by the store_ schema.sql script as follows:

```
CREATE TABLE more_employees (
    employee_id INTEGER
      CONSTRAINT more_employees_pk PRIMARY KEY,
    manager_id INTEGER
      CONSTRAINT more_empl_fk_fk_more_empl
      REFERENCES more_employees(employee_id),
    first_name VARCHAR2(10) NOT NULL,
    last_name VARCHAR2(10) NOT NULL,
    title VARCHAR2(20),
    salary NUMBER(6, 0)
);
```

The manager_id column is a self-reference back to the employee_id column of the more_employees table; manager_id indicates the manager of an employee (if any). The more_employees table contains the following rows:

EMPLOYEE_ID	MANAGER_ID	FIRST_NAME	LAST_NAME	TITLE	SALARY
1		James	Smith	CEO	800000
2	1	Ron	Johnson	Sales Manager	600000
3	2	Fred	Hobbs	Sales Person	200000
4	1	Susan	Jones	Support Manager	500000
5	2	Rob	Green	Sales Person	40000

```
 6       4 Jane      Brown      Support Person     45000
 7       4 John      Grey       Support Manager    30000
 8       7 Jean      Blue       Support Person     29000
 9       6 Henry     Heyson     Support Person     30000
10       1 Kevin     Black      Ops Manager       100000
11      10 Keith     Long       Ops Person         50000
12      10 Frank     Howard     Ops Person         45000
13      10 Doreen    Penn       Ops Person         47000
```

As you can see, it is a little difficult to pick out the various employee relationships from this data. Figure 7-1 shows the relationships in a graphical form.

As you can see from Figure 7-1, the elements—or *nodes*—form a tree. Trees of nodes have some technical terms associated with them, as follows:

- ■ **Root node**   The root is the node at the top of the tree. In the example shown in Figure 7-1, the root node is James Smith, the CEO.

- ■ **Parent node**   A parent is a node that has one or more nodes beneath it. For example, James Smith is the parent to the following nodes: Ron Johnson, Susan Jones, and Kevin Black.

- ■ **Child node**   A child is a node that has one parent node above it. For example, Ron Johnson's parent is James Smith.

- ■ **Leaf node**   A leaf is a node that has no children. For example, Fred Hobbs and Rob Green are leaf nodes.

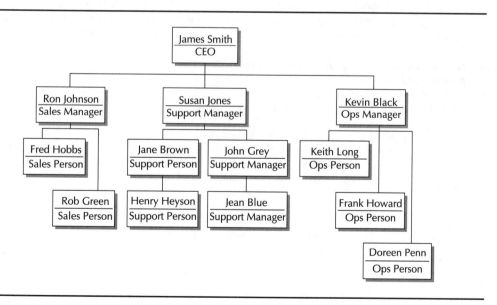

FIGURE 7-1.   *Employee relationships*

You can use the CONNECT BY and START WITH clauses of a SELECT statement to perform hierarchical queries.

Using the CONNECT BY and START WITH Clauses

The syntax for the CONNECT BY and START WITH clauses of a SELECT statement is as follows:

```
SELECT [LEVEL], column, expression, ...
FROM table
[WHERE where_clause]
[[START WITH start_condition] [CONNECT BY PRIOR prior_condition]];
```

where

- LEVEL is a pseudo-column that tells you how far into a tree you are. LEVEL returns 1 for a root node, 2 for a child of the root, and so on.

- *start_condition* specifies where to start the hierarchical query from. You must specify a START WITH clause when writing a hierarchical query. An example *start_ condition* is employee_id = 1, which specifies the query starts from employee #1.

- *prior_condition* specifies the relationship between the parent and child rows. You must specify a CONNECT BY PRIOR clause when writing a hierarchical query. An example *prior_condition* is employee_id = manager_id, which specifies the relationship is between the parent employee_id and the child manager_id—that is, the child's manager_id points to the parent's employee_id.

The following query illustrates the use of the START WITH and CONNECT BY PRIOR clauses. Notice the first row contains the details of James Smith (employee #1), the second row contains the details of Ron Johnson, whose manager_id is 1, and so on down the tree:

```
SELECT employee_id, manager_id, first_name, last_name
FROM more_employees
START WITH employee_id = 1
CONNECT BY PRIOR employee_id = manager_id;
```

```
EMPLOYEE_ID MANAGER_ID FIRST_NAME LAST_NAME
----------- ---------- ---------- ---------
          1            James      Smith
          2          1 Ron        Johnson
          3          2 Fred       Hobbs
          5          2 Rob        Green
          4          1 Susan      Jones
          6          4 Jane       Brown
          9          6 Henry      Heyson
          7          4 John       Grey
          8          7 Jean       Blue
         10          1 Kevin      Black
         11         10 Keith      Long
         12         10 Frank      Howard
         13         10 Doreen     Penn
```

Using the LEVEL Pseudo-Column

The next query illustrates the use of the LEVEL pseudo-column to display the level in the tree:

```
SELECT LEVEL, employee_id, manager_id, first_name, last_name
FROM more_employees
START WITH employee_id = 1
CONNECT BY PRIOR employee_id = manager_id
ORDER BY LEVEL;
```

LEVEL	EMPLOYEE_ID	MANAGER_ID	FIRST_NAME	LAST_NAME
1	1		James	Smith
2	2	1	Ron	Johnson
2	4	1	Susan	Jones
2	10	1	Kevin	Black
3	3	2	Fred	Hobbs
3	7	4	John	Grey
3	12	10	Frank	Howard
3	13	10	Doreen	Penn
3	11	10	Keith	Long
3	5	2	Rob	Green
3	6	4	Jane	Brown
4	9	6	Henry	Heyson
4	8	7	Jean	Blue

The next query uses the COUNT() function and LEVEL to get the number of levels in the tree:

```
SELECT COUNT(DISTINCT LEVEL)
FROM more_employees
START WITH employee_id = 1
CONNECT BY PRIOR employee_id = manager_id;
```

```
COUNT(DISTINCTLEVEL)
--------------------
                   4
```

Formatting the Results from a Hierarchical Query

You can format the results from a hierarchical query using LEVEL and the LPAD() function, which left-pads values with characters. The following query uses LPAD(' ', 2 * LEVEL - 1) to left-pad with 2 * LEVEL - 1 spaces. This is used to indent an employee's name with spaces based on their LEVEL (LEVEL 1 isn't padded, LEVEL 2 is padded by two spaces, LEVEL 3 by four spaces, and so on).

```
SET PAGESIZE 999
COLUMN employee FORMAT A25
SELECT LEVEL,
  LPAD(' ', 2 * LEVEL - 1) || first_name || ' ' ||
  last_name AS employee
FROM more_employees
```

```
START WITH employee_id = 1
CONNECT BY PRIOR employee_id = manager_id;


     LEVEL EMPLOYEE
---------- ------------------
         1 James Smith
         2   Ron Johnson
         3     Fred Hobbs
         3     Rob Green
         2   Susan Jones
         3     Jane Brown
         4       Henry Heyson
         3     John Grey
         4       Jean Blue
         2   Kevin Black
         3     Keith Long
         3     Frank Howard
         3     Doreen Penn
```

Starting at a Node Other than the Root

You don't have to start at the root node when traversing a tree: you can start at any node using the START WITH clause. The following query starts with Susan Jones; notice LEVEL returns 1 for Susan Jones, 2 for Jane Brown, and so on:

```
SELECT LEVEL,
  LPAD(' ', 2 * LEVEL - 1) || first_name || ' ' ||
  last_name AS employee
FROM more_employees
START WITH last_name = 'Jones'
CONNECT BY PRIOR employee_id = manager_id;


     LEVEL EMPLOYEE
---------- ----------------
         1   Susan Jones
         2     Jane Brown
         3       Henry Heyson
         2     John Grey
         3       Jean Blue
```

If the store had more than one employee with the same name, you could simply use the employee_id in the query's START WITH clause. The following query uses Susan Jones' employee_id of 4:

```
SELECT LEVEL,
  LPAD(' ', 2 * LEVEL - 1) || first_name || ' ' ||
  last_name AS employee
FROM more_employees
START WITH employee_id = 4
CONNECT BY PRIOR employee_id = manager_id;
```

This query returns the same rows as the previous one.

Using a Subquery in a START WITH Clause

You can use a subquery in a START WITH clause. For example, the following query uses a subquery to select the employee_id whose name is Kevin Black. This employee_id is passed to the START WITH clause:

```
SELECT LEVEL,
  LPAD(' ', 2 * LEVEL - 1) || first_name || ' ' ||
  last_name AS employee
FROM more_employees
START WITH employee_id = (
  SELECT employee_id
  FROM more_employees
  WHERE first_name = 'Kevin'
  AND last_name = 'Black'
)
CONNECT BY PRIOR employee_id = manager_id;

     LEVEL EMPLOYEE
---------- ---------------
         1 Kevin Black
         2   Keith Long
         2   Frank Howard
         2   Doreen Penn
```

Traversing Upward Through the Tree

You don't have to traverse a tree downward from parents to children: you can start at a child and traverse upward. You do this by switching child and parent columns in the CONNECT BY PRIOR clause. For example, CONNECT BY PRIOR manager_id = employee_id connects the child's manager_id to the parent's employee_id.

The following query starts with Jean Blue and traverses upward all the way to James Smith; notice LEVEL returns 1 for Jean Blue, 2 for John Grey, and so on:

```
SELECT LEVEL,
  LPAD(' ', 2 * LEVEL - 1) || first_name || ' ' ||
  last_name AS employee
FROM more_employees
START WITH last_name = 'Blue'
CONNECT BY PRIOR manager_id = employee_id;

     LEVEL EMPLOYEE
---------- ------------------
         1 Jean Blue
         2   John Grey
         3     Susan Jones
         4       James Smith
```

Eliminating Nodes and Branches from a Hierarchical Query

You can eliminate a particular node from a query tree using a WHERE clause. The following query eliminates Ron Johnson from the results using WHERE last_name != 'Johnson':

```
SELECT LEVEL,
  LPAD(' ', 2 * LEVEL - 1) || first_name || ' ' ||
  last_name AS employee
FROM more_employees
WHERE last_name != 'Johnson'
START WITH employee_id = 1
CONNECT BY PRIOR employee_id = manager_id;

    LEVEL EMPLOYEE
---------- ------------------
        1 James Smith
        3     Fred Hobbs
        3     Rob Green
        2   Susan Jones
        3     Jane Brown
        4       Henry Heyson
        3     John Grey
        4       Jean Blue
        2   Kevin Black
        3     Keith Long
        3     Frank Howard
        3     Doreen Penn
```

You'll notice although Ron Johnson is eliminated from the results, his employees Fred Hobbs and Rob Green are still included. To eliminate an entire branch of nodes from the results of a query, you add an AND clause to your CONNECT BY PRIOR clause. The following query uses AND last_name != 'Johnson' to eliminate Ron Johnson and all his employees from the results:

```
SELECT LEVEL,
  LPAD(' ', 2 * LEVEL - 1) || first_name || ' ' ||
  last_name AS employee
FROM more_employees
START WITH employee_id = 1
CONNECT BY PRIOR employee_id = manager_id
AND last_name != 'Johnson';

    LEVEL EMPLOYEE
---------- ------------------
        1 James Smith
        2   Susan Jones
        3     Jane Brown
        4       Henry Heyson
        3     John Grey
        4       Jean Blue
        2   Kevin Black
        3     Keith Long
        3     Frank Howard
        3     Doreen Penn
```

Including Other Conditions in a Hierarchical Query

You can include other conditions in a hierarchical query using a WHERE clause. The following example uses a WHERE clause to only show employees whose salaries are less than or equal to $50,000:

```
SELECT LEVEL,
  LPAD(' ', 2 * LEVEL - 1) || first_name || ' ' ||
  last_name AS employee, salary
FROM more_employees
WHERE salary <= 50000
START WITH employee_id = 1
CONNECT BY PRIOR employee_id = manager_id;
```

```
    LEVEL EMPLOYEE                       SALARY
---------- ------------------------- ----------
        3     Rob Green                   40000
        3     Jane Brown                  45000
        4       Henry Heyson              30000
        3     John Grey                   30000
        4       Jean Blue                 29000
        3     Keith Long                  50000
        3     Frank Howard                45000
        3     Doreen Penn                 47000
```

This concludes the discussion of hierarchical queries. In the next section, you'll learn about advanced group clauses.

Using the Extended GROUP BY Clauses

In this section, you'll learn about:

■ ROLLUP, which extends the GROUP BY clause to return rows containing a subtotal for each group.

■ CUBE, which extends the GROUP BY clause to return rows containing a subtotal for all combinations of columns along with a total at the end.

First, let's look at the example tables you'll see in this section.

The Example Tables

You'll see the use of three new tables that refine the representation of employees in the company that runs the store.

■ divisions, which stores the divisions within the company

■ jobs, which stores the jobs within the company

■ employees2, which stores the employees

These tables are created by the `store_schema.sql` script. You'll learn the details of the `divisions`, `jobs`, and `employees2` tables in the following sections.

The divisions Table

The `divisions` table is created using the following statement:

```
CREATE TABLE divisions (
    division_id CHAR(3)
      CONSTRAINT divisions_pk PRIMARY KEY,
    name VARCHAR2(15) NOT NULL
);
```

The `divisions` table contains the following rows:

```
DIV NAME
--- ----------
SAL Sales
OPE Operations
SUP Support
BUS Business
```

The jobs Table

The `jobs` table is created using the following statement:

```
CREATE TABLE jobs (
    job_id CHAR(3)
      CONSTRAINT jobs_pk PRIMARY KEY,
    name VARCHAR2(20) NOT NULL
);
```

The `jobs` table contains the following rows:

```
JOB NAME
--- ------------
WOR Worker
MGR Manager
ENG Engineer
TEC Technologist
PRE President
```

The employees2 Table

The `employees2` table is created using the following statement:

```
CREATE TABLE employees2 (
    employee_id INTEGER
      CONSTRAINT employees2_pk PRIMARY KEY,
    division_id CHAR(3)
      CONSTRAINT employees2_fk_divisions
```

```
  REFERENCES divisions(division_id),
 job_id CHAR(3) REFERENCES jobs(job_id),
 first_name VARCHAR2(10) NOT NULL,
 last_name VARCHAR2(10) NOT NULL,
 salary NUMBER(6, 0)
);
```

The following output shows the first five rows in the `employees2` table:

```
EMPLOYEE_ID DIV JOB FIRST_NAME LAST_NAME      SALARY
----------- --- --- ---------- ---------- ----------
          1 BUS PRE James      Smith          800000
          2 SAL MGR Ron        Johnson        350000
          3 SAL WOR Fred       Hobbs          140000
          4 SUP MGR Susan      Jones          200000
          5 SAL WOR Rob        Green          350000
```

NOTE
*The `employees2` table actually contains a lot more rows than this,
but for brevity I've omitted listing them all here.*

Using the ROLLUP Clause

The `ROLLUP` clause extends `GROUP BY` to return a row containing a subtotal for each group
along with a total for all groups. As you saw in Chapter 3, you use `GROUP BY` to group rows
into blocks with a common column value. For example, the following query uses `GROUP BY` to
group the rows from the `employees2` table by `department_id` and uses `SUM()` to get the
sum of the salaries for each `division_id`:

```
SELECT division_id, SUM(salary)
FROM employees2
GROUP BY division_id;
```

```
DIV SUM(SALARY)
--- -----------
BUS     1610000
OPE     1320000
SAL     4936000
SUP     1015000
```

Passing a Single Column to ROLLUP
The following query rewrites the previous example to use `ROLLUP`. Notice the additional row
at the end that contains the total salaries for all groups:

```
SELECT division_id, SUM(salary)
FROM employees2
GROUP BY ROLLUP(division_id);
```

```
DIV  SUM(SALARY)
---  -----------
BUS      1610000
OPE      1320000
SAL      4936000
SUP      1015000
         8881000
```

Passing Multiple Columns to ROLLUP

You can pass multiple columns to ROLLUP, which then groups the rows into blocks with the same column values. The following example passes the division_id and job_id columns of the employees2 table to ROLLUP, which groups the rows by identical values in those columns. Notice the salaries are summed by division_id and job_id, and ROLLUP returns a row with the sum of the salaries in each division_id along with another row at the very end with the total salaries for all groups:

```
SELECT division_id, job_id, SUM(salary)
FROM employees2
GROUP BY ROLLUP(division_id, job_id);
```

```
DIV JOB  SUM(SALARY)
--- ---  -----------
BUS MGR       530000
BUS PRE       800000
BUS WOR       280000
BUS          1610000
OPE ENG       245000
OPE MGR       805000
OPE WOR       270000
OPE          1320000
SAL MGR      4446000
SAL WOR       490000
SAL          4936000
SUP MGR       465000
SUP TEC       115000
SUP WOR       435000
SUP          1015000
             8881000
```

Changing the Position of Columns Passed to ROLLUP

The next example switches division_id and job_id so that job_id is listed before division_id. This causes ROLLUP to return a row with the sum of the salaries in each job_id:

```
SELECT job_id, division_id, SUM(salary)
FROM employees2
GROUP BY ROLLUP(job_id, division_id);
```

```
JOB DIV SUM(SALARY)
--- --- -----------
ENG OPE    245000
ENG        245000
MGR BUS    530000
MGR OPE    805000
MGR SAL   4446000
MGR SUP    465000
MGR       6246000
PRE BUS    800000
PRE        800000
TEC SUP    115000
TEC        115000
WOR BUS    280000
WOR OPE    270000
WOR SAL    490000
WOR SUP    435000
WOR       1475000
          8881000
```

Using Other Aggregate Functions with ROLLUP

You can use any of the aggregate functions with ROLLUP (for a list of the aggregate functions, see Table 3-5 in Chapter 3). The following example uses AVG() to compute average salaries:

```
SELECT division_id, job_id, AVG(salary)
FROM employees2
GROUP BY ROLLUP(division_id, job_id);
```

```
DIV JOB AVG(SALARY)
--- --- -----------
BUS MGR 176666.667
BUS PRE    800000
BUS WOR    280000
BUS        322000
OPE ENG    245000
OPE MGR    201250
OPE WOR    135000
OPE     188571.429
SAL MGR 261529.412
SAL WOR    245000
SAL     259789.474
SUP MGR    232500
SUP TEC    115000
SUP WOR    145000
SUP     169166.667
        240027.027
```

Using the CUBE Clause

The CUBE clause extends GROUP BY to return rows containing a subtotal for all combinations of columns included in the CUBE clause along with a total at the end. The following example passes division_id and job_id to CUBE, which groups the rows by identical values in those columns. Notice the salaries are summed by division_id and job_id, and CUBE returns a row with the sum of the salaries in each division_id, along with the sum of all salaries in each job_id near the end, followed by another row at the very end with the total salaries:

```
SELECT division_id, job_id, SUM(salary)
FROM employees2
GROUP BY CUBE(division_id, job_id);

DIV JOB SUM(SALARY)
--- --- -----------
BUS MGR     530000
BUS PRE     800000
BUS WOR     280000
BUS        1610000
OPE ENG     245000
OPE MGR     805000
OPE WOR     270000
OPE        1320000
SAL MGR    4446000
SAL WOR     490000
SAL        4936000
SUP MGR     465000
SUP TEC     115000
SUP WOR     435000
SUP        1015000
    ENG     245000
    MGR    6246000
    PRE     800000
    TEC     115000
    WOR    1475000
           8881000
```

NOTE
Oracle9i puts the extra rows from the CUBE at the end, but Oracle Database 10g puts the extra rows at the start. So, depending on the version of the database you are using, you may see the rows at the end or the beginning. You can always put in an ORDER BY clause if you must have the rows in a specific order. For example, you could add ORDER BY division_id, job_id to the previous query.

The next example switches division_id and job_id so that job_id is listed before division_id. This still results in CUBE returning the sums of the salaries by job_id and division_id, but the sums by job_id are returned first:

```
SELECT job_id, division_id, SUM(salary)
FROM employees2
GROUP BY CUBE(job_id, division_id);

JOB DIV SUM(SALARY)
--- --- -----------
ENG OPE     245000
ENG         245000
MGR BUS     530000
MGR OPE     805000
MGR SAL    4446000
MGR SUP     465000
MGR        6246000
PRE BUS     800000
PRE         800000
TEC SUP     115000
TEC         115000
WOR BUS     280000
WOR OPE     270000
WOR SAL     490000
WOR SUP     435000
WOR        1475000
    BUS    1610000
    OPE    1320000
    SAL    4936000
    SUP    1015000
           8881000
```

Using the GROUPING() Function

The GROUPING() function accepts a column and returns 0 or 1. GROUPING() returns 1 when
the column value is null, and returns 0 when the column value is non-null. GROUPING() is only
used in queries that use ROLLUP or CUBE. GROUPING() is useful when you want to display a
value when a null would otherwise be returned.

Using GROUPING() with a Single Column in a ROLLUP

As you saw earlier in the section "Passing a Single Column to ROLLUP," the last row in the
example's result set contained a total of the salaries:

```
SELECT division_id, SUM(salary)
FROM employees2
GROUP BY ROLLUP(division_id);

DIV SUM(SALARY)
--- -----------
BUS    1610000
OPE    1320000
SAL    4936000
SUP    1015000
       8881000
```

The division_id column for the last row is null. You can use the GROUPING() function to determine whether this column is null, as shown in the following query. Notice GROUPING() returns 0 for the rows that have non-null division_id values, and 1 for the last row that has a null division_id:

```
SELECT GROUPING(division_id), division_id, SUM(salary)
FROM employees2
GROUP BY ROLLUP(division_id);
```

```
GROUPING(DIVISION_ID) DIV SUM(SALARY)
--------------------- --- -----------
                    0 BUS     1610000
                    0 OPE     1320000
                    0 SAL     4936000
                    0 SUP     1015000
                    1         8881000
```

Using DECODE() to Convert the Returned Value from GROUPING()

You can use the DECODE() function to convert the 1 in the previous example to a meaningful value. The following example uses DECODE() to convert 1 to the string All divisions:

```
SELECT
  DECODE(GROUPING(division_id), 1, 'All divisions', division_id) AS
  div,
  SUM(salary)
FROM employees2
GROUP BY ROLLUP(division_id);
```

```
DIV           SUM(SALARY)
------------- -----------
BUS               1610000
OPE               1320000
SAL               4936000
SUP               1015000
All divisions     8881000
```

Using DECODE() and GROUPING() to Convert Multiple Column Values

The next example extends the idea of replacing null values to a ROLLUP containing both the division_id and job_id. Notice null division_id values are replaced with the string All divisions, and null job_id values are replaced with All jobs:

```
SELECT
  DECODE(GROUPING(division_id), 1, 'All divisions', division_id) AS
  div,
  DECODE(GROUPING(job_id), 1, 'All jobs', job_id) AS job,
  SUM(salary)
FROM employees2
GROUP BY ROLLUP(division_id, job_id);
```

```
DIV             JOB       SUM(SALARY)
-------------   --------  -----------
BUS             MGR           530000
BUS             PRE           800000
BUS             WOR           280000
BUS             All jobs     1610000
OPE             ENG           245000
OPE             MGR           805000
OPE             WOR           270000
OPE             All jobs     1320000
SAL             MGR          4446000
SAL             WOR           490000
SAL             All jobs     4936000
SUP             MGR           465000
SUP             TEC           115000
SUP             WOR           435000
SUP             All jobs     1015000
All divisions All jobs      8881000
```

Using GROUPING() with CUBE

You can use the GROUPING() function with CUBE. For example:

```
SELECT
  DECODE(GROUPING(division_id), 1, 'All divisions', division_id) AS div,
  DECODE(GROUPING(job_id), 1, 'All jobs', job_id) as job,
  SUM(salary)
FROM employees2
GROUP BY CUBE(division_id, job_id);
```

```
DIV             JOB       SUM(SALARY)
-------------   --------  -----------
BUS             MGR           530000
BUS             PRE           800000
BUS             WOR           280000
BUS             All jobs     1610000
OPE             ENG           245000
OPE             MGR           805000
OPE             WOR           270000
OPE             All jobs     1320000
SAL             MGR          4446000
SAL             WOR           490000
SAL             All jobs     4936000
SUP             MGR           465000
SUP             TEC           115000
SUP             WOR           435000
SUP             All jobs     1015000
All divisions ENG           245000
All divisions MGR          6246000
All divisions PRE           800000
All divisions TEC           115000
All divisions WOR          1475000
All divisions All jobs      8881000
```

Using the GROUPING SETS Clause

You use the GROUPING SETS clause to just get the subtotal rows. The following example uses GROUPING SETS to get the subtotals for salaries by division_id and job_id:

```
SELECT division_id, job_id, SUM(salary)
FROM employees2
GROUP BY GROUPING SETS(division_id, job_id);

DIV JOB SUM(SALARY)
--- --- -----------
BUS         1610000
OPE         1320000
SAL         4936000
SUP         1015000
    ENG      245000
    MGR     6246000
    PRE      800000
    TEC      115000
    WOR     1475000
```

Notice only subtotals for the division_id and job_id columns are returned: the total for all salaries is not returned. You'll see how you can get the total as well as the subtotals using the GROUPING_ID() function in the next section.

Using the GROUPING_ID() Function

You can use the GROUPING_ID() function to filter rows using a HAVING clause to exclude rows that don't contain a subtotal or total. The GROUPING_ID() function accepts one or more columns and returns the decimal equivalent of the GROUPING bit vector. The GROUPING bit vector is computed by combining the results of a call to the GROUPING() function for each column in order.

Computing the GROUPING Bit Vector

Earlier in the section "Using the GROUPING() Function," you saw that GROUPING() returns 1 when the column value is null, and returns 0 when the column value is non-null.

For example:

- If both division_id and job_id are non-null, GROUPING() would return 0 for both columns. The result for division_id is combined with the result for job_id, giving a bit vector of 00, whose decimal equivalent is 0. GROUPING_ID() therefore returns 0 when division_id and job_id are non-null.

- If division_id is non-null (the GROUPING bit is 0), but job_id is null (the GROUPING bit is 1), the resulting bit vector is 01 and GROUPING_ID() returns 1.

- If division_id is null (the GROUPING bit is 1), but job_id is non-null (the GROUPING bit is 0), the resulting bit vector is 10 and GROUPING_ID() returns 2.

- If both division_id and job_id are null (both GROUPING bits are 0), the bit vector is 11 and GROUPING_ID() returns 3.

The following table summarizes these results.

division_id	job_id	Bit Vector	GROUPING_ID() Return Value
non-null	non-null	00	0
non-null	null	01	1
null	non-null	10	2
null	null	11	3

An Example Query that Illustrates the Use of GROUPING_ID()

The following example passes division_id and job_id to GROUPING_ID(). Notice the output from the GROUPING_ID() function agrees with the expected returned values documented in the previous section:

```
SELECT
  division_id, job_id,
  GROUPING(division_id) AS DIV_GRP,
  GROUPING(job_id) AS JOB_GRP,
  GROUPING_ID(division_id, job_id) AS grp_id,
  SUM(salary)
FROM employees2
GROUP BY CUBE(division_id, job_id);
```

```
DIV JOB    DIV_GRP    JOB_GRP    GRP_ID SUM(SALARY)
--- ---  ---------- ---------- ---------- -----------
BUS MGR         0          0          0      530000
BUS PRE         0          0          0      800000
BUS WOR         0          0          0      280000
BUS             0          1          1     1610000
OPE ENG         0          0          0      245000
OPE MGR         0          0          0      805000
OPE WOR         0          0          0      270000
OPE             0          1          1     1320000
SAL MGR         0          0          0     4446000
SAL WOR         0          0          0      490000
SAL             0          1          1     4936000
SUP MGR         0          0          0      465000
SUP TEC         0          0          0      115000
SUP WOR         0          0          0      435000
SUP             0          1          1     1015000
    ENG         1          0          2      245000
    MGR         1          0          2     6246000
    PRE         1          0          2      800000
    TEC         1          0          2      115000
    WOR         1          0          2     1475000
                1          1          3     8881000
```

A Useful Application of GROUPING_ID()

One useful application of GROUPING_ID() is to filter rows using a HAVING clause. Your HAVING clause can exclude rows that don't contain a subtotal or total by simply checking if GROUPING_ID() returns a value greater than 0. For example:

```
SELECT
  division_id, job_id,
  GROUPING_ID(division_id, job_id) AS grp_id,
  SUM(salary)
FROM employees2
GROUP BY CUBE(division_id, job_id)
HAVING GROUPING_ID(division_id, job_id) > 0;
```

```
DIV JOB     GRP_ID SUM(SALARY)
--- ---  ---------- -----------
BUS              1     1610000
OPE              1     1320000
SAL              1     4936000
SUP              1     1015000
    ENG          2      245000
    MGR          2     6246000
    PRE          2      800000
    TEC          2      115000
    WOR          2     1475000
                 3     8881000
```

Using a Column Multiple Times in a GROUP BY Clause

You can use a column multiple times in a GROUP BY clause, which can enable you to reorganize your data or report on different groupings of data. For example, the following query contains a GROUP BY clause that uses division_id twice, once to group by division_id and the second in a ROLLUP:

```
SELECT division_id, job_id, SUM(salary)
FROM employees2
GROUP BY division_id, ROLLUP(division_id, job_id);
```

```
DIV JOB SUM(SALARY)
--- --- -----------
BUS MGR      530000
BUS PRE      800000
BUS WOR      280000
OPE ENG      245000
OPE MGR      805000
OPE WOR      270000
SAL MGR     4446000
SAL WOR      490000
SUP MGR      465000
```

```
SUP TEC       115000
SUP WOR        435000
BUS           1610000
OPE           1320000
SAL           4936000
SUP           1015000
BUS           1610000
OPE           1320000
SAL           4936000
SUP           1015000
```

Notice, however, that the last four rows are duplicates of the previous four rows. You can eliminate these duplicates using the GROUP_ID() function, which you'll learn about next.

Using the GROUP_ID() Function

You can use the GROUP_ID() function to remove duplicate rows returned by a GROUP BY clause. GROUP_ID() doesn't accept any parameters. If *n* duplicates exist for a particular grouping, GROUP_ID returns numbers in the range 0 to *n*-1.

The following example rewrites the query shown in the previous section to include the output from GROUP_ID(). Notice GROUP_ID() returns 0 for all rows except the last four, which are duplicates of the previous four rows and GROUP_ID() returns 1:

```
SELECT division_id, job_id, GROUP_ID(), SUM(salary)
FROM employees2
GROUP BY division_id, ROLLUP(division_id, job_id);

DIV JOB GROUP_ID() SUM(SALARY)
--- --- ---------- -----------
BUS MGR          0      530000
BUS PRE          0      800000
BUS WOR          0      280000
OPE ENG          0      245000
OPE MGR          0      805000
OPE WOR          0      270000
SAL MGR          0     4446000
SAL WOR          0      490000
SUP MGR          0      465000
SUP TEC          0      115000
SUP WOR          0      435000
BUS              0     1610000
OPE              0     1320000
SAL              0     4936000
SUP              0     1015000
BUS              1     1610000
OPE              1     1320000
SAL              1     4936000
SUP              1     1015000
```

You can eliminate duplicate rows using a HAVING clause that only allows rows whose GROUP_ID() is 0; for example:

```
SELECT division_id, job_id, GROUP_ID(), SUM(salary)
FROM employees2
GROUP BY division_id, ROLLUP(division_id, job_id)
HAVING GROUP_ID() = 0;
```

```
DIV JOB GROUP_ID() SUM(SALARY)
--- --- ---------- -----------
BUS MGR          0      530000
BUS PRE          0      800000
BUS WOR          0      280000
OPE ENG          0      245000
OPE MGR          0      805000
OPE WOR          0      270000
SAL MGR          0     4446000
SAL WOR          0      490000
SUP MGR          0      465000
SUP TEC          0      115000
SUP WOR          0      435000
BUS              0     1610000
OPE              0     1320000
SAL              0     4936000
SUP              0     1015000
```

This concludes the discussion of the extended GROUP BY clauses.

Using the Analytic Functions

The database has many built-in analytic functions that enable you to perform complex calculations such as finding the top-selling product type for each month, the top salespersons, and so on. The analytic functions are organized into the following categories:

- **Ranking functions** Enable you to calculate ranks, percentiles, and *n*-tiles (tertiles, quartiles, and so on)

- **Inverse percentile functions** Enable you to calculate the value that corresponds to a percentile

- **Window functions** Enable you to calculate cumulative and moving aggregates

- **Reporting functions** Enable you to calculate things like market shares

- **Lag and lead functions** Enable you to get a value in a row where that row is a certain number of rows away from the current row

- **First and last functions** Enable you to get the first and last values in an ordered group

- **Linear regression functions**   Enable you to fit an ordinary-least-squares regression line to a set of number pairs

- **Hypothetical rank and distribution functions**   Enable you to calculate the rank and percentile that a new row would have if you inserted it into a table

You'll learn about these functions shortly, but first let's examine the example table used in this section.

The Example Table

You'll see the use of the `all_sales` table in the following sections. `all_sales` stores the sum of all the sales by dollar amount for a particular year, month, product type, and employee.

The `all_sales` table is created by the `store_schema.sql` script as follows:

```
CREATE TABLE all_sales (
  year INTEGER NOT NULL,
  month INTEGER NOT NULL,
  prd_type_id INTEGER
    CONSTRAINT all_sales_fk_product_types
    REFERENCES product_types(product_type_id),
  emp_id INTEGER
    CONSTRAINT all_sales_fk_employees2
    REFERENCES employees2(employee_id),
  amount NUMBER(8, 2),
  CONSTRAINT all_sales_pk PRIMARY KEY (
    year, month, prd_type_id, emp_id
  )
);
```

As you can see, the `all_sales` table contains five columns, which are as follows:

- **year**   Stores the year the sales took place

- **month**   Stores the month the sales took place (1 to 12)

- **prd_type_id**   Stores the `product_type_id` of the product

- **emp_id**   Stores the `employee_id` of the employee who handled the sales

- **amount**   Stores the total dollar amount of the sales

The following output shows the first 13 rows in the `all_sales` table:

YEAR	MONTH	PRD_TYPE_ID	EMP_ID	AMOUNT
2003	1	1	21	10034.84
2003	2	1	21	15144.65
2003	3	1	21	20137.83
2003	4	1	21	25057.45

2003	5	1	21	17214.56
2003	6	1	21	15564.64
2003	7	1	21	12654.84
2003	8	1	21	17434.82
2003	9	1	21	19854.57
2003	10	1	21	21754.19
2003	11	1	21	13029.73
2003	12	1	21	10034.84
2003	1	1	22	11034.84

NOTE
The all_sales table actually contains a lot more rows than this, but for brevity I've omitted listing them all here.

Let's examine the ranking functions.

Using the Ranking Functions

You use the ranking functions to calculate ranks, percentiles, and *n*-tiles. The ranking functions are shown in Table 7-2.

Let's examine the RANK() and DENSE_RANK() functions first.

Using the RANK() and DENSE_RANK() Functions

You use RANK() and DENSE_RANK() to rank items in a group. The difference between these two functions is in the way they handle items that tie: RANK() leaves a gap in the sequence when there is a tie, but DENSE_RANK() leaves no gaps. For example, if you were ranking sales by product type and two product types tie for first place, RANK() would put the two product types in first place, but the next product type would be in third place. DENSE_RANK() would also put the two product types in first place, but the next product type would be in second place.

Function	Description
RANK()	Returns the rank of items in a group. RANK() leaves a gap in the sequence of rankings in the event of a tie.
DENSE_RANK()	Returns the rank of items in a group. DENSE_RANK() doesn't leave a gap in the sequence of rankings in the event of a tie.
CUME_DIST()	Returns the position of a specified value relative to a group of values; CUME_DIST() is short for cumulative distribution.
PERCENT_RANK()	Returns the percent rank of a value relative to a group of values.
NTILE()	Returns *n*-tiles: tertiles, quartiles, and so on.
ROW_NUMBER()	Returns a number with each row in a group.

TABLE 7-2. *Ranking Functions*

The following query illustrates the use of RANK() and DENSE_RANK() to get the ranking of sales by product type for 2003. Notice the use of the keyword OVER in the syntax when calling the RANK() and DENSE_RANK() functions:

```
SELECT
  prd_type_id, SUM(amount),
  RANK() OVER (ORDER BY SUM(amount) DESC) AS rank,
  DENSE_RANK() OVER (ORDER BY SUM(amount) DESC) AS dense_rank
FROM all_sales
WHERE year = 2003
AND amount IS NOT NULL
GROUP BY prd_type_id
ORDER BY prd_type_id;
```

```
PRD_TYPE_ID SUM(AMOUNT)        RANK DENSE_RANK
----------- -----------  ---------- ----------
          1   905081.84           1          1
          2   186381.22           4          4
          3   478270.91           2          2
          4   402751.16           3          3
```

Notice sales for product type #1 are ranked first, sales for product type #2 are ranked fourth, and so on. Because there are no ties, RANK() and DENSE_RANK() return the same ranks.

The all_sales table actually contains nulls in the amount column for all rows whose prd_type_id column is 5, but the previous query omits these rows because of the inclusion of the line AND amount IS NOT NULL in the WHERE clause. The next example includes these rows by leaving out the AND line from the WHERE clause:

```
SELECT
  prd_type_id, SUM(amount),
  RANK() OVER (ORDER BY SUM(amount) DESC) AS rank,
  DENSE_RANK() OVER (ORDER BY SUM(amount) DESC) AS dense_rank
FROM all_sales
WHERE year = 2003
GROUP BY prd_type_id
ORDER BY prd_type_id;
```

```
PRD_TYPE_ID SUM(AMOUNT)        RANK DENSE_RANK
----------- -----------  ---------- ----------
          1   905081.84           2          2
          2   186381.22           5          5
          3   478270.91           3          3
          4   402751.16           4          4
          5                       1          1
```

Notice the last row contains null for the sum of the amount column and RANK() and DENSE_RANK() return 1 for this row. This is because by default RANK() and DENSE_RANK() assign the highest rank of 1 to null values in descending rankings (that is, DESC is used in the OVER clause), and the lowest rank in ascending rankings (that is, ASC is used in the OVER clause).

Controlling Ranking of Null Values Using the NULLS FIRST and NULLS LAST Clauses   When
using an analytic function, you can explicitly control whether nulls are the highest or lowest in a
group using NULLS FIRST or NULLS LAST. The next example uses NULLS LAST to specify nulls
are the lowest:

```
SELECT
  prd_type_id, SUM(amount),
  RANK() OVER (ORDER BY SUM(amount) DESC NULLS LAST) AS rank,
  DENSE_RANK() OVER (ORDER BY SUM(amount) DESC NULLS LAST) AS
    dense_rank
FROM all_sales
WHERE year = 2003
GROUP BY prd_type_id
ORDER BY prd_type_id;
```

```
PRD_TYPE_ID SUM(AMOUNT)       RANK DENSE_RANK
----------- ----------- ---------- ----------
          1   905081.84          1          1
          2   186381.22          4          4
          3   478270.91          2          2
          4   402751.16          3          3
          5                      5          5
```

Using the PARTITION BY Clause with Analytic Functions   You use the PARTITION BY clause
with the analytic functions when you need to divide the groups into subgroups. For example, if you
need to subdivide the sales amount by month, you can use PARTITION BY month as shown in the
following query:

```
SELECT
  prd_type_id, month, SUM(amount),
  RANK() OVER (PARTITION BY month ORDER BY SUM(amount) DESC) AS rank
FROM all_sales
WHERE year = 2003
AND amount IS NOT NULL
GROUP BY prd_type_id, month
ORDER BY prd_type_id, month;
```

```
PRD_TYPE_ID     MONTH SUM(AMOUNT)       RANK
----------- --------- ----------- ----------
          1         1    38909.04          1
          1         2     70567.9          1
          1         3    91826.98          1
          1         4    120344.7          1
          1         5    97287.36          1
          1         6    57387.84          1
          1         7    60929.04          2
          1         8    75608.92          1
          1         9    85027.42          1
          1        10   105305.22          1
          1        11    55678.38          1
```

1	12	46209.04	2
2	1	14309.04	4
2	2	13367.9	4
2	3	16826.98	4
2	4	15664.7	4
2	5	18287.36	4
2	6	14587.84	4
2	7	15689.04	3
2	8	16308.92	4
2	9	19127.42	4
2	10	13525.14	4
2	11	16177.84	4
2	12	12509.04	4
3	1	24909.04	2
3	2	15467.9	3
3	3	20626.98	3
3	4	23844.7	2
3	5	18687.36	3
3	6	19887.84	3
3	7	81589.04	1
3	8	62408.92	2
3	9	46127.42	3
3	10	70325.29	3
3	11	46187.38	2
3	12	48209.04	1
4	1	17398.43	3
4	2	17267.9	2
4	3	31026.98	2
4	4	16144.7	3
4	5	20087.36	2
4	6	33087.84	2
4	7	12089.04	4
4	8	58408.92	3
4	9	49327.42	2
4	10	75325.14	2
4	11	42178.38	3
4	12	30409.05	3

Using ROLLUP, CUBE, and GROUPING SETS Operators with Analytic Functions   You can use the ROLLUP, CUBE, and GROUPING SETS operators with the analytic functions. The following query uses ROLLUP and RANK() to get the sales rankings by product type ID:

```
SELECT
  prd_type_id, SUM(amount),
  RANK() OVER (ORDER BY SUM(amount) DESC) AS rank
FROM all_sales
WHERE year = 2003
GROUP BY ROLLUP(prd_type_id)
ORDER BY prd_type_id;
```

```
PRD_TYPE_ID SUM(AMOUNT)        RANK
----------- -----------   ----------
          1   905081.84            3
          2   186381.22            6
          3   478270.91            4
          4   402751.16            5
          5                        1
              1972485.13           2
```

The next query uses CUBE and RANK() to get all rankings of sales by product type ID and employee ID:

```
SELECT
 prd_type_id, emp_id, SUM(amount),
 RANK() OVER (ORDER BY SUM(amount) DESC) AS rank
FROM all_sales
WHERE year = 2003
GROUP BY CUBE(prd_type_id, emp_id)
ORDER BY prd_type_id, emp_id;
```

```
PRD_TYPE_ID     EMP_ID SUM(AMOUNT)        RANK
----------- ---------- -----------   ----------
          1         21   197916.96           19
          1         22   214216.96           17
          1         23    98896.96           26
          1         24   207216.96           18
          1         25    93416.96           28
          1         26    93417.04           27
          1              905081.84            9
          2         21    20426.96           40
          2         22    19826.96           41
          2         23    19726.96           42
          2         24    43866.96           34
          2         25    32266.96           38
          2         26    50266.42           31
          2              186381.22           21
          3         21   140326.96           22
          3         22   116826.96           23
          3         23   112026.96           24
          3         24    34829.96           36
          3         25    29129.96           39
          3         26    45130.11           33
          3              478270.91           10
          4         21   108326.96           25
          4         22    81426.96           30
          4         23    92426.96           29
          4         24    47456.96           32
          4         25    33156.96           37
          4         26    39956.36           35
          4              402751.16           13
```

```
        5          21                              1
        5          22                              1
        5          23                              1
        5          24                              1
        5          25                              1
        5          26                              1
        5                                          1
                   21      466997.84              11
                   22      432297.84              12
                   23      323077.84              15
                   24      333370.84              14
                   25      187970.84              20
                   26      228769.93              16
                         1972485.13               8
```

The next query uses GROUPING SETS and RANK() to get just the sales amount subtotal rankings:

```
SELECT
 prd_type_id, emp_id, SUM(amount),
 RANK() OVER (ORDER BY SUM(amount) DESC) AS rank
FROM all_sales
WHERE year = 2003
GROUP BY GROUPING SETS(prd_type_id, emp_id)
ORDER BY prd_type_id, emp_id;
```

```
PRD_TYPE_ID     EMP_ID SUM(AMOUNT)          RANK
----------- ---------- -----------    ----------
          1                905081.84            2
          2                186381.22           11
          3                478270.91            3
          4                402751.16            6
          5                                     1
                   21      466997.84            4
                   22      432297.84            5
                   23      323077.84            8
                   24      333370.84            7
                   25      187970.84           10
                   26      228769.93            9
```

Using the CUME_DIST() and PERCENT_RANK() Functions

You use CUME_DIST() to calculate the position of a specified value relative to a group of values; CUME_DIST() is short for cumulative distribution. You use PERCENT_RANK() to calculate the percent rank of a value relative to a group of values.

The following query illustrates the use of CUME_DIST() and PERCENT_RANK() to get the cumulative distribution and percent rank of sales:

```
SELECT
 prd_type_id, SUM(amount),
 CUME_DIST() OVER (ORDER BY SUM(amount) DESC) AS cume_dist,
```

```
  PERCENT_RANK() OVER (ORDER BY SUM(amount) DESC) AS percent_rank
FROM all_sales
WHERE year = 2003
GROUP BY prd_type_id
ORDER BY prd_type_id;
```

```
PRD_TYPE_ID SUM(AMOUNT)  CUME_DIST PERCENT_RANK
----------- ----------- ---------- ------------
          1  905081.84         .4          .25
          2  186381.22          1            1
          3  478270.91         .6           .5
          4  402751.16         .8          .75
          5                    .2            0
```

Using the NTILE() Function

You use `NTILE(buckets)` to calculate *n*-tiles: tertiles, quartiles, and so on; `bucket` specifies the number of "buckets" into which groups of rows are placed. For example, `NTILE(2)` specifies two buckets and divides the groups of rows in two; `NTILE(4)` divides the groups into four.

The following query illustrates the use of `NTILE()`. Notice 4 is passed to `NTILE()` to split the groups of rows into four buckets:

```
SELECT
  prd_type_id, SUM(amount),
  NTILE(4) OVER (ORDER BY SUM(amount) DESC) AS ntile
FROM all_sales
WHERE year = 2003
AND amount IS NOT NULL
GROUP BY prd_type_id
ORDER BY prd_type_id;
```

```
PRD_TYPE_ID SUM(AMOUNT)      NTILE
----------- ----------- ----------
          1  905081.84          1
          2  186381.22          4
          3  478270.91          2
          4  402751.16          3
```

Using the ROW_NUMBER() Function

You use `ROW_NUMBER()` to return a number with each row in a group, starting at 1. The following query illustrates the use of `ROW_NUMBER()`:

```
SELECT
  prd_type_id, SUM(amount),
  ROW_NUMBER() OVER (ORDER BY SUM(amount) DESC) AS row_number
FROM all_sales
WHERE year = 2003
GROUP BY prd_type_id
ORDER BY prd_type_id;
```

```
PRD_TYPE_ID SUM(AMOUNT) ROW_NUMBER
----------- ----------- ----------
          1   905081.84          2
          2   186381.22          5
          3   478270.91          3
          4   402751.16          4
          5                      1
```

This concludes the discussion of ranking functions.

Using the Inverse Percentile Functions

In the section "Using the CUME_DIST() and PERCENT_RANK() Functions," you saw that CUME_ DIST() is used to calculate the position of a specified value relative to a group of values. You also saw that PERCENT_RANK() is used to calculate the percent rank of a value relative to a group of values.

In this section, you'll see how you use the inverse percentile functions to get the value that corresponds to a percentile. There are two inverse percentile functions: PERCENTILE_DISC(x) and PERCENTILE_CONT(x). They operate in the reverse sense of CUME_DIST() and PERCENT_ RANK(). PERCENTILE_DISC(x) examines the cumulative distribution values in each group until it finds one that is greater than or equal to x. PERCENTILE_CONT(x) examines the percent rank values in each group until it finds one that is greater than or equal to x.

The following query illustrates the use of PERCENTILE_CONT() and PERCENTILE_DISC() to get the sum of the amount whose percentile is greater than or equal to 0.6:

```
SELECT
  PERCENTILE_CONT(0.6) WITHIN GROUP (ORDER BY SUM(amount) DESC)
   AS percentile_cont,
  PERCENTILE_DISC(0.6) WITHIN GROUP (ORDER BY SUM(amount) DESC)
   AS percentile_disc
FROM all_sales
WHERE year = 2003
GROUP BY prd_type_id;

PERCENTILE_CONT PERCENTILE_DISC
--------------- ---------------
      417855.11        402751.16
```

If you compare the sum of the amounts shown in these results with those shown in the earlier section "Using the CUME_DIST() and PERCENT_RANK() Functions," you'll see the sums correspond to those whose cumulative distribution and percent rank are 0.6 and 0.75, respectively.

Using the Window Functions

You use the window functions to calculate things like cumulative sums and moving averages within a specified range of rows, a range of values, or an interval of time. The term "window" is used because processing of results involves a sliding range of rows returned by a query.

You can use windows with the following functions: SUM(), AVG(), MAX(), MIN(), COUNT(), VARIANCE(), and STDDEV(); you saw these functions in Chapter 3. You can also use windows with FIRST_VALUE() and LAST_VALUE(), which return the first and last values in a window. (You'll learn more about the FIRST_VALUE() and LAST_VALUE() functions later in the section "Getting the First and Last Rows Using FIRST_VALUE() and LAST_VALUE()".)

In this section, you'll see how to perform a cumulative sum, a moving average, and a centered average.

Performing a Cumulative Sum

The following query performs a cumulative sum to compute the cumulative sales amount for 2003 starting with January and ending in December. Notice each monthly sales amount is added to the cumulative amount that grows after each month:

```
SELECT
  month, SUM(amount) AS month_amount,
  SUM(SUM(amount)) OVER
    (ORDER BY month ROWS BETWEEN UNBOUNDED PRECEDING AND CURRENT ROW)
    AS cumulative_amount
FROM all_sales
WHERE year = 2003
GROUP BY month
ORDER BY month;
```

MONTH	MONTH_AMOUNT	CUMULATIVE_AMOUNT
1	95525.55	95525.55
2	116671.6	212197.15
3	160307.92	372505.07
4	175998.8	548503.87
5	154349.44	702853.31
6	124951.36	827804.67
7	170296.16	998100.83
8	212735.68	1210836.51
9	199609.68	1410446.19
10	264480.79	1674926.98
11	160221.98	1835148.96
12	137336.17	1972485.13

Notice the previous query uses the following expression to compute the cumulative aggregate:

```
SUM(SUM(amount)) OVER
  (ORDER BY month ROWS BETWEEN UNBOUNDED PRECEDING AND CURRENT ROW)
  AS cumulative_amount
```

Let's break this expression down:

- SUM(amount) computes the sum of an amount. The outer SUM() computes the cumulative amount.

- ORDER BY month orders the rows read by the query by month.

- ROWS BETWEEN UNBOUNDED PRECEDING AND CURRENT ROW defines the start and end of the window. The start includes all rows read by the query as indicated by UNBOUNDED

PRECEDING; the end of the window is the current row. CURRENT ROW is actually the default, and I could have implicitly indicated the window size using ROWS UNBOUNDED PRECEDING and the results of the query would be the same.

So the entire expression means compute the cumulative sum of the amount for each month starting at the first row read by the query.

Each row in the window is processed one at a time, starting with the first row in the window. As each row is processed, the current row's amount is added to the cumulative amount and the end of the window moves down to the next row. Processing continues until the last row read by the query is processed.

CAUTION
Don't confuse the end of the window with the end of the rows read by the query. The end of the window slides down as each current row read from the query is processed. So, in the example, the window starts off with 1 row, increases by 1 row as each row is processed, and ends with 12 rows.

The next query uses a cumulative sum to compute the cumulative sales amount starting with June and ending in December of 2003. Notice the use of ROWS UNBOUNDED PRECEDING to implicitly indicate the end of the window is the current row:

```
SELECT
 month, SUM(amount) AS month_amount,
 SUM(SUM(amount)) OVER (ORDER BY month ROWS UNBOUNDED PRECEDING) AS
  cumulative_amount
FROM all_sales
WHERE year = 2003
AND month BETWEEN 6 AND 12
GROUP BY month
ORDER BY month;
```

```
    MONTH MONTH_AMOUNT CUMULATIVE_AMOUNT
---------- ------------ -----------------
        6    124951.36         124951.36
        7    170296.16         295247.52
        8    212735.68          507983.2
        9    199609.68         707592.88
       10    264480.79         972073.67
       11    160221.98        1132295.65
       12    137336.17        1269631.82
```

Performing a Moving Average
The following query computes the moving average of the sales amount between the current month and the previous three months:

```
SELECT
 month, SUM(amount) AS month_amount,
 AVG(SUM(amount)) OVER
```

```
(ORDER BY month ROWS BETWEEN 3 PRECEDING AND CURRENT ROW)
  AS moving_average
FROM all_sales
WHERE year = 2003
GROUP BY month
ORDER BY month;
```

```
    MONTH MONTH_AMOUNT MOVING_AVERAGE
---------- ------------ --------------
        1     95525.55       95525.55
        2     116671.6      106098.575
        3    160307.92      124168.357
        4     175998.8      137125.968
        5    154349.44       151831.94
        6    124951.36       153901.88
        7    170296.16       156398.94
        8    212735.68       165583.16
        9    199609.68       176898.22
       10    264480.79      211780.578
       11    160221.98      209262.033
       12    137336.17      190412.155
```

Notice the previous query uses the following expression to compute the moving average:

```
AVG(SUM(amount)) OVER
    (ORDER BY month ROWS BETWEEN 3 PRECEDING AND CURRENT ROW)
  AS moving_average
```

Let's break this expression down:

- SUM(amount) computes the sum of an amount. The outer AVG() computes the average.

- ORDER BY month orders the rows read by the query by month.

- ROWS BETWEEN 3 PRECEDING AND CURRENT ROW defines the start of the window as including the three rows preceding the current row; the end of the window is the current row. I could have implicitly indicated the window size using ROWS 3 PRECEDING and the results of the query would be the same.

So the entire expression means compute the moving average of the sales amount between the current month and the previous three months. Because for the first two months less than the full three months of data are available, the moving average is based on only the months available.

Both the start and the end of the window begin at row #1 read by the query. The end of the window moves down after each row is processed. The start of the window only moves down once row #4 has been processed, after which time the start of the window moves down after each row is processed. Processing continues until the last row read by the query is processed.

Performing a Centered Average

The following query computes the moving average of the sales amount centered between the previous and next month from the current month:

```
SELECT
  month, SUM(amount) AS month_amount,
  AVG(SUM(amount)) OVER
    (ORDER BY month ROWS BETWEEN 1 PRECEDING AND 1 FOLLOWING)
    AS moving_average
FROM all_sales
WHERE year = 2003
GROUP BY month
ORDER BY month;
```

MONTH	MONTH_AMOUNT	MOVING_AVERAGE
1	95525.55	106098.575
2	116671.6	124168.357
3	160307.92	150992.773
4	175998.8	163552.053
5	154349.44	151766.533
6	124951.36	149865.653
7	170296.16	169327.733
8	212735.68	194213.84
9	199609.68	225608.717
10	264480.79	208104.15
11	160221.98	187346.313
12	137336.17	148779.075

Notice the previous query uses the following expression to compute the moving average:

```
AVG(SUM(amount)) OVER
  (ORDER BY month ROWS BETWEEN 1 PRECEDING AND 1 FOLLOWING)
  AS moving_average
```

Let's break this expression down:

- SUM(amount) computes the sum of an amount. The outer AVG() computes the average.

- ORDER BY month orders the rows read by the query by month.

- ROWS BETWEEN 1 PRECEDING AND 1 FOLLOWING defines the start of the window as including the row preceding the current row. The end of the window is the row following the current row.

So the entire expression means compute the moving average of the sales amount between the current month and the previous month. Because for the first and last month less than the full three months of data are available, the moving average is based on only the months available.

The start of the window begins at row #1 read by the query. The end of the window begins at row #2 and moves down after each row is processed. The start of the window only moves down once row #2 has been processed. Processing continues until the last row read by the query is processed.

Getting the First and Last Rows Using FIRST_VALUE() and LAST_VALUE()

You use the FIRST_VALUE() and LAST_VALUE() functions to get the first and last rows in a window. The following query uses FIRST_VALUE() and LAST_VALUE() to get the previous and next month's sales amount:

```
SELECT
  month, SUM(amount) AS month_amount,
FIRST_VALUE(SUM(amount)) OVER
  (ORDER BY month ROWS BETWEEN 1 PRECEDING AND 1 FOLLOWING)
  AS previous_month_amount,
LAST_VALUE(SUM(amount)) OVER
  (ORDER BY month ROWS BETWEEN 1 PRECEDING AND 1 FOLLOWING)
  AS next_month_amount
FROM all_sales
WHERE year = 2003
GROUP BY month
ORDER BY month;
```

MONTH	MONTH_AMOUNT	PREVIOUS_MONTH_AMOUNT	NEXT_MONTH_AMOUNT
1	95525.55	95525.55	116671.6
2	116671.6	95525.55	160307.92
3	160307.92	116671.6	175998.8
4	175998.8	160307.92	154349.44
5	154349.44	175998.8	124951.36
6	124951.36	154349.44	170296.16
7	170296.16	124951.36	212735.68
8	212735.68	170296.16	199609.68
9	199609.68	212735.68	264480.79
10	264480.79	199609.68	160221.98
11	160221.98	264480.79	137336.17
12	137336.17	160221.98	137336.17

The next query divides the current month's sales amount by the previous month's sales amount (labeled as curr_div_prev), and also divides the current month's sales amount by the next month's sales amount (labeled as curr_div_next):

```
SELECT
  month, SUM(amount) AS month_amount,
  SUM(amount)/FIRST_VALUE(SUM(amount)) OVER
  (ORDER BY month ROWS BETWEEN 1 PRECEDING AND 1 FOLLOWING)
  AS curr_div_prev,
  SUM(amount)/LAST_VALUE(SUM(amount)) OVER
  (ORDER BY month ROWS BETWEEN 1 PRECEDING AND 1 FOLLOWING)
  AS curr_div_next
FROM all_sales
WHERE year = 2003
GROUP BY month
ORDER BY month;
```

```
MONTH MONTH_AMOUNT CURR_DIV_PREV CURR_DIV_NEXT
----- ------------ ------------- -------------
    1     95525.55             1   .818755807
    2     116671.6    1.22136538   .727796855
    3    160307.92    1.37400978   .910846665
    4     175998.8    1.09787963   1.14026199
    5    154349.44    .876991434   1.23527619
    6    124951.36    .809535558   .733729756
    7    170296.16    1.36289961   .800505867
    8    212735.68    1.24921008   1.06575833
    9    199609.68    .93829902    .754722791
   10    264480.79    1.3249898    1.65071478
   11    160221.98    .605798175   1.16664081
   12    137336.17    .857161858             1
```

This concludes the discussion of window functions.

Using the Reporting Functions

You use the reporting functions to perform calculations across groups and partitions within groups.

You can perform reporting with the following functions: SUM(), AVG(), MAX(), MIN(), COUNT(), VARIANCE(), and STDDEV(). You can also use the RATIO_TO_REPORT() function to compute the ratio of a value to the sum of a set of values.

In this section, you'll see how to perform a report on a sum and use the RATIO_TO_REPORT() function.

Reporting on a Sum

For the first three months of 2003, the following query reports:

- The total sum of all sales for all three months (labeled as total_month_amount)

- The total sum of all sales for all product types (labeled as total_product_type_amount)

```
SELECT
 month, prd_type_id,
 SUM(SUM(amount)) OVER (PARTITION BY month)
  AS total_month_amount,
 SUM(SUM(amount)) OVER (PARTITION BY prd_type_id)
  AS total_product_type_amount
FROM all_sales
WHERE year = 2003
AND month <= 3
GROUP BY month, prd_type_id
ORDER BY month, prd_type_id;
```

```
MONTH PRD_TYPE_ID TOTAL_MONTH_AMOUNT TOTAL_PRODUCT_TYPE_AMOUNT
----- ----------- ------------------ -------------------------
    1           1           95525.55                 201303.92
    1           2           95525.55                  44503.92
    1           3           95525.55                  61003.92
```

1	4	95525.55	65693.31
1	5	95525.55	
2	1	116671.6	201303.92
2	2	116671.6	44503.92
2	3	116671.6	61003.92
2	4	116671.6	65693.31
2	5	116671.6	
3	1	160307.92	201303.92
3	2	160307.92	44503.92
3	3	160307.92	61003.92
3	4	160307.92	65693.31
3	5	160307.92	

Notice the previous query uses the following expression to report the total sum of all sales for all months (labeled as `total_month_amount`).

```
SUM(SUM(amount)) OVER (PARTITION BY month)
  AS total_month_amount
```

Let's break this expression down:

- `SUM(amount)` computes the sum of an amount. The outer `SUM()` computes the total sum.

- `OVER (PARTITION BY month)` causes the outer `SUM()` to compute the sum for each month.

The previous query also uses the following expression to report the total sum of all sales for all product types (labeled as `total_product_type_amount`):

```
SUM(SUM(amount)) OVER (PARTITION BY prd_type_id)
  AS total_product_type_amount
```

Let's break this expression down:

- `SUM(amount)` computes the sum of an amount. The outer `SUM()` computes the total sum.

- `OVER (PARTITION BY prd_type_id)` causes the outer `SUM()` to compute the sum for each product type.

Using the RATIO_TO_REPORT() Function

You use the `RATIO_TO_REPORT()` function to compute the ratio of a value to the sum of a set of values.

For the first three months of 2003, the following query reports:

- The sum of the sales amount by product type for each month (labeled as `prd_type_amount`)

■   The ratio of the product type's sales amount for the entire month's sales (labeled as
     `prd_type_ratio`), which is computed using `RATIO_TO_REPORT()`

```
SELECT
 month, prd_type_id,
 SUM(amount) AS prd_type_amount,
 RATIO_TO_REPORT(SUM(amount)) OVER (PARTITION BY month)
  AS prd_type_ratio
FROM all_sales
WHERE year = 2003
AND month <= 3
GROUP BY month, prd_type_id
ORDER BY month, prd_type_id;
```

```
MONTH PRD_TYPE_ID PRD_TYPE_AMOUNT PRD_TYPE_RATIO
---------- ----------- --------------- --------------
        1           1        38909.04      .40731553
        1           2        14309.04     .149792804
        1           3        24909.04     .260757881
        1           4        17398.43     .182133785
        1           5
        2           1         70567.9     .604842138
        2           2         13367.9     .114577155
        2           3         15467.9     .132576394
        2           4         17267.9     .148004313
        2           5
        3           1        91826.98      .57281624
        3           2        16826.98     .104966617
        3           3        20626.98     .128670998
        3           4        31026.98     .193546145
        3           5
```

Notice the previous query uses the following expression to compute the ratio (labeled as
`prd_type_ratio`):

```
RATIO_TO_REPORT(SUM(amount)) OVER (PARTITION BY month)
 AS prd_type_ratio
```

Let's break this expression down:

■   `SUM(amount)` computes the sum of the amount.

■   `OVER (PARTITION BY month)` causes the outer `SUM()` to compute the sum for each
     month.

■   The ratio is computed by dividing the sum of the amount for each product type by the
     sum of the amount for the entire amount.

This concludes the discussion of reporting functions.

Using the LAG() and LEAD() Functions

You use the LAG() and LEAD() functions to get a value in a row where that row is a certain number of rows away from the current row. The following query uses LAG() and LEAD() to get the previous and next month's sales amount:

```
SELECT
  month, SUM(amount) AS month_amount,
  LAG(SUM(amount), 1) OVER (ORDER BY month) AS previous_month_amount,
  LEAD(SUM(amount), 1) OVER (ORDER BY month) AS next_month_amount
FROM all_sales
WHERE year = 2003
GROUP BY month
ORDER BY month;
```

MONTH	MONTH_AMOUNT	PREVIOUS_MONTH_AMOUNT	NEXT_MONTH_AMOUNT
1	95525.55		116671.6
2	116671.6	95525.55	160307.92
3	160307.92	116671.6	175998.8
4	175998.8	160307.92	154349.44
5	154349.44	175998.8	124951.36
6	124951.36	154349.44	170296.16
7	170296.16	124951.36	212735.68
8	212735.68	170296.16	199609.68
9	199609.68	212735.68	264480.79
10	264480.79	199609.68	160221.98
11	160221.98	264480.79	137336.17
12	137336.17	160221.98	

Notice the previous query uses the following expressions to get the previous and next month's sales:

```
LAG(SUM(amount), 1) OVER (ORDER BY month) AS previous_month_amount,
LEAD(SUM(amount), 1) OVER (ORDER BY month) AS next_month_amount
```

LAG(SUM(amount), 1) gets the previous row's sum of the amount. LEAD(SUM(amount), 1) gets the next row's sum of the amount.

Using the FIRST and LAST Functions

You use the FIRST and LAST functions to get the first and last values in an ordered group. You can use FIRST and LAST with the following functions: MIN(), MAX(), COUNT(), SUM(), AVG(), STDDEV(), and VARIANCE().

The following query uses FIRST and LAST to get the months in 2003 that had the highest and lowest sales:

```
SELECT
  MIN(month) KEEP (DENSE_RANK FIRST ORDER BY SUM(amount))
    AS highest_sales_month,
```

```
MIN(month) KEEP (DENSE_RANK LAST ORDER BY SUM(amount))
  AS lowest_sales_month
FROM all_sales
WHERE year = 2003
GROUP BY month
ORDER BY month;


HIGHEST_SALES_MONTH LOWEST_SALES_MONTH
------------------- ------------------
                  1                 10
```

Using the Linear Regression Functions

You use the linear regression functions to fit an ordinary-least-squares regression line to a set of number pairs. You can use the linear regression functions as aggregate, windowing, or reporting functions. The following table shows the linear regression functions. In the function syntax, y is interpreted by the functions as a variable that depends on x.

Function	Description
REGR_AVGX(y, x)	Returns the average of x after eliminating x and y pairs where either x or y is null.
REGR_AVGY(y, x)	Returns the average of y after eliminating x and y pairs where either x or y is null.
REGR_COUNT(y, x)	Returns the number of non-null number pairs that are used to fit the regression line.
REGR_INTERCEPT(y, x)	Returns the intercept on the y-axis of the regression line.
REGR_R2(y, x)	Returns the coefficient of determination, or R-squared, of the regression line.
REGR_SLOPE(y, x)	Returns the slope of the regression line.
REGR_SXX(y, x)	Returns REG_COUNT(y, x) * VAR_POP(x).
REGR_SXY(y, x)	Returns REG_COUNT(y, x) * COVAR_POP(y, x).
REGR_SYY(y, x)	Returns REG_COUNT(y, x) * VAR_POP(y).

The following query shows the use of the linear regression functions:

```
SELECT
  prd_type_id,
  REGR_AVGX(amount, month) AS avgx,
  REGR_AVGY(amount, month) AS avgy,
  REGR_COUNT(amount, month) AS count,
  REGR_INTERCEPT(amount, month) AS inter,
  REGR_R2(amount, month) AS r2,
  REGR_SLOPE(amount, month) AS slope,
  REGR_SXX(amount, month) AS sxx,
  REGR_SXY(amount, month) AS sxy,
```

```
  REGR_SYY(amount, month) AS syy
FROM all_sales
WHERE year = 2003
GROUP BY prd_type_id;
```

PRD_TYPE_ID	AVGX	AVGY	COUNT	INTER	R2
SLOPE	SXX	SXY	SYY		
1	6.5 12570.5811		72	13318.4543	.003746289
-115.05741	858	-98719.26 3031902717			
2	6.5 2588.62806		72	2608.11268	.0000508
-2.997634	858	-2571.97 151767392			
3	6.5 6642.65153		72	2154.23119	.126338815
690.526206	858 592471.485 3238253324				
4	6.5 5593.76611		72	2043.47164	.128930297
546.199149	858 468638.87 1985337488				
5		0			

Using the Hypothetical Rank and Distribution Functions

You use the hypothetical rank and distribution functions to calculate the rank and percentile that a new row would have if you inserted it into a table. You can perform hypothetical calculations with the following functions: RANK(), DENSE_RANK(), PERCENT_RANK(), and CUME_DIST().

Before you see an example of a hypothetical, the following query uses RANK() and PERCENT_ RANK() to get the rank and percent rank of sales by product type for 2003:

```
SELECT
  prd_type_id, SUM(amount),
  RANK() OVER (ORDER BY SUM(amount) DESC) AS rank,
  PERCENT_RANK() OVER (ORDER BY SUM(amount) DESC) AS percent_rank
FROM all_sales
WHERE year = 2003
AND amount IS NOT NULL
GROUP BY prd_type_id
ORDER BY prd_type_id;
```

PRD_TYPE_ID	SUM(AMOUNT)	RANK	PERCENT_RANK
1	905081.84	1	0
2	186381.22	4	1
3	478270.91	2	.333333333
4	402751.16	3	.666666667

The next query shows the hypothetical rank and percent rank of a sales amount of $500,000:

```
SELECT
 RANK(500000) WITHIN GROUP (ORDER BY SUM(amount) DESC)
  AS rank,
 PERCENT_RANK(500000) WITHIN GROUP (ORDER BY SUM(amount) DESC)
  AS percent_rank
FROM all_sales
WHERE year = 2003
AND amount IS NOT NULL
GROUP BY prd_type_id
ORDER BY prd_type_id;

      RANK PERCENT_RANK
---------- ------------
         2         .25
```

As you can see, the hypothetical rank and percent rank of a sales amount of $500,000 are 2 and .25.

This concludes the discussion of hypothetical functions.

Using the MODEL Clause

You use the new Oracle Database 10*g* MODEL clause to perform inter-row calculations. The MODEL clause allows you to access a column in a row like a cell in an array. This gives you the ability to perform calculations in a similar manner to spreadsheet calculations. For example, the all_sales table contains sales information for the months in 2003. You can use the MODEL clause to calculate sales in future months based on sales in 2003.

An Example of the MODEL Clause

The easiest way to learn how to use the MODEL clause is to see an example. The following query retrieves the sales amount for each month in 2003 made by employee #21 for product types #1 and #2, and computes the predicted sales for January, February, and March of 2004 based on sales in 2003:

```
SELECT prd_type_id, year, month, sales_amount
FROM all_sales
WHERE prd_type_id BETWEEN 1 AND 2
AND emp_id = 21
MODEL
PARTITION BY (prd_type_id)
DIMENSION BY (month, year)
MEASURES (amount sales_amount) (
 sales_amount[1, 2004] = sales_amount[1, 2003],
 sales_amount[2, 2004] =
  sales_amount[2, 2003] + sales_amount[3, 2003],
 sales_amount[3, 2004] = ROUND(sales_amount[3, 2003] * 1.25, 2)
)
ORDER BY prd_type_id, year, month;
```

Let's break this query down:

- ■ PARTITION BY (prd_type_id) specifies the results are partitioned by prd_type_id.

- ■ DIMENSION BY (month, year) specifies the dimensions of the array are month and year. This means you access a column in a row by supplying a month and year.

- ■ MEASURES (amount sales_amount) specifies each cell in the array contains an amount, and the array name is sales_amount. To access the cell in the sales_amount array for January 2003, you use sales_amount[1, 2003], which returns an amount.

- ■ After MEASURES come three lines that compute the future sales for January, February, and March of 2004:

  - ■ sales_amount[1, 2004] = sales_amount[1, 2003] sets the sales amount for January 2004 to the amount for January 2003.

  - ■ sales_amount[2, 2004] = sales_amount[2, 2003] + sales_amount[3, 2003] sets the sales amount for February 2004 to the amount for February 2003 plus March 2003.

  - ■ sales_amount[3, 2004] = ROUND(sales_amount[3, 2003] * 1.25, 2) sets the sales amount for March 2004 to the rounded value of the sales amount for March 2003 multiplied by 1.25.

- ■ ORDER BY prd_type_id, year, month simply orders the results returned by the entire query.

The output from the example query is as follows. Notice the results contain the sales amounts for all months in 2003 for product types #1 and #2, plus the predicted sales amounts for the first three months in 2004 (which I've made bold to make them stand out):

PRD_TYPE_ID	YEAR	MONTH	SALES_AMOUNT
1	2003	1	10034.84
1	2003	2	15144.65
1	2003	3	20137.83
1	2003	4	25057.45
1	2003	5	17214.56
1	2003	6	15564.64
1	2003	7	12654.84
1	2003	8	17434.82
1	2003	9	19854.57
1	2003	10	21754.19
1	2003	11	13029.73
1	2003	12	10034.84
1	**2004**	**1**	**10034.84**
1	**2004**	**2**	**35282.48**

1	**2004**	**3**	**25172.29**
2	2003	1	1034.84
2	2003	2	1544.65
2	2003	3	2037.83
2	2003	4	2557.45
2	2003	5	1714.56
2	2003	6	1564.64
2	2003	7	1264.84
2	2003	8	1734.82
2	2003	9	1854.57
2	2003	10	2754.19
2	2003	11	1329.73
2	2003	12	1034.84
2	**2004**	**1**	**1034.84**
2	**2004**	**2**	**3582.48**
2	**2004**	**3**	**2547.29**

Using Positional and Symbolic Notation to Access Cells

In the previous example, you saw how to access a cell in an array using the following notation: `sales_amount[1, 2004]`, where 1 is the month and 2004 is the year. This is referred to as positional notation because the meaning of the dimensions is determined by their position; the first position contains the month and the second position contains the year.

You can also use symbolic notation to explicitly indicate the meaning of the dimensions, for example, `sales_amount[month=1, year=2004]`. The following query rewrites the previous example to use symbolic notation:

```
SELECT prd_type_id, year, month, sales_amount
FROM all_sales
WHERE prd_type_id BETWEEN 1 AND 2
AND emp_id = 21
MODEL
PARTITION BY (prd_type_id)
DIMENSION BY (month, year)
MEASURES (amount sales_amount) (
 sales_amount[month=1, year=2004] = sales_amount[month=1, year=2003],
 sales_amount[month=2, year=2004] =
  sales_amount[month=2, year=2003] + sales_amount[month=3, year=2003],
 sales_amount[month=3, year=2004] =
  ROUND(sales_amount[month=3, year=2003] * 1.25, 2)
)
ORDER BY prd_type_id, year, month;
```

One difference to be aware of when using positional or symbolic notation is how they handle null values in the dimensions. `sales_amount[null, 2003]` returns the amount whose month is null and year is 2003, but `sales_amount[month=null, year=2004]` won't access a valid cell because `null=null` always returns false.

Accessing a Range of Cells Using BETWEEN and AND

You can access a range of cells using the BETWEEN and AND keywords. For example, the following expression sets the sales amount for January 2004 to the rounded average of the sales between January and March of 2003; notice the use of BETWEEN and AND:

```
sales_amount[1, 2004] =
  ROUND(AVG(sales_amount)[month BETWEEN 1 AND 3, 2003], 2)
```

The following query shows the use of this expression:

```
SELECT prd_type_id, year, month, sales_amount
FROM all_sales
WHERE prd_type_id BETWEEN 1 AND 2
AND emp_id = 21
MODEL
PARTITION BY (prd_type_id)
DIMENSION BY (month, year)
MEASURES (amount sales_amount) (
 sales_amount[1, 2004] =
   ROUND(AVG(sales_amount)[month BETWEEN 1 AND 3, 2003], 2)
)
ORDER BY prd_type_id, year, month;
```

Accessing All Cells Using ANY and IS ANY

You can access all cells using the ANY and IS ANY predicates. You use ANY with positional notation and IS ANY with symbolic notation. For example, the following expression sets the sales amount for January 2004 to the rounded sum of the sales for all months and years; notice the use of ANY and IS ANY:

```
sales_amount[1, 2004] =
  ROUND(SUM(sales_amount)[ANY, year IS ANY], 2)
```

The following query shows the use of this expression:

```
SELECT prd_type_id, year, month, sales_amount
FROM all_sales
WHERE prd_type_id BETWEEN 1 AND 2
AND emp_id = 21
MODEL
PARTITION BY (prd_type_id)
DIMENSION BY (month, year)
MEASURES (amount sales_amount) (
 sales_amount[1, 2004] =
   ROUND(SUM(sales_amount)[ANY, year IS ANY], 2)
)
ORDER BY prd_type_id, year, month;
```

Getting the Current Value of a Dimension Using CURRENTV()

You can get the current value of a dimension using the CURRENTV() function. For example, the following expression sets the sales amount for the first month of 2004 to 1.25 times the sales of the same month in 2003. Notice the use of CURRENTV() to get the current month, which is 1:

```
sales_amount[1, 2004] =
  ROUND(sales_amount[CURRENTV(), 2003] * 1.25, 2)
```

The following query shows the use of this expression:

```
SELECT prd_type_id, year, month, sales_amount
FROM all_sales
WHERE prd_type_id BETWEEN 1 AND 2
AND emp_id = 21
MODEL
PARTITION BY (prd_type_id)
DIMENSION BY (month, year)
MEASURES (amount sales_amount) (
sales_amount[1, 2004] =
  ROUND(sales_amount[CURRENTV(), 2003] * 1.25, 2)
)
ORDER BY prd_type_id, year, month;
```

The output from this query is as follows; I've highlighted the values for 2004 in bold:

PRD_TYPE_ID	YEAR	MONTH	SALES_AMOUNT
1	2003	1	10034.84
1	2003	2	15144.65
1	2003	3	20137.83
1	2003	4	25057.45
1	2003	5	17214.56
1	2003	6	15564.64
1	2003	7	12654.84
1	2003	8	17434.82
1	2003	9	19854.57
1	2003	10	21754.19
1	2003	11	13029.73
1	2003	12	10034.84
1	**2004**	**1**	**12543.55**
2	2003	1	1034.84
2	2003	2	1544.65
2	2003	3	2037.83
2	2003	4	2557.45
2	2003	5	1714.56

2	2003	6	1564.64
2	2003	7	1264.84
2	2003	8	1734.82
2	2003	9	1854.57
2	2003	10	2754.19
2	2003	11	1329.73
2	2003	12	1034.84
2	**2004**	**1**	**1293.55**

Accessing Cells Using a FOR Loop

You can access cells using a FOR loop. For example, the following expression sets the sales amount for the first three months of 2004 to 1.25 times the sales of the same months in 2003. Notice the use of the FOR loop and the INCREMENT keyword that specifies the amount to increment month by during each iteration of the loop:

```
sales_amount[FOR month FROM 1 TO 3 INCREMENT 1, 2004] =
  ROUND(sales_amount[CURRENTV(), 2003] * 1.25, 2)
```

The following query shows the use of this expression:

```
SELECT prd_type_id, year, month, sales_amount
FROM all_sales
WHERE prd_type_id BETWEEN 1 AND 2
AND emp_id = 21
MODEL
PARTITION BY (prd_type_id)
DIMENSION BY (month, year)
MEASURES (amount sales_amount) (
  sales_amount[FOR month FROM 1 TO 3 INCREMENT 1, 2004] =
    ROUND(sales_amount[CURRENTV(), 2003] * 1.25, 2)
)
ORDER BY prd_type_id, year, month;
```

The output from this query is as follows; I've highlighted the values for 2004 in bold:

PRD_TYPE_ID	YEAR	MONTH	SALES_AMOUNT
1	2003	1	10034.84
1	2003	2	15144.65
1	2003	3	20137.83
1	2003	4	25057.45
1	2003	5	17214.56
1	2003	6	15564.64
1	2003	7	12654.84
1	2003	8	17434.82
1	2003	9	19854.57
1	2003	10	21754.19
1	2003	11	13029.73
1	2003	12	10034.84

1	**2004**	**1**	**12543.55**
1	**2004**	**2**	**18930.81**
1	**2004**	**3**	**25172.29**
2	2003	1	1034.84
2	2003	2	1544.65
2	2003	3	2037.83
2	2003	4	2557.45
2	2003	5	1714.56
2	2003	6	1564.64
2	2003	7	1264.84
2	2003	8	1734.82
2	2003	9	1854.57
2	2003	10	2754.19
2	2003	11	1329.73
2	2003	12	1034.84
2	**2004**	**1**	**1293.55**
2	**2004**	**2**	**1930.81**
2	**2004**	**3**	**2547.29**

Handling Null and Missing Values

In this section, you'll learn how to handle null and missing values using the MODEL clause.

Using IS PRESENT

IS PRESENT returns true if the row specified by the cell reference existed prior to the execution of the MODEL clause. For example:

```
sales_amount[CURRENTV(), 2003] IS PRESENT
```

will return true if sales_amount[CURRENTV(), 2003] exists.

The following expression sets the sales amount for the first three months of 2004 to 1.25 times the sales of the same months in 2003; notice the use of IS PRESENT:

```
sales_amount[FOR month FROM 1 TO 3 INCREMENT 1, 2004] =
  CASE WHEN sales_amount[CURRENTV(), 2003] IS PRESENT THEN
   ROUND(sales_amount[CURRENTV(), 2003] * 1.25, 2)
  ELSE
   0
  END
```

The following query shows the use of this expression:

```
SELECT prd_type_id, year, month, sales_amount
FROM all_sales
WHERE prd_type_id BETWEEN 1 AND 2
AND emp_id = 21
MODEL
PARTITION BY (prd_type_id)
DIMENSION BY (month, year)
MEASURES (amount sales_amount) (
```

```
sales_amount[FOR month FROM 1 TO 3 INCREMENT 1, 2004] =
 CASE WHEN sales_amount[CURRENTV(), 2003] IS PRESENT THEN
  ROUND(sales_amount[CURRENTV(), 2003] * 1.25, 2)
 ELSE
  0
 END
)
ORDER BY prd_type_id, year, month;
```

The output of this query is the same as the example in the previous section.

Using PRESENTV()

PRESENTV(*cell*, *expr1*, *expr2*) returns the expression *expr1* if the row specified by the *cell* reference existed prior to the execution of the MODEL clause. If the row doesn't exist, the expression *expr2* is returned. For example:

```
PRESENTV(sales_amount[CURRENTV(), 2003],
 ROUND(sales_amount[CURRENTV(), 2003] * 1.25, 2), 0)
```

will return the rounded sales amount if sales_amount[CURRENTV(), 2003] exists; otherwise, 0 will be returned.

The following query shows the use of this expression:

```
SELECT prd_type_id, year, month, sales_amount
FROM all_sales
WHERE prd_type_id BETWEEN 1 AND 2
AND emp_id = 21
MODEL
PARTITION BY (prd_type_id)
DIMENSION BY (month, year)
MEASURES (amount sales_amount) (
 sales_amount[FOR month FROM 1 TO 3 INCREMENT 1, 2004] =
  PRESENTV(sales_amount[CURRENTV(), 2003],
   ROUND(sales_amount[CURRENTV(), 2003] * 1.25, 2), 0)
)
ORDER BY prd_type_id, year, month;
```

Using PRESENTNNV()

PRESENTNNV(*cell*, *expr1*, *expr2*) returns the expression *expr1* if the row specified by the *cell* reference existed prior to the execution of the MODEL clause and the cell value is not null. If the row doesn't exist or the cell value is null, the expression *expr2* is returned. For example:

```
PRESENTNNV(sales_amount[CURRENTV(), 2003],
 ROUND(sales_amount[CURRENTV(), 2003] * 1.25, 2), 0)
```

will return the rounded sales amount if sales_amount[CURRENTV(), 2003] exists and is not null; otherwise, 0 will be returned.

Using IGNORE NAV and KEEP NAV

IGNORE NAV returns

- 0 for null or missing numeric values

- An empty string for null or missing string values

- 01-JAN-2000 for null or missing date values

KEEP NAV returns null for null or missing numeric values.

NOTE
KEEP NAV is the default.

For example:

```
SELECT prd_type_id, year, month, sales_amount
FROM all_sales
WHERE prd_type_id BETWEEN 1 AND 2
AND emp_id = 21
MODEL IGNORE NAV
PARTITION BY (prd_type_id)
DIMENSION BY (month, year)
MEASURES (amount sales_amount) (
 sales_amount[FOR month FROM 1 TO 3 INCREMENT 1, 2004] =
  ROUND(sales_amount[CURRENTV(), 2003] * 1.25, 2)
)
ORDER BY prd_type_id, year, month;
```

Updating Existing Cells

By default, if the cell referenced on the left side of an expression exists, it is updated. If the cell doesn't exist, a new row in the array is created. You can change this default behavior using RULES UPDATE, which specifies that if the cell doesn't exist, don't create a new row.

The following query uses RULES UPDATE:

```
SELECT prd_type_id, year, month, sales_amount
FROM all_sales
WHERE prd_type_id BETWEEN 1 AND 2
AND emp_id = 21
MODEL
PARTITION BY (prd_type_id)
DIMENSION BY (month, year)
MEASURES (amount sales_amount)
RULES UPDATE (
 sales_amount[FOR month FROM 1 TO 3 INCREMENT 1, 2004] =
  ROUND(sales_amount[CURRENTV(), 2003] * 1.25, 2)
)
ORDER BY prd_type_id, year, month;
```

Because cells for 2004 don't exist and RULES UPDATE is specified, no new rows are created in the array for 2004—and therefore the query doesn't return rows for 2004. The following output shows the output for the query; notice there are no rows for 2004:

PRD_TYPE_ID	YEAR	MONTH	SALES_AMOUNT
1	2003	1	10034.84
1	2003	2	15144.65
1	2003	3	20137.83
1	2003	4	25057.45
1	2003	5	17214.56
1	2003	6	15564.64
1	2003	7	12654.84
1	2003	8	17434.82
1	2003	9	19854.57
1	2003	10	21754.19
1	2003	11	13029.73
1	2003	12	10034.84
2	2003	1	1034.84
2	2003	2	1544.65
2	2003	3	2037.83
2	2003	4	2557.45
2	2003	5	1714.56
2	2003	6	1564.64
2	2003	7	1264.84
2	2003	8	1734.82
2	2003	9	1854.57
2	2003	10	2754.19
2	2003	11	1329.73
2	2003	12	1034.84

Summary

In this chapter, you learned that

- The set operators (UNION ALL, UNION, INTERSECT, and MINUS) allow you to combine rows returned by two or more queries.

- TRANSLATE(*x*, *from_string*, *to_string*) converts the occurrences of characters in *from_string* found in *x* to corresponding characters in *to_string*.

- You use DECODE(*value*, *search_value*, *result*, *default_value*) to compare *value* with *search_value*. If the values are equal, DECODE() returns *search_value*; otherwise, *default_value* is returned. DECODE() allows you to perform if-then-else logic in SQL without having to use PL/SQL.

- You use the CASE expression to perform if-then-else logic in SQL without having to use PL/SQL. CASE works in a similar manner to DECODE(), but you should use CASE since it is ANSI-compliant.

■ You may perform queries against data that is organized into a hierarchy.

■ ROLLUP extends the GROUP BY clause to return rows containing a subtotal for each group.

■ CUBE extends the GROUP BY clause to return rows containing a subtotal for all combinations of columns included in the CUBE clause along with a total at the end.

■ The database has many built-in analytic functions that enable you to perform complex calculations, such as finding the top-selling product type for each month, the top salespersons, and so on.

■ You use the new Oracle Database 10g MODEL clause to perform inter-row calculations. The MODEL clause allows you to access a column in a row like a cell in an array. This gives you the ability to perform calculations in a similar manner to spreadsheet calculations.

In the next chapter, you'll learn about changing the contents of a table.

CHAPTER
8

Changing Table
Contents

In this chapter you'll learn more about changing the contents of tables. Specifically, you'll learn

- How to add, modify, and remove rows using the INSERT, UPDATE, and DELETE statements.

- That a database transaction may consist of multiple INSERT, UPDATE, and DELETE statements.

- How to make the results of your transactions permanent using the COMMIT statement, or undo their results entirely using the ROLLBACK statement.

- How an Oracle database can process multiple transactions at the same time.

Adding Rows Using the INSERT Statement

You use the INSERT statement to add rows to a table. You can specify the following information in an INSERT statement:

- The table into which the row is to be inserted

- A list of columns for which you want to specify column values

- A list of values to store in the specified columns

When adding a row, you typically need to supply a value for the primary key and all other columns that are defined as NOT NULL. You don't have to specify values for NULL columns if you don't want to; by default they will be set to null.

You can find out which columns are defined as NOT NULL using the SQL*Plus DESCRIBE command. The following example describes the customers table:

```
DESCRIBE customers
Name                                      Null?    Type
----------------------------------------- -------- ------------
CUSTOMER_ID                               NOT NULL NUMBER(38)
FIRST_NAME                                NOT NULL VARCHAR2(10)
LAST_NAME                                 NOT NULL VARCHAR2(10)
DOB                                                DATE
PHONE                                              VARCHAR2(12)
```

As you can see, the customer_id, first_name, and last_name columns are NOT NULL, meaning that you must supply a value for these columns. The dob and phone columns don't require a value—you could omit the values when adding a row and these columns would be set to null.

The following INSERT statement adds a row to the customers table. Notice that the order of values in the VALUES clause matches the order in which the columns are specified in the column list. Also notice that the statement has three parts: the table name, the column list, and the values to be added.

```
INSERT INTO customers (
  customer_id, first_name, last_name, dob, phone
```

```
) VALUES (
  6, 'Fred', 'Brown', '01-JAN-1970', '800-555-1215'
);

1 row created.
```

SQL*Plus responds that one row has been created. You can verify this by performing the following SELECT statement:

```
SELECT *
FROM customers;

CUSTOMER_ID FIRST_NAME LAST_NAME   DOB       PHONE
----------- ---------- ----------  --------- ------------
          1 John       Brown       01-JAN-65 800-555-1211
          2 Cynthia    Green       05-FEB-68 800-555-1212
          3 Steve      White       16-MAR-71 800-555-1213
          4 Gail       Black                 800-555-1214
          5 Doreen     Blue        20-MAY-70
          6 Fred       Brown       01-JAN-70 800-555-1215
```

Notice the new row that has been added to the table.

Omitting the Column List

You may omit the column list when supplying values for every column. For example:

```
INSERT INTO customers
VALUES (7, 'Jane', 'Green', '01-JAN-1970', '800-555-1216');
```

When you omit the column list, the order of the values you supply must match the order in which the columns are listed in the output from the DESCRIBE command.

Specifying a Null Value for a Column

You can specify a null value for a column using the NULL keyword. For example, the following INSERT specifies a null value for the dob and phone columns:

```
INSERT INTO customers
VALUES (8, 'Sophie', 'White', NULL, NULL);
```

When you view this row using a query, you won't see a value for the dob and phone columns because they've been set to null values:

```
SELECT *
FROM customers
WHERE customer_id = 8;

CUSTOMER_ID FIRST_NAME LAST_NAME   DOB       PHONE
----------- ---------- ----------  --------- ------------
          8 Sophie     White
```

Notice the dob and phone column values are blank.

Including Single and Double Quotes in a Column Value

You can include a single and double quote in a column value. For example, the following INSERT specifies a last name of O'Malley for a new customer; notice the use of two single quotes in the last name after the letter O:

```
INSERT INTO customers
VALUES (9, 'Kyle', 'O''Malley', NULL, NULL);
```

The next example specifies the name The "Great" Gatsby for a new product:

```
INSERT INTO products (
    product_id, product_type_id, name, description, price
) VALUES (
    13, 1, 'The "Great" Gatsby', NULL, 12.99
);
```

Copying Rows from One Table to Another

You can copy rows from one table to another using a query in the place of the column values in the INSERT statement. The number of columns and the column types in the source and destination must match. The following example uses a SELECT to retrieve the first_name and last_name columns for customer #1 and supplies those columns to an INSERT statement:

```
INSERT INTO customers (customer_id, first_name, last_name)
SELECT 10, first_name, last_name
FROM customers
WHERE customer_id = 1;
```

Notice that the customer_id for the new row is set to 10.

NOTE
Oracle9i introduced the new MERGE statement that allows you to merge rows from one table to another. MERGE is much more flexible than combining an INSERT and a SELECT to copy rows from one table to another. You'll learn about MERGE later in the section "Merging Rows Using MERGE."

Modifying Rows Using the UPDATE Statement

You use the UPDATE statement to change rows in a table. When you typically use the UPDATE statement, you specify the following information:

- The table containing the rows that are to be changed

- A WHERE clause that specifies the rows that are to be changed

- A list of column names, along with their new values, specified using the SET clause

You can change one or more rows using the same UPDATE statement. If more than one row is specified, the same change will be implemented for all of those rows. The following statement updates the last_name column to Orange for the row whose customer_id is 2:

```
UPDATE customers
SET last_name = 'Orange'
WHERE customer_id = 2;
```

```
1 row updated.
```

SQL*Plus confirms that one row was updated. If the WHERE clause were omitted, all the rows would be updated. Notice that the SET clause is used in the UPDATE statement to specify the column and its new value. The following query confirms the change was made:

```
SELECT *
FROM customers
WHERE customer_id = 2;
```

```
CUSTOMER_ID FIRST_NAME LAST_NAME  DOB       PHONE
----------- ---------- ---------- --------- ------------
          2 Cynthia    Orange     05-FEB-68 800-555-1212
```

You can change multiple rows and multiple columns in the same UPDATE statement. For example, the following UPDATE raises the price by 20 percent for all products whose current price is greater than or equal to $20. The UPDATE also changes those products' names to lowercase:

```
UPDATE products
SET
  price = price * 1.20,
  name = LOWER(name)
WHERE
  price >= 20;
```

```
3 rows updated.
```

As you can see, three rows are updated by this statement. You can confirm the change using the following query:

```
SELECT product_id, name, price
FROM products
WHERE price >= (20 * 1.20);
```

```
        ID NAME                           PRICE
---------- ------------------------------ ----------
         2 chemistry                          36
         3 supernova                       31.19
         5 z-files                         59.99
```

NOTE
You can also use a subquery with an UPDATE statement. This was covered in Chapter 6 in the section "Writing an UPDATE Statement Containing a Subquery."

The RETURNING Clause

In Oracle Database 10*g* you can use the RETURNING clause to return the value from an aggregate function such as AVG(). Aggregate functions were covered in Chapter 3.

The following example performs the following tasks:

- Declares a variable named average_product_price

- Decreases the price column of the rows in the products table and saves the average price in the average_product_price variable using the RETURNING clause

- Rolls back the update

- Prints the value of the average_product_price variable

```
VARIABLE average_product_price NUMBER

UPDATE products
SET price =  price * 0.75
RETURNING AVG(price) INTO :average_product_price;
12 rows updated.

ROLLBACK;
Rollback complete.

PRINT average_product_price
AVERAGE_PRODUCT_PRICE
--------------------
          14.7966667
```

Removing Rows Using the DELETE Statement

You use the DELETE statement to remove rows from a table. Generally, you should specify a WHERE clause that limits the rows that you wish to delete. If you don't, *all* the rows will be deleted.

The following DELETE statement removes the row from the customers table whose customer_id is 2:

```
DELETE FROM customers
WHERE customer_id = 2;

1 row deleted.
```

SQL*Plus confirms that one row has been deleted.

You can also use a subquery with a DELETE statement. This was covered in Chapter 6 in the section "Writing a DELETE Statement Containing a Subquery."

NOTE
*If you've been following along with the previous INSERT, UPDATE, and **DELETE** statements, roll them back using ROLLBACK. If you disconnected from the database before performing the rollback, don't worry: simply rerun the* store_schema.sql *script to re-create everything.*

Database Integrity

When you execute a DML statement (an INSERT, UPDATE, or DELETE, for example), the database ensures that the rows in the tables maintain their integrity. This means that any changes you make to the rows in the tables must always be in keeping with the primary key and foreign key relationships set for the tables.

Enforcement of Primary Key Constraints

Let's examine some examples that show the enforcement of a primary key constraint. The customers table's primary key is the customer_id column, which means that every value stored in the customer_id column must be unique. If you try to insert a row with a duplicate value for a primary key column, the database returns the error ORA-00001, for example:

```
SQL> INSERT INTO customers (
  2    customer_id, first_name, last_name, dob, phone
  3  ) VALUES (
  4    1, 'Jason', 'Price', '01-JAN-60', '800-555-1211'
  5  );
INSERT INTO customers (
*
ERROR at line 1:
ORA-00001: unique constraint (STORE.CUSTOMERS_PK) violated
```

If you attempt to update a primary key value to a value that already exists in the table, the database returns the same error:

```
SQL> UPDATE customers
  2    SET customer_id = 1
  3    WHERE customer_id = 2;
UPDATE customers
*
ERROR at line 1:
ORA-00001: unique constraint (STORE.CUSTOMERS_PK) violated
```

Enforcement of Foreign Key Constraints

A foreign key relationship is where a column from one table is referenced in another. The `product_type_id` column in the `products` table references the `product_type_id` column in the `product_types` table using a foreign key relationship. The `product_types` table is known as the *parent* table, and the `products` table is known as the *child* table because the `product_type_id` column in the `products` table is dependent on the `product_type_id` column in the `product_types` table.

If you try to insert a row into the `products` table with a nonexistent `product_type_id`, the database will return the error `ORA-02291`. This error indicates the database couldn't find a matching parent key value (the parent key is the `product_type_id` column of the `product_types` table). For example:

```
SQL> INSERT INTO products (
  2    product_id, product_type_id, name, description, price
  3  ) VALUES (
  4    13, 6, 'Test', 'Test', NULL
  5  );
INSERT INTO products (
*
ERROR at line 1:
ORA-02291: integrity constraint (STORE.PRODUCTS_FK_PRODUCT_TYPES)
 violated - parent key not found
```

Similarly, if you attempt to set the `product_type_id` of a row in the `products` table to a nonexistent parent key value, the database returns the same error. For example:

```
SQL> UPDATE products
  2    SET product_type_id = 6
  3  WHERE product_id = 1;
UPDATE products
*
ERROR at line 1:
ORA-02291: integrity constraint (STORE.PRODUCTS_FK_PRODUCT_TYPES)
 violated - parent key not found
```

If you attempt to delete a row in the parent table that already had dependent child rows, the database returns error `ORA-02292`, which means a child record was found. For example, if you attempt to delete the row with a `product_type_id` of 1 in the `product_types` table, the database will return error `ORA-02292` because the `products` table contains rows with `product_type_id` values equal to that value:

```
SQL> DELETE FROM product_types
  2  WHERE product_type_id = 1;
DELETE FROM product_types
*
ERROR at line 1:
ORA-02292: integrity constraint (STORE.PRODUCTS_FK_PRODUCT_TYPES)
 violated - child record found
```

If the database were to allow this deletion, the child rows would be invalid because they wouldn't point to valid values in the parent table.

Using Default Values

The Oracle9*i* database introduced a new feature that allows you to define a default value for a column. For example, the following statement creates a table named `order_status` that has two columns named `status` and `last_modified`. The `status` column is defaulted to `Order placed` and the `last_modified` column is defaulted to the value returned by the `SYSDATE` function:

```
CREATE TABLE order_status (
  order_status_id INTEGER
    CONSTRAINT default_example_pk PRIMARY KEY,
  status VARCHAR2(20) DEFAULT 'Order placed' NOT NULL,
  last_modified DATE DEFAULT SYSDATE
);
```

NOTE
As with the other tables featured in this book, the `order_status` table is created by the `store_schema.sql` script. This means you don't have to type in the previous `CREATE TABLE` statement yourself. Also, you don't have to type in the `INSERT` statements shown later in this section.

If you were to add a new row to the `order_status` table but didn't specify the values for the `status` and `last_modified` columns, those columns would be set to the default values. For example, the following `INSERT` statement omits values for the `status` and `last_modified` columns:

```
INSERT INTO order_status (order_status_id)
VALUES (1);
```

The `status` column is set to the default value of `Order placed` and the `last_modified` column is set to the current date and time returned by the `SYSDATE` function.

You can override the defaults by specifying a value for the columns, as shown in the following example:

```
INSERT INTO order_status (order_status_id, status, last_modified)
VALUES (2, 'Order shipped', '10-JUN-2004');
```

The following query retrieves the rows from `order_status`:

```
SELECT *
FROM order_status;


ORDER_STATUS_ID STATUS               LAST_MODI
--------------- -------------------- ---------
              1 Order placed         28-DEC-03
              2 Order shipped        10-JUN-04
```

You can update a column and set it back to the default using the DEFAULT keyword in an UPDATE statement. For example, the following UPDATE statement sets the status column to the default:

```
UPDATE order_status
SET status = DEFAULT
WHERE order_status_id = 2;
```

The following query shows the change made by this UPDATE statement:

```
SELECT *
FROM order_status;

ORDER_STATUS_ID STATUS               LAST_MODI
--------------- -------------------- ---------
              1 Order placed         28-DEC-03
              2 Order placed         10-JUN-04
```

Merging Rows Using MERGE

The Oracle9*i* database introduced the MERGE statement that allows you to merge rows from one table into another. For example, you might want to merge changes to products listed in one table into the products table.

The store schema contains a table named product_changes that was created using the following CREATE TABLE statement in store_schema.sql:

```
CREATE TABLE product_changes (
  product_id INTEGER
    CONSTRAINT prod_changes_pk PRIMARY KEY,
  product_type_id INTEGER
    CONSTRAINT prod_changes_fk_product_types
    REFERENCES product_types(product_type_id),
  name VARCHAR2(30) NOT NULL,
  description VARCHAR2(50),
  price NUMBER(5, 2)
);
```

The following query shows the product_id, product_type_id, name, and price columns for the rows in the product_changes table:

```
SELECT product_id, product_type_id, name, price
FROM product_changes;

PRODUCT_ID PRODUCT_TYPE_ID NAME                                PRICE
---------- --------------- ----------------------------------- ----------
         1               1 Modern Science                          40
         2               1 New Chemistry                           35
         3               1 Supernova                            25.99
```

```
13                2 Lunar Landing                         15.99
14                2 Submarine                             15.99
15                2 Airplane                              15.99
```

Let's say the merge should do the following:

■ For existing rows with matching `product_id` values in `products` and `product_changes`, update the rows in `products` with the column values that are listed in `product_changes`. For example, product #1 has a different price in `product_changes` from that in `products`, so product #1's price must be updated in the `products` table. Similarly, product #2 has a different name and price and must be updated in the `products` table. Finally, product #3 has a different `product_type_id` and must be updated in `products`.

■ For new rows in `product_changes`, insert those new rows into the `products` table. Products #13, #14, and #15 are new in `product_changes` and must therefore be inserted into `products`.

The easiest way to learn how to use the MERGE statement is to see an example. The following example performs the merge as defined in the previous bullet points to merge the changes in `product_changes` into `products`:

```
MERGE INTO products p
USING product_changes pc ON (
  p.product_id = pc.product_id
)
WHEN MATCHED THEN
  UPDATE
  SET
    p.product_type_id = pc.product_type_id,
    p.name = pc.name,
    p.description = pc.description,
    p.price = pc.price
WHEN NOT MATCHED THEN
  INSERT (
    p.product_id, p.product_type_id, p.name,
    p.description, p.price
  ) VALUES (
    pc.product_id, pc.product_type_id, pc.name,
    pc.description, pc.price
  );
```

Notice the following points about the MERGE statement:

■ The MERGE INTO clause specifies the name of the table to merge the rows into. In the example, the table to merge rows into is the `products` table, which has an alias of p that is referenced in the rest of the MERGE statement.

■ The USING . . . ON clause specifies a table join. In the example, the join is made on the `product_id` columns in the `products` and `product_changes` tables; the `product_changes` table has an alias of pc that is referenced in the rest of the MERGE statement.

■ The WHEN MATCHED THEN clause specifies the action to take when the USING . . . ON clause is satisfied for a row. In the example, the action is an UPDATE statement that sets the product_type_id, name, description, and price columns of the existing row in the products table to the column values for the matching row in the product_ changes table.

■ The WHEN NOT MATCHED clause specifies the action to take when the USING . . . ON clause is *not* satisfied for a row. In the example, the action is an INSERT statement that adds a row to the products table, taking the column values from the row in the product_ changes table.

If you run the previous MERGE statement, you'll see that it reports six rows are merged, which are the rows with product_id values of 1, 2, 3, 13, 14, and 15. The following query retrieves the six merged rows from the products table:

```
SELECT product_id, product_type_id, name, price
FROM products
WHERE product_id IN (1, 2, 3, 13, 14, 15);
```

```
PRODUCT_ID PRODUCT_TYPE_ID NAME                                     PRICE
---------- --------------- ------------------------------- ----------
         1               1 Modern Science                              40
         2               1 New Chemistry                               35
         3               1 Supernova                                25.99
        13               2 Lunar Landing                           15.99
        14               2 Submarine                               15.99
        15               2 Airplane                                15.99
```

If you compare these rows with those shown in Chapter 1 in the section "The Products Table," you'll see the following changes in the rows returned by the previous query:

■ Product #1 has a new price.

■ Product #2 has a new name and price.

■ Product #3 has a new product type ID.

■ Products #13, #14, and #15 are new.

Now that you've seen how to make changes to the contents of tables, let's move on to database transactions.

Database Transactions

A database *transaction* is a group of SQL statements that are a *logical unit of work*. You can think of a transaction as an inseparable set of SQL statements that should be made permanent in the database (or undone) as a whole. An example of this would be a transfer of money from one bank account to another. One UPDATE statement would subtract from the total amount of money from one account, and another UPDATE would add money to the other account. Both the subtraction and the addition must either be permanently recorded in the database, or they both must be undone—otherwise money will be lost. This simple example uses only two UPDATE statements, but a more realistic transaction may consist of many INSERT, UPDATE, and DELETE statements.

Committing and Rolling Back a Transaction

To permanently record the results of the SQL statements in a transaction, you perform a *commit* with the COMMIT statement. To undo the results of the SQL statements, you perform a *rollback* with the ROLLBACK statement, which resets all the rows back to what they were originally. Any changes you make prior to performing a rollback will be undone, as long as you haven't disconnected from the database beforehand.

The following example adds a row to the customers table and then makes the change permanent by performing a COMMIT:

```
INSERT INTO customers
VALUES (6, 'Fred', 'Green', '01-JAN-1970', '800-555-1215');

1 row created.

COMMIT;

Commit complete.
```

The following example updates a row in the customers table and then undoes the change by performing a ROLLBACK:

```
UPDATE customers
SET first_name = 'Edward'
WHERE customer_id = 1;

1 row updated.

ROLLBACK;

Rollback complete.
```

You can verify the changes to the customers table using the following query:

```
SELECT *
FROM customers;

CUSTOMER_ID FIRST_NAME LAST_NAME  DOB       PHONE
----------- ---------- ---------- --------- ------------
          1 John       Brown      01-JAN-65 800-555-1211
          2 Cynthia    Green      05-FEB-68 800-555-1212
          3 Steve      White      16-MAR-71 800-555-1213
          4 Gail       Black                800-555-1214
          5 Doreen     Blue       20-MAY-70
          6 Fred       Green      01-JAN-70 800-555-1215
```

Notice that the result of the INSERT statement that added customer #6 is indeed made permanent by the COMMIT and that the result of the UPDATE statement that changed the first name of customer #1 is undone by the ROLLBACK.

Starting and Ending a Transaction

As mentioned, transactions are logical units of work you use to split up your database activities. A transaction has both a beginning and an end; it begins when one of the following events occurs:

- You connect to the database and perform the first DML statement.

- A previous transaction ends and you enter another DML statement.

A transaction ends when one of the following events occurs:

- You perform a COMMIT or a ROLLBACK statement.

- You perform a DDL statement, such as a CREATE TABLE statement, in which case a COMMIT is automatically performed.

- You perform a DCL statement, such as a GRANT statement, in which case a COMMIT is automatically performed. You'll learn about GRANT in the next chapter.

- You disconnect from the database. If you exit SQL*Plus normally by entering the EXIT command, a COMMIT is automatically performed for you. If SQL*Plus terminates abnormally—for example, if the computer on which SQL*Plus was running were to crash— a ROLLBACK is automatically performed. This applies to any program that accesses a database. For example, if you wrote a Java program that accessed a database and your program crashed, a ROLLBACK would be automatically performed.

- You perform a DML statement that fails, in which case a ROLLBACK is automatically performed for that individual DML statement.

TIP
It is considered poor practice not to explicitly commit or roll back your transactions once they are complete, so make sure you perform a COMMIT or ROLLBACK at the end of your transactions.

Savepoints

You can also set a *savepoint* at any point within a transaction. These allow you to roll back changes to that point. This might be useful if you have a very long transaction because if you make a mistake after you've set a savepoint, you don't have to roll back the transaction all the way to the start. You should use savepoints sparingly; you might be better off restructuring your transaction into smaller transactions instead. I'll show you an example of using a savepoint, but before we begin, let's check the details for product #1 and product #2:

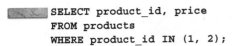
```
SELECT product_id, price
FROM products
WHERE product_id IN (1, 2);
```

```
PRODUCT_ID        PRICE
----------   ----------
         1        19.95
         2           30
```

So far, so good: the price for product #1 is $19.95, and the price for product #2 is $30. Next, let's increase the price of product #1 by 20 percent:

```
UPDATE products
SET price = price * 1.20
WHERE product_id = 1;
```

Set a savepoint here named save1. This will allow you to roll back any further DML statements and preserve the previous UPDATE:

```
SAVEPOINT save1;
```

Next, let's increase the price of product #2 by 30 percent:

```
UPDATE products
SET price = price * 1.30
WHERE product_id = 2;
```

Let's check the prices of the two products, just to make sure everything's set as we expect:

```
SELECT product_id, price
FROM products
WHERE product_id IN (1, 2);
```

```
PRODUCT_ID        PRICE
----------   ----------
         1        23.94
         2           39
```

Everything looks good: product #1's price is 20 percent greater, and product #2's price is 30 percent greater. Okay, let's roll back the transaction to the savepoint established earlier:

```
ROLLBACK TO SAVEPOINT save1;
```

This should preserve the new price set for product #1, but it will roll back the price for product #2 to its original price before we began, because the savepoint was set before the change to product #2's price was made:

```
SELECT product_id, price
FROM products
WHERE product_id IN (1, 2);
```

```
PRODUCT_ID        PRICE
----------   ----------
         1        23.94
         2           30
```

These are the expected results: product #1's new price is $23.94 and product #2's price is back to the original. Finally, roll back the entire transaction:

```
ROLLBACK;
```

This rolls back the changes all the way to the start of the transaction and undoes the change made to the price of product #1.

ACID Transaction Properties

Earlier, I defined a transaction as being a *logical unit of work*, that is, a grouping of related SQL statements that are either committed or rolled back as one unit. One example of this is a transfer of money from one bank account to another using two UPDATE statements, one that takes money out of one account, and another that puts that money into a different account. Both UPDATE statements may be considered to be a single transaction because both statements must be either committed or rolled back together; otherwise, money might be lost.

Database theory has a more rigorous definition of a transaction and states that a transaction has four fundamental properties, known as *ACID* properties:

- **Atomicity**   Transactions are committed or rolled back as a group, and are atomic, meaning that all SQL statements contained in a transaction are considered to be a single indivisible unit.

- **Consistency**   Transactions ensure that the database state remains consistent, meaning that the database starts at one consistent state and ends in another consistent state when the transaction finishes.

- **Isolation**   Separate transactions should appear to run without interfering with each other.

- **Durability**   Once a transaction has been committed, the database changes are preserved, even if the machine on which the database software runs later crashes.

The Oracle database software ensures that each transaction possesses these ACID properties and has extensive recovery facilities for restoring databases that may have crashed for one reason or another.

Concurrent Transactions

The Oracle database supports many users interacting with the database at the same time, with each user running their own transactions at the same time. These transactions are known as *concurrent* transactions.

If users are running transactions that affect the same table, the effects of those transactions are separated from each other until a COMMIT is performed. The following sequence of events, based on two transactions named T1 and T2 accessing the customers table, illustrates the separation of transactions:

1. T1 and T2 perform a SELECT that retrieves all the rows from the customers table.

2. T1 performs an INSERT to add a row in the customers table, but T1 doesn't perform a COMMIT.

3. T2 performs another SELECT and retrieves the same rows as those in step 1. T2 doesn't "see" the new row added by T1 in step 2.

4. T1 finally performs a COMMIT to permanently record the new row added in step 2.

5. T2 performs another SELECT and finally sees the new row added by T1.

To summarize: T2 doesn't see the changes made by T1 until T1 commits its changes. This is the default level of isolation between transactions. As you'll learn later in the section "Transaction Isolation Levels," you can change this level of isolation.

Table 8-1 shows example SQL statements that further illustrate concurrent transactions. The table shows the interleaved order in which statements are to be performed by two transactions named T1 and T2. T1 retrieves rows, adds a row, and updates a row in the customers table. T2 retrieves rows from the customers table. T2 doesn't see the changes made by T1 until T1 commits its changes.

You can enter the statements shown in Table 8-1 and see their results by starting two separate SQL*Plus sessions and connect as the store user for both sessions. Enter the statements in the interleaved order shown in the table into the SQL*Plus sessions.

Transaction 1 T1	Transaction 2 T2
`SELECT *` `FROM customers;`	`SELECT *` `FROM customers;`

`INSERT INTO customers (`
`   customer_id, first_name, last_name`
`) VALUES (`
`   7, 'Jason', 'Price'`
`);`	

`UPDATE customers`
`SET last_name = 'Orange'`
`WHERE customer_id = 2;`	

`SELECT *`
`FROM customers;`
The returned result set contains the new row and the update.
	`SELECT *`
	`FROM customers;`
	The returned result set doesn't contain the new row or the update made by T1. Instead, the result set contains the original rows.

`COMMIT;`	

	`SELECT *`
	`FROM customers;`
	The returned result set contains the new row and the update made by T1.

TABLE 8-1. *Concurrent Transactions*

Transaction Locking

To support concurrent transactions, an Oracle database must ensure that the data in the tables remains valid. It does this through the use of *locks*. Consider the following example in which two transactions named T1 and T2 attempt to modify customer #1 in the `customers` table:

1. T1 performs an UPDATE to modify customer #1, but T1 doesn't perform a COMMIT. T1 is said to have "locked" the row.

2. T2 also attempts to perform an UPDATE to modify customer #1, but since this row is already locked by T1, T2 is prevented from getting a lock on the row. T2's UPDATE statement has to wait until T1 ends and frees the lock on the row.

3. T1 ends by performing a COMMIT, thus freeing the lock on the row.

4. T2 gets the lock on the row and the UPDATE is performed. T2 holds the lock on the row until T2 ends.

To summarize: A transaction cannot get a lock on a row while another transaction already holds the lock on that row.

NOTE
The easiest way to understand default locking is: readers don't block readers, writers don't block readers, and writers only block writers when they attempt to modify the same row.

Transaction Isolation Levels

The *transaction isolation level* is the degree to which the changes made by one transaction are separated from other transactions running concurrently. Before you see the details of the various transaction isolation levels, you need to understand the types of problems that may occur when current transactions attempt to access the same rows in a table.

In the following bullets, you'll see examples of two concurrent transactions that are accessing the same rows to illustrate the three types of potential transaction processing problems:

- **Phantom reads**   T1 reads a set of rows returned by a specified WHERE clause. T2 then inserts a new row, which also happens to satisfy the WHERE clause of the query previously used by T1. T1 then reads the rows again using the same query, but now sees the additional row just inserted by T2. This new row is known as a "phantom" because to T1 this row seems to have magically appeared.

- **Nonrepeatable reads**   T1 reads a row, and T2 updates the same row just read by T1. T1 then reads the same row again and discovers that the row it read earlier is now different. This is known as a "nonrepeatable" read, because the row originally read by T1 has been changed.

- **Dirty reads**   T1 updates a row, but doesn't commit the update. T2 reads the updated row. T1 then performs a rollback, undoing the previous update. Now the row just read by T2 is no longer valid (it's "dirty") because the update made by T1 wasn't committed when the row was read by T2.

To deal with these potential problems, databases implement various levels of transaction isolation to prevent concurrent transactions from interfering with each other. The SQL standard defines the following transaction isolation levels, shown in order of increasing isolation:

- **READ UNCOMMITTED**   Phantom reads, nonrepeatable reads, and dirty reads are permitted.

- **READ COMMITTED**   Phantom reads and nonrepeatable reads are permitted, but dirty reads are not.

- **REPEATABLE READ**   Phantom reads are permitted, but nonrepeatable and dirty reads are not.

- **SERIALIZABLE**   Phantom reads, nonrepeatable reads, and dirty reads are not permitted.

The Oracle database supports the READ COMMITTED and SERIALIZABLE transaction isolation levels. It doesn't support READ UNCOMMITTED or REPEATABLE READ levels.

The default transaction isolation level defined by the SQL standard is SERIALIZABLE, but the default used by the Oracle database is READ COMMITTED, which is usually acceptable for nearly all applications.

CAUTION
Although you can use SERIALIZABLE with the Oracle database, it may increase the time your SQL statements take to complete, so you should only use SERILIZABLE if you absolutely have to.

You set the transaction isolation level using the SET TRANSACTION statement. For example, the following statement sets the transaction isolation level to SERIALIZABLE:

```
SET TRANSACTION ISOLATION LEVEL SERIALIZABLE;
```

You'll see an example of a transaction that uses the isolation level of SERIALIZABLE next.

A SERIALIZABLE Transaction Example

In this section, you'll see an example that shows the effect of setting the transaction isolation level to SERIALIZABLE.

The example uses two transactions named T1 and T2. T1 has the default isolation level of READ COMMITTED; T2 has a transaction isolation level of SERIALIZABLE. T1 and T2 will read the rows in the customers table, and then T1 will insert a new row and update an existing row in the customers table. Because T2 is SERIALIZABLE, it doesn't "see" the inserted row or the update made to the existing row by T1, even *after* T1 commits its changes. That's because reading the inserted row would be a phantom read, and reading the update would be a nonrepeatable read, which is not permitted by SERIALIZABLE transactions.

Table 8-2 shows the SQL statements that make up T1 and T2 in the interleaved order in which the statements are to be performed.

Transaction 1 T1 (READ COMMITTED)	Transaction 2 T2 (SERIALIZABLE)
	SET TRANSACTION ISOLATION LEVEL SERIALIZABLE;
SELECT * FROM customers;	SELECT * FROM customers;

INSERT INTO customers (
  customer_id, first_name, last_name
) VALUES (
  8, 'Steve', 'Button'
);	

UPDATE customers SET last_name = 'Yellow' WHERE customer_id = 3;	
COMMIT;	
SELECT * FROM customers; The returned result set contains the new row and the update.	SELECT * FROM customers; The returned result set *still* doesn't contain the new row or the update made by T1. That's because T2 is SERIALIZABLE.

TABLE 8-2. *Serializable Transactions*

Query Flashbacks

If you mistakenly commit changes and you want to view rows as they originally were, you can use a query flashback. You can then use the results of a query flashback to manually change rows back to their original values if you need to.

In addition, flashbacks can be based on a datetime or system change number (SCN). The database uses SCNs to track changes made to data, and you can use them to flash back to a particular SCN in the database.

Granting the Privilege for Using Flashbacks

Flashbacks use the PL/SQL DBMS_FLASHBACK package, for which you must have the EXECUTE privilege. The following example connects as the sys user and grants the EXECUTE privilege on DBMS_FLASHBACK to the store user:

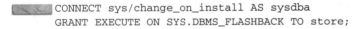
```
CONNECT sys/change_on_install AS sysdba
GRANT EXECUTE ON SYS.DBMS_FLASHBACK TO store;
```

> **NOTE**
> *Speak with your DBA if you get errors when performing these statements. You'll learn more about privileges in the next chapter. You'll learn more about PL/SQL packages in Chapter 11.*

Time Query Flashbacks

The following example connects as `store` and retrieves the `product_id`, `name`, and `price` columns for the first five rows from the `products` table:

```
CONNECT store/store_password
SELECT product_id, name, price
FROM products
WHERE product_id <= 5;

PRODUCT_ID NAME                                PRICE
---------- ------------------------------ ----------
         1 Modern Science                      19.95
         2 Chemistry                              30
         3 Supernova                           25.99
         4 Tank War                            13.95
         5 Z Files                             49.99
```

The next example reduces the price of these rows, commits the change, and retrieves the rows again so you can see the new prices:

```
UPDATE products
SET price = price * 0.75
WHERE product_id <= 5;
COMMIT;
SELECT product_id, name, price
FROM products
WHERE product_id <= 5;

PRODUCT_ID NAME                                PRICE
---------- ------------------------------ ----------
         1 Modern Science                      14.96
         2 Chemistry                            22.5
         3 Supernova                           19.49
         4 Tank War                            10.46
         5 Z Files                             37.49
```

The next example executes the `DBMS_FLASHBACK.ENABLE_AT_TIME()` procedure, which enables you to perform a flashback to a particular datetime. This procedure accepts a datetime, and the example passes `SYSDATE - 10 / 1440` to the procedure, which is ten minutes in the past:

```
EXECUTE DBMS_FLASHBACK.ENABLE_AT_TIME(SYSDATE - 10 / 1440);
```

NOTE
*24 hours * 60 minutes per hour = 1440 minutes.*

Any queries you execute now will display the rows as they were ten minutes ago. Assuming you performed the earlier UPDATE less than ten minutes ago, the following query will display the prices as they were before you updated them.

```
SELECT product_id, name, price
FROM products
WHERE product_id <= 5;

PRODUCT_ID NAME                                PRICE
---------- ----------------------------- ----------
         1 Modern Science                      19.95
         2 Chemistry                              30
         3 Supernova                           25.99
         4 Tank War                            13.95
         5 Z Files                             49.99
```

To disable a flashback, you execute DBMS_FLASHBACK.DISABLE(), as shown in the following example:

```
EXECUTE DBMS_FLASHBACK.DISABLE();
```

CAUTION
You must disable a flashback before you can enable it again.

Now when you perform queries, the rows as they currently exist will be retrieved. For example:

```
SELECT product_id, name, price
FROM products
WHERE product_id <= 5;

PRODUCT_ID NAME                                PRICE
---------- ----------------------------- ----------
         1 Modern Science                      14.96
         2 Chemistry                            22.5
         3 Supernova                           19.49
         4 Tank War                            10.46
         5 Z Files                             37.49
```

System Change Number Query Flashbacks

Flashbacks based on system change numbers (SCNs) can be more precise than those based on a time, because the database uses SCNs to track changes. To get the current SCN, you can execute DBMS_FLASHBACK.GET_SYSTEM_CHANGE_NUMBER(). For example:

```
VARIABLE current_scn NUMBER
EXECUTE :current_scn := DBMS_FLASHBACK.GET_SYSTEM_CHANGE_NUMBER();
PRINT current_scn

CURRENT_SCN
-----------
     292111
```

The next example adds a row to the `products` table, commits the change, and retrieves the new row:

```
INSERT INTO products (
  product_id, product_type_id, name, description, price
) VALUES (
  15, 1, 'Physics', 'Textbook on physics', 39.95
);
COMMIT;
SELECT *
FROM products
WHERE product_id = 15;


PRODUCT_ID PRODUCT_TYPE_ID NAME
---------- --------------- -----------------------------
DESCRIPTION                                           PRICE
-------------------------------------------------- ----------
        15               1 Physics
Textbook on physics                                   39.95
```

The next example executes the `DBMS_FLASHBACK.ENABLE_AT_SYSTEM_CHANGE_NUMBER()` procedure, which enables you to perform a flashback to an SCN. This procedure accepts an SCN and the example passes the `current_scn` variable to the procedure:

```
EXECUTE DBMS_FLASHBACK.ENABLE_AT_SYSTEM_CHANGE_NUMBER(:current_scn);
```

Any queries you execute now will display the rows as they were at the SCN stored in `current_scn` before you performed the `INSERT`. The following query attempts to get the row with a `product_id` of 15 and fails because that new row was added after the SCN stored in `current_scn`:

```
SELECT product_id
FROM products
WHERE product_id = 15;


no rows selected
```

To disable a flashback, you execute `DBMS_FLASHBACK.DISABLE()`, as shown in the following example:

```
EXECUTE DBMS_FLASHBACK.DISABLE();
```

If you perform the previous query again, you'll see the new row that was added by the `INSERT`.

NOTE
If you followed along with the examples, go ahead and rerun the `store_schema.sql` *script to re-create everything. That way, the results of your SQL statements will match mine as you progress through the rest of this book.*

Summary

In this chapter, you learned

- How to add rows using the INSERT statement.

- How to modify rows using the UPDATE statement.

- How to remove rows using the DELETE statement.

- How the database maintains referential integrity through the enforcement of constraints.

- How to use the DEFAULT keyword to specify default values for columns.

- How to merge rows using the MERGE statement.

- That a database transaction is a group of SQL statements that comprise a logical unit of work.

- That an Oracle database can handle multiple transactions that are performed concurrently.

In the next chapter, you'll learn about database security.

CHAPTER
9

Database Security

In this chapter, you will

- Learn more about users
- See how privileges are used to enable users to perform tasks in the database
- Explore how privileges are divided into two types: system privileges and object privileges
- Learn how system privileges allow you to perform actions such as execute DDL statements
- See how object privileges allow you to perform actions such as execute DML statements
- Explore how to manage privileges using roles

NOTE
You'll need to type in the SQL statements shown in this chapter.

Users

In this section, you'll learn how to create a user, alter a user's password, and drop a user.

Creating a User

To create a user in the database, you use the CREATE USER statement. The simplified syntax for the CREATE USER statement is as follows:

```
CREATE USER user_name IDENTIFIED BY password
[DEFAULT TABLESPACE def_tabspace]
[TEMPORARY TABLESPACE temp_tabspace];
```

where

- *user_name* specifies the name of the database user.
- *password* specifies the password for the database user.
- *def_tabspace* specifies the default tablespace where objects are stored. These objects include tables. If you omit a default tablespace, the default SYSTEM tablespace is used, which always exists in a database. Note: Tablespaces are used by the database to separate objects. For more details on tablespaces, speak with your DBA or consult the Oracle reference documentation.
- *temp_tabspace* specifies the default tablespace where temporary objects are stored. These objects include temporary tables that you'll learn about in the next chapter. If you omit a temporary tablespace, the default SYSTEM tablespace is used.

The following example connects as system and creates a user named jason with a password of price:

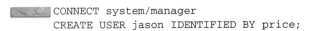
```
CONNECT system/manager
CREATE USER jason IDENTIFIED BY price;
```

NOTE

If you want to follow along with these examples you'll need to connect to the database as a privileged user. I used the system user in the example, which has a default password of manager in my database. If you're not acting as your own DBA, you'll need to speak with your DBA to get the password for a privileged user who is able to create users.

The next example creates a user named henry and specifies a default and temporary tablespace:

```
CREATE USER henry IDENTIFIED BY hooray
DEFAULT TABLESPACE users
TEMPORARY TABLESPACE temp;
```

NOTE

*If your database doesn't have tablespaces named users and temp, you can skip this example. The henry user isn't used elsewhere in this book, and I included the example only so you can see how to specify tablespaces for a user. You can view all the tablespaces in a database by connecting as the system user and running the query SELECT * FROM dba_tablespaces.*

If you want a user to be able to do things in the database, that user must be granted the necessary permissions to do those things. For example, to connect to the database a user must be granted the permission to create a session, which is the CREATE SESSION system privilege. Permissions are granted by a privileged user (system, for example) using the GRANT statement.

The following example grants the CREATE SESSION permission to jason:

```
GRANT CREATE SESSION TO jason;
```

You are now able to connect as jason.

The following example creates other users used in this chapter and grants the CREATE SESSION privilege to those users:

```
CREATE USER steve IDENTIFIED BY button;
CREATE USER gail IDENTIFIED BY seymour;
GRANT CREATE SESSION TO steve, gail;
```

Changing a User's Password

You can change a user's password using the ALTER USER statement. For example, the following ALTER USER statement changes the password for jason to marcus:

```
ALTER USER jason IDENTIFIED BY marcus;
```

You can also change the password for the user you're currently logged in as using the PASSWORD command. After you enter PASSWORD, SQL*Plus prompts you to enter the old password and the new password twice for confirmation. The following example connects as jason and executes PASSWORD:

```
CONNECT jason/marcus
PASSWORD
Changing password for JASON
Old password: ******
New password: ******
Retype new password: ******
Password changed
```

Deleting a User

You delete a user using the DROP USER statement. The following example connects as system and uses DROP USER to delete jason:

```
CONNECT system/manager
DROP USER jason;
```

> **NOTE**
> *You must add the keyword CASCADE after the user's name in the DROP USER statement if that user's schema contains objects such as tables and so on.*

System Privileges

A *system privilege* allows a user to perform certain actions within the database—such as executing DDL statements. For example, CREATE TABLE allows a user to create a table in their schema. Some of the commonly used system privileges are shown in Table 9-1.

> **NOTE**
> *You can get the full list of system privileges in the Oracle SQL Reference manual.*

Granting System Privileges to a User

As mentioned, you use GRANT to grant a system privilege to a user. The following example grants some system privileges to steve using GRANT (assuming you're still connected to the database as system):

```
GRANT CREATE SESSION, CREATE USER, CREATE TABLE TO steve;
```

You can also use WITH ADMIN OPTION to enable a user to grant a privilege to another user. The following example grants the EXECUTE ANY PROCEDURE privilege with the ADMIN option to steve:

```
GRANT EXECUTE ANY PROCEDURE TO steve WITH ADMIN OPTION;
```

System Privilege	Allows You to ...
CREATE SESSION	Connect to a database.
CREATE SEQUENCE	Create a sequence. A sequence is a series of numbers, which are typically used to automatically populate a primary key column. You'll learn about sequences in the next chapter.
CREATE SYNONYM	Create a synonym. A synonym allows you to reference a table in another schema. You'll learn about synonyms later in this chapter.
CREATE TABLE	Create a table.
CREATE ANY TABLE	Create a table in any schema.
DROP TABLE	Drop a table.
DROP ANY TABLE	Drop a table from any schema.
CREATE PROCEDURE	Create a stored procedure.
EXECUTE ANY PROCEDURE	Execute a procedure in any schema.
CREATE USER	Create a user.
DROP USER	Drop a user.
CREATE VIEW	Create a view. A view is a stored query that allows you to access multiple tables and columns. You may then query the view as you would a table. You'll learn about views in the next chapter.

TABLE 9-1. *Commonly Used System Privileges*

The EXECUTE ANY PROCEDURE can then be granted to another user by steve. The following example connects as steve and grants EXECUTE ANY PROCEDURE to gail:

```
CONNECT steve/button
GRANT EXECUTE ANY PROCEDURE TO gail;
```

You can grant a privilege to all users by granting to PUBLIC. The following example connects as system and grants the EXECUTE ANY PROCEDURE privilege to PUBLIC:

```
CONNECT system/manager
GRANT EXECUTE ANY PROCEDURE TO PUBLIC;
```

Every user in the database now has the EXECUTE ANY PROCEDURE privilege.

Checking System Privileges Granted to a User

You can check which system privileges a user has by querying user_sys_privs. Table 9-2 describes the columns in user_sys_privs.

Column	Type	Description
username	VARCHAR2(30)	Name of the current user.
privilege	VARCHAR2(40)	System privilege.
admin_option	VARCHAR2(3)	Whether the user is able to grant the privilege to another user.

TABLE 9-2. *Some Columns in* user_sys_privs

NOTE
user_sys_privs *forms part of the Oracle database's data dictionary.*
The data dictionary stores information on the database.

The following example connects as steve and queries user_sys_privs:

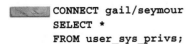

```
CONNECT steve/button
SELECT *
FROM user_sys_privs;

USERNAME                 PRIVILEGE                           ADM
------------------------ ----------------------------------- ---
PUBLIC                   EXECUTE ANY PROCEDURE               NO
STEVE                    CREATE SESSION                      NO
STEVE                    CREATE TABLE                        NO
STEVE                    CREATE USER                         NO
STEVE                    EXECUTE ANY PROCEDURE               YES
```

The next example connects as gail and queries user_sys_privs:

```
CONNECT gail/seymour
SELECT *
FROM user_sys_privs;

USERNAME                 PRIVILEGE                           ADM
------------------------ ----------------------------------- ---
GAIL                     CREATE SESSION                      NO
GAIL                     EXECUTE ANY PROCEDURE               NO
PUBLIC                   EXECUTE ANY PROCEDURE               NO
```

Notice gail has EXECUTE ANY PROCEDURE that was granted earlier by steve.

Making Use of System Privileges
Once a user has been granted a system privilege, they can use it to perform the specified task. For example, steve has the CREATE USER privilege, so he is able to create a user:

```
CONNECT steve/button
CREATE USER roy IDENTIFIED BY williams;
```

If `steve` were to attempt to use a system privilege he doesn't have, the database will return the error `ORA-01031: insufficient privileges`. For example, `steve` doesn't have the `DROP USER` privilege, and in the following example `steve` attempts to drop `roy` and fails:

```
SQL> DROP USER roy;
DROP USER roy
*
ERROR at line 1:
ORA-01031: insufficient privileges
```

Revoking System Privileges from a User

You revoke system privileges from a user using `REVOKE`. The following example connects as `system` and revokes the `CREATE TABLE` privilege from `steve`:

```
CONNECT system/manager
REVOKE CREATE TABLE FROM steve;
```

The next example revokes `EXECUTE ANY PROCEDURE` from `steve`:

```
REVOKE EXECUTE ANY PROCEDURE FROM steve;
```

When you revoke `EXECUTE ANY PROCEDURE` from `steve`—who has already passed on this privilege to `gail`—`gail` still gets to keep the privilege:

```
CONNECT gail/seymour
SELECT *
FROM user_sys_privs;
```

```
USERNAME            PRIVILEGE                       ADM
------------------  ------------------------------  ---
GAIL                CREATE SESSION                  NO
GAIL                EXECUTE ANY PROCEDURE           NO
PUBLIC              EXECUTE ANY PROCEDURE           NO
```

Object Privileges

An *object privilege* allows a user to perform certain actions on database objects, such as executing DML statements on tables. For example, `INSERT ON store.products` allows a user to insert rows into the `products` table of the `store` schema. Some of the commonly used object privileges are shown in Table 9-3.

NOTE
You can get the full list of object privileges in the Oracle SQL Reference manual.

Object Privilege	Allows a User to ...
SELECT	Perform a select
INSERT	Perform an insert
UPDATE	Perform an update
DELETE	Perform a delete
EXECUTE	Execute a stored procedure

TABLE 9-3.   *Commonly Used Object Privileges*

Granting Object Privileges to a User

You use GRANT to grant an object privilege to a user. The following example connects as store and grants the SELECT, INSERT, and UPDATE object privileges on the products table to steve along with the SELECT privilege on the employees table:

```
CONNECT store/store_password
GRANT SELECT, INSERT, UPDATE ON store.products TO steve;
GRANT SELECT ON store.employees TO steve;
```

The next example grants the UPDATE privilege on the last_name and salary columns to steve:

```
GRANT UPDATE (last_name, salary) ON store.employees TO steve;
```

You can also use the GRANT option to enable a user to grant a privilege to another user. The following example grants the SELECT privilege on the customers table with the GRANT option to steve:

```
GRANT SELECT ON store.customers TO steve WITH GRANT OPTION;
```

NOTE
You use the GRANT option when enabling a user to grant an object privilege to another user, and you use the ADMIN option when enabling a user to grant a system privilege to another user.

The SELECT ON store.customers privilege can then be granted to another user by steve. The following example connects as steve and grants this privilege to gail:

```
CONNECT steve/button
GRANT SELECT ON store.customers TO gail;
```

Checking Object Privileges Made

You can check which table object privileges a user has made to other users by querying user_tab_privs_made. Table 9-4 documents the columns in user_tab_privs_made.

Column	Type	Description
grantee	VARCHAR2(30)	User to whom the privilege was granted.
table_name	VARCHAR2(30)	Name of the object (such as a table) on which privilege was granted.
grantor	VARCHAR2(30)	User who granted the privilege.
privilege	VARCHAR2(40)	Privilege on the object.
grantable	VARCHAR2(3)	Whether the grantee can grant the privilege to another. Equal to YES or NO.
hierarchy	VARCHAR2(3)	Whether the privilege forms part of a hierarchy. Equal to YES or NO.

TABLE 9-4. *Some Columns in user_tab_privs_made*

The following example connects as store and queries user_tab_privs_made. Since there are so many rows, I'll limit the retrieved rows to those where table_name is PRODUCTS:

```
CONNECT store/store_password
SELECT *
FROM user_tab_privs_made
WHERE table_name = 'PRODUCTS';

GRANTEE                  TABLE_NAME
--------------------    ----------------------------
GRANTOR                  PRIVILEGE                    GRA HIE
--------------------    ----------------------------  --- ---
PRODUCT_MANAGER          PRODUCTS
STORE                    DELETE                        NO  NO

PRODUCT_MANAGER          PRODUCTS
STORE                    INSERT                        NO  NO

PRODUCT_MANAGER          PRODUCTS
STORE                    SELECT                        NO  NO

PRODUCT_MANAGER          PRODUCTS
STORE                    UPDATE                        NO  NO

STEVE                    PRODUCTS
STORE                    INSERT                        NO  NO

STEVE                    PRODUCTS
STORE                    SELECT                        NO  NO

STEVE                    PRODUCTS
STORE                    UPDATE                        NO  NO
```

You can check which column object privileges a user has made by querying user_col_privs_made. Table 9-5 documents the columns in user_col_privs_made.

Column	Type	Description
grantee	VARCHAR2(30)	User to whom the privilege was granted.
table_name	VARCHAR2(30)	Name of the object on which privilege was granted.
column_name	VARCHAR2(30)	Name of the object on which privilege was granted.
grantor	VARCHAR2(30)	User who granted the privilege.
privilege	VARCHAR2(40)	Privilege on the object.
grantable	VARCHAR2(3)	Whether the grantee can grant the privilege to another. Equal to YES or NO.

TABLE 9-5. *Some Columns in* user_col_privs_made

The following example queries user_col_privs_made:

```
SELECT *
FROM user_col_privs_made;

GRANTEE                                 TABLE_NAME
--------------------------------------- -------------
COLUMN_NAME                             GRANTOR
--------------------------------------- -------------
PRIVILEGE                                         GRA
--------------------------------------- ---
STEVE                                   EMPLOYEES
LAST_NAME                               STORE
UPDATE                                            NO

STEVE                                   EMPLOYEES
SALARY                                  STORE
UPDATE                                            NO
```

Checking Object Privileges Received

You can check which object privileges on a table a user has received by querying the user_tab_privs_recd table. Table 9-6 documents the columns in user_tab_privs_recd.

The next example connects as steve and queries user_tab_privs_recd:

```
CONNECT steve/button
SELECT *
FROM user_tab_privs_recd;

OWNER                           TABLE_NAME
------------------------------- -----------------
```

```
GRANTOR
------------------------------
PRIVILEGE                            GRA HIE
------------------------------------ --- ---
STORE                     CUSTOMERS
STORE
SELECT                               YES NO

STORE                     PRODUCTS
STORE
INSERT                               NO  NO

STORE                     PRODUCTS
STORE
SELECT                               NO  NO

STORE                     PRODUCTS
STORE
UPDATE                               NO  NO

STORE                     EMPLOYEES
STORE
SELECT                               NO  NO
```

You can check which column object privileges a user has received by querying `user_col_privs_recd`. Table 9-7 documents the columns in `user_col_privs_recd`.

Column	Type	Description
owner	VARCHAR2(30)	User who owns the object.
table_name	VARCHAR2(30)	Name of the object on which the privilege was granted.
grantor	VARCHAR2(30)	User who granted the privilege.
privilege	VARCHAR2(40)	Privilege on the object.
grantable	VARCHAR2(3)	Whether the grantee can grant the privilege to another. Equal to YES or NO.
hierarchy	VARCHAR2(3)	Whether the privilege forms part of a hierarchy. Equal to YES or NO.

TABLE 9-6.   *Some Columns in* `user_tab_privs_recd`

Column	Type	Description
owner	VARCHAR2(30)	User who owns the object.
table_name	VARCHAR2(30)	Name of the table on which the privilege was granted.
column_name	VARCHAR2(30)	Name of the column on which privilege was granted.
grantor	VARCHAR2(30)	User who granted the privilege.
privilege	VARCHAR2(40)	Privilege on the object.
grantable	VARCHAR2(3)	Whether the grantee can grant the privilege to another. Equal to YES or NO.

TABLE 9-7. *Some Columns in* user_col_privs_recd

The following example queries user_col_privs_recd:

```
SELECT *
FROM user_col_privs_recd;

OWNER                                   TABLE_NAME
--------------------------------------- -------------
COLUMN_NAME                             GRANTOR
--------------------------------------- -------------
PRIVILEGE                                         GRA
--------------------------------------- ---
STORE                                   EMPLOYEES
LAST_NAME                               STORE
UPDATE                                             NO

STORE                                   EMPLOYEES
SALARY                                  STORE
UPDATE                                             NO
```

Making Use of Object Privileges

Once a user has been granted an object privilege, they can use it to perform the specified task. For example, steve has the SELECT privilege on store.customers:

```
CONNECT steve/button
SELECT *
FROM store.customers;

CUSTOMER_ID FIRST_NAME LAST_NAME  DOB       PHONE
----------- ---------- ---------- --------- ------------
          1 John       Brown      01-JAN-65 800-555-1211
          2 Cynthia    Green      05-FEB-68 800-555-1212
```

```
     3 Steve      White       16-MAR-71 800-555-1213
     4 Gail       Black                 800-555-1214
     5 Doreen     Blue        20-MAY-70
```

If `steve` were to attempt to retrieve from the `purchases` table—for which he doesn't have any permissions—the database will return the error `ORA-00942: table or view does not exist`:

```
SQL> SELECT *
  2  FROM store.purchases;
FROM store.purchases
           *
ERROR at line 2:
ORA-00942: table or view does not exist
```

Synonyms

In the examples in the previous section, you saw that you can access tables in another schema by specifying the schema name followed by the table. For example, when `steve` retrieved rows from the `customers` table in the `store` schema, he performed a `SELECT` from `store.customers`. You can avoid having to enter the schema name by creating a *synonym* for a table, which you create using the `CREATE SYNONYM` statement.

Let's take a look at an example. First, connect as `system` and grant the `CREATE SYNONYM` system privilege to `steve`:

```
CONNECT system/manager
GRANT CREATE SYNONYM TO steve;
```

Next, connect as `steve` and perform a `CREATE SYNONYM` statement to create a synonym for the `store.customers` table:

```
CONNECT steve/button
CREATE SYNONYM customers FOR store.customers;
```

To retrieve rows from `store.customers`, all `steve` has to do is to reference the `customers` synonym in the `FROM` clause of a `SELECT` statement. For example:

```
SELECT *
FROM customers;
```

```
CUSTOMER_ID FIRST_NAME LAST_NAME  DOB       PHONE
----------- ---------- ---------- --------- ------------
          1 John       Brown      01-JAN-65 800-555-1211
          2 Cynthia    Green      05-FEB-68 800-555-1212
          3 Steve      White      16-MAR-71 800-555-1213
          4 Gail       Black                800-555-1214
          5 Doreen     Blue       20-MAY-70
```

Public Synonyms

You can also create a *public* synonym for a table. When you do this, all users see the synonym. The following statements perform the following tasks:

1. Connect as `system`

2. Grant the `CREATE PUBLIC SYNONYM` system privilege to `store`

3. Connect as `store`

4. Create a public synonym named `products` for `store.products`

   ```
   CONNECT system/manager
   GRANT CREATE PUBLIC SYNONYM TO store;
   CONNECT store/store_password
   CREATE PUBLIC SYNONYM products FOR store.products;
   ```

If you connect as `steve`, who has the `SELECT` privilege on `store.products`, you can retrieve from `store.products` through the `products` public synonym:

```
CONNECT steve/button
SELECT *
FROM products;
```

Even though a public synonym has been created for `store.products`, a user still needs object privileges on that table to actually access the table. For example, `gail` can see the `products` public synonym, but `gail` doesn't have any object privileges on `store.products`. Therefore, if `gail` attempts to retrieve rows from `products`, the database returns the error `ORA-00942: table or view does not exist`:

```
SQL> CONNECT gail/seymour
Connected.
SQL> SELECT * FROM products;
SELECT * FROM products
              *
ERROR at line 1:
ORA-00942: table or view does not exist
```

If `gail` had the `SELECT` object privilege on the `store.products` table, the previous `SELECT` would succeed.

If a user has other object privileges, that user can exercise those object privileges through a synonym. For example, if `gail` had the `INSERT` object privilege on the `store.products` table, `gail` would be able to add a row to `store.products` through the `products` synonym.

Revoking Object Privileges

You revoke object privileges using `REVOKE`. The following example connects as `store` and revokes the `INSERT` privilege on the `products` table from `steve`:

```
CONNECT store/store_password
REVOKE INSERT ON products FROM steve;
```

The next example revokes the SELECT privilege on the customers table from steve:

```
REVOKE SELECT ON store.customers FROM steve;
```

When you revoke SELECT ON store.customers from steve—who has already passed on this privilege to gail—gail also loses the privilege.

Roles

A *role* is a group of privileges that you can assign to a user or another role. The following points summarize the benefits of roles:

- Rather than assigning privileges one at a time directly to a user, you can create a role, assign privileges to that role, and then grant that role to multiple users and roles.

- When you add or delete a privilege from a role, all users and roles assigned that role automatically receive or lose that privilege.

- You can assign multiple roles to a user or role.

- You can assign a password to a role.

As you can see from these points, roles can help you manage multiple privileges assigned to multiple users.

Creating Roles

To create a role, you must have the CREATE ROLE system privilege. As you'll see in a later example, the store user also needs the ability to grant the CREATE USER system privilege with the ADMIN option. The following example connects as system, and grants the required privileges to store:

```
CONNECT system/manager
GRANT CREATE ROLE TO store;
GRANT CREATE USER TO store WITH ADMIN OPTION;
```

Table 9-8 shows the roles you'll create shortly.

You create a role using the CREATE ROLE statement. The following statements connect as store and create the three roles shown in Table 9-8:

```
CONNECT store/store_password
CREATE ROLE product_manager;
CREATE ROLE hr_manager;
CREATE ROLE overall_manager IDENTIFIED by manager_password;
```

Notice overall_manager has a password of manager_password.

Granting Privileges to Roles

You grant privileges to a role using the GRANT statement. You can grant both system and object privileges to a role, as well as grant another role to a role. The following example grants the

Role Name	Has Permissions to …
product_manager	Perform SELECT, INSERT, UPDATE, and DELETE operations on the product_types and products tables.
hr_manager	Perform SELECT, INSERT, UPDATE, and DELETE operations on the salary_grades and employees tables. Also, hr_manager is able to create users.
overall_manager	Perform SELECT, INSERT, UPDATE, and DELETE operations on all the tables shown in the previous roles; overall_manager will be granted the previous roles.

TABLE 9-8. *Roles to be Created*

required privileges to the product_manager and hr_manager roles, and grants these two roles to overall_manager:

```
GRANT SELECT, INSERT, UPDATE, DELETE
  ON product_types TO product_manager;
GRANT SELECT, INSERT, UPDATE, DELETE
  ON products TO product_manager;
GRANT SELECT, INSERT, UPDATE, DELETE
  ON salary_grades TO hr_manager;
GRANT SELECT, INSERT, UPDATE, DELETE
  ON employees TO hr_manager;
GRANT CREATE USER TO hr_manager;
GRANT product_manager, hr_manager TO overall_manager;
```

Granting Roles to a User

You grant a role to a user using GRANT. The following example grants the overall_manager role to steve:

```
GRANT overall_manager TO steve;
```

Checking Roles Granted to a User

You can check which roles have been granted to a user by querying user_role_privs. Table 9-9 defines the columns in user_role_privs.

The following example connects as steve and queries user_role_privs:

```
CONNECT steve/button
SELECT *
FROM user_role_privs;

USERNAME             GRANTED_ROLE              ADM DEF OS_
-------------------- ------------------------- --- --- ---
STEVE                OVERALL_MANAGER           YES YES NO
```

Column	Type	Description
username	VARCHAR2(30)	Name of the user to whom the role has been granted.
granted_role	VARCHAR2(30)	Name of the role granted to the user.
admin_option	VARCHAR2(3)	Whether the user is able to grant the role to another user or role. Equal to YES or NO.
default_role	VARCHAR2(3)	Whether the role is enabled by default when the user connects to the database. Equal to YES or NO.
os_granted	VARCHAR2(3)	Whether the role was granted by the operating system.

TABLE 9-9. *Some Columns in* user_role_privs

A user who creates a role is also granted that role by default. The following example connects as store and queries user_role_privs:

```
CONNECT store/store_password
SELECT *
FROM user_role_privs;
```

```
USERNAME              GRANTED_ROLE               ADM DEF OS_
----------------      -------------------------  --- --- ---
STORE                 CONNECT                    NO  YES NO
STORE                 HR_MANAGER                 YES YES NO
STORE                 OVERALL_MANAGER            YES YES NO
STORE                 PRODUCT_MANAGER            YES YES NO
STORE                 RESOURCE                   NO  YES NO
```

Notice store has the roles CONNECT and RESOURCE in addition to the roles store created earlier.

NOTE
CONNECT and RESOURCE are built-in roles that were granted to store when you ran the store_schema.sql script. As you'll see in the next section, the CONNECT and RESOURCE roles contain multiple privileges.

Checking System Privileges Granted to a Role

You can check which system privileges have been granted to a role by querying role_sys_privs. Table 9-10 defines the columns in role_sys_privs.

Column	Type	Description
role	VARCHAR2(30)	Name of the role.
privilege	VARCHAR2(40)	System privilege granted to the role.
admin_option	VARCHAR2(3)	Whether the privilege was granted with the ADMIN option. Equal to YES or NO.

TABLE 9-10. *Some Columns in* role_sys_privs

The following example retrieves the rows from role_sys_privs (assuming you're still connected as store):

```
SELECT *
FROM role_sys_privs;

ROLE                            PRIVILEGE                           ADM
------------------------------  ----------------------------------  ---
CONNECT                         ALTER SESSION                       NO
CONNECT                         CREATE CLUSTER                      NO
CONNECT                         CREATE DATABASE LINK                NO
CONNECT                         CREATE SEQUENCE                     NO
CONNECT                         CREATE SESSION                      NO
CONNECT                         CREATE SYNONYM                      NO
CONNECT                         CREATE TABLE                        NO
CONNECT                         CREATE VIEW                         NO
HR_MANAGER                      CREATE USER                         NO
RESOURCE                        CREATE CLUSTER                      NO
RESOURCE                        CREATE INDEXTYPE                    NO
RESOURCE                        CREATE OPERATOR                     NO
RESOURCE                        CREATE PROCEDURE                    NO
RESOURCE                        CREATE SEQUENCE                     NO
RESOURCE                        CREATE TABLE                        NO
RESOURCE                        CREATE TRIGGER                      NO
RESOURCE                        CREATE TYPE                         NO
```

Checking Object Privileges Granted to a Role

You can check which object privileges have been granted to a role by querying role_tab_privs. Table 9-11 defines the columns in role_tab_privs.

The following example queries role_tab_privs where role equals HR_MANAGER:

```
SELECT *
FROM role_tab_privs
WHERE role='HR_MANAGER';

ROLE                            OWNER
------------------------------  ------------------------------
TABLE_NAME                      COLUMN_NAME
------------------------------  ------------------------------
```

```
PRIVILEGE                                     GRA
------------------------------------------- ---
HR_MANAGER                     STORE
EMPLOYEES
DELETE                                        NO

HR_MANAGER                     STORE
EMPLOYEES
INSERT                                        NO

HR_MANAGER                     STORE
EMPLOYEES
SELECT                                        NO

HR_MANAGER                     STORE
EMPLOYEES
UPDATE                                        NO

HR_MANAGER                     STORE
SALARY_GRADES
DELETE                                        NO

HR_MANAGER                     STORE
SALARY_GRADES
INSERT                                        NO

HR_MANAGER                     STORE
SALARY_GRADES
SELECT                                        NO

HR_MANAGER                     STORE
SALARY_GRADES
UPDATE                                        NO
```

Column	Type	Description
role	VARCHAR2(30)	User to whom the privilege was granted.
owner	VARCHAR2(30)	User who owns the object.
table_name	VARCHAR2(30)	Name of the object on which privilege was granted.
column_name	VARCHAR2(30)	Name of the column (if applicable).
privilege	VARCHAR2(40)	Privilege on the object.
grantable	VARCHAR2(3)	Whether the privilege was granted with the GRANT option. Equal to YES or NO.

TABLE 9-11.   *Some Columns in* `role_tab_privs`

Making Use of Privileges Granted to a Role

Once a user has been granted a privilege via a role, they can use that privilege to perform the specified task. For example, `steve` has the `overall_manager` role. `overall_manager` was granted the `product_manager` and `hr_manager` roles. `product_manager` was granted the `SELECT` object privilege on the `products` and `product_types` tables. Therefore, `steve` is able to retrieve rows from these tables as shown in the following example:

```
CONNECT steve/button
SELECT p.name, pt.name
FROM store.products p, store.product_types pt
WHERE p.product_type_id = pt.product_type_id;
```

```
NAME                               NAME
--------------------------------   ----------
Modern Science                     Book
Chemistry                          Book
Supernova                          Video
Tank War                           Video
Z Files                            Video
2412: The Return                   Video
Space Force 9                      DVD
From Another Planet                DVD
Classical Music                    CD
Pop 3                              CD
Creative Yell                      CD
```

Default Roles

By default, when a role is granted to a user, that role is enabled for that user. This means when the user connects to the database, the role is automatically available to them. To enhance security, you can disable a role by default; when the user connects, they will have to enable the role themselves before they can use it. If the role has a password, the user must enter that password before the role is enabled. For example, the `overall_manager` role has a password of `manager_passsword`, and `overall_manager` is granted to `steve`. In the example you'll see next, you'll disable `overall_manager` so that `steve` has to enable this role and enter the password before he can use it.

You can alter a role so that it is no longer a default role using the `ALTER ROLE` statement. The following example connects as `system` and alters `steve` so that `overall_manager` is no longer a default role:

```
CONNECT system/manager
ALTER USER steve DEFAULT ROLE ALL EXCEPT overall_manager;
```

When you connect as `steve`, you need to enable `overall_manager` using `SET ROLE`:

```
CONNECT steve/button
SET ROLE overall_manager IDENTIFIED BY manager_password;
```

Once you've set the role, you can use the privileges granted to that role. You can set your role to none using the following statement:

```
SET ROLE NONE;
```

You can also set your role to everything except `overall_manager` using the following statement:

```
SET ROLE ALL EXCEPT overall_manager;
```

By assigning passwords to roles and setting roles to not be enabled by default for a user, you introduce an additional level of security.

Revoking a Role

You revoke a role using REVOKE. The following example connects as `store` and revokes the `overall_manager` role from `steve`:

```
CONNECT store/store_password
REVOKE overall_manager FROM steve;
```

Revoking Privileges from a Role

You revoke a privilege from a role using REVOKE. The following example connects as `store` and revokes all privileges on the `products` and `product_types` tables from `product_manager` (assuming you're still connected as `store`):

```
REVOKE ALL ON products FROM product_manager;
REVOKE ALL ON product_types FROM product_manager;
```

Dropping a Role

You drop a role using DROP ROLE. The following example drops the `overall_manager`, `product_manager`, and `hr_manager` roles (assuming you're still connected as `store`):

```
DROP ROLE overall_manager;
DROP ROLE product_manager;
DROP ROLE hr_manager;
```

Summary

In this chapter, you learned that

- A user is created using the CREATE USER statement.
- System privileges allow you to perform certain actions within the database, such as executing DDL statements.

■ Object privileges allow you to perform certain actions on database objects, such as executing DML statements on tables.

■ You can avoid having to enter the schema name by creating a synonym for a table.

■ A role is a group of privileges that you can assign to a user or another role.

In the next chapter, you'll learn more about creating tables and see how to create indexes, sequences, and views.

CHAPTER
10

Creating Tables,
Sequences, Indexes,
and Views

In this chapter, you will

- Learn more about tables

- See how to create and use sequences; a sequence generates a series of numbers

- Explore how to create and use indexes; an index can improve the performance of queries

- Learn how to create and use views, which are predefined queries on one or more tables; among other benefits, views allow you to hide complexity from a user, and implement another layer of security by only allowing a view to access a limited set of data in the tables

Let's plunge in and examine tables.

Tables

In this section, you'll learn more about creating a table. You'll see how to modify and drop a table. You'll also learn how to get information about tables from the data dictionary, which contains information about the database itself.

Creating a Table

As you know from Chapter 1, you use the CREATE TABLE statement to create a table. The simplified syntax for the CREATE TABLE statement is as follows:

```
CREATE [GLOBAL TEMPORARY] TABLE table_name (
    column_name type [CONSTRAINT constraint_def DEFAULT default_exp]
    [, column_name type [CONSTRAINT constraint_def DEFAULT default_exp] ...]
)
[ON COMMIT {DELETE | PRESERVE} ROWS]
TABLESPACE tab_space;
```

where

- GLOBAL TEMPORARY specifies that the table's rows are temporary and such tables are known as temporary tables. The duration of the contents are specified by the ON COMMIT clause. A temporary table is visible to all sessions, but rows are specific to a session.

- table_name specifies the name you assign to the table.

- column_name specifies the name you assign to a column.

- type specifies the type of a column.

- constraint_def specifies the definition of a constraint on a column.

- default_exp specifies the expression used to assign a default value to a column.

- ON COMMIT controls the duration of the rows in a temporary table. DELETE specifies the rows are deleted at the end of a transaction. PRESERVE specifies the rows are deleted at the end of a session. If you omit ON COMMIT for a temporary table, the default is DELETE.

- *tab_space* specifies the tablespace for the table. If you don't provide a tablespace, the table is stored in the user's default tablespace.

NOTE
The full CREATE TABLE syntax is far richer than that shown above.
For full details, see the SQL Reference manual from Oracle Corporation.

The following example connects as `store` and creates a table named `order_status2`:

```
CONNECT store/store_password
CREATE TABLE order_status2 (
  id INTEGER
    CONSTRAINT order_status2_pk PRIMARY KEY,
  status VARCHAR2(10),
  last_modified DATE DEFAULT SYSDATE
);
```

NOTE
If you want to follow along with the examples in this chapter, you'll
*need to enter and run the SQL statements using SQL*Plus.*

The next example creates a temporary table named `order_status_temp` whose rows will be deleted at the end of a session by specifying ON COMMIT PRESERVE ROWS:

```
CREATE GLOBAL TEMPORARY TABLE order_status_temp (
  id INTEGER,
  status VARCHAR2(10),
  last_modified DATE DEFAULT SYSDATE
)
ON COMMIT PRESERVE ROWS;
```

The next example performs the following:

- Adds a row to `order_status_temp`.

- Disconnects from the database to end the session, which causes the row in `order_status_temp` to be deleted.

- Reconnects as `store` and queries `order_status_temp` to show there are no rows in this table.

```
INSERT INTO order_status_temp (
  id, status
) VALUES (
  1, 'New'
);
1 row created.
```

```
DISCONNECT
CONNECT store/store_password
SELECT *
FROM order_status_temp;
no rows selected
```

Getting Information on Tables

You can get information about your tables by:

- Performing a DESCRIBE command on the table. You've already seen examples that use the DESCRIBE command in earlier chapters.

- Querying user_tables, which forms part of the data dictionary.

Table 10-1 describes some of the columns in user_tables.

NOTE
You can get information on all the tables you have access to using
all_tables.

The following example retrieves the table_name, tablespace_name, and temporary columns from user_tables where table_name is order_status2 or order_status_temp:

```
SELECT table_name, tablespace_name, temporary
FROM user_tables
WHERE table_name IN ('ORDER_STATUS2', 'ORDER_STATUS_TEMP');
```

```
TABLE_NAME                      TABLESPACE_NAME               T
------------------------------  ----------------------------  -
ORDER_STATUS2                   SYSTEM                        N
ORDER_STATUS_TEMP                                             Y
```

Notice the order_status_temp table is temporary.

Column	Type	Description
table_name	VARCHAR2(30)	Name of the table.
tablespace_name	VARCHAR2(30)	Name of the tablespace in where the table is stored. A tablespace is an area used by the database to store objects such as tables.
temporary	VARCHAR2(1)	Whether the table is temporary. Set to Y if temporary or N if not temporary.

TABLE 10-1. *Some Columns in user_tables*

Getting Information on Columns in Tables

You can get information about the columns in your tables from `user_tab_columns`. Table 10-2 describes some of the columns in `user_tab_columns`.

NOTE
You can get information on all the columns in tables you have access to using `all_tab_columns`.

The following example retrieves the `column_name`, `data_type`, `data_length`, `data_precision`, and `data_scale` from `user_tab_columns` for the `products` table:

```
COLUMN column_name FORMAT a15
COLUMN data_type FORMAT a10
SELECT
  column_name, data_type, data_length, data_precision, data_scale
FROM user_tab_columns
WHERE table_name = 'PRODUCTS';

COLUMN_NAME      DATA_TYPE   DATA_LENGTH DATA_PRECISION DATA_SCALE
---------------  ----------  ----------- -------------- ----------
PRODUCT_ID       NUMBER               22                         0
PRODUCT_TYPE_ID  NUMBER               22                         0
NAME             VARCHAR2             30
DESCRIPTION      VARCHAR2             50
PRICE            NUMBER               22              5          2
```

Column	Type	Description
table_name	VARCHAR2(30)	Name of the table.
column_name	VARCHAR2(30)	Name of the column.
data_type	VARCHAR2(106)	Data type of the column.
data_length	NUMBER	Length of the data.
data_precision	NUMBER	Precision of a numeric column if a precision was specified for the column.
data_scale	NUMBER	Scale of a numeric column.

TABLE 10-2. *Some Columns in `user_tab_columns`*

Altering a Table

You alter a table using the ALTER TABLE statement. You can use ALTER TABLE to perform tasks such as:

- Add, modify, or drop a column
- Add or drop a constraint
- Enable or disable a constraint

In the following sections, you'll learn how to use ALTER TABLE to perform each of these tasks. You'll also see how to view the details of constraints established on a table and its columns.

Adding a Column

The following example uses ALTER TABLE to add a column named modified_by to order_status2:

```
ALTER TABLE order_status2
ADD modified_by INTEGER;
```

Notice the data type of modified_by is INTEGER.
The next example adds a column named initially_created to order_status2:

```
ALTER TABLE order_status2
ADD initially_created DATE DEFAULT SYSDATE NOT NULL;
```

You can verify the addition of the new column by executing a DESCRIBE command on order_status2:

```
DESCRIBE order_status2
```

Name	Null?	Type
ID	NOT NULL	NUMBER(38)
STATUS		VARCHAR2(10)
LAST_MODIFIED		DATE
MODIFIED_BY		NUMBER(38)
INITIALLY_CREATED	NOT NULL	DATE

Modifying a Column

The following list shows some of the aspects of a column you can modify using ALTER TABLE:

- Change the size of a column if the column's data type is one whose length may be changed, such as CHAR or VARCHAR2, for example
- Change the precision of a numeric column
- Change the data type of a column
- Change the default value of a column

You'll see examples of how to change these aspects of a column in the following sections.

Changing the Size of a Column

The following example uses ALTER TABLE to increase the length of the status column of order_status2 from 10 to 15 (status is of type VARCHAR2):

```
ALTER TABLE order_status2
MODIFY status VARCHAR2(15);
```

You can only *decrease* the length of a column if there are no rows in the table or all the columns contain null values.

Changing the Precision of a Numeric Column

The following example uses ALTER TABLE to change the precision of the id column of order_status2 from 38 to 5 (id is of type NUMBER):

```
ALTER TABLE order_status2
MODIFY id NUMBER(5);
```

You can only *decrease* the precision of a numeric column if there are no rows in the table or the column contains null values.

Changing the Data Type of a Column

The following example uses ALTER TABLE to change the data type of the status column from VARCHAR2 to CHAR:

```
ALTER TABLE order_status2
MODIFY status CHAR(15);
```

If the table is empty or the column contains null values, you can change the column to any data type (including a data type that is shorter). Otherwise you can only change the data type of a column to a compatible data type. For example, you can change a VARCHAR2 to CHAR (and vice versa) as long as you don't make the column shorter, but you cannot change a DATE to a NUMBER.

Changing the Default Value of a Column

The following example uses ALTER TABLE to change the default value for the last_modified column to SYSDATE - 1:

```
ALTER TABLE order_status2
MODIFY last_modified DEFAULT SYSDATE - 1;
```

The default value only applies to new rows added to the table.

Dropping a Column

The following example uses ALTER TABLE to drop the initially_created column from order_status2:

```
ALTER TABLE order_status2
DROP COLUMN initially_created;
```

Adding a Constraint

In earlier chapters, you've seen examples of tables with PRIMARY KEY, FOREIGN KEY, and NOT NULL constraints. These constraints, along with the other types of constraints, are summarized in Table 10-3. The constraint type in Table 10-3 identifies how an Oracle database represents the type of the constraint.

You'll see how to add some of the constraints shown in Table 10-3 in the following sections.

Adding a CHECK Constraint

The following example uses ALTER TABLE to add a CHECK constraint to the status column of the order_status2 table:

```
ALTER TABLE order_status2
ADD CONSTRAINT order_status2_status_ck
CHECK (status IN ('PLACED', 'PENDING', 'SHIPPED'));
```

Constraint	Constraint Type	Meaning
CHECK	C	Specifies the value for a column, or group of columns, must satisfy a certain condition.
NOT NULL	C	Specifies a column doesn't allow storage of null values. This is actually enforced as a CHECK constraint. You can check NOT NULL columns using the DESCRIBE command.
PRIMARY KEY	P	Specifies the primary key of a table. A primary key is made up of one or more columns that uniquely identify each row in a table.
FOREIGN KEY	R	Specifies a foreign key for a table. A foreign key references a column in another table, or a column in the same table in the case of a self-reference.
UNIQUE	U	Specifies a column, or group of columns, can only store unique values.
CHECK OPTION	V	Specifies that DML operations on a view must satisfy the subquery. You'll learn about views later in the section "Views."
READ ONLY	O	Specifies that a view may only be read from.

TABLE 10-3. *Constraints*

Notice the constraint enforces the `status` value is in the supplied list of values in the `IN` clause. The following `INSERT` adds a row to the `order_status2` table whose `status` value is `PENDING`:

```
INSERT INTO order_status2 (
  id, status, last_modified, modified_by
) VALUES (
  1, 'PENDING', '01-JAN-2005', 1
);
```

If you attempt to add a row that doesn't satisfy a check constraint, the database returns the error ORA-02290. For example, the following `INSERT` attempts to add a row whose `status` value isn't in the list of valid values:

```
INSERT INTO order_status2 (
  id, status, last_modified, modified_by
) VALUES (
  2, 'CLEARED', '01-JAN-2005', 2
);
INSERT INTO order_status2 (
*
ERROR at line 1:
ORA-02290: check constraint (STORE.ORDER_STATUS2_STATUS_CK) violated
```

You can use other comparison operators with a `CHECK` constraint. The next example adds a `CHECK` constraint that enforces the `id` value is greater than zero:

```
ALTER TABLE order_status2
ADD CONSTRAINT order_status2_id_ck CHECK (id > 0);
```

To add a constraint, any existing rows in the table must satisfy the constraint. For example, if the `order_status2` table contained rows, to add the `order_status2_id_ck` constraint the `id` column would have to be greater than zero; otherwise the attempt to enable the constraint would fail with an error.

NOTE
There is an exception to the previous rule: you can disable a constraint when you add it. You'll learn how to disable and enable constraints later in the sections "Disabling a Constraint" and "Enabling a Constraint." You can also choose to apply a constraint to new data only by specifying `ENABLE NOVALIDATE`, *which you'll learn more about in the "Enabling a Constraint" section.*

Adding a NOT NULL Constraint

The following example uses ALTER TABLE to add a NOT NULL constraint on the status column of the order_status2 table:

```
ALTER TABLE order_status2
MODIFY status CONSTRAINT order_status2_status_nn NOT NULL;
```

Notice you use MODIFY to add a NOT NULL constraint rather than ADD CONSTRAINT. The next example adds a NOT NULL constraint on the modified_by column:

```
ALTER TABLE order_status2
MODIFY modified_by CONSTRAINT order_status2_modified_by_nn NOT NULL;
```

The next example adds a NOT NULL constraint on the last_modified column:

```
ALTER TABLE order_status2
MODIFY last_modified NOT NULL;
```

Notice I didn't supply a name for the constraint. The database automatically assigns a name to the constraint like SYS_C003381, which isn't particularly meaningful to a human being. You'll see how to view the details of constraints later in the section "Getting Information on Constraints."

TIP
Always specify a meaningful name to your constraints so that when a constraint error occurs in an application you can easily identify the problem.

Adding a FOREIGN KEY Constraint

The following example uses ALTER TABLE to first drop the modified_by column from order_status2 and then adds a FOREIGN KEY constraint that references the employees.employee_id column:

```
ALTER TABLE order_status2
DROP COLUMN modified_by;

ALTER TABLE order_status2
ADD CONSTRAINT order_status2_modified_by_fk
modified_by REFERENCES employees(employee_id);
```

You use the ON DELETE CASCADE clause with a FOREIGN KEY constraint to specify that when a row in the parent table is deleted, any matching rows in the child table are also deleted. The following example drops the modified_by column and rewrites the previous example to include the ON DELETE CASCADE clause:

```
ALTER TABLE order_status2
DROP COLUMN modified_by;
```

```
ALTER TABLE order_status2
ADD CONSTRAINT order_status2_modified_by_fk
modified_by REFERENCES employees(employee_id) ON DELETE CASCADE;
```

When a row is deleted from employees, any matching rows in `order_status2` are also deleted.

You use the ON DELETE SET NULL clause with a FOREIGN KEY constraint to specify that when a row in the parent table is deleted, the foreign key column for the row (or rows) in the child table is set to null. The following example drops the `modified_by` column from `order_status2` and rewrites the previous example to include the ON DELETE SET NULL clause:

```
ALTER TABLE order_status2
DROP COLUMN modified_by;
```

```
ALTER TABLE order_status2
ADD CONSTRAINT order_status2_modified_by_fk
modified_by REFERENCES employees(employee_id) ON DELETE SET NULL;
```

When a row is deleted from `employees`, the `modified_by` column for any matching rows in `order_status2` is set to null. To clean up, the following statement drops the `modified_by` column:

```
ALTER TABLE order_status2
DROP COLUMN modified_by;
```

Adding a UNIQUE Constraint

The following example uses ALTER TABLE to add a UNIQUE constraint to the `status` column of the `order_status2` table:

```
ALTER TABLE order_status2
ADD CONSTRAINT order_status2_status_uq UNIQUE (status);
```

Dropping a Constraint

You drop a constraint using the DROP CONSTRAINT clause of ALTER TABLE. The following example drops the `order_status2_status_uq` constraint:

```
ALTER TABLE order_status2
DROP CONSTRAINT order_status2_status_uq;
```

Disabling a Constraint

By default, a constraint is enabled when you create it. You can disable a constraint when you create it by adding DISABLE to the end of the CONSTRAINT clause. The following example adds a constraint to `order_status2` but disables it:

```
ALTER TABLE order_status2
ADD CONSTRAINT order_status2_status_uq UNIQUE (status) DISABLE;
```

You can disable an existing constraint using the DISABLE CONSTRAINT clause of ALTER TABLE. The following example disables the order_status2_status_nn constraint:

```
ALTER TABLE order_status2
DISABLE CONSTRAINT order_status2_status_nn;
```

You can add CASCADE to the end of a DISABLE CONSTRAINT clause to disable any integrity constraints that depend on the specified integrity constraint. You must use CASCADE when you disable a primary key or unique constraint that is part of a foreign key constraint.

Enabling a Constraint

You can enable an existing constraint using the ENABLE CONSTRAINT clause of ALTER TABLE. The following example enables the order_status2_status_uq constraint:

```
ALTER TABLE order_status2
ENABLE CONSTRAINT order_status2_status_uq;
```

To enable a constraint, all the rows in the table must satisfy the constraint. For example, if the order_status2 table contained rows, to enable the order_status2_status_uq constraint the status column would have to contain unique values, otherwise the attempt to enable the constraint would fail with an error.

You can also choose to apply a constraint to new data only by specifying ENABLE NOVALIDATE. For example:

```
ALTER TABLE order_status2
ENABLE NOVALIDATE CONSTRAINT order_status2_status_uq;
```

NOTE
The default is ENABLE VALIDATE.

Deferred Constraints

A deferred constraint is one that is enforced when a transaction is committed. You specify a constraint is deferrable using the DEFERRABLE clause when you initially add a constraint. Once you've added a constraint, you cannot change it to DEFERRABLE; instead, you must drop and re-create the constraint.

When you add a DEFERRABLE constraint, you can mark it as INITIALLY IMMEDIATE or INITIALLY DEFERRED. INITIALLY IMMEDIATE means that the constraint is checked whenever you add, update, or delete rows from a table (this is the same as the default behavior of a constraint). INITIALLY DEFERRED means that the constraint is only checked when a transaction is committed. Let's take a look at an example.

The following statement drops the order_status2_status_uq constraint:

```
ALTER TABLE order_status2
DROP CONSTRAINT order_status2_status_uq;
```

The next example adds the `order_status2_status_uq` constraint, setting it to `DEFERRABLE INITIALLY DEFERRED`:

```
ALTER TABLE order_status2
ADD CONSTRAINT order_status2_status_uq UNIQUE (status)
DEFERRABLE INITIALLY DEFERRED;
```

If you add rows to `order_status2`, the `order_status2_status_uq` constraint isn't enforced until you perform a commit.

Getting Information on Constraints

You can get information on your constraints by querying `user_constraints`. Table 10-4 describes some of the columns in `user_constraints`.

NOTE
You can get information on all the constraints you have access to using
`all_constraints`.

Column	Type	Description
owner	VARCHAR2(30)	Owner of the constraint.
constraint_name	VARCHAR2(30)	Name of the constraint.
constraint_type	VARCHAR2(1)	Constraint type. Set to P, R, C, U, V, or O—see Table 10-3 shown earlier for the constraint type meanings.
table_name	VARCHAR2(30)	Name of the table on which the constraint is defined.
status	VARCHAR2(8)	Constraint status. Set to ENABLED or DISABLED.
deferrable	VARCHAR2(14)	Whether the constraint is deferrable. Set to DEFERRABLE or NOT DEFERRABLE.
deferred	VARCHAR2(9)	Whether the deferred. Set to IMMEDIATE or DEFERRED.

TABLE 10-4.   *Some Columns in user_constraints*

The following example retrieves the constraint_name, constraint_type, status, deferrable, and deferred from user_constraints for the order_staus2 table:

```
SELECT
  constraint_name, constraint_type, status, deferrable, deferred
FROM user_constraints
WHERE table_name = 'ORDER_STATUS2';
```

```
CONSTRAINT_NAME                 C STATUS   DEFERRABLE     DEFERRED
------------------------------- - -------- -------------- ---------
ORDER_STATUS2_PK                P ENABLED  NOT DEFERRABLE IMMEDIATE
ORDER_STATUS2_STATUS_CK         C ENABLED  NOT DEFERRABLE IMMEDIATE
ORDER_STATUS2_ID_CK             C ENABLED  NOT DEFERRABLE IMMEDIATE
ORDER_STATUS2_STATUS_NN         C DISABLED NOT DEFERRABLE IMMEDIATE
ORDER_STATUS2_STATUS_UQ         U ENABLED  DEFERRABLE     DEFERRED
SYS_C004807                     C ENABLED  NOT DEFERRABLE IMMEDIATE
```

Notice all the constraints except one have the name that was supplied when the constraint was added by the ALTER TABLE statement. One constraint has the database-generated name of SYS_C004807. Since this name is automatically generated, the name of the constraint in your database will be different.

Getting Information on the Constraints on a Column

You can get information on the constraints on a column by querying user_cons_columns. Table 10-5 describes some of the columns in user_cons_columns.

NOTE
You can get information on all the column constraints you have access to using all_cons_columns.

Column	Type	Description
owner	VARCHAR2(30)	Owner of the constraint.
constraint_name	VARCHAR2(30)	Name of the constraint.
table_name	VARCHAR2(30)	Name of the table on which the constraint is defined.
column_name	VARCHAR2(4000)	Name of the column on which the constraint is defined.

TABLE 10-5. *Some Columns in user_cons_columns*

The following example retrieves the `constraint_name` and `column_name` from `user_cons_columns` for the `order_staus2` table:

```
COLUMN column_name FORMAT a15
SELECT constraint_name, column_name
FROM user_cons_columns
WHERE table_name = 'ORDER_STATUS2';
```

CONSTRAINT_NAME	COLUMN_NAME
ORDER_STATUS2_ID_CK	ID
ORDER_STATUS2_PK	ID
ORDER_STATUS2_STATUS_CK	STATUS
ORDER_STATUS2_STATUS_NN	STATUS
ORDER_STATUS2_STATUS_UQ	STATUS
SYS_C004807	LAST_MODIFIED

The next example joins `user_constraints` and `user_cons_columns` to get the `column_name`, `constraint_name`, `constraint_type`, and `status`:

```
SELECT
 ucc.column_name, ucc.constraint_name, uc.constraint_type, uc.status
FROM user_constraints uc, user_cons_columns ucc
WHERE uc.table_name = ucc.table_name
AND uc.constraint_name = ucc.constraint_name
AND ucc.table_name = 'ORDER_STATUS2';
```

COLUMN_NAME	CONSTRAINT_NAME	C	STATUS
ID	ORDER_STATUS2_ID_CK	C	ENABLED
ID	ORDER_STATUS2_PK	P	ENABLED
STATUS	ORDER_STATUS2_STATUS_CK	C	ENABLED
STATUS	ORDER_STATUS2_STATUS_NN	C	DISABLED
STATUS	ORDER_STATUS2_STATUS_UQ	U	ENABLED
LAST_MODIFIED	SYS_C004807	C	ENABLED

Renaming a Table

You rename a table using the RENAME statement. The following example renames `order_status2` to `order_state`:

```
RENAME order_status2 TO order_state;
```

The next example changes the table name back to the original:

```
RENAME order_state TO order_status2;
```

NOTE
If you use the table name in your constraint name, renaming the table will also mean you should change the names of your constraints.

Adding a Comment to a Table

A comment can help you remember what the table or column is used for. You add a comment to a table or column using the COMMENT statement. The following example adds a comment to the order_status2 table:

```
COMMENT ON TABLE order_status2 IS
'order_status2 stores the state of an order';
```

The next example adds a comment to the order_status2.last_modified column:

```
COMMENT ON COLUMN order_status2.last_modified IS
'last_modified stores the date and time the order was modified last';
```

Getting Table Comments

You can get the comments on your tables using user_tab_comments. For example:

```
SELECT *
FROM user_tab_comments
WHERE table_name = 'ORDER_STATUS2';

TABLE_NAME                      TABLE_TYPE
------------------------------- -----------
COMMENTS
------------------------------------------
ORDER_STATUS2                   TABLE
order_status2 stores the state of an order
```

Getting Column Comments

You can get the comments on your columns using user_col_comments. For example:

```
SELECT *
FROM user_col_comments
WHERE table_name = 'ORDER_STATUS2';

TABLE_NAME                      COLUMN_NAME
------------------------------- ------------------------------
COMMENTS
-----------------------------------------------------------------
ORDER_STATUS2                   ID

ORDER_STATUS2                   STATUS

ORDER_STATUS2                   LAST_MODIFIED
last_modified stores the date and time the order was modified last
```

Truncating a Table

You truncate a table using the TRUNCATE statement. This removes *all* the rows from a table and resets the storage area for a table. The following example truncates order_status2:

```
TRUNCATE TABLE order_status2;
```

TIP
If you need to remove all the rows from a table, you should use
TRUNCATE rather than DELETE. This is because TRUNCATE resets
the storage area for a table ready to receive new rows. Issuing a
TRUNCATE statement also doesn't require any undo space in the
database and doesn't require you issue a COMMIT to make the delete
permanent.

Dropping a Table

You drop a table using the DROP TABLE statement. The following example drops the order_
status2 table:

```
DROP TABLE order_status2;
```

This concludes the discussion of tables. In the next section, you'll learn about sequences.

Sequences

A *sequence* is a database item that generates a sequence of integers. You typically use the integers
generated by a sequence to populate a numeric primary key column. In this section, you'll learn
how to:

- Create a sequence
- Get information on a sequence from the data dictionary
- Use a sequence
- Modify a sequence
- Drop a sequence

Creating a Sequence

You create a sequence using the CREATE SEQUENCE statement, which has the following syntax:

```
CREATE SEQUENCE sequence_name
[START WITH start_num]
[INCREMENT BY increment_num]
[ { MAXVALUE maximum_num | NOMAXVALUE } ]
[ { MINVALUE minimum_num | NOMINVALUE } ]
[ { CYCLE | NOCYCLE } ]
[ { CACHE cache_num | NOCACHE } ]
[ { ORDER | NOORDER } ];
```

where

- *sequence_name* specifies the name you assign to the sequence.

- START WITH *start_num* specifies the integer to start the sequence. The default start number is 1.

- INCREMENT BY *increment_num* specifies the integer to increment the sequence by. The default increment number is 1. The absolute value of *increment_num* must be less than the difference between *maximum_num* and *minimum_num*.

- MINVALUE *minimum_num* specifies the maximum integer of the sequence. *minimum_num* must be less than or equal to *start_num*, and *minimum_num* must be less than *maximum_num*.

- NOMINVALUE specifies the maximum is 1 for an ascending sequence or -10^{26} for a descending sequence. NOMINVALUE is the default.

- MAXVALUE *maximum_num* specifies the maximum integer of the sequence. *maximum_num* must be greater than or equal to *start_num*, and *maximum_num* must be greater than *minimum_num*.

- NOMAXVALUE specifies the maximum is 10^{27} for an ascending sequence or -1 for a descending sequence. NOMAXVALUE is the default.

- CYCLE specifies the sequence generates integers even after reaching its maximum or minimum value. When an ascending sequence reaches its maximum value, the next value generated is the minimum. When a descending sequence reaches its minimum value, the next value generated is the maximum.

- NOCYCLE specifies the sequence cannot generate any more integers after reaching its maximum or minimum value. NOCYCLE is the default.

- CACHE *cache_num* specifies the number of integers to keep in memory. The default number of integers to cache is 20. The minimum number of integers that may be cached is 2. The maximum integers that may be cached is determined by the formula CEIL (*maximum_num* − *minimum_num*) /ABS (*increment_num*).

- NOCACHE specifies no integers are to be stored.

- ORDER guarantees the integers are generated in the order of the request. You typically use ORDER when using Real Application Clusters.

- NOORDER doesn't guarantee the integers are generated in the order of the request. NOORDER is the default.

The following example creates a sequence named test_seq:

```
CREATE SEQUENCE test_seq;
```

Since this CREATE SEQUENCE statement omits the optional parameters, the default values are used. This means that parameters such as start number and the increment by numbers are set to the default of 1.

The next example creates a sequence named `test2_seq` that supplies values for the optional parameters:

```
CREATE SEQUENCE test2_seq
START WITH 10 INCREMENT BY 5
MINVALUE 10 MAXVALUE 20
CYCLE CACHE 2 ORDER;
```

The final example creates a sequence named `test3_seq` that starts at 10 and counts down to 1:

```
CREATE SEQUENCE test3_seq
START WITH 10 INCREMENT BY -1
MINVALUE 1 MAXVALUE 10
CYCLE CACHE 5;
```

Getting Information on Sequences

You get information on your sequences from `user_sequences`, which forms part of the data dictionary. Table 10-6 describes the columns in `user_sequences`.

NOTE
You can get information on all the sequences you have access to using `all_sequences`.

Column	Type	Description
sequence_name	VARCHAR2(30)	Name of the sequence.
min_value	NUMBER	Minimum value.
max_value	NUMBER	Maximum value.
increment_by	NUMBER	Number to increment or decrement sequence by.
cycle_flag	VARCHAR2(1)	Whether the sequence cycles. Set to Y or N.
order_flag	VARCHAR2(1)	Whether the sequence is ordered. Set to Y or N.
cache_size	NUMBER	Number of sequence values stored in memory.
last_number	NUMBER	Last number that was generated or cached by the sequence.

TABLE 10-6. *Some Columns in `user_sequences`*

The following example retrieves the details for the sequences from `user_sequences`:

```
COLUMN sequence_name FORMAT a6
SELECT * FROM user_sequences;
```

SEQUEN	MIN_VALUE	MAX_VALUE	INCREMENT_BY	C	O	CACHE_SIZE	LAST_NUMBER
ORDER_STATUS2_SEQ	1	1.0000E+27	1	N	N	20	21
TEST_SEQ	1	1.0000E+27	1	N	N	20	21
TEST2_SEQ	10	20	5	Y	Y	2	20
TEST3_SEQ	1	10	-1	Y	N	5	5

Using a Sequence

A sequence generates a series of numbers. A sequence contains two pseudo columns named `currval` and `nextval` that you use to get the current value and the next value from the sequence.

Before retrieving the current value you must initialize a sequence by retrieving the next value. When you select `test_seq.nextval` the sequence is initialized to 1. For example, the following `SELECT` statement retrieves `test_seq.nextval`; notice you use `dual` in the `FROM` clause:

```
SELECT test_seq.nextval FROM dual;

  NEXTVAL
----------
        1
```

The first value in `test_seq` sequence is 1. Once initialized, you can get the current value from the sequence using `currval`. For example:

```
SELECT test_seq.currval FROM dual;

  CURRVAL
----------
        1
```

When you select `currval`, `nextval` remains unchanged; `nextval` only changes when you select `nextval` to get the next value. The following example selects `test_seq.nextval` and `test_seq.currval`. Notice these values are both 2:

```
SELECT test_seq.nextval, test_seq.currval FROM dual;

  NEXTVAL    CURRVAL
---------- ----------
        2          2
```

Selecting `test_seq.nextval` gets the next value in the sequence, which is 2; `test_seq.currval` is also 2 at that point.

The next example initializes `test2_seq` by selecting `test_seq2.nextval`. Notice the first value in the sequence is 10:

```
SELECT test2_seq.nextval FROM dual;

 NEXTVAL
----------
      10
```

The maximum value for `test_seq2` is 20, and the sequence was created with the CYCLE option, which means the sequence will cycle back to 10 once it reaches the maximum of 20:

```
SELECT test2_seq.nextval FROM dual;

 NEXTVAL
----------
      15
```

```
SELECT test2_seq.nextval FROM dual;

 NEXTVAL
----------
      20
```

```
SELECT test2_seq.nextval FROM dual;

 NEXTVAL
----------
      10
```

The next example initializes `test3_seq` and retrieves some of the values:

```
SELECT test3_seq.nextval FROM dual;

 NEXTVAL
----------
      10
```

```
SELECT test3_seq.nextval FROM dual;

 NEXTVAL
----------
       9
```

```
SELECT test3_seq.nextval FROM dual;

 NEXTVAL
----------
       8
```

Populating a Primary Key Using a Sequence

You'll typically use a sequence to populate a primary key of a table when that primary key is an integer. The following statement recreates the `order_status2` table. You'll be using a sequence to populate the `id` column of `order_status2`:

```
CREATE TABLE order_status2 (
  id INTEGER
    CONSTRAINT order_status2_pk PRIMARY KEY,
  status VARCHAR2(10),
  last_modified DATE DEFAULT SYSDATE
);
```

The following example creates a sequence named `order_status2_seq` that will be used to populate the `id` column of the `order_status2` table:

```
CREATE SEQUENCE order_status2_seq NOCACHE;
```

TIP
When using a sequence to populate a primary key column, you should typically use NOCACHE to avoid gaps in the sequence of numbers. The gaps occur because when the database is shut down any cached values are lost.

The following `INSERT` statements add rows to `order_status2`. Notice the value for the `id` column is set using `order_status2_seq.nextval`:

```
INSERT INTO order_status2 (
  id, status, last_modified
) VALUES (
  order_status2_seq.nextval, 'PLACED', '01-JAN-2006'
);

INSERT INTO order_status2 (
  id, status, last_modified
) VALUES (
  order_status2_seq.nextval, 'PENDING', '01-FEB-2006'
);
```

The following `SELECT` statement retrieves the rows from `order_status2`. Notice the `id` column is set to the first two values (1 and 2) from the `order_status2_seq` sequence:

```
SELECT * FROM order_status2;

        ID STATUS     LAST_MODI
---------- ---------- ---------
         1 PLACED     01-JAN-06
         2 PENDING    01-FEB-06
```

Modifying a Sequence

You modify a sequence using the ALTER SEQUENCE statement. There are some limitations on what you can modify in a sequence, which include the following:

- You cannot change the start value of a sequence.
- The minimum value cannot be more than the current value of the sequence (currval).
- The maximum value cannot be less than the current value of the sequence (currval).

The following example modifies test_seq to increment the sequence of numbers by 2:

```
ALTER SEQUENCE test_seq
INCREMENT BY 2;
```

When you modify test_seq the new values generated by the sequence will be incremented by 2. For example, the last number generated by test_seq in the previous section was 2, so when you retrieve test_seq.nextval the value returned is 4. The following examples get the current value and next value of test_seq using test_seq.currval and test_seq.nextval:

```
SELECT test_seq.currval FROM dual;

    CURRVAL
----------
          2

SELECT test_seq.nextval FROM dual;

    NEXTVAL
----------
          4
```

Dropping a Sequence

You drop a sequence using DROP SEQUENCE. The following example drops test3_seq:

```
DROP SEQUENCE test3_seq;
```

This concludes the discussion of sequences. In the next section, you'll learn about indexes.

Indexes

When looking for a particular topic in a book, you can either scan the whole book looking for your topic, or you can use the book's index to find the exact location of the topic directly. An index for a database table is similar in concept to a book index, except that database indexes are used to find specific rows in a table. The downside of indexes is that when a row is added to the table, additional time is required to update the index for the new row.

Generally, you should only create an index on a column when you find that you are retrieving a small number of rows from a table containing many rows. A good rule of thumb is that an index is useful when you expect any single query to retrieve 10 percent or less of the total rows in a table.

This means that the candidate column for an index should be used to store a wide range of values. A good candidate for indexing would be a column containing a unique number for each record, while a poor candidate for indexing would be a column that only contains a small range of numeric codes such as 1, 2, 3, or 4. This consideration applies to all database types, not just numbers. An Oracle database automatically creates an index for the primary key of a table and for columns included in a unique constraint.

NOTE
Normally, the DBA is responsible for creating indexes, but as an application developer you will be able to provide the DBA with feedback on which columns are good candidates for indexing. This is because you may know more about the application than the DBA.

In this section, you'll learn how to:

- Create an index
- Create a function-based index
- Get information on an index from the data dictionary
- Modify an index
- Drop an index

Creating an Index

You create an index using CREATE INDEX, which has the following simplified syntax:

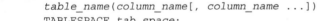

```
CREATE [UNIQUE] INDEX index_name ON
table_name(column_name[, column_name ...])
TABLESPACE tab_space;
```

where

- UNIQUE specifies the values in the indexed columns must be unique.
- *index_name* specifies the name you assign to the index.
- *table_name* specifies the name of the table on which the index is created.
- *column_name* specifies the name of the column on which the index is created. You can create an index on multiple columns; such an index is known as a *composite index*.
- *tab_space* specifies the tablespace for the index. If you don't provide a tablespace, the index is stored in the user's default tablespace.

TIP
For performance reasons you should typically store indexes in a different tablespace from tables, but for simplicity the examples in this chapter use the default tablespace. In your own database you should have the DBA create separate tablespaces for tables and indexes.

I'll now guide you through the thought processes you should follow when creating an index. Then you'll see an example CREATE INDEX statement. Assume that the customers table contains a large number of rows, and you regularly retrieve rows from the customers table using a SELECT that contains a WHERE clause that filters the rows based on the last_name column; for example:

```
SELECT customer_id, first_name, last_name
FROM customers
WHERE last_name = 'Brown';
```

Also assume that the last_name column contains fairly unique values, so that any query using the last_name column in a WHERE clause will return less than 10 percent of the total number of rows in the table. The last_name column is therefore a good candidate for indexing.

The following CREATE INDEX statement creates an index named customers_last_name_idx on the last_name column of the customers table:

```
CREATE INDEX customers_last_name_idx ON customers(last_name);
```

Once the index has been created, queries such as the previous one that searched for specific last names should take less time to complete than was required without the index.

You can enforce uniqueness of values in a column using a unique index. For example, the following statement creates a unique index named customers_phone_idx on the customers .phone column:

```
CREATE UNIQUE INDEX customers_phone_idx ON customers(phone);
```

You can also create a composite index on multiple columns. For example, the following statement creates a composite index named employees_first_last_name_idx on the first_name and last_name columns of the employees table:

```
CREATE INDEX employees_first_last_name_idx ON
employees(first_name, last_name);
```

Creating a Function-Based Index

In the previous section you saw the index customers_last_name_idx, which was created as follows:

```
CREATE INDEX customers_last_name_idx ON customers(last_name);
```

Let's say you issue the following query:

```
SELECT first_name, last_name
FROM customers
WHERE last_name = UPPER('PRICE');
```

Because this query uses a function—UPPER() in this case—the customers_last_name_idx index isn't used. If you want an index to be based on the results of a function you must create a function-based index. For example:

```
CREATE INDEX customers_last_name_func_idx
ON customers(UPPER(last_name));
```

In addition, your DBA must set the initialization parameter `QUERY_REWRITE_ENABLED` to true (the default is false) in order to take advantage of function-based indexes. For example:

```
CONNECT system/manager
ALTER SYSTEM SET QUERY_REWRITE_ENABLED=TRUE;
```

Getting Information on Indexes

You can get information on your indexes from `user_indexes`. Table 10-7 describes some of the columns in `user_indexes`.

NOTE
You can get information on all the indexes you have access to using `all_indexes`.

The following example retrieves the `index_name`, `table_name`, `uniqueness`, and `status` from `user_indexes` for the `customers` and `employees` tables. Notice the list of indexes includes `customers_pk`, which is a unique index automatically created by the database for the `customer_id` primary key column of the `customers` table:

```
SELECT index_name, table_name, uniqueness, status
FROM user_indexes
WHERE table_name IN ('CUSTOMERS', 'EMPLOYEES');
```

INDEX_NAME	TABLE_NAME	UNIQUENES	STATUS
CUSTOMERS_LAST_NAME_IDX	CUSTOMERS	NONUNIQUE	VALID
CUSTOMERS_PHONE_IDX	CUSTOMERS	UNIQUE	VALID
CUSTOMERS_PK	CUSTOMERS	UNIQUE	VALID
CUSTOMERS_LAST_NAME_FUNC_IDX	CUSTOMERS	NONUNIQUE	VALID
EMPLOYEES_FIRST_LAST_NAME_IDX	EMPLOYEES	NONUNIQUE	VALID
EMPLOYEES_PK	EMPLOYEES	UNIQUE	VALID

Getting Information on the Indexes on a Column

You can get information on the indexes on a column by querying `user_ind_columns`. Table 10-8 describes some of the columns in `user_ind_columns`.

NOTE
You can get information on all the indexes you have access to using `all_ind_columns`.

Column	Type	Description
index_name	VARCHAR2(30)	Name of the index.
table_owner	VARCHAR2(30)	The user who owns the table on which the index was created.
table_name	VARCHAR2(30)	The name of the table on which the index was created.
uniqueness	VARCHAR2(9)	Indicates whether the index is unique. Set to UNIQUE or NONUNIQUE.
status	VARCHAR2(8)	Indicates whether the index is valid. Set to VALID or INVALID.

TABLE 10-7. *Some Columns in* user_indexes

The following example retrieves the index_name, table_name, and column_name from user_ind_columns for the customers and employees tables:

```
COLUMN table_name FORMAT a15
COLUMN column_name FORMAT a15
SELECT index_name, table_name, column_name
FROM user_ind_columns
WHERE table_name IN ('CUSTOMERS', 'EMPLOYEES');

INDEX_NAME                        TABLE_NAME        COLUMN_NAME
--------------------------------- ----------------- ---------------
CUSTOMERS_PK                      CUSTOMERS         CUSTOMER_ID
CUSTOMERS_LAST_NAME_IDX           CUSTOMERS         LAST_NAME
CUSTOMERS_PHONE_IDX               CUSTOMERS         PHONE
EMPLOYEES_PK                      EMPLOYEES         EMPLOYEE_ID
EMPLOYEES_FIRST_LAST_NAME_IDX     EMPLOYEES         FIRST_NAME
EMPLOYEES_FIRST_LAST_NAME_IDX     EMPLOYEES         LAST_NAME
```

Column	Type	Description
index_name	VARCHAR2(30)	Name of the index.
table_name	VARCHAR2(30)	The name of the table on which the index was created.
column_name	VARCHAR2(4000)	Name of the column in which the index was created.

TABLE 10-8. *Some Columns in* user_ind_columns

Modifying an Index

You modify an index using ALTER INDEX. The following example renames the customers_phone_idx index to customers_phone_number_idx:

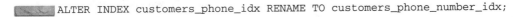

```
ALTER INDEX customers_phone_idx RENAME TO customers_phone_number_idx;
```

Dropping an Index

You drop an index using the DROP INDEX statement. The following example drops the customers_phone_number_idx index:

```
DROP INDEX customers_phone_number_idx;
```

This concludes the discussion of indexes. In the next section, you'll learn about views.

Views

A view is basically a predefined query on one or more tables (known as *base tables*). Retrieving information from a view is done in the same manner as retrieving from a table: you simply include the view in the FROM clause of a SELECT statement. With some views you can also perform DML operations on the base tables.

NOTE
Views don't store data, they only access rows in the base tables.

You've already seen some examples of retrieving information from views when you selected rows from the data dictionary, which is accessed through views. For example, user_tables, user_sequences, and user_indexes are all views.

Views offer you several benefits, such as:

- Only allow a user to retrieve data through a view. This allows you to hide the underlying base tables on which a view is built from an end user.

- Write complex queries as a view. This allows you to hide complexity from an end user.

- Only allow a view to access certain rows in the base tables. This allows you to implement another layer of security and allows you to hide rows from an end user.

In this section, you'll learn how to:

- Create and use a view

- Get details of a view from the data dictionary

- Modify a view

- Drop a view

Creating and Using a View

You create a view using CREATE VIEW, which has the following simplified syntax:

```
CREATE [OR REPLACE] VIEW [{FORCE | NOFORCE}] VIEW view_name
[(alias_name[, alias_name ...])] AS subquery
[WITH {CHECK OPTION | READ ONLY} CONSTRAINT constraint_name];
```

where

- OR REPLACE specifies the view is to replace an existing view if present.

- FORCE specifies the view is to be created even if the base tables don't exist.

- NOFORCE specifies the view is not to be created if the base tables don't exist; NOFORCE is the default.

- view_name specifies the name of the view.

- alias_name specifies the name of an alias for an expression in the subquery. There must be the same number of aliases as there are expressions in the subquery.

- subquery specifies the subquery that retrieves from the base tables. If you've supplied aliases, you can use those aliases in the list after the SELECT clause.

- WITH CHECK OPTION specifies that only the rows that would be retrieved by the subquery can be inserted, updated, or deleted. By default, rows are not checked that they are retrievable by the subquery before they are inserted, updated, or deleted.

- constraint_name specifies the name of the WITH CHECK OPTION or READ ONLY constraint.

- WITH READ ONLY specifies that rows may only read from the base tables.

There are two basic types of views:

- Simple views, which contain a subquery that retrieves from one base table

- Complex views, which contain a subquery that:

    - Retrieves from multiple base tables

    - Groups rows using a GROUP BY or DISTINCT clause

    - Contains a function call

You'll learn how to create and use these types of views in the following sections.

Creating and Using Simple Views

Simple views access one base table. The following example creates a view named cheap_products_view whose subquery only retrieves products where the price is less than $15:

```
CREATE VIEW cheap_products_view AS
SELECT *
FROM products
WHERE price < 15;
```

The next example creates a view named employees_view whose subquery retrieves all the columns from the employees table except salary:

```
CREATE VIEW employees_view AS
SELECT employee_id, manager_id, first_name, last_name, title
FROM employees;
```

Performing a SELECT on a View

Once you've created a view, you can use it to access the base table. The following example performs a SELECT on cheap_products_view:

```
SELECT product_id, name, price
FROM cheap_products_view;
```

```
PRODUCT_ID NAME                                    PRICE
---------- ------------------------------ ----------
         4 Tank War                                13.95
         6 2412: The Return                        14.95
         7 Space Force 9                           13.49
         8 From Another Planet                     12.99
         9 Classical Music                         10.99
        11 Creative Yell                           14.99
        12 My Front Line                           13.49
```

The next example retrieves from employees_view:

```
SELECT *
FROM employees_view;
```

```
EMPLOYEE_ID MANAGER_ID FIRST_NAME LAST_NAME  TITLE
----------- ---------- ---------- ---------- -------------
          1            James      Smith      CEO
          2          1 Ron        Johnson    Sales Manager
          3          2 Fred       Hobbs      Salesperson
          4          2 Susan      Jones      Salesperson
```

Performing an INSERT Using a View

You can also perform DML operations using cheap_products_view. The following example performs an INSERT into cheap_products_view and then retrieves the row:

```
INSERT INTO cheap_products_view (
  product_id, product_type_id, name, price
) VALUES (
  13, 1, 'Westerrn Front', 13.50
);

1 row created.

SELECT *
FROM cheap_products_view
WHERE product_id = 13;

PRODUCT_ID PRODUCT_TYPE_ID NAME
---------- --------------- ------------------------------
DESCRIPTION                                             PRICE
-------------------------------------------------- ----------
        13               1 Westerrn Front
                                                         13.5
```

NOTE
You can only perform DML operations with simple views. Complex views don't support DML.

Because `cheap_products_view` didn't use `WITH CHECK OPTION`, you can insert, update, and delete rows that aren't retrievable by the subquery. The following example inserts a row using `cheap_products_view` whose price is $16.50, which is greater than $15 and therefore not retrievable by the subquery:

```
INSERT INTO cheap_products_view (
  product_id, product_type_id, name, price
) VALUES (
  14, 1, 'Eastern Front', 16.50
);

1 row created.

SELECT *
FROM cheap_products_view
WHERE product_id = 14;

no rows selected
```

The view `employees_view` contains a subquery that selects every column from `employees` except `salary`. When you perform an `INSERT` using `employees_view`, the `salary` column in the `employees` base table will be set to null; for example:

```
INSERT INTO employees_view (
  employee_id, manager_id, first_name, last_name, title
) VALUES (
```

```
    5, 1, 'Jeff', 'Jones', 'CTO'
);
```

```
1 row created.
```

```
SELECT *
FROM employees
WHERE employee_id = 5;
```

```
EMPLOYEE_ID MANAGER_ID FIRST_NAME LAST_NAME  TITLE          SALARY
----------- ---------- ---------- ---------- -------------- ---------
          5          1 Jeff       Jones      CTO
```

Notice `salary` is null in the employees table for the new row.

Creating a View with a CHECK OPTION Constraint

You can specify that DML operations on a view must satisfy the subquery by adding a CHECK OPTION constraint to the view. For example, the following CREATE VIEW statement creates a view named `cheap_products_view2` that has a CHECK OPTION constraint:

```
CREATE VIEW cheap_products_view2 AS
SELECT *
FROM products
WHERE price < 15
WITH CHECK OPTION CONSTRAINT cheap_products_view2_price;
```

The next example attempts to insert a row using `cheap_products_view2` with a price of $19.50. Notice the database returns an error because the row isn't retrievable by the view:

```
INSERT INTO cheap_products_view2 (
    product_id, product_type_id, name, price
) VALUES (
    15, 1, 'Southern Front', 19.50
);
INSERT INTO cheap_products_view2 (
              *
ERROR at line 1:
ORA-01402: view WITH CHECK OPTION where-clause violation
```

Creating a View with a READ ONLY Constraint

You can make a view read only by adding a READ ONLY constraint to the view. For example, the following CREATE VIEW statement creates a view named `cheap_products_view3` that has a READ ONLY constraint:

```
CREATE VIEW cheap_products_view3 AS
SELECT *
FROM products
WHERE price < 15
WITH READ ONLY CONSTRAINT cheap_products_view3_read_only;
```

The following example attempts to insert a row using cheap_products_view3. Notice the database returns an error because the view is read only and doesn't allow DML operations:

```
INSERT INTO cheap_products_view3 (
  product_id, product_type_id, name, price
) VALUES (
  16, 1, 'Northen Front', 19.50
);
product_id, product_type_id, name, price
  *
ERROR at line 2:
ORA-01733: virtual column not allowed here
```

Getting Information on View Definitions

You get information on view definitions using the DESCRIBE command and the data dictionary. The following example uses the DESCRIBE command on cheap_products_view3:

```
DESCRIBE cheap_products_view3
Name                                       Null?    Type
----------------------------------------- -------- ------------
PRODUCT_ID                                 NOT NULL NUMBER(38)
PRODUCT_TYPE_ID                                     NUMBER(38)
NAME                                       NOT NULL VARCHAR2(30)
DESCRIPTION                                         VARCHAR2(50)
PRICE                                               NUMBER(5,2)
```

You can get information about your views from user_views. Table 10-9 describes some of the columns in user_views.

NOTE
You can get information on all the indexes you have access to using
all_views.

Column	Type	Description
view_name	VARCHAR2(30)	Name of the view.
text_length	NUMBER	Number of characters in the view's subquery.
text	LONG	Text of the view's subquery.

TABLE 10-9.   *Some Columns in* user_views

The following example retrieves the `view_name`, `text_length`, and `text` from `user_views`:

```
SELECT view_name, text_length, text
FROM user_views;

VIEW_NAME                          TEXT_LENGTH
-----------------------------      -----------
TEXT
-----------------------------------------------------------------
CHEAP_PRODUCTS_VIEW                         97
SELECT "PRODUCT_ID","PRODUCT_TYPE_ID","NAME","DESCRIPTION","PRICE"
FROM products

CHEAP_PRODUCTS_VIEW2                        116
SELECT "PRODUCT_ID","PRODUCT_TYPE_ID","NAME","DESCRIPTION","PRICE"
FROM products

CHEAP_PRODUCTS_VIEW3                        112
SELECT "PRODUCT_ID","PRODUCT_TYPE_ID","NAME","DESCRIPTION","PRICE"
FROM products

EMPLOYEES_VIEW                              75
SELECT employee_id, manager_id, first_name, last_name, title
FROM employees
```

Getting Information on View Constraints

Earlier you saw you can add CHECK OPTION and READ ONLY constraints to a view. The view `cheap_products_view2` contained a CHECK OPTION constraint to ensure the price was less than $15. The view `cheap_products_view3` contained a READ ONLY constraint to prevent modifications to the rows in the base table.

You get information on view constraints from `user_constraints`; for example:

```
SELECT
  constraint_name, constraint_type, status, deferrable, deferred
FROM user_constraints
WHERE table_name IN ('CHEAP_PRODUCTS_VIEW2', 'CHEAP_PRODUCTS_VIEW3');

CONSTRAINT_NAME                 C STATUS   DEFERRABLE     DEFERRED
-----------------------------   - -------- -------------- ---------
CHEAP_PRODUCTS_VIEW2_PRICE      V ENABLED  NOT DEFERRABLE IMMEDIATE
CHEAP_PRODUCTS_VIEW3_READ_ONLY  O ENABLED  NOT DEFERRABLE IMMEDIATE
```

The `constraint_type` for CHEAP_PRODUCTS_VIEW2_PRICE is V, which from Table 10-3 shown earlier corresponds to a CHECK OPTION constraint. The `constraint_type` for CHEAP_PRODUCTS_VIEW3_READ_ONLY is O, which corresponds to a READ ONLY constraint.

Creating and Using Complex Views

Complex views contain subqueries that:

- Retrieve from multiple base tables

- Group rows using a GROUP BY or DISTINCT clause

- Contain a function call

The following example creates a view named products_and_types_view whose subquery performs a full outer join on the products and product_types tables using the SQL/92 syntax:

```
CREATE VIEW products_and_types_view AS
SELECT p.name product_name, pt.name product_type_name, p.price
FROM products p FULL OUTER JOIN product_types pt
USING (product_type_id);
```

The following example queries products_and_types_view:

```
SELECT *
FROM products_and_types_view;
```

```
PRODUCT_NAME                     PRODUCT_TY       PRICE
------------------------------   ----------    ----------
Eastern Front                    Book              16.5
Westerrn Front                   Book              13.5
Chemistry                        Book                30
Modern Science                   Book             19.95
2412: The Return                 Video            14.95
Z Files                          Video            49.99
Tank War                         Video            13.95
Supernova                        Video            25.99
From Another Planet              DVD              12.99
Space Force 9                    DVD              13.49
Creative Yell                    CD               14.99
Pop 3                            CD               15.99
Classical Music                  CD               10.99
My Front Line                                     13.49
                                 Magazine
```

The next example creates a view named employee_salary_grades_view whose subquery uses an inner join to retrieve the salary grades for the employees, which is determined using the BETWEEN operator:

```
CREATE VIEW employee_salary_grades_view AS
SELECT e.first_name, e.last_name, e.title, e.salary,
 sg.salary_grade_id
FROM employees e INNER JOIN salary_grades sg
ON e.salary BETWEEN sg.low_salary AND sg.high_salary;
```

The following example queries `products_average_view`:

```
SELECT *
FROM employee_salary_grades_view;
```

```
FIRST_NAME LAST_NAME  TITLE                    SALARY SALARY_GRADE_ID
---------- ---------- -------------------- ---------- ---------------
Fred       Hobbs      Salesperson              150000               1
Susan      Jones      Salesperson              500000               2
Ron        Johnson    Sales Manager            600000               3
James      Smith      CEO                      800000               4
```

The next example creates a view named `product_average_view` whose subquery uses

- A `WHERE` clause to filter the rows from the `products` table to those whose `price` is less than $15
- A `GROUP BY` clause to group the remaining rows by the `product_type_id` column
- A `HAVING` clause to filter the row groups to those whose average price is greater than $13

```
CREATE VIEW product_average_view AS
SELECT product_type_id, AVG(price) average_price
FROM products
WHERE price < 15
GROUP BY product_type_id
HAVING AVG(price) > 13;
```

The following example queries `product_average_view`:

```
SELECT *
FROM product_average_view;
```

```
PRODUCT_TYPE_ID AVERAGE_PRICE
--------------- -------------
              1          13.5
              2         14.45
              3         13.24
                        13.49
```

Modifying a View

You can completely replace a view using `CREATE OR REPLACE`; you can alter the constraints on a view using `ALTER VIEW`. The following example uses `CREATE OR REPLACE` to replace `product_average_view`:

```
CREATE OR REPLACE VIEW product_average_view AS
SELECT product_type_id, AVG(price) average_price
FROM products
```

```
WHERE price < 12
GROUP BY product_type_id
HAVING AVG(price) > 11;
```

The next example uses ALTER VIEW to drop the `cheap_products_view2_price` constraint from `cheap_products_view2`:

```
ALTER VIEW cheap_products_view2
DROP CONSTRAINT cheap_products_view2_price;
```

Dropping a View

You drop a view using DROP VIEW. The following example drops `cheap_products_view2`:

```
DROP VIEW cheap_products_view2;
```

> **NOTE**
> *Go ahead and rerun* `store_schema.sql` *to recreate the store tables so that your queries match mine in the rest of this book.*

Summary

In this chapter, you learned that

- A table is created using the CREATE TABLE statement.

- A sequence is a database item that generates a sequence of integers. You typically use the integers generated by a sequence to populate a numeric primary key column.

- An index for a database table is similar in concept to a book index, except that database indexes are used to find specific rows in a table.

- Generally, you should only create an index on a column when you find that you are retrieving a small number of rows from a table containing many rows.

- A view is basically a predefined query on one or more base tables. Among other benefits, views allow you to hide complexity from a user, and implement another layer of security by only allowing a view to access a limited set of data in the base tables.

In the next chapter, you'll learn about PL/SQL programming.

CHAPTER
11

Introducing PL/SQL
Programming

Oracle added a procedural programming language known as PL/SQL (Procedural Language/SQL) to the database. PL/SQL is built on top of SQL and enables you to write programs that contain SQL statements. PL/SQL is a third-generation language and contains the standard programming constructs you would expect from such a language, such as:

- Block structure
- Variables and types
- Conditional logic
- Loops
- Cursors, which hold the results returned by a query
- Procedures
- Functions
- Packages, which may be used to group procedures and functions together in one unit

You typically use PL/SQL to add business logic to the database. This centralized code may be called by any program that can access the database, including SQL*Plus, a C program, or a Java program.

> **NOTE**
> *For full details on how to access a database through Java, see my book* Oracle9*i* JDBC Programming *(Oracle Press, 2002).*

In this chapter, you'll learn about PL/SQL programming. You'll also learn how to create triggers, which are blocks of code that are run when a certain event occurs in the database. Let's plunge in and examine block structure.

Block Structure

PL/SQL programs are divided up into structures known as *blocks*, with each block containing PL/SQL and SQL statements. A typical PL/SQL block has the following structure:

```
[DECLARE
   declaration_statements
]
BEGIN
   executable_statements
[EXCEPTION
   exception_handling_statements
]
END;
```

The declaration and exception blocks are optional, and the elements for the above syntax are as follows:

- *declaration_statements* are contained within a declaration block, and declare the variables subsequently used in the rest of the block. These variables are local to that block, meaning that they cannot be referenced outside of that block. Declarations are always placed at the start of the block.

- *executable_statements* are the actual executable statements for the block, which may include statements for performing tasks such as loops, conditional logic, and so on.

- *exception_handling_statements* are statements that handle any errors that might occur due to the executable statements.

Every statement is terminated by a semicolon (;), and a block is terminated using the END keyword. Before I get into the details of PL/SQL, you'll see a simple example to get a feel of the language. The following PL/SQL example calculates the width of a rectangle given its area and height:

```
DECLARE
  width  INTEGER;
  height INTEGER := 2;
  area   INTEGER;
BEGIN
  area := 6;
  width := area / height;
  DBMS_OUTPUT.PUT_LINE('width = ' || width);
EXCEPTION
  WHEN ZERO_DIVIDE THEN
    DBMS_OUTPUT.PUT_LINE('Division by zero');
END;
/
```

As you can see, three INTEGER variables are declared: width, height, and area. The height variable is initialized to 2 when it is declared, and area is set to 6 later. The width variable is calculated by dividing area by height. The call to the DBMS_OUTPUT.PUT_LINE() method displays the value set for the area variable on the screen (you must enter the command SET SERVEROUTPUT ON in SQL*Plus to see the output). The EXCEPTION block handles any attempts to divide a number by zero by catching the ZERO_DIVIDE exception. In the example, no attempt is actually made to divide by zero, but if you change height to 0 and run the code you'll see the exception.

NOTE
The slash character (/) at the end of the example executes the PL/SQL.

The following listing shows the block being entered and run in SQL*Plus:

```
SQL> SET SERVEROUTPUT ON
SQL> DECLARE
  2    width  INTEGER;
  3    height INTEGER := 2;
  4    area   INTEGER;
  5  BEGIN
  6    area := 6;
  7    width := area / height;
  8    DBMS_OUTPUT.PUT_LINE('width = ' || width);
  9  EXCEPTION
 10    WHEN ZERO_DIVIDE THEN
 11      DBMS_OUTPUT.PUT_LINE('Division by zero');
 12  END;
 13  /
width = 3

PL/SQL procedure successfully completed.
```

Notice the slash character at line 13 runs the PL/SQL.

Variables and Types

Variables declared within the DECLARE section of a PL/SQL block may only be referenced within that block. As you saw in the previous example, a variable declaration has both a name and a type. For example, the width variable was declared as:

```
width INTEGER;
```

NOTE
The PL/SQL types are similar to the database column types. You can see all the available types in Appendix A.

The following example illustrates some more variable declarations that may be used to store the column values from the products table:

```
product_id       INTEGER;
product_type_id  INTEGER;
name             VARCHAR2(30);
description      VARCHAR2(50);
price            NUMBER(5, 2);
```

You may also specify a variable's type using the %TYPE keyword, which tells PL/SQL to use the same type as a specified column in a table. The following example uses %TYPE to declare a variable of the same type as the price column of the products table, which is NUMBER(5, 2):

```
product_price products.price%TYPE;
```

Conditional Logic

You may use the IF, THEN, ELSE, ELSIF, and END IF keywords in PL/SQL for performing conditional logic. The following syntax illustrates the use of conditional logic:

```
IF condition1 THEN
  statements1
ELSIF condition2 THEN
  statements2
ELSE
  statements3
END IF;
```

where

- *condition1* and *condition2* are Boolean expressions that evaluate to true or false.

- *statements1*, *statements2*, and *statements3* are PL/SQL statements.

This conditional logic flows as follows:

- If *condition1* is true, then *statements1* is executed.

- If *condition1* is false but *condition2* is true, then *statements2* is executed.

- If neither *condition1* nor *condition2* are true, then *statements3* is executed.

You can also embed IF statements within another IF statement, as shown in the following example:

```
IF count > 0 THEN
  message := 'count is positive';
  IF area > 0 THEN
    message := 'count and area are positive';
  END IF
ELSIF count = 0 THEN
  message := 'count is zero';
ELSE
  message := 'count is negative';
END IF;
```

Loops

You may use a loop to run one or more statements multiple times. There are three types of loops in PL/SQL:

- **Simple loops** Run until you explicitly end the loop

- **WHILE loops** Run until a specified condition occurs

- **FOR loops** Run a predetermined number of times

You'll learn about these loops in the following sections.

Simple Loops

A simple loop runs until you explicitly end the loop. The syntax for a simple loop is as follows:

```
LOOP
    statements
END LOOP;
```

To end the loop, you use either an EXIT or EXIT WHEN statement. The EXIT statement ends a loop immediately, and the EXIT WHEN statement ends a loop when a specified condition occurs.

The following example shows a simple loop. A variable named counter is initialized to 0 prior to the beginning of the loop, and the loop adds 1 to counter. The loop exits when counter is equal to 5 using an EXIT WHEN statement.

```
counter := 0;
LOOP
  counter := counter + 1;
  EXIT WHEN counter = 5;
END LOOP;
```

NOTE
The EXIT WHEN statement can appear anywhere in the loop code.

WHILE Loops

A WHILE loop runs until a specified condition occurs. The syntax for a WHILE loop is as follows:

```
WHILE condition LOOP
    statements
END LOOP;
```

The following example shows a WHILE loop that executes while the counter variable is less than 6:

```
counter := 0;
WHILE counter < 6 LOOP
  counter := counter + 1;
END LOOP;
```

FOR Loops

A FOR loop runs a predetermined number of times; you determine the number of times the loop runs by specifying the *lower* and *upper bounds* for a loop variable. The loop variable is then incremented (or decremented) each time around the loop. The syntax for a FOR loop is as follows:

```
FOR loop_variable IN [REVERSE] lower_bound..upper_bound LOOP
    statements
END LOOP;
```

where

- *loop_variable* specifies the loop variable. You can use a variable that already exists for the loop variable, or you can just have the loop create one for you (this occurs if the variable specified doesn't exist). The loop variable value is increased (or decreased if you use the REVERSE keyword) by 1 each time through the loop.

- REVERSE specifies that the loop variable value is to be decremented each time through the loop. The loop variable is initialized to the upper bound and is decremented by 1 until the loop variable reaches the lower bound. You must still specify the lower bound before the upper bound.

- *lower_bound* specifies the loop's lower bound. The loop variable is initialized to this lower bound as long as REVERSE is not used.

- *upper_bound* specifies the loop's upper bound. If REVERSE is used, the loop variable is initialized to this upper bound.

The following example shows a FOR loop. Notice that the variable count2 isn't explicitly declared—the FOR loop automatically creates an INTEGER variable in this case:

```
FOR count2 IN 1..5 LOOP
  DBMS_OUTPUT.PUT_LINE(count2);
END LOOP;
```

If REVERSE was used in this example, the loop variable counter would start at 5, be decremented by 1 each time through the loop, and end at 1.

Cursors

You use a *cursor* when you have a SELECT statement that returns more than one row from the database. A cursor is basically a set of rows that you can access one at a time. You retrieve the rows into the cursor using your SELECT statement and then fetch the rows from the cursor. You may follow five steps when using a cursor:

1. Declare variables to store the column values from the SELECT statement.

2. Declare the cursor, specifying your SELECT statement.

3. Open the cursor.

4. Fetch the rows from the cursor.

5. Close the cursor.

You'll learn the details of these five steps in the following sections. You'll also learn how to access the rows in a cursor using a FOR loop.

Step 1: Declare the Variables to Store the Column Values

The first step is to declare the variables that will be used to store the column values. These variables must be compatible with the column types.

> **TIP**
> *Earlier you saw that %TYPE may be used to get the type of a column. If you use %TYPE when declaring your variables, your variables will automatically be of the correct type.*

The following example declares three variables to store the product_id, name, and price columns from the products table using %TYPE:

```
DECLARE
    v_product_id  products.product_id%TYPE;
    v_name        products.name%TYPE;
    v_price       products.price%TYPE;
```

Step 2: Declare the Cursor

A cursor declaration consists of a name that you assign to the cursor and the SELECT statement that you want to execute—this SELECT statement is not actually run until you open the cursor. The cursor declaration, like all other declarations, is placed in the declaration section. The syntax for declaring a cursor is as follows:

```
CURSOR cursor_name IS
    SELECT_statement;
```

where

- ■ *cursor_name* specifies the name of the cursor.

- ■ *SELECT_statement* is a SELECT statement.

The following example declares a cursor named cv_product_cursor whose SELECT statement retrieves the product_id, name, and price columns from the products table:

```
CURSOR cv_product_cursor IS
    SELECT product_id, name, price
    FROM products
    ORDER BY product_id;
```

Step 3: Open the Cursor

The next step is to open the cursor, which runs the SELECT statement. You open a cursor using the OPEN statement, which must be placed in the executable section of the block.

The following example opens cv_product_cursor, and therefore also runs the SELECT statement that retrieves the rows from the products table:

```
OPEN cv_product_cursor;
```

Step 4: Fetch the Rows from the Cursor

To read each row from the cursor, you can use the FETCH statement. The FETCH statement reads the column values into the variables that you specify; FETCH uses the following syntax:

```
FETCH cursor_name
INTO variable[, variable ...];
```

where

- *cursor_name* specifies the name of the cursor.

- *variable* is a previously declared variable into which values from the cursor's SELECT statement are stored.

The following example uses FETCH to retrieve a row from cv_product_cursor and stores the column values in the v_product_id, v_name, and v_price variables created earlier in step 1:

```
FETCH cv_product_cursor
INTO v_product_id, v_name, v_price;
```

Of course, a cursor may contain many rows; therefore, a loop is required is to read each row in turn. To determine when the loop is to end, you can use the Boolean variable cv_product_cursor%NOTFOUND. This variable is true when the FETCH statement has reached the end of the rows in the cursor, and there are no further rows to read. The following example shows a loop that reads each row from cv_product_cursor:

```
LOOP

    FETCH cv_product_cursor
    INTO v_product_id, v_name, v_price;

    -- exit the loop when there are no more rows, as indicated by
    -- the Boolean variable cv_product_cursor%NOTFOUND (= true when
    -- there are no more rows)
    EXIT WHEN cv_product_cursor%NOTFOUND;

    -- use DBMS_OUTPUT.PUT_LINE() to display the variables
    DBMS_OUTPUT.PUT_LINE(
      'v_product_id = ' || v_product_id || ', v_name = ' || v_name ||
      ', v_price = ' || v_price
    );

END LOOP;
```

Notice I've used DBMS_OUTPUT.PUT_LINE() to display the v_product_id, v_name, and v_price variables that were read for each row.

Step 5: Close the Cursor

Once you've finished with the cursor, the final step is to close the cursor using the CLOSE statement. Closing your cursors frees up system resources. The following example closes cv_product_cursor:

```
CLOSE cv_product_cursor;
```

The following section shows a complete example script that you can run using SQL*Plus. This script contains all of the five steps for using a cursor.

Complete Example: product_cursor.sql

The SQL*Plus script product_cursor.sql is contained in the SQL directory where you unzipped the files for this book. The product_cursor.sql script is as follows:

```
-- product_cursor.sql displays the product_id, name,
-- and price columns from the products table using a cursor

SET SERVEROUTPUT ON

DECLARE

  -- step 1: declare the variables
  v_product_id products.product_id%TYPE;
  v_name       products.name%TYPE;
  v_price      products.price%TYPE;

  -- step 2: declare the cursor
  CURSOR cv_product_cursor IS
    SELECT product_id, name, price
    FROM products
    ORDER BY product_id;

BEGIN

  -- step 3: open the cursor
  OPEN cv_product_cursor;

  LOOP

    -- step 4: fetch the rows from the cursor
    FETCH cv_product_cursor
    INTO v_product_id, v_name, v_price;

    -- exit the loop when there are no more rows, as indicated by
    -- the Boolean variable cv_product_cursor%NOTFOUND (= true when
    -- there are no more rows)
    EXIT WHEN cv_product_cursor%NOTFOUND;
```

```
   -- use DBMS_OUTPUT.PUT_LINE() to display the variables
   DBMS_OUTPUT.PUT_LINE(
     'v_product_id = ' || v_product_id || ', v_name = ' || v_name ||
     ', v_price = ' || v_price
   );

 END LOOP;

 -- step 5: close the cursor
 CLOSE cv_product_cursor;

END;
/
```

To run this script, follow these steps:

1. Start SQL*Plus.

2. Connect to the database as `store` with the password `store_password`.

3. Run the `product_cursor.sql` script using a command similar to the following:

   ```
   @ C:\SQL\product_cursor.sql
   ```

NOTE
If your `product_cursor.sql` script is in a different directory from
C:\SQL, you should use that directory in the previous command.

The output from `product_cursor.sql` is as follows:

```
v_product_id = 1, v_name = Modern Science, v_price = 19.95
v_product_id = 2, v_name = Chemistry, v_price = 30
v_product_id = 3, v_name = Supernova, v_price = 25.99
v_product_id = 4, v_name = Tank War, v_price = 13.95
v_product_id = 5, v_name = Z Files, v_price = 49.99
v_product_id = 6, v_name = 2412: The Return, v_price = 14.95
v_product_id = 7, v_name = Space Force 9, v_price = 13.49
v_product_id = 8, v_name = From Another Planet, v_price = 12.99
v_product_id = 9, v_name = Classical Music, v_price = 10.99
v_product_id = 10, v_name = Pop 3, v_price = 15.99
v_product_id = 11, v_name = Creative Yell, v_price = 14.99
v_product_id = 12, v_name = My Front Line, v_price = 13.49
```

Cursors and FOR Loops

You can combine the power of a FOR loop to access the rows in a cursor. When you use a FOR loop, you don't have to explicitly open and close the cursor—the FOR loop does this automatically for you. The following `product_cursor2.sql` script uses a FOR loop to access the rows in `cv_product_cursor`. Notice how concise the FOR loop is:

```
-- product_cursor2.sql displays the product_id, name,
-- and price columns from the products table using a cursor
-- and a FOR loop

SET SERVEROUTPUT ON

DECLARE
  CURSOR cv_product_cursor IS
    SELECT product_id, name, price
    FROM products
    ORDER BY product_id;
BEGIN
  FOR v_product IN cv_product_cursor LOOP
    DBMS_OUTPUT.PUT_LINE(
      'product_id = ' || v_product.product_id ||
      ', name = ' || v_product.name ||
      ', price = ' || v_product.price
    );
  END LOOP;
END;
/
```

To run the `product_cursor2.sql` script, you issue a command similar to the following:

```
@ C:\SQL\product_cursor2.sql
```

The output from this script is as follows:

```
product_id = 1, name = Modern Science, price = 19.95
product_id = 2, name = Chemistry, price = 30
product_id = 3, name = Supernova, price = 25.99
product_id = 4, name = Tank War, price = 13.95
product_id = 5, name = Z Files, price = 49.99
product_id = 6, name = 2412: The Return, price = 14.95
product_id = 7, name = Space Force 9, price = 13.49
product_id = 8, name = From Another Planet, price = 12.99
product_id = 9, name = Classical Music, price = 10.99
product_id = 10, name = Pop 3, price = 15.99
product_id = 11, name = Creative Yell, price = 14.99
product_id = 12, name = My Front Line, price = 13.49
```

Exceptions

Exceptions are used to handle errors that occur in your PL/SQL code. Earlier you saw an example PL/SQL block that contained an EXCEPTION block to handle attempts to divide a number by zero; that block handled the ZERO_DIVIDE exception. This exception and some of the other exceptions are shown in Table 11-1.

Exception	Error	Description
ACCESS_INTO_NULL	ORA-06530	Attempt was made to assign values to the attributes of an uninitialized object. You'll learn about objects in Chapter 12.
CASE_NOT_FOUND	ORA-06592	None of the WHEN clauses of a CASE statement was selected, and there is no default ELSE clause.
COLLECTION_IS_NULL	ORA-06531	You'll learn about collections in Chapter 13. Attempt was made to apply collection methods other than EXISTS to an uninitialized nested table or varray, or an attempt was made to assign values to the elements of an uninitialized nested table or varray.
CURSOR_ALREADY_OPEN	ORA-06511	Attempt was made to open an already open cursor. Cursor must be closed before it can be reopened.
DUP_VAL_ON_INDEX	ORA-00001	Attempt was made to store duplicate values in a column that is constrained by a unique index.
INVALID_CURSOR	ORA-01001	Your program attempts an illegal cursor operation such as closing an unopened cursor.
INVALID_NUMBER	ORA-01722	Attempt to convert a character string into a number failed because the string does not represent a valid number. Note: In procedural statements VALUE_ERROR is raised instead of INVALID_NUMBER.
LOGIN_DENIED	ORA-01017	Attempt was made to connect to a database with an invalid user name or password.
NO_DATA_FOUND	ORA-01403	SELECT INTO statement returns no rows, or an attempt was made to access a deleted element in a nested table or an uninitialized element in an index by table.
NOT_LOGGED_ON	ORA-01012	Attempt was made to access a database item without first being connected to a database.
PROGRAM_ERROR	ORA-06501	PL/SQL had an internal problem.

TABLE 11-1. *Predefined Exceptions*

Exception	Error	Description
`ROWTYPE_MISMATCH`	ORA-06504	Host cursor variable and PL/SQL cursor variable involved in an assignment have incompatible return types. For example, when an open host cursor variable is passed to a stored procedure or function, the return types of the actual and formal parameters must be compatible.
`SELF_IS_NULL`	ORA-30625	Attempt was made to call a `MEMBER` method on a null instance. That is, the built-in parameter `SELF` (which is always the first parameter passed to a `MEMBER` method) is null.
`STORAGE_ERROR`	ORA-06500	PL/SQL ran out of memory or the memory has been corrupted.
`SUBSCRIPT_BEYOND_COUNT`	ORA-06533	Attempt was made to reference a nested table or varray element using an index number larger than the number of elements in the collection.
`SUBSCRIPT_OUTSIDE_LIMIT`	ORA-06532	Attempt was made to reference a nested table or varray element using an index number (–1, for example) that is outside the legal range.
`SYS_INVALID_ROWID`	ORA-01410	Conversion of a character string to a universal rowid fails because the character string does not represent a valid rowid.
`TIMEOUT_ON_RESOURCE`	ORA-00051	A timeout occurred while the database was waiting for a resource.
`TOO_MANY_ROWS`	ORA-01422	`SELECT INTO` statement returned more than one row.
`VALUE_ERROR`	ORA-06502	An arithmetic, conversion, truncation, or size-constraint error occurred. For example, when selecting a column value into a character variable, if the value is longer than the declared length of the variable, PL/SQL aborts the assignment and raises `VALUE_ERROR`. In procedural statements `VALUE_ERROR` is raised if the conversion of a character string into a number fails. Note: In SQL statements `INVALID_NUMBER` is raised instead of `VALUE_ERROR`.
`ZERO_DIVIDE`	ORA-01476	Attempt was made to divide a number by zero.

TABLE 11-1. *Predefined Exceptions* (continued)

The following sections show examples that raise some of the exceptions shown in Table 11-1.

ZERO_DIVIDE Exception

The ZERO_DIVIDE exception is raised when an attempt is made to divide a number by zero. The following example attempts to divide 1 by 0 and therefore causes the ZERO_DIVIDE exception to be raised:

```
BEGIN
  DBMS_OUTPUT.PUT_LINE(1 / 0);
EXCEPTION
  WHEN ZERO_DIVIDE THEN
    DBMS_OUTPUT.PUT_LINE('Division by zero');
END;
/
```

```
Division by zero
```

When the exception occurs, program control passes to the EXCEPTION block where the WHEN clause is examined for a matching exception. If no matching exception is found, the exception is propagated to the enclosing block. For example, if the EXCEPTION block was omitted from the previous example, the exception is propagated up and is sent to SQL*Plus:

```
BEGIN
  DBMS_OUTPUT.PUT_LINE(1 / 0);
END;
BEGIN
*
ERROR at line 1:
ORA-01476: divisor is equal to zero
ORA-06512: at line 2
```

DUP_VAL_ON_INDEX Exception

The DUP_VAL_ON_INDEX exception is raised when an attempt is made to store duplicate values in a column that is constrained by a unique index. The following example attempts to insert a row in the customers table with a customer_id of 1. This causes DUP_VAL_ON_INDEX to be raised because the customers table already contains a row with a customer_id of 1:

```
BEGIN
  INSERT INTO customers (
    customer_id, first_name, last_name
  ) VALUES (
    1, 'Greg', 'Green'
  );
EXCEPTION
  WHEN DUP_VAL_ON_INDEX THEN
    DBMS_OUTPUT.PUT_LINE('Duplicate value on an index');
END;
/
```

```
Duplicate value on an index
```

INVALID_NUMBER Exception

The INVALID_NUMBER exception is raised when an attempt is made to convert an invalid character string into a number. The following example attempts to convert the string 123X to a number that is used in an insert, which causes INVALID_NUMBER to be raised because 123X is not a valid number:

```
BEGIN
  INSERT INTO customers (
    customer_id, first_name, last_name
  ) VALUES (
    '123X', 'Greg', 'Green'
  );
EXCEPTION
  WHEN INVALID_NUMBER THEN
    DBMS_OUTPUT.PUT_LINE('Conversion of string to number failed');
END;
/

Conversion of string to number failed
```

OTHERS Exception

You can use the OTHERS exception to handle all exceptions. For example:

```
BEGIN
  DBMS_OUTPUT.PUT_LINE(1 / 0);
EXCEPTION
  WHEN OTHERS THEN
    DBMS_OUTPUT.PUT_LINE('An exception occurred');
END;
/

An exception occurred
```

Because OTHERS handles all exceptions, you must list it after any specific exceptions in your EXCEPTION block. If you attempt to list OTHERS elsewhere, the database returns the error PLS-00370. For example:

```
SQL> BEGIN
  2    DBMS_OUTPUT.PUT_LINE(1 / 0);
  3  EXCEPTION
  4    WHEN OTHERS THEN
  5      DBMS_OUTPUT.PUT_LINE('An exception occurred');
  6    WHEN ZERO_DIVIDE THEN
  7      DBMS_OUTPUT.PUT_LINE('Division by zero');
  8  END;
  9  /
WHEN OTHERS THEN
     *
```

```
ERROR at line 4:
ORA-06550: line 4, column 3:
PLS-00370: OTHERS handler must be last among the exception
 handlers of a block
ORA-06550: line 0, column 0:
PL/SQL: Compilation unit analysis terminated
```

Procedures

You can create a procedure that contains a group of SQL and PL/SQL statements. Procedures allow you to centralize your business logic in the database and may be used by any program that accesses the database.

In this section, you'll learn how to:

- Create a procedure
- Call a procedure
- Get information on procedures
- Drop a procedure
- View errors in a procedure

Creating a Procedure

You create a procedure using the CREATE PROCEDURE statement. The simplified syntax for the CREATE PROCEDURE statement is as follows:

```
CREATE [OR REPLACE] PROCEDURE procedure_name
[(parameter_name [IN | OUT | IN OUT] type [, ...])]
{IS | AS}
BEGIN
  procedure_body
END procedure_name;
```

where

- OR REPLACE specifies the procedure is to replace an existing procedure if present. You can use this option when you want to modify a procedure.
- *procedure_name* specifies.the name of the procedure.
- *parameter_name* specifies the parameter name. A procedure may be passed multiple parameters.
- IN | OUT | IN OUT specifies the *mode* of the parameter. You may pick one of the following modes for each parameter:
  - IN is the default mode for a parameter. This mode is specified for parameters that already have a value when the procedure is run and that value may not be changed in the body.

■ OUT is specified for parameters whose values are only set in the body.

■ IN OUT is specified for parameters that may already have a value when the procedure is called, but their value may also be changed in the body.

■ *type* specifies the type of the parameter.

■ *procedure_body* contains the SQL and PL/SQL statements to perform the procedure's task.

The following statement defines a procedure named update_product_price(). This statement is contained in the store_schema.sql script. The update_product_price() procedure multiplies the price of a product by a factor—the product ID and the factor are passed as parameters to the procedure. If the specified product doesn't exist, the procedure takes no action, otherwise it updates the product price by the factor.

```
CREATE OR REPLACE PROCEDURE update_product_price(
   p_product_id IN products.product_id%TYPE,
   p_factor     IN NUMBER
) AS
   v_product_count INTEGER;
BEGIN
   -- count the number of products with the
   -- supplied product_id (should be 1 if the product exists)
   SELECT COUNT(*)
   INTO v_product_count
   FROM products
   WHERE product_id = p_product_id;

   -- if the product exists (v_product_count = 1) then
   -- update that product's price
   IF v_product_count = 1 THEN
     UPDATE products
     SET price = price * p_factor
     WHERE product_id = p_product_id;
     COMMIT;
   END IF;
EXCEPTION
   WHEN OTHERS THEN
     ROLLBACK;
END update_product_price;
/
```

As you can see from this listing, the procedure takes two parameters named p_product_id and p_factor. Notice that both of these parameters use the IN mode, which means their values cannot be changed in the body.

The declaration section contains an INTEGER variable named v_product_count:

```
v_product_count INTEGER;
```

The body of the procedure follows this declaration section, starting with BEGIN. The first statement in the body uses a SELECT statement that counts the number of products with the specified ID. The count is performed using the COUNT() function:

```
-- count the number of products with the
-- supplied product_id (should be 1 if the product exists)
SELECT COUNT(*)
INTO v_product_count
FROM products
WHERE product_id = p_product_id;
```

NOTE
COUNT(*) counts the rows and returns the total.

If the product exists in the table, v_product_count will be set to 1. If the product doesn't exist, v_product_count will be 0. If the value in v_product_count is 1, the price column can be multiplied by p_factor using an UPDATE statement, and the change can be committed. The following IF statement is

```
-- if the product exists (v_product_count = 1) then
-- update that product's price
IF v_product_count = 1 THEN
  UPDATE products
  SET price = price * p_factor
  WHERE product_id = p_product_id;
  COMMIT;
END IF;
```

The EXCEPTION block performs a ROLLBACK if an exception is raised:

```
EXCEPTION
  WHEN OTHERS THEN
    ROLLBACK;
```

Finally, the END keyword is used to mark the end of the procedure:

```
END update_product_price;
/
```

NOTE
The repetition of the procedure name at the end is not required, but it is good programming practice to put it in.

Calling a Procedure

You call a procedure using the CALL statement. The example you'll see in this section will multiply the price of product #1 by 1.5 using the update_product_price() procedure shown in the previous section. First, the following query retrieves the price of product #1 so you can compare with the modified price later:

```
SELECT price
FROM products
WHERE product_id = 1;

    PRICE
----------
    19.95
```

The following statement calls update_product_price(), passing the parameter values 1 (the product_id) and 1.5 (the factor to multiply the price of the product by):

```
CALL update_product_price(1, 1.5);
```

The next query retrieves the details for product #1 again; notice the price has increased:

```
SELECT price
FROM products
WHERE product_id = 1;

    PRICE
----------
    29.93
```

Getting Information on Procedures

You can get information on your procedures from the user_procedures view. Table 11-2 describes some of the columns in user_procedures.

NOTE
You can get information on all the procedures you have access to using all_procedures.

The following example retrieves the object_name, aggregate, and parallel columns from user_procedures for update_product_price():

```
SELECT object_name, aggregate, parallel
FROM user_procedures
WHERE object_name = 'UPDATE_PRODUCT_PRICE';

OBJECT_NAME                      AGG PAR
------------------------------   --- ---
UPDATE_PRODUCT_PRICE             NO  NO
```

Column	Type	Description
OBJECT_NAME	VARCHAR2(30)	Name of the object, which may be a procedure, function, or package name.
PROCEDURE_NAME	VARCHAR2(30)	Name of the procedure.
AGGREGATE	VARCHAR2(3)	Whether the procedure is an aggregate function. Set to YES or NO.
IMPLTYPEOWNER	VARCHAR2(30)	Name of the owner of the implementation type (if any).
IMPLTYPENAME	VARCHAR2(30)	Name of the implementation type (if any).
PARALLEL	VARCHAR2(3)	Whether or not the procedure or function is enabled for parallel queries. Set to YES or NO.

TABLE 11-2. *Some Columns in* `user_procedures`

Dropping a Procedure

You drop a procedure using DROP PROCEDURE. For example, the following statement drops
update_product_price():

```
DROP PROCEDURE update_product_price;
```

Viewing Errors in a Procedure

If the database reports an error when you create a procedure (or function), you can view the errors
by issuing a SHOW ERRORS command. For example, the following CREATE PROCEDURE statement
attempts to create a procedure that has a syntax error at line 6 (the parameter should be p_dob,
not p_dobs):

```
SQL> CREATE OR REPLACE PROCEDURE update_customer_dob (
  2    p_customer_id INTEGER, p_dob DATE
  3  ) AS
  4  BEGIN
  5    UPDATE customers
  6    SET dob = p_dobs
  7    WHERE customer_id = p_customer_id;
  8  END update_customer_dob;
  9  /

Warning: Procedure created with compilation errors.
```

As you can see, the database reports a compilation error in the procedure. To view the errors, you issue the SHOW ERRORS command, for example:

```
SQL> SHOW ERRORS
Errors for PROCEDURE UPDATE_CUSTOMER_DOB:

LINE/COL ERROR
-------- --------------------------------------------
5/3      PL/SQL: SQL Statement ignored
6/13     PL/SQL: ORA-00904: invalid column name
```

As you can see, line 5 was ignored because an invalid column name was referenced in line 6 of the CREATE PROCEDURE statement. You can fix the error by issuing an EDIT command, changing p_dobs to p_dob, and rerunning the CREATE PROCEDURE statement by entering /.

Functions

A function is similar to a procedure except that a function must return a value to the statement from which it is called. Together, stored procedures and functions are sometimes referred to as *stored subprograms* because they are, in one sense, small programs.

In this section, you'll learn how to:

- Create a function
- Call a function
- Get information on functions
- Drop a function

Creating a Function

You create a function using the CREATE FUNCTION statement. The simplified syntax for the CREATE FUNCTION statement is as follows:

```
CREATE [OR REPLACE] FUNCTION function_name
[(parameter_name [IN | OUT | IN OUT] type [, ...])]
RETURN type
{IS | AS}
BEGIN
  function_body
END function_name;
```

where

- OR REPLACE specifies the function that is to replace an existing function if present. You can use this option when you want to modify the definition of a function.

- *function_name* specifies the name of the function.

- *parameter_name* specifies the parameter name. A function may be passed multiple parameters.

- IN |OUT | IN OUT specifies the mode of the parameter.

- *type* specifies the PL/SQL type of the parameter.

- *function_body* contains the SQL and PL/SQL statements to perform the function's task. Unlike a procedure, the body of a function must return a value of the PL/SQL type specified in the RETURN clause.

The following CREATE FUNCTION statement creates a function named circle_area(), which returns the area of a circle. The radius of the circle is passed as a parameter to circle_ area(). This function is created when you run the store_schema.sql script:

```
CREATE OR REPLACE FUNCTION circle_area (
  p_radius IN NUMBER
) RETURN NUMBER AS
  v_pi   NUMBER := 3.1415926;
  v_area NUMBER;
BEGIN
  v_area := v_pi * POWER(p_radius, 2);
  RETURN v_area;
END circle_area;
/
```

Notice circle_area() returns a NUMBER whose value is set to the computed area of a circle.

The next example creates a function named average_product_price(), which returns the average price of products whose product_type_id equals the parameter value. This function is created by the store_schema.sql script:

```
CREATE OR REPLACE FUNCTION average_product_price (
  p_product_type_id IN INTEGER
) RETURN NUMBER AS
  v_average_product_price NUMBER;
BEGIN
  SELECT AVG(price)
  INTO v_average_product_price
  FROM products
  WHERE product_type_id = p_product_type_id;
  RETURN v_average_product_price;
END average_product_price;
/
```

Calling a Function

You call your own functions as you would call any of the built-in database functions; you saw how to call built-in functions in Chapter 3. Just to refresh your memory, you can call a function using a `SELECT` statement that uses the `dual` table in the `FROM` clause. The following example calls `circle_area()`, passing a radius of 2 meters to the function:

```
SELECT circle_area(2)
FROM dual;

CIRCLE_AREA(2)
-------------
   12.5663704
```

The next example calls `average_product_price()`, passing the parameter value 1 to the function to get the average price of products whose `product_type_id` is 1:

```
SELECT average_product_price(1)
FROM dual;

AVERAGE_PRODUCT_PRICE(1)
-----------------------
                 29.965
```

Getting Information on Functions

You can get information on your functions from the `user_procedures` view; this view was covered earlier in the section "Getting Information on Procedures." The following example retrieves the `object_name`, `aggregate`, and `parallel` columns from `user_procedures` for `circle_area()` and `average_product_price()`:

```
SELECT object_name, aggregate, parallel
FROM user_procedures
WHERE object_name IN ('CIRCLE_AREA', 'AVERAGE_PRODUCT_PRICE');

OBJECT_NAME                  AGG PAR
---------------------------- --- ---
AVERAGE_PRODUCT_PRICE        NO  NO
CIRCLE_AREA                  NO  NO
```

Dropping a Function

You drop a function using `DROP FUNCTION`. For example, the following statement drops `circle_area()`:

```
DROP FUNCTION circle_area;
```

Packages

In this section, you'll learn how to group procedures and functions together into *packages*. Packages allow you to encapsulate related functionality into one self-contained unit. By modularizing your PL/SQL code in such a manner, you can potentially build up your own libraries of code that other programmers could reuse.

Packages are typically made up of two components: a *specification* and a *body*. The package specification contains information about the package, and it lists the available procedures and functions. These are potentially available to all database users, so I'll refer to these procedures and functions as being *public* (although only users who have the privileges to access your package can use it). The specification generally doesn't contain the code that makes up those procedures and functions—the package body contains the actual code.

The procedures and functions listed in the specification are available to the outside world, but any procedures and functions only contained in the body are only available within that body— they are *private* to that body. By using a combination of public and private procedures and functions, you can build up very complex packages whose complexity is hidden from the outside world. This is one of the primary goals of all programming: hide complexity from your users.

Creating a Package Specification

You create a package specification using the CREATE PACKAGE statement. The simplified syntax for the CREATE PACKAGE statement is as follows:

```
CREATE [OR REPLACE] PACKAGE package_name
{IS | AS}
  package_specification
END package_name;
```

where

- *package_name* specifies the name of the package.

- *package_specification* specifies the list of procedures and functions (along with any variables, type definitions, and cursors) that are available to your package's users.

The following example creates a package specification for a package named product_ package:

```
CREATE OR REPLACE PACKAGE product_package AS
  TYPE t_ref_cursor IS REF CURSOR;
  FUNCTION get_products_ref_cursor RETURN t_ref_cursor;
  PROCEDURE update_product_price (
    p_product_id IN products.product_id%TYPE,
    p_factor     IN NUMBER
  );
END product_package;
/
```

NOTE
The package defines a type named t_ref_cursor. PL/SQL enables you to create your own types, and you'll learn more about that in the next chapter.

The type `t_ref_cursor` uses the PL/SQL REF CURSOR type. A REF CURSOR is similar to a pointer in the C programming language, and it basically points to rows retrieved from the database using a PL/SQL cursor. In the following section, you'll see the use of a REF CURSOR to point to the result set returned by a SELECT statement that retrieves rows from the `products` table using a PL/SQL cursor. This is done using the function `get_products_ref_cursor()`, which returns a variable of type `t_ref_cursor`.

Creating a Package Body

You create a package body using the CREATE PACKAGE BODY statement. The simplified syntax for the CREATE PACKAGE BODY statement is as follows:

```
CREATE [OR REPLACE] PACKAGE BODY package_name
{IS | AS}
  package_body
END package_name;
```

where

- *package_name* specifies the name of the package, which must match the package name previously set in the package specification.

- *package_body* specifies the code for the procedures and functions, along with any variables and cursors.

The following example creates the package body for `product_package`:

```
CREATE OR REPLACE PACKAGE BODY product_package AS
  FUNCTION get_products_ref_cursor
  RETURN t_ref_cursor IS
    products_ref_cursor t_ref_cursor;
  BEGIN
    -- get the REF CURSOR
    OPEN products_ref_cursor FOR
      SELECT product_id, name, price
      FROM products;
    -- return the REF CURSOR
    RETURN products_ref_cursor;
  END get_products_ref_cursor;

  PROCEDURE update_product_price (
    p_product_id IN products.product_id%TYPE,
    p_factor     IN NUMBER
  ) AS
    v_product_count INTEGER;
  BEGIN
    -- count the number of products with the
    -- supplied product_id (should be 1 if the product exists)
    SELECT COUNT(*)
    INTO v_product_count
    FROM products
```

```
    WHERE product_id = p_product_id;
    -- if the product exists (v_product_count = 1) then
    -- update that product's price
    IF v_product_count = 1 THEN
      UPDATE products
      SET price = price * p_factor
      WHERE product_id = p_product_id;
      COMMIT;
    END IF;
  EXCEPTION
    WHEN OTHERS THEN
      -- perform a rollback when an exception occurs
      ROLLBACK;
  END update_product_price;
END product_package;
/
```

The get_products_ref_cursor() function opens a cursor and retrieves the product_
id, name, and price columns from the products table The reference to this cursor (the REF
CURSOR) is then returned by the function. This REF CURSOR may then be accessed to read the
column values. The update_product_price() procedure updates the price of a product.

Calling Functions and Procedures in a Package

When calling functions and procedures in a package, you include the package name in the call.
The following example calls product_package.get_products_ref_cursor(), which
returns a cursor containing the product_id, name, and price for the products:

```
SELECT product_package.get_products_ref_cursor
FROM dual;

GET_PRODUCTS_REF_CUR
--------------------
CURSOR STATEMENT : 1

CURSOR STATEMENT : 1

PRODUCT_ID NAME                                     PRICE
---------- -------------------------------- ----------
         1 Modern Science                           19.95
         2 Chemistry                                   30
         3 Supernova                                25.99
         4 Tank War                                 13.95
         5 Z Files                                  49.99
         6 2412: The Return                         14.95
         7 Space Force 9                            13.49
         8 From Another Planet                      12.99
         9 Classical Music                          10.99
        10 Pop 3                                    15.99
        11 Creative Yell                            14.99
        12 My Front Line                            13.49
```

The next example calls `product_package.update_product_price()` to multiply product #3's price by 1.25:

```
CALL product_package.update_product_price(3, 1.25);
```

The next query retrieves the details for product #3; notice the price has increased:

```
SELECT price
FROM products
WHERE product_id = 3;

    PRICE
----------
    32.49
```

Getting Information on Functions and Procedures in a Package

You can get information on your functions and procedures in a package from the `user_procedures` view; this view was covered earlier in the section "Getting Information on Procedures." The following example retrieves the `object_name`, and `procedure_name` columns from `user_procedures` for `product_package`:

```
SELECT object_name, procedure_name
FROM user_procedures
WHERE object_name = 'PRODUCT_PACKAGE';

OBJECT_NAME                        PROCEDURE_NAME
-------------------------------    -------------------------------
PRODUCT_PACKAGE                    GET_PRODUCTS_REF_CURSOR
PRODUCT_PACKAGE                    UPDATE_PRODUCT_PRICE
```

Dropping a Package

You drop a package using DROP PACKAGE. For example, the following statement drops `product_package`:

```
DROP PACKAGE product_package;
```

Triggers

A *trigger* is a procedure that is run automatically by the database—or in technical terms, *fired*—when a specified SQL DML INSERT, UPDATE, or DELETE statement is run against a specified database table. Triggers are useful for doing things like advanced auditing of changes made to column values in a table.

When a Trigger Runs

A trigger can fire before or after the SQL statement runs. Also, since a DML statement can affect more than one row at the same time, the procedure code for the trigger may be run once for every row affected (such a trigger is known as a *row-level trigger*), or just once for all the rows (known as a *statement-level trigger*). For example, if you had an UPDATE statement that modified ten rows and you had also created a row trigger that would fire for this UPDATE statement, then that trigger would run ten times—once for each row. If, however, your trigger was a statement-level trigger, the trigger would only fire once for the whole UPDATE statement.

> **NOTE**
> *A row-level trigger has access to the old and new column values when the trigger fires as a result of an UPDATE statement on that column.*

The firing of a trigger may also be limited using a trigger *condition*, for example, when a column value is less than a specified value.

Set Up for the Example Trigger

Triggers are useful for doing advanced auditing of changes made to column values. In the next section, you'll see a trigger that records when a product's price is lowered by more than 25 percent. When this event occurs, the trigger will add a row to the product_price_audit table, which is created by the following CREATE TABLE statement in the store_schema.sql script:

```
CREATE TABLE product_price_audit (
  product_id INTEGER
    CONSTRAINT price_audit_fk_products
    REFERENCES products(product_id),
  old_price  NUMBER(5, 2),
  new_price  NUMBER(5, 2)
);
```

As you can see, the product_id column of the product_price_audit table is a foreign key to the product_id column of the products table. The old_price column will be used to store the old price of a product prior to the change, and the new_price column will be used to store the new price after the change.

Creating a Trigger

You create a trigger using the CREATE TRIGGER statement. The simplified syntax for the CREATE TRIGGER statement is as follows:

```
CREATE [OR REPLACE] TRIGGER trigger_name
{BEFORE | AFTER | INSTEAD OF} trigger_event
ON table_name
```

```
[FOR EACH ROW [WHEN trigger_condition]]
BEGIN
  trigger_body
END trigger_name;
```

where

- OR REPLACE specifies the trigger is to replace an existing trigger if present. You can use this option when you want to modify the definition of a trigger.

- *trigger_name* specifies the trigger name.

- BEFORE specifies the trigger fires before the triggering event is performed. AFTER specifies the trigger fires after the triggering event is performed. INSTEAD OF specifies the trigger fires instead of performing the triggering event.

- *trigger_event* specifies the event that causes the trigger to fire.

- *table_name* specifies the table that the trigger references.

- FOR EACH ROW specifies the trigger is a row-level trigger, which means the code contained within *trigger_body* is run for each row when the trigger fires. If you omit FOR EACH ROW, the trigger is a statement-level trigger, which means the code within *trigger_body* is run once when the trigger fires regardless of the number of rows affected.

- *trigger_condition* specifies a Boolean condition that limits when a trigger actually runs its code.

- *trigger_body* contains the SQL and PL/SQL statements that perform the trigger's task.

The example trigger you'll see in this section will fire before an update of the price column from the products table, and therefore I'll name the trigger before_product_price_update. Also, because I want to use the price column values before and after any UPDATE statement modifies the price column's value, I must use a row-level trigger. Finally, since I only want to audit a price change when the new price is lowered by more than 25 percent of the old value, I'll need to specify a trigger condition. The following statement creates the before_product_price_update trigger:

```
CREATE OR REPLACE TRIGGER before_product_price_update
BEFORE UPDATE OF price
ON products
FOR EACH ROW WHEN (new.price < old.price * 0.75)
BEGIN
  dbms_output.put_line('product_id = ' || :old.product_id);
  dbms_output.put_line('Old price = ' || :old.price);
  dbms_output.put_line('New price = ' || :new.price);
  dbms_output.put_line('The price reduction is more than 25%');

  -- insert row into the product_price_audit table
```

```
  INSERT INTO product_price_audit (
    product_id, old_price, new_price
  ) VALUES (
    :old.product_id, :old.price, :new.price
  );
END before_product_price_update;
/
```

There are five things you should notice about this statement:

- The BEFORE UPDATE OF clause specifies that the trigger is to fire before the update of the price column.

- The FOR EACH ROW clause identifies this as a row-level trigger, which means the trigger code contained within the BEGIN and END keywords is to be run once for each row.

- The trigger condition is (new.price < old.price * 0.75), which means the trigger code will only be run when the new price is less than 75 percent of the old price—that is, when the price is reduced by more than 25 percent.

- The new and old column values are accessed using the :old and :new aliases in the trigger.

- The trigger code displays the product ID, the old and new prices, and a message stating that the price reduction is more than 25 percent. The code then adds a row to the product_price_audit table containing the product ID and the old and new prices.

Firing a Trigger

To fire the before_product_price_update trigger, you must reduce a product's price by more than 25 percent. Before you see that, the following example retrieves the product_id and price columns from the products table:

```
SELECT product_id, price
FROM products
ORDER BY product_id;
```

```
       ID      PRICE
---------- ----------
        1      29.93
        2         30
        3      32.49
        4      13.95
        5      49.99
        6      14.95
        7      13.49
        8      12.99
        9      10.99
```

```
10      15.99
11      14.99
12      13.49
```

To see the output from the trigger, you need to run the SET SERVEROUTPUT ON command:

```
SET SERVEROUTPUT ON
```

Go ahead and perform the following UPDATE statement to reduce the price of products #5 and #10 by 30 percent (this is achieved by multiplying the price column by .7). This UPDATE will cause the before_product_price_update trigger to fire:

```
UPDATE products
SET price = price * .7
WHERE product_id IN (5, 10);

product_id = 10
Old price = 15.99
New price = 11.19
The price reduction is more than 25%
product_id = 5
Old price = 49.99
New price = 34.99
The price reduction is more than 25%

2 rows updated.
```

As you can see, the trigger fired for products #10 and #5. You can see that the trigger did indeed add the two required rows containing the product IDs, along with the old and new prices, to the product_price_audit table using the following query:

```
SELECT *
FROM product_price_audit;

PRODUCT_ID   OLD_PRICE   NEW_PRICE
----------   ---------   ---------
        10       15.99       11.19
         5       49.99       34.99
```

Getting Information on Triggers

You can get information on your triggers from the user_triggers view. Table 11-3 describes some of the columns in user_triggers.

NOTE
You can get information on all the triggers you have access to using all_triggers.

Column	Type	Description
TRIGGER_NAME	VARCHAR2(30)	Name of the trigger.
TRIGGER_TYPE	VARCHAR2(16)	Type of the trigger.
TRIGGERING_EVENT	VARCHAR2(227)	Event that causes the trigger to fire.
TABLE_OWNER	VARCHAR2(30)	User who owns the table that the trigger references.
BASE_OBJECT_TYPE	VARCHAR2(16)	Type of the object referenced by the trigger.
TABLE_NAME	VARCHAR2(30)	Name of the table referenced by the trigger.
COLUMN_NAME	VARCHAR2(4000)	Name of the column referenced by the trigger.
REFERENCING_NAMES	VARCHAR2(128)	Name of the old and new aliases.
WHEN_CLAUSE	VARCHAR2(4000)	Trigger condition that limits when the trigger runs its code.
STATUS	VARCHAR2(8)	Whether the trigger is enabled or disabled. Set to ENABLED or DISABLED.
DESCRIPTION	VARCHAR2(4000)	Description of trigger.
ACTION_TYPE	VARCHAR2(11)	Action type of the trigger. Set to CALL or PL/SQL.
TRIGGER_BODY	LONG	Code contained in the trigger body. The LONG type allows storage of large amounts of text. You'll learn about the LONG type in Chapter 14.

TABLE 11-3. *Some Columns in* user_triggers

The following example retrieves the details of the before_product_price_update trigger from user_triggers:

```
SELECT *
FROM user_triggers
WHERE trigger_name = 'BEFORE_PRODUCT_PRICE_UPDATE';

TRIGGER_NAME                    TRIGGER_TYPE
------------------------------ ----------------
TRIGGERING_EVENT
-----------------------------------------------------------
TABLE_OWNER                    BASE_OBJECT_TYPE TABLE_NAME
------------------------------ ---------------- -----------
COLUMN_NAME
```

```
------------------------------------------------------------
REFERENCING_NAMES
------------------------------------------------------------
WHEN_CLAUSE
------------------------------------------------------------
STATUS
--------
DESCRIPTION
------------------------------------------------------------
ACTION_TYPE
-----------
TRIGGER_BODY
------------------------------------------------------------
BEFORE_PRODUCT_PRICE_UPDATE     BEFORE EACH ROW
UPDATE
STORE                           TABLE            PRODUCTS

REFERENCING NEW AS NEW OLD AS OLD
new.price < old.price * 0.75
ENABLED
before_product_price_update
BEFORE UPDATE OF
  price
ON
  products
FOR EACH ROW
PL/SQL
BEGIN

  dbms_output.put_line('product_id = ' || :old.product_id);
  dbms_output
```

Disabling and Enabling Trigger

You can stop a trigger from firing by disabling it using the ALTER TRIGGER statement. For example, the following statement disables the before_product_price_update trigger:

```
ALTER TRIGGER before_product_price_update DISABLE;
```

The following example enables the before_product_price_update trigger:

```
ALTER TRIGGER before_product_price_update ENABLE;
```

Dropping a Trigger

You drop a trigger using DROP TRIGGER. For example, the following statement drops the before_product_price_update trigger:

```
DROP TRIGGER before_product_price_update;
```

Summary

In this chapter, you learned that

- PL/SQL (Procedural Language/SQL) is built on top of SQL and is a third generation programming language.

- PL/SQL programs are divided up into blocks with each block containing PL/SQL and SQL statements.

- You may use a loop, such as a WHILE or FOR loop, to run one or more statements multiple times.

- You use a cursor when you have a SELECT statement that returns more than one row from the database. You retrieve the rows into the cursor using your SELECT statement and then fetch the rows from the cursor.

- Exceptions are used to handle errors that occur in your PL/SQL code.

- A procedure contains a group of SQL and PL/SQL statements. Procedures allow you to centralize your business logic in the database and may be used by any program that accesses the database.

- A function is similar to a procedure except that a function must return a value to the statement from which it is called.

- You can group procedures and functions together into packages, which allow you to encapsulate related functionality into one self-contained unit. Packages are typically made up of two components: a specification and a body.

- A trigger is a procedure that is run automatically by the database when a specified SQL DML INSERT, UPDATE, or DELETE statement is run against a specified database table. Triggers are useful for doing things like advanced auditing of changes made to column values in a table.

In the next chapter, you'll learn about database objects.

CHAPTER
12

Database Objects

In this chapter, you will

- Be introduced to objects in the database
- Learn how to create object types
- Use object types to define column objects and object tables
- Perform DML operations with objects
- Use objects in PL/SQL
- Learn how a type may inherit from another type
- Define your own constructors

Introducing Objects

Object-oriented programming languages such as Java and C++ allow you to define classes. These classes act as templates from which you can create objects. Classes define attributes and methods. Attributes are used to store an object's state, and methods are used to model an object's behaviors.

With the release of the Oracle8 database, objects became available within the database. The availability of objects in the database was a major breakthrough because they enable you to define your own classes, known as *object types*, in the database. Like classes in Java, database object types can contain attributes and methods. Object types are also sometimes known as user-defined types.

A simple example of an object type would be a type that models a product. This object type could contain attributes for the product's name, description, price, and in the case of a product that is perishable, the number of days the product can sit on the shelves before it must be thrown away. This product object type could also contain a method that returns the sell-by date of the product, based on the shelf life of the product and the current date. Another example of an object type might be one that models a person; this object type could store attributes for the person's first name, last name, date of birth, and address. The address itself could be an object type, and it could store things like the street, city, state, and zip code. You'll see examples of object types that represent a product, person, and address in this chapter. You'll also see how to create tables from those object types and populate those tables with rows.

Creating Object Types

You create an object type using the CREATE [OR REPLACE] TYPE statement. The following example uses the CREATE TYPE statement to create an object type named address_typ. This object type is used to represent an address and contains four attributes named street, city, state, and zip:

```
CREATE TYPE address_typ AS OBJECT (
    street VARCHAR2(15),
    city   VARCHAR2(15),
    state  CHAR(2),
    zip    VARCHAR2(5)
);
/
```

NOTE
I've provided a SQL*Plus script named `object_schema.sql` *in the* `SQL` *directory, which creates a user named* `object_user` *with a password of* `object_password`. *The* `object_schema.sql` *script creates the types, and tables, and performs the various* `INSERT` *statements shown in this section. You can run the* `object_schema.sql` *script if you are using an Oracle8 database or above.*

As you can see from the previous example, each attribute is defined using a database type. For example, `street` is defined as `VARCHAR2(15)`. As you'll see shortly, the type of an attribute can itself be an object type. You'll notice I add `_typ` to the end of my object types. You can follow this standard when creating your own object types or you can use your own standard—just be sure to use your standard consistently.

As I mentioned at the start of this chapter, I'm going to represent a person using an object type. The following statement creates an object type named `person_typ`. Notice that `person_typ` uses `address_typ` to define an attribute named `address`:

```
CREATE TYPE person_typ AS OBJECT (
    id          NUMBER,
    first_name  VARCHAR2(10),
    last_name   VARCHAR2(10),
    dob         DATE,
    phone       VARCHAR2(12),
    address     address_typ
);
/
```

The next example creates an object type named `product_typ` that will be used to represent products. Notice that `product_typ` declares a function named `get_sell_by_date()`. This function will return the date by which the product must be sold based on the `days_valid` attribute and the current date:

```
CREATE TYPE product_typ AS OBJECT (
    id          NUMBER,
    name        VARCHAR2(15),
    description VARCHAR2(22),
    price       NUMBER(5, 2),
    days_valid  NUMBER,

    -- declare the get_sell_by_date() member function,
    -- get_sell_by_date() returns the date by which the
    -- product must be sold
    MEMBER FUNCTION get_sell_by_date RETURN DATE
);
/
```

The `MEMBER FUNCTION` clause is used to declare the `get_sell_by_date()` function. You can declare a procedure using `MEMBER PROCEDURE`. A procedure is similar to a function except that a procedure doesn't typically return a value.

Since `product_typ` contains a method declaration, a *body* for `product_typ` must also be created. The body defines the code for the method, and a body is created using the CREATE TYPE BODY statement. The following example creates the body for `product_typ`. Notice that this body contains the code definition for the `get_sell_by_date()` method:

```
CREATE TYPE BODY product_typ AS
  -- define the get_sell_by_date() member function,
  -- get_sell_by_date() returns the date by which the
  -- product must be sold
  MEMBER FUNCTION get_sell_by_date RETURN DATE IS
    v_sell_by_date DATE;
  BEGIN
    -- calculate the sell by date by adding the days_valid attribute
    -- to the current date (SYSDATE)
    SELECT days_valid + SYSDATE
    INTO v_sell_by_date
    FROM dual;

    -- return the sell by date
    RETURN v_sell_by_date;
  END;
END;
/
```

As you can see, `get_sell_by_date()` calculates and returns the date by which the product must be sold by adding the `days_valid` attribute to the current date. The current date is obtained from the database using SYSDATE.

You can also create a synonym and a public synonym for a type. The following example creates a public synonym named `pub_product_typ` for `product_typ`:

```
CREATE PUBLIC SYNONYM pub_product_typ FOR product_typ;
```

NOTE
You must have the CREATE PUBLIC SYNONYM privilege to run this statement.

Using DESCRIBE to Get Information on Object Types

You can use the DESCRIBE command to get information on object types. The following examples describe `address_typ` and `person_typ`:

```
DESCRIBE address_typ
 Name                                    Null?    Type
 --------------------------------------- -------- ------------
 STREET                                           VARCHAR2(15)
 CITY                                             VARCHAR2(15)
```

```
    STATE                                          CHAR(2)
    ZIP                                            VARCHAR2(5)


DESCRIBE person_typ
Name                                     Null?    Type
---------------------------------------- -------- ------------
    ID                                             NUMBER
    FIRST_NAME                                     VARCHAR2(10)
    LAST_NAME                                      VARCHAR2(10)
    DOB                                            DATE
    PHONE                                          VARCHAR2(12)
    ADDRESS                                        ADDRESS_TYP
```

You can set the depth to which DESCRIBE will show information using SET DESCRIBE DEPTH. The following example sets the depth to 2 and then describes person_typ again. Notice the attributes of address are displayed (address is of type address_typ):

```
SET DESCRIBE DEPTH 2
DESCRIBE person_typ
Name                                     Null?    Type
---------------------------------------- -------- ------------
    ID                                             NUMBER
    FIRST_NAME                                     VARCHAR2(10)
    LAST_NAME                                      VARCHAR2(10)
    DOB                                            DATE
    PHONE                                          VARCHAR2(12)
    ADDRESS                                        ADDRESS_TYP
      STREET                                       VARCHAR2(15)
      CITY                                         VARCHAR2(15)
      STATE                                        CHAR(2)
      ZIP                                          VARCHAR2(5)
```

Using Object Types to Define Column Objects and Object Tables

You can use an object type to define a column in a table, and the column is known as a *column object*. Also, when an object type contains an embedded object type, that embedded object type is also a column object. An example of this is person_typ, which contains an embedded address_typ column object named address.

The following example creates a table named products that contains a column object of product_typ. Notice that this table also contains a NUMBER column named quantity_in_stock, which is used to store the number of those products currently in stock:

```
CREATE TABLE products (
  product           product_typ,
  quantity_in_stock NUMBER
);
```

You can also use an object type to define an entire table, and the table is known as an *object table*. The following examples create two object tables, named `object_products` and `object_customers`, which are defined using `product_typ` and `person_typ`, respectively. Notice the use of the `OF` clause to identify each table as an object table:

```
CREATE TABLE object_products OF product_typ;
CREATE TABLE object_customers OF person_typ;
```

One difference between a table containing a column object and an object table is that the former can have more than one column. For example, I added the additional `quantity_in_stock` column to the `products` table.

Object References and Object Identifiers

Another difference of object tables is that you use *object references* to model relationships between object tables, rather than foreign keys. Object references are defined using the `REF` type and are basically pointers to objects in an object table. Each object in an object table has a unique *object identifier* (OID) that you can then store in a `REF` column. The following example creates a table named `purchases` that contains two `REF` columns:

```
CREATE TABLE purchases (
    id        NUMBER PRIMARY KEY,
    customer REF person_typ   SCOPE IS object_customers,
    product  REF product_typ SCOPE IS object_products
);
```

The `SCOPE IS` clause restricts the object reference to point to objects in a specific table. For example, the `customer` column is restricted to point to objects in the `object_customers` table; similarly, the `product` column is restricted to point to objects in the `object_products` table.

In the following sections, you'll learn how to perform SQL DML operations on the `products`, `object_products`, `object_customers`, and `purchases` tables.

Performing DML on the products Table

In this section, you'll see how to perform SQL DML statements to insert, select, update, and delete rows in the `products` table. The `products` table was created using the following statement:

```
CREATE TABLE products (
    product           product_typ,
    quantity_in_stock NUMBER
);
```

Inserting Rows into the products Table

When inserting a row into a table containing a column object, you must supply the attribute values for that object using a *constructor*. The constructor for the object has the same name as the object type and accepts parameters for the attributes of the object. The following examples insert two rows into the `products` table. Notice the use of the `product_typ` constructor to supply the attribute values for the `product` column object:

```
INSERT INTO products (
   product,
   quantity_in_stock
) VALUES (
   product_typ(1, 'Pasta', '20 oz bag of pasta', 3.95, 10),
   50
);

INSERT INTO products (
   product,
   quantity_in_stock
) VALUES (
   product_typ(2, 'Sardines', '12 oz box of sardines', 2.99, 5),
   25
);
```

NOTE
The SQL*Plus script object_schema.sql *contains these two* INSERT *statements, along with the other* INSERT *statements featured in this chapter.*

Selecting Rows from the products Table

The following example selects all the rows from the products table. Notice that the product column object's attributes are displayed within a constructor for product_typ:

```
SELECT *
FROM products;

PRODUCT(ID, NAME, DESCRIPTION, PRICE, DAYS_VALID)
------------------------------------------------------------
QUANTITY_IN_STOCK
----------------
PRODUCT_TYP(1, 'Pasta', '20 oz bag of pasta', 3.95, 10)
                50

PRODUCT_TYP(2, 'Sardines', '12 oz box of sardines', 2.99, 5)
                25
```

You can select an individual column object from a table. To do this, you must supply a table alias through which you select the object. The following example selects a single product column object from the products table. Notice the use of the table alias p through which the product object's id attribute is specified:

```
SELECT p.product
FROM products p
WHERE p.product.id = 1;
```

```
PRODUCT(ID, NAME, DESCRIPTION, PRICE, DAYS_VALID)
------------------------------------------------------------
PRODUCT_TYP(1, 'Pasta', '20 oz bag of pasta', 3.95, 10)
```

Earlier, you saw that the `product_typ` object type contains a function named `get_sell_by_date()` that calculates and returns the date by which the product must be sold. It does this by adding the `days_valid` attribute to the current date, which is obtained from the database using the `sysdate` variable. You can call the `get_sell_by_date()` function using a table alias, for example:

```
SELECT p.product.get_sell_by_date()
FROM products p;
```

```
P.PRODUCT
---------
12-OCT-03
07-OCT-03
```

Of course, if you run this example your dates will be different because they are calculated using SYSDATE.

Updating a Row in the products Table

The following example updates a row in the `products` table. Notice that a table alias is used to access the `product` column object:

```
UPDATE products p
SET p.product.description = '30 oz bag of pasta'
WHERE p.product.id = 1;
```

```
1 row updated.
```

Deleting a Row from the products Table

The following example deletes a row from the `products` table. Notice that a table alias is used to access the `product` column object:

```
DELETE FROM products p
WHERE p.product.id = 2;
```

```
1 row deleted.
```

```
ROLLBACK;
```

NOTE
If you're entering this UPDATE and the previous DELETE statements in SQL*Plus, make sure you execute the ROLLBACK, or you can run the object_schema.sql script again to re-create the schema and populate the tables.

Performing DML on the object_products Table

The `object_products` table is an object table consisting of `product_typ` objects. This table was created using the following statement:

```
CREATE TABLE object_products OF product_typ;
```

In this section, you'll see how to perform SQL DML statements to insert, update, and delete rows in the `object_products` table. You'll also see how to select rows from the `object_products` table.

Inserting Rows into the object_products Table

When inserting a row into an object table, you can choose whether to use a constructor to supply attribute values, or to supply the values in the same way that you would supply column values in a relational table. The following example inserts a row into the `object_products` table using the constructor for `product_typ`:

```
INSERT INTO object_products VALUES (
  product_typ(1, 'Pasta', '20 oz bag of pasta', 3.95, 10)
);
```

The next example omits the constructor for `product_typ` when inserting a row into `object_products`. Notice that the attribute values for `product_typ` are supplied in the same way that columns would be in a relational table:

```
INSERT INTO object_products (
  id, name, description, price, days_valid
) VALUES (
  2, 'Sardines', '12 oz box of sardines', 2.99, 5
);
```

Selecting Rows from the object_products Table

The following example selects all the rows from the `object_products` table:

```
SELECT *
FROM object_products;

        ID NAME       DESCRIPTION                 PRICE DAYS_VALID
---------- ---------- ---------------------- ---------- ----------
         1 Pasta      20 oz bag of pasta          3.95         10
         2 Sardines   12 oz box of sardines       2.99          5
```

You can use the built-in Oracle database `VALUE()` function to select a row from an object table. This treats the row as an actual object and returns the attributes for the object within a constructor for the object type. The `VALUE()` function accepts a parameter containing a table alias, and the next example uses the VALUE() function when selecting the rows from object_products:

```
SELECT VALUE(op)
FROM object_products op;

VALUE(OP)(ID, NAME, DESCRIPTION, PRICE, DAYS_VALID)
-------------------------------------------------------
PRODUCT_TYP(1, 'Pasta', '20 oz bag of pasta', 3.95, 10)
PRODUCT_TYP(2, 'Sardines', '12 oz box of sardines', 2.99, 5)
```

Updating a Row in the object_products Table
The following example updates a row in the object_products table. Notice that the attributes are treated like columns in a relational table:

```
UPDATE object_products
SET description = '25 oz bag of pasta'
WHERE id = 1;

1 row updated.
```

Deleting a Row from the object_products Table
The following example deletes a row from the object_products table. Notice that the id attribute is again treated like a relational column:

```
DELETE FROM object_products
WHERE id = 2;

1 row deleted.

ROLLBACK;
```

Performing DML on the object_customers Table
The object_customers table is an object table of person_typ; person_typ contains an embedded address_typ column object named address. The object_customers table is defined as follows:

```
CREATE TABLE object_customers OF person_typ;
```

In this section, you'll see how to perform SQL DML statements to insert and select rows in the object_customers table. Since updates and deletes for object_customers are conceptually similar to the previous examples for object_products, I won't show examples of an update and delete for object_products.

Inserting Rows into the object_customers Table

The following examples insert two rows into object_customers. The first example uses constructors for person_typ and address_typ, while the second example omits the person_typ constructor:

```
INSERT INTO object_customers VALUES (
  person_typ(1, 'John', 'Brown', '01-FEB-1955', '800-555-1211',
    address_typ('2 State Street', 'Beantown', 'MA', '12345')
  )
);

INSERT INTO object_customers (
  id, first_name, last_name, dob, phone,
  address
) VALUES (
  2, 'Cynthia', 'Green', '05-FEB-1968', '800-555-1212',
  address_typ('3 Free Street', 'Middle Town', 'CA', '12345')
);
```

Selecting Rows from the object_customers Table

The object_customers table is an object table of person_typ; person_typ contains an embedded address_typ column object named address. The following example selects all the rows from the object_customers table. Notice that the attributes for the embedded address column object are displayed within the address_typ constructor:

```
SELECT *
FROM object_customers;

        ID FIRST_NAME LAST_NAME  DOB       PHONE
---------- ---------- ---------- --------- ------------
ADDRESS(STREET, CITY, STATE, ZIP)
----------------------------------------------------------
         1 John       Brown      01-FEB-55 800-555-1211
ADDRESS_TYP('2 State Street', 'Beantown', 'MA', '12345')

         2 Cynthia    Green      05-FEB-68 800-555-1212
ADDRESS_TYP('3 Free Street', 'Middle Town', 'CA', '12345')
```

The next example selects a single row from object_customers. Notice the use of the table alias oc through which the id attribute is specified:

```
SELECT *
FROM object_customers oc
WHERE oc.id = 1;
```

```
          ID FIRST_NAME LAST_NAME  DOB        PHONE
---------- ---------- ---------- --------- ------------
ADDRESS(STREET, CITY, STATE, ZIP)
------------------------------------------------------
           1 John       Brown      01-FEB-55 800-555-1211
ADDRESS_TYP('2 State Street', 'Beantown', 'MA', '12345')
```

In the following example, a row is selected based on the state attribute of the address column object:

```
SELECT *
FROM object_customers oc
WHERE oc.address.state = 'MA';
```

```
          ID FIRST_NAME LAST_NAME  DOB        PHONE
---------- ---------- ---------- --------- ------------
ADDRESS(STREET, CITY, STATE, ZIP)
-------------------------------------------------------------------
           1 John       Brown      01-FEB-55 800-555-1211
ADDRESS_TYP('2 State Street', 'Beantown', 'MA', '12345')
```

Performing DML on the purchases Table

The purchases table contains a NUMBER column named id, along with two REF columns named customer and product. The purchases table is defined as follows:

```
CREATE TABLE purchases (
   id       NUMBER PRIMARY KEY,
   customer REF person_typ   SCOPE IS object_customers,
   product  REF product_typ  SCOPE IS object_products
);
```

In this section, you'll see how to perform SQL DML statements to insert and update a row in the purchases table. You'll also see how to select rows from the purchases table.

Inserting a Row into the purchases Table

As I mentioned, each object in an object table has a unique object identifier that you can store in a REF column. You can access this object identifier using the REF() function and store the returned object identifier in a REF column. The following example inserts a row into the purchases table. Notice the use of the REF() function to read the object identifiers for the rows from the object_customers and object_products tables:

```
INSERT INTO purchases (
   id,
   customer,
   product
) VALUES (
   1,
   (SELECT REF(oc) FROM object_customers oc WHERE oc.id = 1),
   (SELECT REF(op) FROM object_products  op WHERE op.id = 1)
);
```

This example records that customer #1 purchased product #1.

Selecting a Row from the purchases Table

The following example selects the row from the `purchases` table. Notice that the `customer` and `product` columns contain long strings of numbers and letters. These are the object identifiers for the rows in the `object_customers` and `object_products` tables:

```
SELECT *
FROM purchases;

        ID
----------
CUSTOMER
--------------------------------------------------------------------
PRODUCT
--------------------------------------------------------------------
         1
0000220208662E2AB6256711D6A1B50010A4E7AE8A662E2AB3256711D6A1B50010A4E
7AE8A
0000220208662E2AB4256711D6A1B50010A4E7AE8A662E2AB2256711D6A1B50010A4E
7AE8A
```

You can access the rows in the object tables that are pointed to by REF column values using the DEREF() function; this function accepts a REF column as a parameter. The following example uses the DEREF() function to access the rows pointed to by the `customer` and `product` columns of the `purchases` table:

```
SELECT DEREF(customer), DEREF(product)
FROM purchases;

DEREF(CUSTOMER)(ID, FIRST_NAME, LAST_NAME, DOB, PHONE,
 ADDRESS(STREET, CITY, STATE, ZIP))
--------------------------------------------------------
DEREF(PRODUCT)(ID, NAME, DESCRIPTION, PRICE, DAYS_VALID)
--------------------------------------------------------
PERSON_TYP(1, 'John', 'Brown', '01-FEB-55', '800-555-1211',
 ADDRESS_TYP('2 State Street', 'Beantown', 'MA', '12345'))
PRODUCT_TYP(1, 'Pasta', '20 oz bag of pasta', 3.95, 10)
```

Updating a Row in the purchases Table

The following example updates the row in the `purchases` table. Notice that the `product` column is changed to point to product #2 in the `object_products` table.

```
UPDATE purchases SET product = (
  SELECT REF(op) FROM object_products op WHERE op.id = 2
) WHERE id = 1;

1 row updated.
```

Using Objects in PL/SQL

You can use objects in PL/SQL. In this section, you'll see a package named `product_package` that contains the following items:

- A function named `get_products()` that returns the objects in the `object_products` table
- A procedure named `insert_product()` that adds an object to the `object_products` table

The `object_product.sql` script contains the following package specification:

```
CREATE OR REPLACE PACKAGE product_package AS
  TYPE ref_cursor_typ IS REF CURSOR;
  FUNCTION get_products RETURN ref_cursor_typ;
  PROCEDURE insert_product (
    p_id          IN object_products.id%TYPE,
    p_name        IN object_products.name%TYPE,
    p_description IN object_products.description%TYPE,
    p_price       IN object_products.price%TYPE,
    p_days_valid  IN object_products.days_valid%TYPE
  );
END product_package;
/
```

The `object_product.sql` script contains the following package body:

```
CREATE OR REPLACE PACKAGE BODY product_package AS
  FUNCTION get_products
  RETURN ref_cursor_typ IS
    products_ref_cursor ref_cursor_typ;
  BEGIN
    -- get the REF CURSOR
    OPEN products_ref_cursor FOR
      SELECT VALUE(op)
      FROM object_products op;
    -- return the REF CURSOR
    RETURN products_ref_cursor;
  END get_products;

  PROCEDURE insert_product (
    p_id          IN object_products.id%TYPE,
    p_name        IN object_products.name%TYPE,
    p_description IN object_products.description%TYPE,
```

```
       p_price         IN object_products.price%TYPE,
       p_days_valid  IN object_products.days_valid%TYPE
    ) AS
       product product_typ :=
         product_typ(
            p_id, p_name, p_description, p_price, p_days_valid
         );
    BEGIN
       INSERT INTO object_products VALUES (product);
       COMMIT;
    EXCEPTION
       WHEN OTHERS THEN
          ROLLBACK;
    END insert_product;
END product_package;
/
```

Notice the following about `product_package`:

- The `get_products()` function returns the contents of the `object_products` table as `product_typ` objects using `VALUE`.

- The `insert_product()` procedure accepts a number of parameters that are used to set the attributes of the `product` object, which is of type `product_typ`. The `product` object is then inserted into the `object_products` table.

The following example calls `product_package.insert_product()` to add a new row to the `object_products` table:

```
CALL product_package.insert_product(4, 'salsa',
  '15 oz jar of salsa', 1.50, 20);
```

The next example calls `product_package.get_products()` to retrieve the products from `object_products`:

```
SELECT product_package.get_products
FROM dual;

GET_PRODUCTS
-------------------
CURSOR STATEMENT : 1

CURSOR STATEMENT : 1

VALUE(OP)(ID, NAME, DESCRIPTION, PRICE, DAYS_VALID)
-----------------------------------------------------------
PRODUCT_TYP(1, 'Pasta', '20 oz bag of pasta', 3.95, 10)
PRODUCT_TYP(2, 'Sardines', '12 oz box of sardines', 2.99, 5)
PRODUCT_TYP(3, 'salsa', '15 oz jar of salsa', 1.5, 20)
```

Type Inheritance

With the release of the Oracle9*i* database, you can use object type *inheritance*. This allows you to define hierarchies of database types. For example, you might want to define a business person object type and have that type inherit existing attributes from `person_typ`. The business person type could extend `person_typ` with attributes to store the person's job title and the name of the company they work for. For `person_typ` to be inherited from, it must be defined using the NOT FINAL clause:

```
CREATE TYPE person_typ AS OBJECT (
    id          NUMBER,
    first_name  VARCHAR2(10),
    last_name   VARCHAR2(10),
    dob         DATE,
    phone       VARCHAR2(12),
    address     address_typ
) NOT FINAL;
/
```

The NOT FINAL clause indicates that `person_typ` can be inherited from when defining another type. The default is FINAL, meaning that the object type cannot be inherited from.

NOTE
I've provided a SQL*Plus script named `object_schema2.sql` *in the* `SQL` *directory that creates a user named* `object_user2` *with a password of* `object_password`. *The* `object_schema2.sql` *script creates the types, tables, and performs the various INSERT statements shown in the rest of this chapter. You can run the* `object_schema2.sql` *script if you are using an Oracle9i database or above.*

To have a new type inherit attributes and methods from an existing type, you use the UNDER clause when defining your new type. Our example business person type, which I'll name `business_person_typ`, uses the UNDER clause to inherit the attributes from `person_typ`:

```
CREATE TYPE business_person_typ UNDER person_typ (
    title   VARCHAR2(20),
    company VARCHAR2(20)
);
/
```

In this example, `person_typ` is known as the *supertype*, and `business_person_typ` is known as the *subtype*. You can then use `business_person_typ` when defining column objects or object tables. For example, the following statement creates an object table named `object_business_customers`:

```
CREATE TABLE object_business_customers OF business_person_typ;
```

The following example inserts a row into `object_business_customers`. Notice that the two additional `title` and `company` attributes are supplied:

```
INSERT INTO object_business_customers VALUES (
  business_person_typ(1, 'John', 'Brown', '01-FEB-1955', '800-555-1211',
    address_typ('2 State Street', 'Beantown', 'MA', '12345'),
    'Manager', 'XYZ Corp'
  )
);
```

The final example selects this row:

```
SELECT *
FROM object_business_customers;

        ID FIRST_NAME LAST_NAME  DOB       PHONE
---------- ---------- ---------- --------- ------------
ADDRESS(STREET, CITY, STATE, ZIP)
---------------------------------------------------------
TITLE                COMPANY
-------------------- --------------------
         1 John       Brown      01-FEB-55 800-555-1211
ADDRESS_TYP('2 State Street', 'Beantown', 'MA', '12345')
Manager              XYZ Corp
```

NOT INSTANTIABLE Object Types

You can mark an object type as NOT INSTANTIABLE, which prevents objects of that type from being created. You might want to mark an object type as NOT INSTANTIABLE when you want to use that type only as a supertype. For example, you could create a type to represent vehicles and use it as a supertype for another type to represent cars and motorcycles. The following statement creates a type named `vehicle_typ`, which is marked as NOT INSTANTIABLE:

```
CREATE TYPE vehicle_typ AS OBJECT (
  id    NUMBER,
  make  VARCHAR2(15),
  model VARCHAR2(15)
) NOT FINAL NOT INSTANTIABLE;
/
```

NOTE
`vehicle_typ` is also marked as NOT FINAL. A NOT INSTANTIABLE type cannot be FINAL because you wouldn't be able to use it as a supertype, and that's why `vehicle_typ` is marked as NOT FINAL.

The next example creates a type named `car_typ` that inherits from the `vehicle_typ` supertype. Notice `car_typ` has an additional attribute named `convertible` that records whether the car is a convertible:

```
CREATE TYPE car_typ UNDER vehicle_typ (
    convertible CHAR(1)
);
/
```

The following example creates a type named `motorcycle_typ` that inherits from the `vehicle_typ` supertype. Notice `motorcycle_typ` has an additional attribute named `sidecar` that records whether the motorcycle has a sidecar:

```
CREATE TYPE motorcycle_typ UNDER vehicle_typ (
    sidecar CHAR(1)
);
/
```

The next example creates tables named `vehicles`, `cars` and `motorcycles`, which are object tables that use the types `vehicle_typ`, `car_typ` and `motorcycle_typ`:

```
CREATE TABLE vehicles OF vehicle_typ;
CREATE TABLE cars OF car_typ;
CREATE TABLE motorcycles OF motorcycle_typ;
```

Because `vehicle_typ` is NOT INSTANTIABLE, you cannot add a row to the `vehicles` table. If you attempt to do so, the database returns an error; for example:

```
SQL> INSERT INTO vehicles VALUES (
  2    vehicle_typ(1, 'Toyota', 'MR2', '01-FEB-1955')
  3  );
    vehicle_typ(1, 'Toyota', 'MR2', '01-FEB-1955')
    *
ERROR at line 2:
ORA-22826: cannot construct an instance of a non instantiable type
```

The following examples add rows to the `cars` and `motorcycles` tables:

```
INSERT INTO cars VALUES (
    car_typ(1, 'Toyota', 'MR2', 'Y')
);

INSERT INTO motorcycles VALUES (
    motorcycle_typ(1, 'Harley-Davidson', 'V-Rod', 'N')
);
```

The final example queries the `cars` and `motorcycles` tables:

```
SELECT *
FROM cars;

         ID MAKE            MODEL            C
---------- --------------- --------------- -
          1 Toyota          MR2              Y

SELECT *
FROM motorcycles;

         ID MAKE            MODEL            S
---------- --------------- --------------- -
          1 Harley-Davidson V-Rod            N
```

User-Defined Constructors

Like other object-oriented languages, you can define your own constructors to initialize the attributes of an object. You can define your own constructor to do things like programmatically default one or more attributes of an object.

The following example creates a type named `person_typ2` that declares two constructor method signatures:

```
CREATE OR REPLACE TYPE person_typ2 AS OBJECT (
  id          NUMBER,
  first_name VARCHAR2(10),
  last_name  VARCHAR2(10),
  dob         DATE,
  phone       VARCHAR2(12),
  CONSTRUCTOR FUNCTION person_typ2(
    p_id         NUMBER,
    p_first_name VARCHAR2,
    p_last_name  VARCHAR2
  ) RETURN SELF AS RESULT,
  CONSTRUCTOR FUNCTION person_typ2(
    p_id         NUMBER,
    p_first_name VARCHAR2,
    p_last_name  VARCHAR2,
    p_dob        DATE,
    p_phone      VARCHAR2
  ) RETURN SELF AS RESULT
);
/
```

Notice the following about the constructors:

- The keywords CONSTRUCTOR FUNCTION are used to identify constructors.

- The keywords RETURN SELF AS RESULT indicate an object of the same type as person_typ2 is returned by each constructor.

■ The first constructor accepts three parameters, and the second constructor accepts five parameters.

The constructor signatures don't contain the actual code bodies for the constructors; the code is contained in the following statement:

```
CREATE OR REPLACE TYPE BODY person_typ2 AS
  CONSTRUCTOR FUNCTION person_typ2(
    p_id          NUMBER,
    p_first_name VARCHAR2,
    p_last_name  VARCHAR2
  ) RETURN SELF AS RESULT IS
  BEGIN
    SELF.id := p_id;
    SELF.first_name := p_first_name;
    SELF.last_name := p_last_name;
    SELF.dob := SYSDATE;
    SELF.phone := '555-1212';
    RETURN;
  END;
  CONSTRUCTOR FUNCTION person_typ2(
    p_id          NUMBER,
    p_first_name VARCHAR2,
    p_last_name  VARCHAR2,
    p_dob         DATE,
    p_phone       VARCHAR2
  ) RETURN SELF AS RESULT IS
  BEGIN
    SELF.id := p_id;
    SELF.first_name := p_first_name;
    SELF.last_name := p_last_name;
    SELF.dob := p_dob;
    SELF.phone := p_phone;
    RETURN;
  END;
END;
/
```

Notice the following:

■ The constructors use SELF to set the attributes of the object. For example, SELF.id := p_id sets the id attribute of the object to the p_id parameter that is passed to the constructor.

■ The first constructor sets the dob attribute to the datetime returned by the SYSDATE() function, and sets phone to 555-1212. The second constructor simply sets the attributes to the parameters passed to the constructor.

The following example describes person_typ2:

```
DESC person_typ2;
```

```
Name                                      Null?    Type
----------------------------------------- -------- -------------------
ID                                                 NUMBER
FIRST_NAME                                         VARCHAR2(10)
LAST_NAME                                          VARCHAR2(10)
DOB                                                DATE
PHONE                                              VARCHAR2(12)

METHOD
------
FINAL MEMBER FUNCTION PERSON_TYP2 RETURNS PERSON_TYP2
Argument Name                     Type                     In/Out Default?
--------------------------------- ------------------------ ------ --------
P_ID                              NUMBER                   IN
P_FIRST_NAME                      VARCHAR2                 IN
P_LAST_NAME                       VARCHAR2                 IN

METHOD
------
FINAL MEMBER FUNCTION PERSON_TYP2 RETURNS PERSON_TYP2
Argument Name                     Type                     In/Out Default?
--------------------------------- ------------------------ ------ --------
P_ID                              NUMBER                   IN
P_FIRST_NAME                      VARCHAR2                 IN
P_LAST_NAME                       VARCHAR2                 IN
P_DOB                             DATE                     IN
P_PHONE                           VARCHAR2                 IN
```

You can then create a table of type person_typ2; for example:

```
CREATE TABLE object_customers2 OF person_typ2;
```

Summary

In this chapter, you learned that

- The Oracle database allows you to create object types. An object type is like a class in Java.

- An object type may contain attributes and methods.

- A simple example of an object type would be a type that models a product. This object type could contain attributes for the product's name, description, and price, along with a method that gets the sell-by date of the product.

- You create an object type using the CREATE TYPE statement.

- You can use an object type to define a column in a table, and the column is known as a column object.

■ You can also use an object type to define an entire table, and the table is known as an object table.

■ You use object references to model relationships between object tables, rather than foreign keys. Object references are defined using the REF type and are basically pointers to objects in an object table. Each object in an object table has a unique object identifier (OID) that you can then store in a REF column.

■ With the release of the Oracle9*i* database, you can use object type inheritance. This allows you to define hierarchies of database types.

■ You can mark an object type as NOT INSTANTIABLE, which prevents objects of that type from being created. You might want to mark an object type as NOT INSTANTIABLE when you want to use that type as a supertype.

■ You can define your own constructors.

In the next chapter, you'll learn about collections.

CHAPTER
13

Collections

In this chapter, you will

- Be introduced to collections
- Learn how to create collection types
- Use collection types to define columns in tables
- Perform DML operations with collections
- Learn how a collection type may contain elements that are also collection types
- Use collections in PL/SQL
- Examine Oracle10*g* enhancements to collections

Introducing Collections

The Oracle8 database introduced two new database types known as *collections*, which allow you to store sets of elements. The Oracle9*i* database extends these features to include multilevel collections, which allow you to create a collection that is itself a collection. The Oracle10*g* database further improves collections to include more ANSI functionality along with other enhancements.

There are three types of collections:

- **Varrays**   A varray is similar to an array in Java. You can use a varray to store an ordered set of elements with each element having an index associated with it. The elements in a varray are of the same type, and a varray has one dimension. A varray has a maximum size that you set when creating it, but you can change the size later.

- **Nested tables**   A nested table is a table that is embedded within another table. You can insert, update, and delete individual elements in a nested table. Because you can modify individual elements in a nested table, this makes them more flexible than a varray because elements in a varray can only be modified as a whole, not individually. A nested table doesn't have a maximum size, and you can store an arbitrary number of elements in a nested table.

- **Associative arrays (formerly known as index-by tables)**   New for Oracle10g, an associative array is a set of key and value pairs. You can get the value from the array using the key (which may be a string) or an integer that specifies the position of the value in the array. An associative array is similar to a hash table in programming languages such as Java. You'll learn how to use associative arrays later in the section "Associative Arrays."

You create a collection type using the SQL DDL CREATE TYPE statement, and you then use these types to define columns in a table. The elements stored in a varray are stored with the table when the size of the varray is 4KB or less, otherwise the varray is stored outside of the table.

The elements for nested tables are stored in separate tables. When a varray is stored with the table, accessing its elements is faster than accessing elements in a nested table. An associative array is a PL/SQL construct, not a SQL construct. An associative array cannot be stored persistently in a table.

You might be asking yourself why you would want to use collections in the first place. After all, using two tables with a foreign key already allows you to model relationships between data. The answer is that the data stored in the collection may be accessed more rapidly by the database than if you were to use two tables instead. Typically, you'll want to use a collection if you have data that is only used by one table. For example, this chapter uses collections to store addresses for customers, and those addresses are used only within the tables they are stored in.

Varrays

You use a varray to store an ordered set of elements, with each element having an index associated with it that corresponds to its position in the array. A varray has a maximum size that you can change dynamically.

>
> **NOTE**
> *I've provided a SQL*Plus script named* `collection_schema.sql` *in the SQL directory where you unzipped the files for this book. This script may be run against an Oracle8 or higher database. This script creates a user named* `collection_user` *with a password of* `collection_password` *and creates the collection types and tables used in the first part of this chapter. This script also populates the tables with sample data. I've also provided scripts named* `collection_schema_9i.sql` *and* `collection_schema_10g.sql` *that are referred to later in this chapter (don't run these additional scripts yet).*

Creating a Varray Type

You create a varray type using the SQL DDL `CREATE TYPE` statement, and you specify the maximum size and the type of elements stored in the varray when creating the type. You can change the maximum size of a varray using the `ALTER TYPE` statement. The following `CREATE TYPE` statement creates a varray type named `varray_address_typ` that can store up to two `VARCHAR2` strings:

```
CREATE TYPE varray_address_typ AS VARRAY(2) OF VARCHAR2(50);
/
```

Each `VARCHAR2` can be used to represent a different address for a customer of our imaginary store. One address could be the customer's shipping address where they receive products, and the other their billing address where they receive the bill for the product (both addresses could, of course, be the same). You can also store object types in a collection, and you'll see an example of that when I show you how to create a nested table type later.

Using a Varray Type to Define a Column in a Table

Once you define your varray type, you can use it to define a column in a table. For example, the following table named `customers_with_varray` uses `varray_address_typ` to define a column named `addresses`:

```
CREATE TABLE customers_with_varray (
    id          INTEGER PRIMARY KEY,
    first_name VARCHAR2(10),
    last_name  VARCHAR2(10),
    addresses  varray_address_typ
);
```

Notice that `customers_with_varray` also contains columns named `id`, `first_name`, and `last_name` in addition to the `addresses` column.

Getting Information on Varrays

You can use the `DESCRIBE` command to get information on your varray types. The following example describes the varray type `varray_address_typ`:

```
DESCRIBE varray_address_typ
varray_address_typ VARRAY(2) OF VARCHAR2(50)
```

The next example describes the table `customers_with_varray` whose addresses column is of type `varray_address_typ`:

```
DESCRIBE customers_with_varray
Name                              Null?     Type
-------------------------------- --------- -------------------
ID                               NOT NULL NUMBER(38)
FIRST_NAME                                VARCHAR2(10)
LAST_NAME                                 VARCHAR2(10)
ADDRESSES                                 VARRAY_ADDRESS_TYP
```

You can also get information on your varrays from the `user_varrays` view. Table 13-1 describes some of the columns in `user_varrays`. I've only mentioned some of the more useful

Column	Type	Description
parent_table_name	VARCHAR2(30)	Name of the table that contains the varray.

TABLE 13-1. *Some Columns in* `user_varrays`

Column	Type	Description
parent_table_column	VARCHAR2(4000)	Name of the column in the parent table containing the varray.
type_owner	VARCHAR2(30)	User who owns the varray type.
type_name	VARCHAR2(30)	Name of the varray type.
lob_name	VARCHAR2(30)	Name of the large object (LOB) if the varray is stored in a LOB. You'll learn about LOBs in the next chapter.
storage_spec	VARCHAR2(30)	Storage specification for the varray.
return_type	VARCHAR2(20)	Return type of the column.

TABLE 13-1.   *Some Columns in* user_varrays (continued)

columns in user_varrays in the table; you can get information on all the columns in user_varrays from the Oracle SQL reference manuals.

NOTE
You can get information on all the tables you have access to using
all_varrays.

The following example retrieves the columns from user_varrays (assuming you're connected to the database as collection_user):

```
SELECT *
FROM user_varrays;

PARENT_TABLE_NAME
-------------------------------
PARENT_TABLE_COLUMN
-----------------------------------------------------------------
TYPE_OWNER                      TYPE_NAME
-----------------------------   -----------------------------
LOB_NAME                        STORAGE_SPEC
-----------------------------   -----------------------------
RETURN_TYPE
--------------------
CUSTOMERS_WITH_VARRAY
ADDRESSES
COLLECTION_USER                 VARRAY_ADDRESS_TYP
                                                       DEFAULT
            VALUE
```

Populating a Varray with Elements

You initially populate the elements in a varray using an INSERT statement. The following
INSERT statement adds a row to the customers_with_varray table. Notice the use of the
varray_address_typ constructor to specify two strings for the addresses varray column:

```
INSERT INTO customers_with_varray VALUES (
  1, 'Steve', 'Brown',
  varray_address_typ(
    '2 State Street, Beantown, MA, 12345',
    '4 Hill Street, Lost Town, CA, 54321'
  )
);
```

Selecting Varray Elements

You select the elements in a varray using a SELECT statement. The following SELECT statement
selects the row from the customers_with_varray table:

```
SELECT *
FROM customers_with_varray;

        ID FIRST_NAME LAST_NAME
---------- ---------- ----------
ADDRESSES
-------------------------------------------------------------
         1 Steve      Brown
VARRAY_ADDRESS_TYP('2 State Street, Beantown, MA, 12345',
 '4 Hill Street, Lost Town, CA, 54321')
```

Modifying Varray Elements

As I mentioned earlier, the elements in a varray can only be modified as a whole. This means that
even if you only want to modify one element, you must supply all the elements for the varray. The
following UPDATE statement modifies the first address of customer #1 in the customers_with_
varray table. Notice that the second address is also supplied even though it hasn't changed:

```
UPDATE customers_with_varray
  SET addresses = varray_address_typ(
    '3 New Street, Middle Town, CA, 123435',
    '4 Hill Street, Lost Town, CA, 54321'
  )
WHERE id = 1;
```

The following query shows the change:

```
SELECT *
FROM customers_with_varray;

        ID FIRST_NAME LAST_NAME
---------- ---------- ----------
```

```
ADDRESSES
--------------------------------------------------------------------------------
       1 Steve       Brown
VARRAY_ADDRESS_TYP('3 New Street, Middle Town, CA, 123435',
 '4 Hill Street, Lost Town, CA, 54321')
```

Nested Tables

A *nested table* is an unordered set of any number of *elements*, all of the same data type. A nested table has a single column, and the type of that column may be a built-in database type or an object type that you previously created (object types were covered in the previous chapter). If the column in a nested table is an object type, the table can also be viewed as a multicolumn table, with a column for each attribute of the object type. You can insert, update, and delete individual elements in a nested table.

Creating a Nested Table Type

In this section, I'll show you how to create a nested table type that stores address_typ object types. You saw the use of address_typ in the previous chapter; it is used to represent an address and is defined as follows:

```
CREATE TYPE address_typ AS OBJECT (
   street VARCHAR2(15),
   city   VARCHAR2(15),
   state  CHAR(2),
   zip    VARCHAR2(5)
);
/
```

You create a nested table type using the CREATE TYPE statement, and the following example creates a nested table type named nested_table_address_typ that stores address_typ object types:

```
CREATE TYPE nested_table_address_typ AS TABLE OF address_typ;
/
```

Notice that you don't specify the maximum size of a nested table. That's because you can insert any number of elements in a nested table.

Using a Nested Table Type to Define a Column in a Table

Once you have defined your nested table type, you can use it to define a column in a table. For example, the following table named customers_with_nested_table uses nested_table_address_typ to define a column named addresses:

```
CREATE TABLE customers_with_nested_table (
   id          INTEGER PRIMARY KEY,
   first_name VARCHAR2(10),
   last_name  VARCHAR2(10),
```

```
  addresses  nested_table_address_typ
)
NESTED TABLE
  addresses
STORE AS
  nested_addresses;
```

The NESTED TABLE clause identifies the name of the nested table column (addresses), and the STORE AS clause specifies the name of the actual nested table (nested_addresses). You cannot access the nested table independently of the table in which it is embedded.

Getting Information on Nested Tables

You can use the DESCRIBE command to get information on your nested table types. The following example describes nested_table_address_typ:

DESCRIBE nested_table_address_typ
```
nested_table_address_typ TABLE OF ADDRESS_TYP
 Name                                    Null?     Type
 --------------------------------------- --------  -----------
 STREET                                            VARCHAR2(15)
 CITY                                              VARCHAR2(15)
 STATE                                             CHAR(2)
 ZIP                                               VARCHAR2(5)
```

The next example describes the table customers_with_nested_table whose addresses column is of type nested_table_address_typ:

DESCRIBE customers_with_nested_table
```
 Name                              Null?     Type
 --------------------------------- --------  ------------------------
 ID                                NOT NULL  NUMBER(38)
 FIRST_NAME                                  VARCHAR2(10)
 LAST_NAME                                   VARCHAR2(10)
 ADDRESSES                                   NESTED_TABLE_ADDRESS_TYP
```

If you set the depth to 2 and describe customers_with_nested_table, then you can see the attributes that make up nested_table_address_typ:

SET DESCRIBE DEPTH 2
DESCRIBE customers_with_nested_table
```
 Name                              Null?     Type
 --------------------------------- --------  ------------------------
 ID                                NOT NULL  NUMBER(38)
 FIRST_NAME                                  VARCHAR2(10)
 LAST_NAME                                   VARCHAR2(10)
 ADDRESSES                                   NESTED_TABLE_ADDRESS_TYP
    STREET                                   VARCHAR2(15)
    CITY                                     VARCHAR2(15)
```

```
STATE                          CHAR(2)
ZIP                            VARCHAR2(5)
```

You can also get information on your nested tables from the `user_nested_tables` view.
Table 13-2 describes some of the more useful columns in `user_nested_tables`.

NOTE
You can get information on all the tables you have access to using
`all_nested_tables`*.*

The following example retrieves the columns from `user_nested_tables`:

```
SELECT *
FROM user_nested_tables;
```

```
TABLE_NAME                        TABLE_TYPE_OWNER
--------------------------------  --------------------------
TABLE_TYPE_NAME                   PARENT_TABLE_NAME
--------------------------------  --------------------------
PARENT_TABLE_COLUMN
--------------------------------------------------------------
STORAGE_SPEC                      RETURN_TYPE
--------------------------------  --------------------
NESTED_ADDRESSES                  COLLECTION_USER
NESTED_TABLE_ADDRESS_TYP          CUSTOMERS_WITH_NESTED_TABLE
ADDRESSES
                    DEFAULT                   VALUE
```

Column	Type	Description
table_name	VARCHAR2(30)	Name of the nested table
table_type_owner	VARCHAR2(30)	User who owns the nested table type
table_type_name	VARCHAR2(30)	Name of the nested table type
parent_table_name	VARCHAR2(30)	Name of the parent table that contains the nested table
parent_table_column	VARCHAR2(4000)	Name of the column in the parent table containing the nested table
storage_spec	VARCHAR2(30)	Storage specification for the nested table
return_type	VARCHAR2(20)	Return type of the column

TABLE 13-2.   *Some Columns in* `user_nested_tables`

Populating a Nested Table with Elements

You initially populate the elements in a nested table using an INSERT statement. The following INSERT statement adds a row to customers_with_nested_table. Notice the use of the nested_table_address_typ and address_typ constructors to specify the addresses:

```
INSERT INTO customers_with_nested_table VALUES (
  1, 'Steve', 'Brown',
  nested_table_address_typ(
    address_typ('2 State Street', 'Beantown', 'MA', '12345'),
    address_typ('4 Hill Street', 'Lost Town', 'CA', '54321')
  )
);
```

As you can see, this row has two addresses, but any number of addresses can be stored in a nested table. You'll see how to add additional addresses to the nested table shortly in the section "Modifying Nested Table Elements."

Selecting Nested Table Elements

You select the elements in a nested table using a SELECT statement. The following SELECT statement selects the row from customers_with_nested_table:

```
SELECT *
FROM customers_with_nested_table;

        ID FIRST_NAME LAST_NAME
---------- ---------- ----------
ADDRESSES(STREET, CITY, STATE, ZIP)
-----------------------------------------------------------
         1 Steve      Brown
NESTED_TABLE_ADDRESS_TYP(
 ADDRESS_TYP('2 State Street', 'Beantown', 'MA', '12345'),
 ADDRESS_TYP('4 Hill Street', 'Lost Town', 'CA', '54321'))
```

Modifying Nested Table Elements

Unlike a varray, elements in a nested table can be modified individually: you can insert, update, and delete elements in a nested table. You do this using the TABLE clause in conjunction with a subquery that selects the nested table. The following example inserts an address at the end of the addresses nested table column for customer #1 in customer_with_nested_table:

```
INSERT INTO TABLE (
  SELECT addresses FROM customers_with_nested_table WHERE id = 1
) VALUES (
  address_typ('5 Main Street', 'Uptown', 'NY', '55512')
);
```

The next example updates the first address of customer #1 in customers_with_nested_table. Notice the use of the alias addr to identify the first address and subsequently set it:

```
UPDATE TABLE (
  SELECT addresses FROM customers_with_nested_table WHERE id = 1
) addr
SET
  VALUE(addr) = address_typ(
    '1 Market Street', 'Main Town', 'MA', '54321'
  )
WHERE
  VALUE(addr) = address_typ(
    '2 State Street', 'Beantown', 'MA', '12345'
  );
```

The final example deletes the second address for customer #1 in customers_with_
nested_table:

```
DELETE FROM TABLE (
  SELECT addresses FROM customers_with_nested_table WHERE id = 1
) addr
WHERE
  VALUE(addr) = address_typ(
    '4 Hill Street', 'Lost Town', 'CA', '54321'
  );
```

The following query verifies the changes:

```
SELECT *
FROM customers_with_nested_table;

        ID FIRST_NAME LAST_NAME
---------- ---------- ----------
ADDRESSES(STREET, CITY, STATE, ZIP)
------------------------------------------------------------
         1 Steve      Brown
NESTED_TABLE_ADDRESS_TYP(
 ADDRESS_TYP('1 Market Street', 'Main Town', 'MA', '54321'),
 ADDRESS_TYP('5 Main Street', 'Uptown', 'NY', '55512'))
```

Multilevel Collection Types

With the release of the Oracle9*i* database, you can create a collection type in the database
whose elements are also a collection type; this is known as a *multilevel collection type*. The
following list shows the valid multilevel collection types:

- A nested table containing a nested table type

- A nested table containing a varray type

- A varray containing a varray type

- A varray containing a nested table type
- A varray or nested table of an object type that has an attribute that is a varray or nested table type

NOTE
I've provided a SQL*Plus script named collection_schema_9i.sql *in the SQL directory that creates a user named* collection_user2 *with a password of* collection_password, *along with the types and the table described in this section. You can run this script if you are using an Oracle9i database or higher. You'll notice I create a completely different user named* collection_user2 *that has its own types and tables separate from* collection_user *you saw earlier in this chapter.*

To consider an example of a multilevel collection type, let's say you wanted to store a set of phone numbers that are associated with each address of a customer. The following example creates a varray type of three VARCHAR2 strings named varray_phone_typ to represent phone numbers:

```
CREATE TYPE varray_phone_typ AS VARRAY(3) OF VARCHAR2(14);
/
```

Next, the following example creates an object type named address_typ that contains an attribute named phone_numbers; this attribute is defined using varray_phone_typ:

```
CREATE TYPE address_typ AS OBJECT (
    street         VARCHAR2(15),
    city           VARCHAR2(15),
    state          CHAR(2),
    zip            VARCHAR2(5),
    phone_numbers varray_phone_typ
);
/
```

The next example creates a nested table type of address_typ objects:

```
CREATE TYPE nested_table_address_typ AS TABLE OF address_typ;
/
```

The following example creates a table named customers_with_nested_table that contains a column named addresses of nested_table_address_typ:

```
CREATE TABLE customers_with_nested_table (
    id          INTEGER PRIMARY KEY,
    first_name VARCHAR2(10),
    last_name  VARCHAR2(10),
    addresses  nested_table_address_typ
)
NESTED TABLE
```

```
  addresses
STORE AS
  nested_addresses;
```

Finally, the next example inserts a row into `customers_with_nested_table`; notice the use of the constructors for the three types in the `INSERT` statement:

```
INSERT INTO customers_with_nested_table VALUES (
  1, 'Steve', 'Brown',
  nested_table_address_typ(
    address_typ('2 State Street', 'Beantown', 'MA', '12345',
      varray_phone_typ(
        '(800)-555-1211',
        '(800)-555-1212',
        '(800)-555-1213'
      )
    ),
    address_typ('4 Hill Street', 'Lost Town', 'CA', '54321',
      varray_phone_typ(
        '(800)-555-1211',
        '(800)-555-1212'
      )
    )
  )
);
```

You can see that the first address has three phone numbers, while the second address only has two. Multilevel collection types are a very powerful extension to the Oracle9*i* database, and you might want to consider using them in any database designs you contribute to.

Using Collections in PL/SQL

You can use collections in PL/SQL. In this section, you'll see how to perform the following tasks in PL/SQL:

- Manipulate varrays
- Manipulate nested tables
- Use collection methods

Manipulating Varrays

In this section, you'll see a package named `varray_package` that contains the following items:

- A function named `get_customers()` that returns the rows in the `customers_with_varray` table.

- A procedure named `insert_customer()` that adds a row to the `customers_with_varray` table.

The `collection_user.sql` script contains the following package specification and body:

```
CREATE OR REPLACE PACKAGE varray_package AS
   TYPE ref_cursor_typ IS REF CURSOR;
   FUNCTION get_customers RETURN ref_cursor_typ;
   PROCEDURE insert_customer (
     p_id         IN customers_with_varray.id%TYPE,
     p_first_name IN customers_with_varray.first_name%TYPE,
     p_last_name  IN customers_with_varray.last_name%TYPE,
     p_addresses  IN customers_with_varray.addresses%TYPE
   );
END varray_package;
/

CREATE OR REPLACE PACKAGE BODY varray_package AS
  FUNCTION get_customers
  RETURN ref_cursor_typ IS
    customers_ref_cursor ref_cursor_typ;
  BEGIN
    -- get the REF CURSOR
    OPEN customers_ref_cursor FOR
      SELECT *
      FROM customers_with_varray;
    -- return the REF CURSOR
    RETURN customers_ref_cursor;
  END get_customers;

  PROCEDURE insert_customer (
    p_id         IN customers_with_varray.id%TYPE,
    p_first_name IN customers_with_varray.first_name%TYPE,
    p_last_name  IN customers_with_varray.last_name%TYPE,
    p_addresses  IN customers_with_varray.addresses%TYPE
  ) IS
  BEGIN
    INSERT INTO customers_with_varray
    VALUES (p_id, p_first_name, p_last_name, p_addresses);
    COMMIT;
  EXCEPTION
    WHEN OTHERS THEN
      ROLLBACK;
  END insert_customer;
END varray_package;
/
```

NOTE

*varray_package (and the other packages you'll see in this chapter)
is created by* `collection_schema.sql`, *so to follow along with
the examples you must have already run this script and then you
connect to the database as* `collection_user` *with a password
of* `collection_password`. *The package is* not *created by*
`collection_schema_9i.sql`, *so don't try and run the package
while connected as* `collection_user2` *as it won't work!*

The following example calls `varray_package.insert_customer()` to add a new row
to the `customers_with_varray` table:

```
CALL varray_package.insert_customer(
  2, 'James', 'Red',
  varray_address_typ(
    '10 Main Street, Green Town, CA, 22212',
    '20 State Street, Blue Town, FL, 22213'
  )
);
```

The next example calls `varray_package.get_products()` to retrieve the rows from
`customers_with_varray`:

```
SELECT varray_package.get_customers
FROM dual;

GET_CUSTOMERS
--------------------
CURSOR STATEMENT : 1

CURSOR STATEMENT : 1

        ID FIRST_NAME LAST_NAME
---------- ---------- ----------
ADDRESSES
------------------------------------------
         1 Steve      Brown
VARRAY_ADDRESS_TYP(
 '2 State Street, Beantown, MA, 12345',
 '4 Hill Street, Lost Town, CA, 54321')

         2 James      Red
VARRAY_ADDRESS_TYP(
 '10 Main Street, Green Town, CA, 22212',
 '20 State Street, Blue Town, FL, 22213')
```

Manipulating Nested Tables

In this section, you'll see a package named `nested_table_package` that contains the
following items:

- A function named `get_customers()` that returns the rows in the table `customers_`
  `with_nested_table`

- A procedure named `insert_customer()` that adds a row to the table `customers_`
  `with_nested_table`

The `collection_user.sql` script contains the following package specification and body:

```
CREATE OR REPLACE PACKAGE nested_table_package AS
  TYPE ref_cursor_typ IS REF CURSOR;
  FUNCTION get_customers RETURN ref_cursor_typ;
  PROCEDURE insert_customer (
    p_id         IN customers_with_nested_table.id%TYPE,
    p_first_name IN customers_with_nested_table.first_name%TYPE,
    p_last_name  IN customers_with_nested_table.last_name%TYPE,
    p_addresses  IN customers_with_nested_table.addresses%TYPE
  );
END nested_table_package;
/

CREATE OR REPLACE PACKAGE BODY nested_table_package AS
  FUNCTION get_customers
  RETURN ref_cursor_typ IS
    customers_ref_cursor ref_cursor_typ;
  BEGIN
    -- get the REF CURSOR
    OPEN customers_ref_cursor FOR
      SELECT *
      FROM customers_with_nested_table;
    -- return the REF CURSOR
    RETURN customers_ref_cursor;
  END get_customers;

  PROCEDURE insert_customer (
    p_id         IN customers_with_nested_table.id%TYPE,
    p_first_name IN customers_with_nested_table.first_name%TYPE,
    p_last_name  IN customers_with_nested_table.last_name%TYPE,
    p_addresses  IN customers_with_nested_table.addresses%TYPE
  ) IS
  BEGIN
    INSERT INTO customers_with_nested_table
    VALUES (p_id, p_first_name, p_last_name, p_addresses);
    COMMIT;
  EXCEPTION
```

```
    WHEN OTHERS THEN
        ROLLBACK;
  END insert_customer;
END nested_table_package;
/
```

The following example calls `nested_table_package.insert_customer()` to add
a new row to `customers_with_nested_table`:

```
CALL nested_table_package.insert_customer(
  2, 'James', 'Red',
  nested_table_address_typ(
    address_typ('10 Main Street', 'Green Town', 'CA', '22212'),
    address_typ('20 State Street', 'Blue Town', 'FL', '22213')
  )
);
```

The next example calls `nested_table_package.get_products()` to retrieve the rows
from `customers_with_nested_table`:

```
SELECT nested_table_package.get_customers
FROM dual;

GET_CUSTOMERS
-------------------
CURSOR STATEMENT : 1

CURSOR STATEMENT : 1

       ID FIRST_NAME LAST_NAME
---------- ---------- ----------
ADDRESSES(STREET, CITY, STATE, ZIP)
------------------------------------------------------------
        1 Steve      Brown
NESTED_TABLE_ADDRESS_TYP(
 ADDRESS_TYP('2 State Street', 'Beantown', 'MA', '12345'),
 ADDRESS_TYP('4 Hill Street', 'Lost Town', 'CA', '54321'))

        2 James      Red
NESTED_TABLE_ADDRESS_TYP(
 ADDRESS_TYP('10 Main Street', 'Green Town', 'CA', '22212'),
 ADDRESS_TYP('20 State Street', 'Blue Town', 'FL', '22213'))
```

Collection Methods

In this section, you'll see some of the methods you can use with collections. Table 13-3
summarizes the collection methods.

In the following sections, you'll see the use of the methods shown in Table 13-3.

Method	Description
COUNT	Returns the number of elements in the collection.
DELETE DELETE(*n*) DELETE(*n*, *m*)	Removes elements from a collection. There are three forms of DELETE: ■ DELETE removes all elements. ■ DELETE(*n*) removes the *n*th element. ■ DELETE(*n*, *m*) removes elements *n* through *m*.
EXISTS(*n*)	Returns true if the *n*th element in a collection exists.
EXTEND EXTEND(*n*) EXTEND(*n*, *m*)	Increases the size of a collection. There are three forms of EXTEND: ■ EXTEND adds one element, which is set to null. ■ EXTEND(*n*) adds *n* elements, which are set to null. ■ EXTEND(*n*, *m*) adds *n* elements, which are set to *m*.
FIRST	Returns the first (smallest) index number in a collection. If the collection is empty, FIRST returns null.
LAST	Returns the last (greatest) index number in a collection. If the collection is empty, LAST returns null.
NEXT(*n*)	Returns the index number of the element after *n*. If there are no elements after *n*, NEXT returns null.
PRIOR(*n*)	Returns the index number of the element before *n*. If there are no elements before *n*, PRIOR returns null.
TRIM TRIM(*n*)	Removes elements from the end of a collection. There are two forms of TRIM: ■ TRIM removes one element from the end. ■ TRIM(*n*) removes *n* elements from the end.

TABLE 13-3. *Collection Methods*

NOTE
The following sections will use a package named collection_
method_examples *that is created by the* collection_schema.sql
*script. You'll see the individual methods defined in this package in the
following sections.*

Using COUNT
You use COUNT to get the number of elements in the collection. The following initialize_
addresses() function is defined in the collection_method_examples package and
performs the following tasks:

■ Accepts a parameter named id_par that specifies the ID of a row in the table
customers_with_nested_table to retrieve

- Declares an object named `addresses_var` of type `nested_table_address_typ`

- Retrieves the addresses column from `customers_with_nested_table` into `addresses_var`

- Displays the number of elements in `addresses_var` using `COUNT`

```
FUNCTION initialize_addresses(
  id_par customers_with_nested_table.id%TYPE
) RETURN nested_table_address_typ IS
  addresses_var nested_table_address_typ;
BEGIN
  DBMS_OUTPUT.PUT_LINE('Initializing addresses');
  SELECT addresses
  INTO addresses_var
  FROM customers_with_nested_table
  WHERE id = id_par;
  DBMS_OUTPUT.PUT_LINE(
    'Number of addresses = '|| addresses_var.COUNT
  );
  RETURN addresses_var;
END initialize_addresses;
```

The following example connects as `collection_user`, turns the server output on, and calls `collection_method_examples.initialize_addresses()`:

```
CONNECT collection_user/collection_password
SET SERVEROUTPUT ON
SELECT collection_method_examples.initialize_addresses(1) addresses
FROM dual;
ADDRESSES(STREET, CITY, STATE, ZIP)
--------------------------------------------------------
NESTED_TABLE_ADDRESS_TYP(
 ADDRESS_TYP('2 State Street', 'Beantown', 'MA', '12345'),
 ADDRESS_TYP('4 Hill Street', 'Lost Town', 'CA', '54321'))
```

The following `display_addresses()` procedure performs the following tasks:

- Accepts a parameter named `addresses_par` of type `nested_table_address_typ` that contains a list of addresses

- Declares an object named `addresses_var` of type `nested_table_address_typ`

- Displays the number of addresses in `address_var` using `COUNT`

- Uses a `FOR` loop to display the addresses in `address_var`

```
PROCEDURE display_addresses(
  addresses_par nested_table_address_typ
) IS
  count_var INTEGER;
```

```
BEGIN
  DBMS_OUTPUT.PUT_LINE(
    'Current number of addresses = '|| addresses_par.COUNT
  );
  FOR count_var IN 1..addresses_par.COUNT LOOP
    DBMS_OUTPUT.PUT_LINE('Address #' || count_var || ':');
    DBMS_OUTPUT.PUT(addresses_par(count_var).street || ', ');
    DBMS_OUTPUT.PUT(addresses_par(count_var).city || ', ');
    DBMS_OUTPUT.PUT(addresses_par(count_var).state || ', ');
    DBMS_OUTPUT.PUT_LINE(addresses_par(count_var).zip);
  END LOOP;
END display_addresses;
```

You'll see the use of `collection_method_examples.display_addresses()` shortly.

Using DELETE

You use `DELETE` to remove elements from a collection. The following `delete_address()` procedure performs the following tasks:

- Accepts a parameter named `address_num_par` that specifies the position of the address to remove

- Declares an object named `addresses_var` of type `nested_table_address_typ`

- Calls `initialize_addresses()` to populate `addresses_var` with the addresses of customer #1

- Displays the addresses in `addresses_var` using `display_addresses()`

- Removes the address specified by `address_num_par` from `addresses_var` using `DELETE`

- Displays the addresses in `addresses_var` again using `display_addresses()`

```
PROCEDURE delete_address(
  address_num_par INTEGER
) IS
  addresses_var nested_table_address_typ;
BEGIN
  addresses_var := initialize_addresses(1);
  display_addresses(addresses_var);
  DBMS_OUTPUT.PUT_LINE('Deleting address #' || address_num_par);
  addresses_var.DELETE(address_num_par);
  display_addresses(addresses_var);
END delete_address;
```

The following example calls `collection_method_examples.delete_address(2)` to remove address #2:

```
CALL collection_method_examples.delete_address(2);
Initializing addresses
Number of addresses = 2
Current number of addresses = 2
Address #1:
2 State Street, Beantown, MA, 12345
Address #2:
4 Hill Street, Lost Town, CA, 54321
Deleting address #2
Current number of addresses = 1
Address #1:
2 State Street, Beantown, MA, 12345
```

Using EXTEND

You use EXTEND to add elements to the end of a collection. The following extend_addresses()
procedure performs the following tasks:

- Declares an object named addresses_var of type nested_table_address_typ

- Calls initialize_addresses() to populate addresses_var with the addresses of
  customer #1

- Displays the addresses in addresses_var using display_addresses()

- Copies address #1 twice to the end of addresses_var using EXTEND

- Displays the addresses in addresses_var again using display_addresses()

```
PROCEDURE extend_addresses IS
  addresses_var nested_table_address_typ;
BEGIN
  addresses_var := initialize_addresses(1);
  display_addresses(addresses_var);
  DBMS_OUTPUT.PUT_LINE('Extending addresses');
  addresses_var.EXTEND(2, 1);
  display_addresses(addresses_var);
END extend_addresses;
```

The following example calls collection_method_examples.extend_addresses():

```
CALL collection_method_examples.extend_addresses();
Initializing addresses
Number of addresses = 2
Current number of addresses = 2
Address #1:
2 State Street, Beantown, MA, 12345
Address #2:
4 Hill Street, Lost Town, CA, 54321
Extending addresses
Current number of addresses = 4
Address #1:
```

```
2 State Street, Beantown, MA, 12345
Address #2:
4 Hill Street, Lost Town, CA, 54321
Address #3:
2 State Street, Beantown, MA, 12345
Address #4:
2 State Street, Beantown, MA, 12345
```

Using FIRST

You use `FIRST` to get the first (smallest) index number in a collection. If the collection is empty, `FIRST` returns null. The following `first_address()` procedure performs the following tasks:

- Declares an object named `addresses_var` of type `nested_table_address_typ`

- Calls `initialize_addresses()` to populate `addresses_var` with the addresses of customer #1

- Displays the index of the first address in `addresses_var` using `FIRST`

- Removes address #1 from `addresses_var` using `DELETE`

- Displays the index of the first address in `addresses_var` again using `FIRST`

```
PROCEDURE first_address IS
  addresses_var nested_table_address_typ;
BEGIN
  addresses_var := initialize_addresses(1);
  DBMS_OUTPUT.PUT_LINE('First address = ' || addresses_var.FIRST);
  DBMS_OUTPUT.PUT_LINE('Deleting address #1');
  addresses_var.DELETE(1);
  DBMS_OUTPUT.PUT_LINE('First address = ' || addresses_var.FIRST);
END first_address;
```

The following example calls `collection_method_examples.first_address()`:

```
CALL collection_method_examples.first_address();
Initializing addresses
Number of addresses = 2
First address = 1
Deleting address #1
First address = 2
```

Using LAST

You use `LAST` to get the last (greatest) index number in a collection. If the collection is empty, `LAST` returns null. The following `last_address()` procedure performs the following tasks:

- Declares an object named `addresses_var` of type `nested_table_address_typ`

- Calls `initialize_addresses()` to populate `addresses_var` with the addresses of customer #1

- Displays the index of the last address in `addresses_var` using `LAST`

- Removes address #2 from `addresses_var` using `DELETE`

- Displays the index of the last address in `addresses_var` again using `LAST`

```
PROCEDURE last_address IS
  addresses_var nested_table_address_typ;
BEGIN
  addresses_var := initialize_addresses(1);
  DBMS_OUTPUT.PUT_LINE('Last address = ' || addresses_var.LAST);
  DBMS_OUTPUT.PUT_LINE('Deleting address #2');
  addresses_var.DELETE(2);
  DBMS_OUTPUT.PUT_LINE('Last address = ' || addresses_var.LAST);
END last_address;
```

The following example calls `collection_method_examples.last_address()`:

```
CALL collection_method_examples.last_address();
Initializing addresses
Number of addresses = 2
Last address = 2
Deleting address #2
Last address = 1
```

Using NEXT

You use `NEXT(n)` to get the index number of the element after *n*. If there are no elements after *n*, `NEXT` returns null.

The following `next_address()` procedure performs the following tasks:

- Declares an object named `addresses_var` of type `nested_table_address_typ`

- Calls `initialize_addresses()` to populate `addresses_var` with the addresses of customer #1

- Displays the index of the next address after #1 in `addresses_var` using `NEXT`

- Displays the index of the next address after #2 in `addresses_var` using `NEXT`, which is null since there is no address after #2

```
PROCEDURE next_address IS
  addresses_var nested_table_address_typ;
BEGIN
  addresses_var := initialize_addresses(1);
  DBMS_OUTPUT.PUT_LINE(
    'addresses_var.NEXT(1) = ' || addresses_var.NEXT(1)
  );
  DBMS_OUTPUT.PUT_LINE(
    'addresses_var.NEXT(2) = ' || addresses_var.NEXT(2)
  );
END next_address;
```

The following example calls `collection_method_examples.next_address()`; notice `addresses_var.NEXT(2)` is null:

```
CALL collection_method_examples.next_address();
Initializing addresses
Number of addresses = 2
addresses_var.NEXT(1) = 2
addresses_var.NEXT(2) =
```

Using PRIOR

You use `PRIOR(n)` to get the index number of the element before *n*. If there are no elements before *n*, `PRIOR` returns null.

The following `prior_address()` procedure performs the following tasks:

■ Declares an object named `addresses_var` of type `nested_table_address_typ`

■ Calls `initialize_addresses()` to populate `addresses_var` with the addresses of customer #1

■ Displays the index of the address before #2 in `addresses_var` using `PRIOR`

■ Displays the index of the address before #1 in `addresses_var` using `NEXT`, which is null since there is no address before #1

```
PROCEDURE prior_address IS
  addresses_var nested_table_address_typ;
BEGIN
  addresses_var := initialize_addresses(1);
  DBMS_OUTPUT.PUT_LINE(
    'addresses_var.PRIOR(2) = ' || addresses_var.PRIOR(2)
  );
  DBMS_OUTPUT.PUT_LINE(
    'addresses_var.PRIOR(1) = ' || addresses_var.PRIOR(1)
  );
END prior_address;
```

The following example calls `collection_method_examples.prior_address()`; notice `addresses_var.PRIOR(1)` is null:

```
CALL collection_method_examples.prior_address();
Initializing addresses
Number of addresses = 2
addresses_var.PRIOR(2) = 1
addresses_var.PRIOR(1) =
```

Using TRIM

You use `TRIM` to remove elements from the end of a collection. The following `trim_addresses()` procedure performs the following tasks:

■ Declares an object named `addresses_var` of type `nested_table_address_typ`

- Calls `initialize_addresses()` to populate `addresses_var` with the addresses of customer #1

- Displays the addresses in `addresses_var` using `display_addresses()`

- Copies address #1 three times to the end of `addresses_var` using `EXTEND`

- Displays the addresses in `addresses_var` again using `display_addresses()`

- Removes two addresses from the end of `addresses_var` using `TRIM`

- Displays the addresses in `addresses_var` again using `display_addresses()`

```
PROCEDURE trim_addresses IS
  addresses_var nested_table_address_typ;
BEGIN
  addresses_var := initialize_addresses(1);
  display_addresses(addresses_var);
  DBMS_OUTPUT.PUT_LINE('Extending addresses');
  addresses_var.EXTEND(3, 1);
  display_addresses(addresses_var);
  DBMS_OUTPUT.PUT_LINE('Trimming 2 addresses from end');
  addresses_var.TRIM(2);
  display_addresses(addresses_var);
END trim_addresses;
```

The following example calls `collection_method_examples.trim_addresses()`:

```
CALL collection_method_examples.trim_addresses();
Initializing addresses
Number of addresses = 2
Current number of addresses = 2
Address #1:
2 State Street, Beantown, MA, 12345
Address #2:
4 Hill Street, Lost Town, CA, 54321
Extending addresses
Current number of addresses = 5
Address #1:
2 State Street, Beantown, MA, 12345
Address #2:
4 Hill Street, Lost Town, CA, 54321
Address #3:
2 State Street, Beantown, MA, 12345
Address #4:
2 State Street, Beantown, MA, 12345
Address #5:
2 State Street, Beantown, MA, 12345
Trimming 2 addresses from end
Current number of addresses = 3
Address #1:
2 State Street, Beantown, MA, 12345
```

```
Address #2:
4 Hill Street, Lost Town, CA, 54321
Address #3:
2 State Street, Beantown, MA, 12345
```

Oracle10*g* Enhancements to Collections

In this section, you'll learn about the following enhancements made to collections in Oracle10*g*:

- Associative arrays

- Ability to change the size or precision of an element type

- Ability to increase the number of elements in a varray

- Ability to use varray columns in temporary tables

- Ability to use a different tablespace for a nested table's storage table

- ANSI support for nested tables

NOTE
The various DDL statements that create the items shown in this section are contained in the `collection_schema_10g.sql` *script. The script connects as* `collection_user` *with a password of* `collection_password`*, so if you're using a different password (or you're using a service name), you'll need to edit the script first. Also, you must have first run* `collection_schema.sql` *before you attempt to run* `collection_schema_10g.sql`*.*

Associative Arrays

An associative array is a set of key and value pairs. You can get the value from the array using the key (which may be a string) or an integer that specifies the position of the value in the array. The following example procedure `customers_associative_array()` performs the following tasks:

- Creates an associative array type named `assoc_array_typ`.

- Creates an object named `customer_array` of the type `assoc_array_typ`. `customer_array` is used to store the ages of customers by name. The key in `customer_array` is the name, and the value is the age.

- Assigns age values to customers by name in `customer_array`.

- Displays the contents of `customer_array` using `DBMS_OUTPUT.PUT_LINE()`.

  ```
  CREATE OR REPLACE PROCEDURE customers_associative_array AS
    TYPE assoc_array_typ IS TABLE OF NUMBER INDEX BY VARCHAR2(15);
    customer_array assoc_array_typ;
  BEGIN
    customer_array('Jason') := 32;
  ```

```
      customer_array('Steve') := 28;
      customer_array('Fred') := 43;
      customer_array('Cynthia') := 27;

    DBMS_OUTPUT.PUT_LINE(
      'customer_array[''Jason''] = ' || customer_array('Jason')
    );
    DBMS_OUTPUT.PUT_LINE(
      'customer_array[''Steve''] = ' || customer_array('Steve')
    );
    DBMS_OUTPUT.PUT_LINE(
      'customer_array[''Fred''] = ' || customer_array('Fred')
    );
    DBMS_OUTPUT.PUT_LINE(
      'customer_array[''Cynthia''] = ' || customer_array('Cynthia')
    );
  END customers_associative_array;
  /
```

The following example connects as `collection_user`, sets server output on, and calls `customers_associative_array()`:

```
CONNECT collection_user/collection_password
SET SERVEROUTPUT ON
CALL customers_associative_array();
customer_array['Jason'] = 32
customer_array['Steve'] = 28
customer_array['Fred'] = 43
customer_array['Cynthia'] = 27
```

Changing the Size or Precision of an Element Type

You can change the size of an element type in a varray or nested table when the element type is one of the character, numeric, or raw types. Earlier in the section "Creating a Varray Type," you saw the following example that creates a varray type and table:

```
CREATE TYPE varray_address_typ AS VARRAY(2) OF VARCHAR2(50);
/
CREATE TABLE customers_with_varray (
  id           INTEGER PRIMARY KEY,
  first_name VARCHAR2(10),
  last_name  VARCHAR2(10),
  addresses  varray_address_typ
);
```

The following example changes the size of the VARCHAR2 elements in `varray_address_typ` to 60:

```
ALTER TYPE varray_address_typ
MODIFY ELEMENT TYPE VARCHAR2(60) CASCADE;
```

The CASCADE option propagates the change to the dependent objects in the database. In the example, the dependent object is the customers_with_varray table. You can also use the INVALIDATE option to invalidate dependent objects to immediately recompile the type.

Increasing the Number of Elements in a Varray

You can increase the number of elements in a varray. The following example increases the number of elements in varray_address_typ to 5:

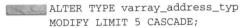

```
ALTER TYPE varray_address_typ
MODIFY LIMIT 5 CASCADE;
```

Using Varrays in Temporary Tables

You can use varrays in temporary tables. The following example creates a temporary table named cust_with_varray_temp_table that contains a varray named addresses of type varray_address_typ:

```
CREATE GLOBAL TEMPORARY TABLE cust_with_varray_temp_table (
    id          INTEGER PRIMARY KEY,
    first_name VARCHAR2(10),
    last_name   VARCHAR2(10),
    addresses   varray_address_typ
);
```

NOTE
This table (along with the other tables featured in the rest of this chapter) is created by the collection_schema_10g.sql *script.*

Using a Different Tablespace for a Nested Table's Storage Table

By default, a nested table's storage table is created in the same tablespace as the parent table. In Oracle10g, you can specify a different tablespace for a nested table's storage table. The following example creates a table named cust_with_nested_table that contains a nested table named addresses of type nested_table_address_typ. Notice the tablespace for the storage table nested_addresses2 is to be stored in the users tablespace:

```
CREATE TABLE cust_with_nested_table (
    id          INTEGER PRIMARY KEY,
    first_name VARCHAR2(10),
    last_name   VARCHAR2(10),
    addresses   nested_table_address_typ
)
NESTED TABLE
    addresses
STORE AS
    nested_addresses2 TABLESPACE users;
```

You must have a tablespace named `users` in order for this example to work. For this reason I've commented out the example in the `collection_schema_10g.sql` script. You can see all the tablespaces you have access to by performing the following query:

```
SELECT tablespace_name
FROM user_tablespaces;
```

You can then use one of your available tablespaces in the previous `CREATE TABLE` example. Just edit the example in the `collection_schema_10g.sql` script and run the `CREATE TABLE` example by cutting and pasting the statement into SQL*Plus.

ANSI Support for Nested Tables

The American National Standards Institute (ANSI) specification includes a number of operators for multisets and arrays that are now implemented in Oracle varrays and nested tables. You'll learn about these new operators in the following sections.

Equal and Not-Equal Operators

You use the equal (=) and not-equal (<>) operators to compare nested tables, which are considered equal when they satisfy all the following conditions:

- All the tables are the same type.

- All the tables are the same cardinality—that is, they contain the same number of elements.

- All the elements are equal.

The following procedure `equal_example()` performs the following tasks:

- Creates a type named `nested_table_typ`.

- Creates objects named `customer_nested_table1`, `customer_nested_table2`, and `customer_nested_table3` of the type `nested_table_typ`. These objects are used to store names of customers.

- Assigns the names Fred, George, and Susan to `customer_nested_table1` and `customer_nested_table2`. Assigns the names John, George, and Susan to `customer_nested_table3`.

- Uses = to compare `customer_nested_table1` and `customer_nested_table2`, which are equal. Displays the results using `DBMS_OUTPUT.PUT_LINE()`.

- Uses <> to compare `customer_nested_table1` and `customer_nested_table3`, which are not equal because the first names are different. Displays the results using `DBMS_OUTPUT.PUT_LINE()`.

```
CREATE OR REPLACE PROCEDURE equal_example AS
  TYPE nested_table_typ IS TABLE OF VARCHAR2(10);
  customer_nested_table1 nested_table_typ;
  customer_nested_table2 nested_table_typ;
```

```
          customer_nested_table3 nested_table_typ;
          result BOOLEAN;
      BEGIN
          customer_nested_table1 :=
            nested_table_typ('Fred', 'George', 'Susan');
          customer_nested_table2 :=
            nested_table_typ('Fred', 'George', 'Susan');
          customer_nested_table3 :=
            nested_table_typ('John', 'George', 'Susan');

          result := customer_nested_table1 = customer_nested_table2;
          IF result THEN
            DBMS_OUTPUT.PUT_LINE(
              'customer_nested_table1 equal to customer_nested_table2'
            );
          END IF;

          result := customer_nested_table1 <> customer_nested_table3;
          IF result THEN
            DBMS_OUTPUT.PUT_LINE(
              'customer_nested_table1 not equal to customer_nested_table3'
            );
          END IF;
      END equal_example;
      /
```

The following example calls `equal_example()`, assuming you're still logged in as `collection_user`:

```
CALL equal_example();
customer_nested_table1 equal to customer_nested_table2
customer_nested_table1 not equal to customer_nested_table3
```

IN and NOT IN Operators

You can use the `IN` and `NOT IN` operators to check if the contents of one nested table appear or don't appear in the contents of another nested table. The following procedure `in_example()` illustrates the use of `IN` and `NOT IN`:

```
CREATE OR REPLACE PROCEDURE in_example AS
    TYPE nested_table_typ IS TABLE OF VARCHAR2(10);
    customer_nested_table1 nested_table_typ;
    customer_nested_table2 nested_table_typ;
    customer_nested_table3 nested_table_typ;
    result BOOLEAN;
BEGIN
    customer_nested_table1 :=
      nested_table_typ('Fred', 'George', 'Susan');
    customer_nested_table2 :=
      nested_table_typ('John', 'George', 'Susan');
```

```
    customer_nested_table3 :=
      nested_table_typ('Fred', 'George', 'Susan');

    result := customer_nested_table3 IN (customer_nested_table1);
    IF result THEN
      DBMS_OUTPUT.PUT_LINE(
        'customer_nested_table3 in customer_nested_table1'
      );
    END IF;

    result := customer_nested_table3 NOT IN (customer_nested_table2);
    IF result THEN
      DBMS_OUTPUT.PUT_LINE(
        'customer_nested_table3 not in customer_nested_table2'
      );
    END IF;
END in_example;
/
```

The following example calls in_example():

```
CALL in_example();
customer_nested_table3 in customer_nested_table1
customer_nested_table3 not in customer_nested_table2
```

SUBMULTISET Operator

You use the SUBMULTISET operator to check whether the contents of one nested table are a subset of another nested table. For example, Fred, George, and Susan are a subset of George, Fred, and Susan.

The following procedure submultiset_example() illustrates the use of SUBMULTISET:

```
CREATE OR REPLACE PROCEDURE submultiset_example AS
  TYPE nested_table_typ IS TABLE OF VARCHAR2(10);
  customer_nested_table1 nested_table_typ;
  customer_nested_table2 nested_table_typ;
  customer_nested_table3 nested_table_typ;
  result BOOLEAN;
BEGIN
  customer_nested_table1 :=
    nested_table_typ('Fred', 'George', 'Susan');
  customer_nested_table2 :=
    nested_table_typ('George', 'Fred', 'Susan');

  result :=
    customer_nested_table1 SUBMULTISET OF customer_nested_table2;
  IF result THEN
    DBMS_OUTPUT.PUT_LINE(
      'customer_nested_table1 subset of customer_nested_table2'
    );
  END IF;
END submultiset_example;
/
```

The following example calls `submultiset_example()`:

```
CALL submultiset_example();
customer_nested_table1 subset of customer_nested_table2
```

MULTISET Operator

You use the `MULTISET` operator to get a nested table whose elements are set to certain elements of two nested tables that are input to `MULTISET`. There are three `MULTISET` operators:

- **MULTISET UNION**   Returns a nested table whose elements are set to the elements of the two input nested tables.

- **MULTISET INTERSECT**   Returns a nested table whose elements are set to the elements that are common to the two input nested tables.

- **MULTISET EXCEPT**   Returns a nested table whose elements are in the first input nested table but not in the second.

You may also use one of the following options with `MULTISET`:

- **ALL**   Indicates that all applicable elements in the input nested tables are set in the returned nested table. `ALL` is the default.

- **DISTINCT**   Indicates that only the distinct non-duplicate elements in the input nested tables are set in the returned nested table.

The following procedure `multiset_example()` illustrates the use of `MULTISET`:

```
CREATE OR REPLACE PROCEDURE multiset_example AS
    TYPE nested_table_typ IS TABLE OF VARCHAR2(10);
    customer_nested_table1 nested_table_typ;
    customer_nested_table2 nested_table_typ;
    customer_nested_table3 nested_table_typ;
    count_var INTEGER;
BEGIN
    customer_nested_table1 :=
      nested_table_typ('Fred', 'George', 'Susan');
    customer_nested_table2 :=
      nested_table_typ('George', 'Steve', 'Rob');

    customer_nested_table3 :=
      customer_nested_table1 MULTISET UNION customer_nested_table2;
    DBMS_OUTPUT.PUT('UNION: ');
    FOR count_var IN 1..customer_nested_table3.COUNT LOOP
      DBMS_OUTPUT.PUT(customer_nested_table3(count_var) || ' ');
    END LOOP;
    DBMS_OUTPUT.PUT_LINE(' ');

    customer_nested_table3 :=
      customer_nested_table1 MULTISET UNION DISTINCT customer_nested_table2;
```

```
    DBMS_OUTPUT.PUT('UNION DISTINCT: ');
    FOR count_var IN 1..customer_nested_table3.COUNT LOOP
      DBMS_OUTPUT.PUT(customer_nested_table3(count_var) || ' ');
    END LOOP;
    DBMS_OUTPUT.PUT_LINE(' ');

    customer_nested_table3 :=
      customer_nested_table1 MULTISET INTERSECT customer_nested_table2;
    DBMS_OUTPUT.PUT('INTERSECT: ');
    FOR count_var IN 1..customer_nested_table3.COUNT LOOP
      DBMS_OUTPUT.PUT(customer_nested_table3(count_var) || ' ');
    END LOOP;
    DBMS_OUTPUT.PUT_LINE(' ');

    customer_nested_table3 :=
      customer_nested_table1 MULTISET EXCEPT customer_nested_table2;
    DBMS_OUTPUT.PUT_LINE('EXCEPT: ');
    FOR count_var IN 1..customer_nested_table3.COUNT LOOP
      DBMS_OUTPUT.PUT(customer_nested_table3(count_var) || ' ');
    END LOOP;
END multiset_example;
/
```

The following example calls `multiset_example()`:

```
CALL multiset_example();
UNION: Fred George Susan George Steve Rob
UNION DISTINCT: Fred George Susan Steve Rob
INTERSECT: George
EXCEPT:
```

CARDINALITY Operator

You use the `CARDINALITY` operator to get the number of elements in a nested table. The following procedure `cardinality_example()` illustrates the use of `CARDINALITY`:

```
CREATE OR REPLACE PROCEDURE cardinality_example AS
  TYPE nested_table_typ IS TABLE OF VARCHAR2(10);
  customer_nested_table1 nested_table_typ;
  cardinality_var INTEGER;
BEGIN
  customer_nested_table1 :=
    nested_table_typ('Fred', 'George', 'Susan');
  cardinality_var := CARDINALITY(customer_nested_table1);
  DBMS_OUTPUT.PUT_LINE('cardinality_var = ' || cardinality_var);
END cardinality_example;
/
```

The following example calls `cardinality_example()`:

```
CALL cardinality_example();
cardinality_var = 3
```

MEMBER OF Operator

You use the MEMBER OF operator to check whether an element is in a nested table. The following procedure member_of_example() illustrates the use of MEMBER OF:

```
CREATE OR REPLACE PROCEDURE member_of_example AS
    TYPE nested_table_typ IS TABLE OF VARCHAR2(10);
    customer_nested_table1 nested_table_typ;
    result BOOLEAN;
BEGIN
    customer_nested_table1 :=
      nested_table_typ('Fred', 'George', 'Susan');
    result := 'George' MEMBER OF customer_nested_table1;
    IF result THEN
      DBMS_OUTPUT.PUT_LINE('''George'' is a member');
    END IF;
END member_of_example;
/
```

The following example calls member_of_example():

```
CALL member_of_example();
    'George' is a member
```

SET Operator

The SET operator first converts a nested table into a set, removes duplicate elements from the set, and returns the set as a nested table. The following procedure set_example() illustrates the use of SET:

```
CREATE OR REPLACE PROCEDURE set_example AS
    TYPE nested_table_typ IS TABLE OF VARCHAR2(10);
    customer_nested_table1 nested_table_typ;
    customer_nested_table2 nested_table_typ;
    count_var INTEGER;
BEGIN
    customer_nested_table1 :=
      nested_table_typ('Fred', 'George', 'Susan', 'George');
    customer_nested_table2 := SET(customer_nested_table1);
    DBMS_OUTPUT.PUT('customer_nested_table2: ');
    FOR count_var IN 1..customer_nested_table2.COUNT LOOP
      DBMS_OUTPUT.PUT(customer_nested_table2(count_var) || ' ');
    END LOOP;
    DBMS_OUTPUT.PUT_LINE(' ');
END set_example;
/
```

The following example calls set_example():

```
CALL set_example();
    customer_nested_table2: Fred George Susan
```

IS A SET Operator

You use the IS A SET operator to check if the elements in a nested table are distinct. The following procedure is_a_set_example() illustrates the use of IS A SET:

```
CREATE OR REPLACE PROCEDURE is_a_set_example AS
  TYPE nested_table_typ IS TABLE OF VARCHAR2(10);
  customer_nested_table1 nested_table_typ;
  result BOOLEAN;
BEGIN
  customer_nested_table1 :=
    nested_table_typ('Fred', 'George', 'Susan', 'George');
  result := customer_nested_table1 IS A SET;
  IF result THEN
    DBMS_OUTPUT.PUT_LINE('Elements are all unique');
  ELSE
    DBMS_OUTPUT.PUT_LINE('Elements contain duplicates');
  END IF;
END is_a_set_example;
/
```

The following example calls is_a_set_example():

```
CALL is_a_set_example();
Elements contain duplicates
```

IS EMPTY Operator

You use the IS EMPTY operator to check if a nested table doesn't contain elements. The following procedure, is_empty_example(), illustrates the use of IS EMPTY:

```
CREATE OR REPLACE PROCEDURE is_empty_example AS
  TYPE nested_table_typ IS TABLE OF VARCHAR2(10);
  customer_nested_table1 nested_table_typ;
  result BOOLEAN;
BEGIN
  customer_nested_table1 :=
    nested_table_typ('Fred', 'George', 'Susan');
  result := customer_nested_table1 IS EMPTY;
  IF result THEN
    DBMS_OUTPUT.PUT_LINE('Nested table is empty');
  ELSE
    DBMS_OUTPUT.PUT_LINE('Nested table contains elements');
  END IF;
END is_empty_example;
/
```

The following example calls is_empty_example():

```
CALL is_empty_example();
Nested table contains elements
```

COLLECT Operator

You use the COLLECT operator to get a list of values as a nested table. You can cast the returned nested table to a nested table type using the CAST operator. The following query illustrates the use of COLLECT:

```
SELECT COLLECT(first_name)
FROM customers_with_varray;

COLLECT(FIRST_NAME)
-------------------------------------
SYSTPxBtv6XzZXLjgNAADug9CQQ==('Steve')
```

POWERMULTISET Operator

You use the POWERMULTISET operator to get a sub-nested table from an input nested table. The following query illustrates the use of POWERMULTISET:

```
SELECT *
FROM TABLE(
  POWERMULTISET(nested_table_typ('This', 'is', 'a', 'test'))
);

COLUMN_VALUE
-------------------------------------------
NESTED_TABLE_TYP('This')
NESTED_TABLE_TYP('is')
NESTED_TABLE_TYP('This', 'is')
NESTED_TABLE_TYP('a')
NESTED_TABLE_TYP('This', 'a')
NESTED_TABLE_TYP('is', 'a')
NESTED_TABLE_TYP('This', 'is', 'a')
NESTED_TABLE_TYP('test')
NESTED_TABLE_TYP('This', 'test')
NESTED_TABLE_TYP('is', 'test')
NESTED_TABLE_TYP('This', 'is', 'test')
NESTED_TABLE_TYP('a', 'test')
NESTED_TABLE_TYP('This', 'a', 'test')
NESTED_TABLE_TYP('is', 'a', 'test')
NESTED_TABLE_TYP('This', 'is', 'a', 'test')
```

NOTE
You cannot use POWERMULTISET in PL/SQL.

POWERMULTISET_BY_CARDINALITY Operator

You use the POWERMULTISET_BY_CARDINALITY operator to get a sub-nested table from an input nested table with a specified length (cardinality). The following query illustrates the use of POWERMULTISET_BY_CARDINALITY:

```
SELECT *
FROM TABLE(
  POWERMULTISET_BY_CARDINALITY(
    nested_table_typ('This', 'is', 'a', 'test'), 3
  )
);

COLUMN_VALUE
------------------------------------
NESTED_TABLE_TYP('This', 'is', 'a')
NESTED_TABLE_TYP('This', 'is', 'test')
NESTED_TABLE_TYP('This', 'a', 'test')
NESTED_TABLE_TYP('is', 'a', 'test')
```

NOTE
You cannot use POWERMULTISET_BY_CARDINALITY in PL/SQL.

Summary

In this chapter, you learned that

- Collections allow you to store sets of elements.

- There are three types of collections: varrays, nested tables, and associative arrays.

- A varray is similar to an array in Java; you can use a varray to store an ordered set of elements with each element having an index associated with it. The elements in a varray are of the same type, and a varray has one dimension. A varray has a maximum size that you set when creating it, but you can change the size later.

- A nested table is a table that is embedded within another table, and you can insert, update, and delete individual elements in a nested table. Because you can modify individual elements in a nested table, this makes them more flexible than a varray because elements in a varray can only be modified as a whole, not individually. A nested table doesn't have a maximum size, and you can store an arbitrary number of elements in a nested table.

- An associative array is a set of key and value pairs. You can get the value from the array using the key (which may be a string) or an integer that specifies the position of the value in the array. An associative array is similar to a hash table in programming languages such as Java.

- A multilevel collection type contains elements that are also collection types.

- Collections can be manipulated using SQL and PL/SQL.

- Oracle10*g* features many enhancements to collections.

In the next chapter, you'll learn about large objects.

CHAPTER
14

Large Objects

I n this chapter, you will

- Be introduced to large objects (LOBs)
- See files whose content will be used to populate example LOBs
- Understand the differences between the different types of LOBs
- Create tables containing LOBs
- Use LOBs in SQL
- Use LOBs in PL/SQL
- Use LONG and LONG RAW types
- Examine some of the Oracle Database 10*g* enhancements to LOBs

Introducing Large Objects (LOBs)

Today's applications and web sites demand more than just the storage and retrieval of text and numbers: they may also require multimedia to make the user experience friendlier. Because of this, databases are now being called upon to store things like images, sounds, and video. Prior to the release of Oracle8, you had to store large blocks of character data using the LONG database type, and large blocks of binary data had to be stored using either the LONG RAW type or the shorter RAW type.

After the release of Oracle8 a new class of types known as *large objects* (LOBs) was introduced. LOBs may be used to store binary data, character data, and references to external files. LOBs are widely used to store documents such as Word and PDF documents. LOBs can store a maximum of 128 terabytes of data depending on the block size of your database.

The Example Files

Some of the examples you'll see in this chapter read files, but the contents of a LOB doesn't have to come from a file—the content can come from any valid source that can be read as a string of characters or bytes. Files are used in the examples because they are an easy and common way of handling large blocks of data.

You'll see the use of the following two files in the examples:

- **textContent.txt**   A text file
- **binaryContent.doc**   A Word 2000 file

NOTE
The files are contained in the directory sample_files, *which will be created when you extract the example files from the Zip file available from this book's web site.*

The file `textContent.txt` contains an extract from Shakespeare's play *Macbeth*. The following text shows the speech made by Macbeth shortly before he is killed:

To-morrow, and to-morrow, and to-morrow,
Creeps in this petty pace from day to day,
To the last syllable of recorded time;
And all our yesterdays have lighted fools
The way to a dusty death. Out, out, brief candle!
Life's but a walking shadow; a poor player,
That struts and frets his hour upon the stage,
And then is heard no more: it is a tale
Told by an idiot, full of sound and fury,
Signifying nothing.

The file `binaryContent.doc` is a Word document containing the same text as the `textContent.txt` file, but is a binary file.

Understanding the Large Object Types

There are four LOB types:

- **CLOB** The character LOB type, which is used to store character data.

- **NCLOB** The national language character LOB type, which is used to store multiple byte character data (typically used for non-English characters).

- **BLOB** The binary LOB type, which is used to store binary data.

- **BFILE** The binary FILE type, which is used to store pointers to files located in the file system—that is, outside of the database. These external files can be on a hard disk, a CD, a DVD, or through any other device that is accessible through the computer's file system.

As mentioned earlier, prior to Oracle8 your only choice for storing large amounts of character or binary data was to use the LONG and LONG RAW types (for smaller binary files, you could also use the RAW type). Columns created using CLOB and BLOB types have three advantages over those created using the older LONG and LONG RAW types:

- LOB columns can store up to 128 terabytes of data. This is far more data than you can store in a LONG and LONG RAW column, which may only store up to 2 gigabytes of data. Note: The RAW type may store up to 4 kilobytes of data.

- A table can have multiple LOB columns, but a table can only have one LONG or LONG RAW column.

- LOB data can be accessed in random order; LONG and LONG RAW data can only be accessed in sequential order.

A LOB consists of two parts:

- **The LOB *locator*** A pointer that specifies the location of the LOB content
- **The LOB *content*** The actual character or byte data stored in the LOB

Depending on the size of the LOB content, the actual data will either be stored in the table or out of the table. If the LOB content is less than 4 kilobytes in size, the content is stored in the table containing the LOB column. If it's bigger, the content is stored outside the table. With `BFILE` columns, only the locator is stored in the database—the locator points to the external file containing the LOB content.

Creating Tables Containing Large Objects

I'll use three tables for the examples in this section:

- The `clob_content` table, which contains a `CLOB` column named `clob_column`. This column is used to store the character data contained in the `textContent.txt` file.
- The `blob_content` table, which contains a `BLOB` column named `blob_column`. This column is used to store the binary data stored in the `binaryContent.doc` file.
- The `bfile_content` table, which contains a `BFILE` column named `bfile_column`. This column is used to store pointers to the two external files.

NOTE
I've provided a SQL*Plus script named `lob_schema.sql` in the SQL directory where you unzipped the files for this book. This script may be run against an Oracle8 or higher database. This script creates a user named `lob_user` with a password of `lob_password` and creates the various items used in the first part of this chapter; this script also populates the tables with sample data. I've also provided an additional script named `lob_schema_10g.sql` that is referred to later in this chapter (don't run this additional script yet).

The example tables contain a column to store the name of the file that was used to populate the LOB column. The three tables are defined as follows:

```
CREATE TABLE clob_content (
    id          INTEGER PRIMARY KEY,
    clob_column CLOB NOT NULL
);

CREATE TABLE blob_content (
    id          INTEGER PRIMARY KEY,
    blob_column BLOB NOT NULL
);
```

```
CREATE TABLE bfile_content (
  id              INTEGER PRIMARY KEY,
  bfile_column BFILE NOT NULL
);
```

Using Large Objects in SQL

In this section, you'll learn how to use large objects from within SQL, starting with CLOB and BLOB objects and followed by BFILE objects.

Using CLOBs and BLOBs

LOB columns store a locator that points to the LOB contents.

Initializing a CLOB and BLOB

Before you can actually write content to a LOB, you must first initialize the LOB column. You do this by calling an Oracle database function that generates and returns a value for the locator. To initialize a CLOB or NCLOB column, you use the EMPTY_CLOB() function. A BLOB column must be initialized using the EMPTY_BLOB() function.

The following INSERT statements use EMPTY_CLOB() to initialize clob_column of two new rows in the clob_content table:

```
INSERT INTO clob_content(
  id, clob_column
) VALUES (
  1, EMPTY_CLOB()
);

INSERT INTO clob_content (
  id, clob_column
) VALUES (
  2, EMPTY_CLOB()
);
```

The next INSERT uses EMPTY_BLOB() to initialize blob_column in the blob_content table:

```
INSERT INTO blob_content(
  id, blob_column
) VALUES (
  1, EMPTY_BLOB()
);
```

Adding Content to a CLOB and BLOB

The following UPDATE statements set clob_column to some text for the two rows in clob_content:

```
UPDATE clob_content
SET clob_column = 'Creeps in this petty pace'
```

```
WHERE id = 1;

UPDATE clob_content
SET clob_column = ' from day to day'
WHERE id = 2;
```

The following query retrieves the row from `clob_content`:

```
SELECT *
FROM clob_content;

        ID
----------
CLOB_COLUMN
------------------------
         1
Creeps in this petty pace

         2
 from day to day
```

The next UPDATE sets `blob_column` to a binary number:

```
UPDATE blob_content
SET blob_column = '100111010101011111'
WHERE id = 1;
```

The following query attempts to retrieve the contents of `blob_content` and fails:

```
SELECT *
FROM blob_content;
SP2-0678: Column or attribute type can not be displayed by SQL*Plus
```

This example fails because SQL*Plus cannot display the binary content in a BLOB. You'll learn how to access the content in a BLOB later in the section "Using Large Objects in PL/SQL."

Using BFILEs

The BFILE LOB type enables you to store a *pointer* to a file that is accessible through the computer's file system. The important point to note is that these files are located outside of the database. BFILE columns can point to files located on any media: a hard disk, CD, DVD, and so on.

NOTE
A BFILE contains a pointer to an external file. The actual file itself is not stored in the database, only a pointer to that file. The file must be accessible through the file system.

Creating a Directory Object

Before you can store a pointer to a file in a BFILE column, you must first create a *directory* object in the database that represents the directory in the file system where your files are stored. You create a directory object using the CREATE DIRECTORY statement. To perform such a statement, you must have the CREATE ANY DIRECTORY database privilege.

The following example creates a directory object named SAMPLE_FILES_DIR for the file system directory C:\sample_files:

```
CREATE OR REPLACE DIRECTORY SAMPLE_FILES_DIR AS 'C:\sample_files';
```

NOTE
Windows uses the backslash character (\) in directories, while Linux and Unix use the forward slash character (/).

When you create a directory object you must ensure that

- The actual directory exists in the file system.

- The user account in the operating system that was used to install the Oracle software has read permission on the directory and on any files that are to be pointed to by a BFILE column in the database.

If you are using Windows, you shouldn't need to worry about the second point. The Oracle database software should have been installed using a user account that has administrator privileges, and such a user account has read permission on everything in the file system. If you are using Linux or Unix, you may have to grant read access to the physical directory and to the files, using the chmod command, for example.

Populating a BFILE Column with a Pointer to a File

Because a BFILE is just a pointer to an external file, populating a BFILE column is very simple. All you have to do is to use the Oracle database's BFILENAME() function to populate the BFILE column with a pointer to your external file. The BFILENAME() function accepts two parameters: the database directory object's name (which was created earlier) and the name of the file.

The following INSERT adds a row to the bfile_content table using the BFILENAME() function to populate bfile_column with a pointer to the textContent.txt file:

```
INSERT INTO bfile_content (
  id,
  bfile_column
) VALUES (
  1,
  BFILENAME('SAMPLE_FILES_DIR', 'textContent.txt')
);
```

A BFILE column doesn't care what format a file is stored in. This example stores a pointer to a text file. A similar statement can be used to add a row containing a pointer to a binary file. The next INSERT adds a row to the bfile_content table using the BFILENAME() function to populate bfile_column with a pointer to the binaryContent.doc file:

```
INSERT INTO bfile_content (
    id,
    bfile_column
) VALUES (
    2,
    BFILENAME('SAMPLE_FILES_DIR', 'binaryContent.doc')
);
```

The following query attempts to retrieve the rows from bfile_content and fails because SQL*Plus cannot display the content in a BFILE:

```
SELECT *
FROM bfile_content;
SP2-0678: Column or attribute type can not be displayed by SQL*Plus
```

In order to access the content in a BFILE (or a BLOB) you may use PL/SQL, which you'll learn how to do next.

Using Large Objects in PL/SQL

In this section, you'll learn how to use LOBs from within PL/SQL. To do this, you use the methods in the DBMS_LOB package that comes with the Oracle database. Table 14-1 summarizes the methods in the DBMS_LOB package.

In the following sections, you'll learn more about the methods shown in Table 14-1. You'll also see examples of some of the methods.

Method	Description
APPEND(*dest_lob, src_lob*)	Adds the contents of the source LOB to the end of the destination LOB
CLOSE(*lob_loc*)	Closes a previously opened LOB
COMPARE(*lob1, lob2, amount, offset1, offset2*)	Compares two entire LOBs or parts of two LOBs
COPY(*dest_lob, src_lob, amount, dest_offset, src_offset*)	Copies all or part of the source LOB to the destination LOB
CREATETEMPORARY(*lob, cache, duration*)	Creates a temporary BLOB or CLOB and its corresponding index in the user's default temporary tablespace
ERASE(*lob, amount, offset*)	Erases all or part of a LOB

TABLE 14-1.   *DBMS_LOB Methods*

Method	Description
FILECLOSE(*bfile*)	Closes a BFILE
FILECLOSEALL()	Closes all previously opened BFILEs
FILEEXISTS(*bfile*)	Checks if a file exists on the server
FILEGETNAME(*bfile, dir_alias, filename*)	Gets the directory alias and file name
FILEISOPEN(*bfile*)	Checks if the file is open
FILEOPEN(*bfile, open_mode*)	Opens a file
FREETEMPORARY(*lob*)	Frees the temporary BLOB or CLOB in the default temporary tablespace of the user
GETCHUNKSIZE(*lob*)	Gets the amount of space used in the LOB chunk to store the LOB value
GET_STORAGE_LIMIT()	Gets the storage limit of a LOB
GETLENGTH(*lob*)	Gets the length of the LOB value
INSTR(*lob, pattern, offset, n*)	Gets the matching position of the nth occurrence of the pattern in the LOB
ISOPEN(*lob*)	Checks if the LOB was already opened using the input locator
ISTEMPORARY(*lob*)	Checks if the locator is pointing to a temporary LOB
LOADFROMFILE(*dest_lob, src_bfile, amount, dest_offset, src_offset*)	Loads BFILE data into an internal LOB
LOADBLOBFROMFILE(*dest_lob, src_bfile, amount, dest_offset, src_offset*)	Loads BFILE data into an internal BLOB
LOADCLOBFROMFILE(*dest_lob, src_bfile, amount, dest_offset, src_offset, src_csid, lang_context, warning*)	Loads BFILE data into an internal CLOB
OPEN(*lob, open_mode*)	Opens a LOB (internal, external, or temporary) in the indicated mode
READ(*lob, amount, offset, buffer*)	Reads data into the buffer from the LOB starting at the specified offset
SUBSTR(*lob, amount, offset*)	Reads part of the LOB value starting at the specified offset
TRIM(*lob, newlen*)	Trims the LOB value to the specified shorter length
WRITE(*lob, amount, offset, buffer*)	Writes data from the buffer to the LOB at the specified offset
WRITEAPPEND(*lob, amount, buffer*)	Writes data from the buffer to the end of a LOB

TABLE 14-1. *DBMS_LOB Methods* (continued)

NOTE
The following sections show example methods that are created by the
`lob_schema.sql` *script.*

READ()

You use `READ()` to read data from the LOB starting at the specified offset. There are three versions of `READ()` and they have the following syntax:

```
DBMS_LOB.READ(
    lob    IN                    BLOB,
    amount IN OUT NOCOPY BINARY_INTEGER,
    offset IN                    INTEGER,
    buffer OUT                   RAW
);

DBMS_LOB.READ(
    lob    IN                    CLOB CHARACTER SET ANY_CS,
    amount IN OUT NOCOPY BINARY_INTEGER,
    offset IN                    INTEGER,
    buffer OUT                   VARCHAR2 CHARACTER SET lob%CHARSET
);

DBMS_LOB.READ(
    bfile  IN                    BFILE,
    amount IN OUT NOCOPY BINARY_INTEGER,
    offset IN                    INTEGER,
    buffer OUT                   RAW
);
```

where

- *lob* is the CLOB or BLOB to read from.
- *bfile* is the BFILE to read from.
- *amount* is the number of characters to read from the CLOB or the number of bytes to read from the BLOB or BFILE.
- *offset* is the offset in characters to read from the CLOB or the number of bytes to read from the BLOB or BFILE (offset starts at 1).
- *buffer* is the storage variable where the output from the read is to be stored.
- CHARACTER SET ANY_CS specifies any character set.
- CHARACTER SET *lob*%CHARSET is the character set of *lob*.

Table 14-2 shows the exceptions thrown by READ().

Exception	Thrown When
VALUE_ERROR	Any of the input parameters are null.
INVALID_ARGVAL	Either: ■ *amount* < 1 ■ *amount* > MAXBUFSIZE ■ *amount* > capacity of buffer in bytes or characters ■ *offset* < 1 ■ *offset* > LOBMAXSIZE
NO_DATA_FOUND	The end of the LOB was reached and there are no more bytes or characters to read from the LOB.

TABLE 14-2. *Exceptions Thrown by READ()*

The following `initialize_clob()` procedure performs the following tasks:

■ Accepts an IN OUT parameter named `clob_par` of type CLOB, which is initialized in the procedure.

■ Accepts an IN parameter named `id_par` of type INTEGER, which specifies the ID of the CLOB to select.

■ Selects `clob_column` from `clob_content` into `clob_par` where id is `id_par`.

```
CREATE OR REPLACE PROCEDURE initialize_clob(
  clob_par IN OUT CLOB,
  id_par IN INTEGER
) IS
BEGIN
  SELECT clob_column
  INTO clob_par
  FROM clob_content
  WHERE id = id_par;
END initialize_clob;
/
```

The following `initialize_blob()` procedure performs the following tasks:

■ Accepts an IN OUT parameter named `blob_par` of type BLOB.

■ Accepts an IN parameter named `id_par` of type INTEGER.

■ Selects `blob_column` from `blob_content` into `blob_par` where id is `id_par`.

```
CREATE OR REPLACE PROCEDURE initialize_blob(
  blob_par IN OUT BLOB,
```

```
    id_par IN INTEGER
) IS
BEGIN
  SELECT blob_column
  INTO blob_par
  FROM blob_content
  WHERE id = id_par;
END initialize_blob;
/
```

The following `read_clob_example()` procedure performs the following tasks:

- Calls `initialize_clob()` to initialize `clob_var`.

- Uses `READ()` to read the contents of `clob_var` into a `VARCHAR2` variable named `char_buffer_var`.

- Outputs the contents of `char_buffer_var`.

```
CREATE OR REPLACE PROCEDURE read_clob_example(
  id_par IN INTEGER
) IS
  clob_var CLOB;
  char_buffer_var VARCHAR2(50);
  offset_var INTEGER := 1;
  amount_var INTEGER := 50;
BEGIN
  initialize_clob(clob_var, id_par);
  DBMS_LOB.READ(clob_var, amount_var, offset_var, char_buffer_var);
  DBMS_OUTPUT.PUT_LINE('char_buffer_var = ' || char_buffer_var);
  DBMS_OUTPUT.PUT_LINE('amount_var = ' || amount_var);
END read_clob_example;
/
```

The following `read_blob_example()` procedure performs the following tasks:

- Calls `initialize_blob()` to initialize `blob_var`.

- Calls `READ()` to read the contents of `blob_var` into a `RAW` variable named `binary_buffer_var`.

- Outputs the contents of `binary_buffer_var`.

```
CREATE OR REPLACE PROCEDURE read_blob_example(
  id_par IN INTEGER
) IS
  blob_var BLOB;
  binary_buffer_var RAW(25);
  offset_var INTEGER := 1;
  amount_var INTEGER := 25;
```

```
BEGIN
  initialize_blob(blob_var, id_par);
  DBMS_LOB.READ(blob_var, amount_var, offset_var, binary_buffer_var);
  DBMS_OUTPUT.PUT_LINE('binary_buffer_var = ' || binary_buffer_var);
  DBMS_OUTPUT.PUT_LINE('amount_var = ' || amount_var);
END read_blob_example;
/
```

The following example connects as `lob_user`, turns the server output on, and calls `read_clob_example()` and `read_blob_example()`:

```
CONNECT lob_user/lob_password
SET SERVEROUTPUT ON
CALL read_clob_example(1);
char_buffer_var = Creeps in this petty pace
amount_var = 25

Call completed.

CALL read_blob_example(1);
binary_buffer_var = 100111010101011111
amount_var = 9

Call completed.
```

WRITE()

You use `WRITE()` to write data to the LOB at a specified offset. There are two versions of `WRITE()` and they have the following syntax:

```
DBMS_LOB.WRITE(
  lob     IN OUT NOCOPY BLOB,
  amount  IN            BINARY_INTEGER,
  offset  IN            INTEGER,
  buffer  IN            RAW
);

DBMS_LOB.WRITE(
  lob     IN OUT NOCOPY CLOB CHARACTER SET ANY_CS,
  amount  IN            BINARY_INTEGER,
  offset  IN            INTEGER,
  buffer  IN            VARCHAR2 CHARACTER SET lob%CHARSET
);
```

where

- *lob* is the CLOB or BLOB to write to.

- *amount* is the number of characters to write to the CLOB or the number of bytes to write to the BLOB.

- *offset* is the offset in characters to write to the CLOB or the number of bytes to write to the BLOB (offset starts at 1).

- *buffer* is the storage variable where the input to the write is to be read from.

Table 14-3 shows the exceptions thrown by WRITE().

The following write_example() procedure performs the following tasks:

- Accepts an IN parameter named id_par of type INTEGER.

- Selects clob_column into a CLOB variable named clob_var from clob_content where id is id_par. The select uses the FOR UPDATE clause to lock the row for update. FOR UPDATE is used because clob_var will be written to using WRITE().

- Calls read_clob_example() to read and display the contents of clob_var.

- Calls WRITE() to write the contents of a VARCHAR2 variable named char_buffer_var to clob_var.

- Calls read_clob_example() again to read and display the contents of clob_var.

- Performs a ROLLBACK to undo the write.

```
CREATE OR REPLACE PROCEDURE write_example(
  id_par IN INTEGER
) IS
  clob_var CLOB;
  char_buffer_var VARCHAR2(10) := 'pretty';
  offset_var INTEGER := 7;
  amount_var INTEGER := 6;
BEGIN
  SELECT clob_column
  INTO clob_var
  FROM clob_content
  WHERE id = 1
  FOR UPDATE;

  read_clob_example(1);
  DBMS_LOB.WRITE(clob_var, amount_var, offset_var, char_buffer_var);
  read_clob_example(1);

  ROLLBACK;
END write_example;
/
```

The following example calls write_example():

```
CALL write_example(1);
char_buffer_var = Creeps in this petty pace
amount_var = 25
char_buffer_var = Creepsprettyis petty pace
amount_var = 25
```

Exception	Thrown When
VALUE_ERROR	Any of the input parameters are null or invalid.
INVALID_ARGVAL	Either: ■ *amount* < 1 ■ *amount* > MAXBUFSIZE ■ *offset* < 1 ■ *offset* > LOBMAXSIZE

TABLE 14-3. *Exceptions Thrown by* WRITE()

APPEND()

You use APPEND() to add the contents of the source LOB to the end of the destination LOB. There are two versions of APPEND() and they have the following syntax:

```
DBMS_LOB.APPEND(
   dest_lob IN OUT NOCOPY BLOB,
   src_lob  IN            BLOB
);

DBMS_LOB.APPEND(
   dest_lob IN OUT NOCOPY CLOB CHARACTER SET ANY_CS,
   src_lob  IN            CLOB CHARACTER SET dest_lob%CHARSET
);
```

where

- *dest_lob* is the destination LOB to which content is added.

- *src_lob* is the source LOB from which content is copied.

Table 14-4 shows the exception thrown by APPEND().
The following append_example() procedure performs the following tasks:

- Selects clob_column into src_clob_var from clob_content where id is 2.

- Selects clob_column into dest_clob_var from clob_content where id is 1 for update.

Exception	Thrown When
VALUE_ERROR	Either *dest_lob* or *src_lob* is null.

TABLE 14-4. *Exception Thrown by* APPEND()

- Calls `read_clob_example()` to read and display the contents of `dest_clob_var`.

- Calls `APPEND()` to add the contents of `src_clob_var` to `dest_clob_var`.

- Calls `read_clob_example()` to read and display the contents of `dest_clob_var`, which now contains the contents of `src_clob_var` at the end.

- Performs a `ROLLBACK` to undo the append.

```
CREATE OR REPLACE PROCEDURE append_example IS
  src_clob_var CLOB;
  dest_clob_var CLOB;
BEGIN
  SELECT clob_column
  INTO src_clob_var
  FROM clob_content
  WHERE id = 2;

  SELECT clob_column
  INTO dest_clob_var
  FROM clob_content
  WHERE id = 1
  FOR UPDATE;

  read_clob_example(1);
  DBMS_LOB.APPEND(dest_clob_var, src_clob_var);
  read_clob_example(1);

  ROLLBACK;
END append_example;
/
```

The following example calls `append_example()`:

```
CALL append_example();
char_buffer_var = Creeps in this petty pace
amount_var = 25
char_buffer_var = Creeps in this petty pace from day to day
amount_var = 41
```

CLOSE()

You use `CLOSE()` to close a previously opened LOB. There are three versions of `CLOSE()` and they have the following syntax:

```
DBMS_LOB.CLOSE(
    lob IN OUT NOCOPY BLOB
);
```

```
DBMS_LOB.CLOSE(
  lob IN OUT NOCOPY CLOB CHARACTER SET ANY_CS
);

DBMS_LOB.CLOSE(
  lob IN OUT NOCOPY BFILE
);
```

where

- ■ *lob* is the LOB to be closed.

COMPARE()

You use COMPARE() to compare two entire LOBs or parts of two LOBs.

```
DBMS_LOB.COMPARE(
  lob1    IN BLOB,
  lob2    IN BLOB,
  amount  IN INTEGER := 4294967295,
  offset1 IN INTEGER := 1,
  offset2 IN INTEGER := 1
) RETURN INTEGER;

DBMS_LOB.COMPARE(
  lob1    IN CLOB  CHARACTER SET ANY_CS,
  lob2    IN CLOB  CHARACTER SET lob_1%CHARSET,
  amount  IN INTEGER := 4294967295,
  offset1 IN INTEGER := 1,
  offset2 IN INTEGER := 1
) RETURN INTEGER;

DBMS_LOB.COMPARE(
  lob1    IN BFILE,
  lob2    IN BFILE,
  amount  IN INTEGER,
  offset1 IN INTEGER := 1,
  offset2 IN INTEGER := 1
) RETURN INTEGER;
```

where

- ■ *lob1* and *lob2* are the LOBs to compare.

- ■ *amount* is the number of characters when reading from a CLOB, and the number of bytes when reading from a BLOB or BFILE.

- ■ *offset1* and *offset2* are the offsets in characters or bytes in *lob1* and *lob2* to start the comparison.

COMPARE() returns

- 0 if the LOBs are identical.

- 1 if the LOBs aren't identical.

- Null if:

  - *amount* < 1

  - *amount* > LOBMAXSIZE (Note: LOBMAXSIZE is the maximum size of the LOB)

  - *offset1* or *offset2* < 1

  - *offset1* or *offset2* > LOBMAXSIZE

Table 14-5 shows the exceptions thrown by COMPARE().
The following compare_example() procedure performs the following tasks:

- Selects clob_column into clob_var1 from clob_content where id is 1.

- Selects clob_column into clob_var2 from clob_content where id is 2 for update.

- Calls COMPARE() to compare the contents of clob_var1 with clob_var2. COMPARE() returns 1 because the contents of clob_var1 and clob_var2 are different.

- Calls COMPARE() to compare the contents of clob_var1 with clob_var1. COMPARE() returns 0 because the contents are the same.

```
CREATE OR REPLACE PROCEDURE compare_example IS
  clob_var1 CLOB;
  clob_var2 CLOB;
  return_var INTEGER;
BEGIN
  SELECT clob_column
  INTO clob_var1
  FROM clob_content
  WHERE id = 1;

  SELECT clob_column
  INTO clob_var2
  FROM clob_content
  WHERE id = 2;

  DBMS_OUTPUT.PUT_LINE('Comparing clob_var1 with clob_var2');
  return_var := DBMS_LOB.COMPARE(clob_var1, clob_var2);
  DBMS_OUTPUT.PUT_LINE('return_var = ' || return_var);

  DBMS_OUTPUT.PUT_LINE('Comparing clob_var1 with clob_var1');
  return_var := DBMS_LOB.COMPARE(clob_var1, clob_var1);
  DBMS_OUTPUT.PUT_LINE('return_var = ' || return_var);
END compare_example;
/
```

Exception	Thrown When
UNOPENED_FILE	The file hasn't been opened yet.
NOEXIST_DIRECTORY	The directory doesn't exist.
NOPRIV_DIRECTORY	You don't have privileges to access the directory.
INVALID_DIRECTORY	The directory is invalid.
INVALID_OPERATION	The file exists, but you don't have privileges to access the file.

TABLE 14-5. *Exceptions Thrown by COMPARE ()*

The following example calls compare_example():

```
CALL compare_example();
Comparing clob_var1 with clob_var2
return_var = 1
Comparing clob_var1 with clob_var1
return_var = 0
```

Notice return_var is 1 when comparing clob_var1 with clob_var2, which indicates the LOBs are different. return_var is 0 when comparing clob_var1 with clob_var1, which indicates the LOBs are identical.

COPY()

You use COPY() to copy all or part of the source LOB to the destination LOB.

```
DBMS_LOB.COPY(
   dest_lob     IN OUT NOCOPY BLOB,
   src_lob      IN            BLOB,
   amount       IN            INTEGER,
   dest_offset  IN            INTEGER := 1,
   src_offset   IN            INTEGER := 1
);

DBMS_LOB.COPY(
   dest_lob     IN OUT NOCOPY CLOB CHARACTER SET ANY_CS,
   src_lob      IN            CLOB CHARACTER SET dest_lob%CHARSET,
   amount       IN            INTEGER,
   dest_offset  IN            INTEGER := 1,
   src_offset   IN            INTEGER := 1
);
```

where

■   *dest_lob* and *src_lob* are the LOBs to copy to and read from.

■ *amount* is the number of characters when reading from a CLOB, and the number of bytes when reading from a BLOB or BFILE.

■ *dest_offset* and *src_offset* are the offsets in characters or bytes in *dest_lob* and *src_lob* to start the copy.

Table 14-6 shows the exceptions thrown by COPY().

The following copy_example() procedure performs the following tasks:

■ Selects clob_column into src_clob_var from clob_content where id is 2.

■ Selects clob_column into dest_clob_var from clob_content where id is 1 for update.

■ Calls read_clob_example() to read and display the contents of dest_clob_var.

■ Calls COPY() to copy part of the contents of src_clob_var to dest_clob_var.

■ Calls read_clob_example() again to read and display the contents of dest_clob_var.

■ Performs a ROLLBACK to undo the copy.

```
CREATE OR REPLACE PROCEDURE copy_example IS
  src_clob_var CLOB;
  dest_clob_var CLOB;
  src_offset_var INTEGER := 1;
  dest_offset_var INTEGER := 7;
  amount_var INTEGER := 5;
BEGIN
  SELECT clob_column
  INTO src_clob_var
  FROM clob_content
  WHERE id = 2;

  SELECT clob_column
  INTO dest_clob_var
  FROM clob_content
  WHERE id = 1
  FOR UPDATE;

  read_clob_example(1);
  DBMS_LOB.COPY(
    dest_clob_var, src_clob_var, amount_var,
    dest_offset_var, src_offset_var
  );
  read_clob_example(1);

  ROLLBACK;
END copy_example;
/
```

Exception	Thrown When
VALUE_ERROR	Any of the parameters are null.
INVALID_ARGVAL	Either: ■ *src_offset* < 1 ■ *dest_offset* < 1 ■ *src_offset* > LOBMAXSIZE ■ *dest_offset* > LOBMAXSIZE ■ *amount* < 1 ■ *amount* > LOBMAXSIZE

TABLE 14-6. *Exceptions Thrown by* COPY()

The following example calls copy_example():

```
CALL copy_example();
char_buffer_var = Creeps in this petty pace
amount_var = 25
char_buffer_var = Creeps fromhis petty pace
amount_var = 25
```

CREATETEMPORARY()

You use CREATETEMPORARY() to create a temporary BLOB or CLOB and its corresponding index in the user's default temporary tablespace.

```
DBMS_LOB.CREATETEMPORARY(
  lob      IN OUT NOCOPY BLOB,
  cache    IN            BOOLEAN,
  duration IN            PLS_INTEGER := 10
);

DBMS_LOB.CREATETEMPORARY (
  lob      IN OUT NOCOPY CLOB CHARACTER SET ANY_CS,
  cache    IN            BOOLEAN,
  duration IN            PLS_INTEGER := 10
);
```

where

- *lob* is the LOB to create.

- *cache* specifies whether the LOB should be read into the buffer cache.

- *duration* is either SESSION or CALL, which indicates whether the temporary LOB is removed at the end of the session or call. The default is SESSION.

Exception	Thrown When
VALUE_ERROR	The *lob* parameter is null.

TABLE 14-7. *Exception Thrown by* CREATETEMPORARY()

Table 14-7 shows the exception thrown by CREATETEMPORARY().
The following temporary_lob_example() procedure performs the following tasks:

- Calls CREATETEMPORARY() to create a temporary CLOB named clob_var.

- Calls WRITE() to write the contents of a VARCHAR2 variable named char_buffer_var to clob_var.

- Calls ISTEMPORARY() to check if clob_var is temporary.

- Calls READ() to read the contents of clob_var into char_buffer_var.

- Displays the contents of char_buffer_var.

- Calls FREETEMPORARY() to free clob_var.

```
CREATE OR REPLACE PROCEDURE temporary_lob_example IS
  clob_var CLOB;
  amount_var INTEGER := 19;
  offset_var INTEGER := 1;
  char_buffer_var VARCHAR2(19) := 'Juliet is the sun';
BEGIN
  DBMS_LOB.CREATETEMPORARY(clob_var, TRUE);
  DBMS_LOB.WRITE(clob_var, amount_var, offset_var, char_buffer_var);

  IF (DBMS_LOB.ISTEMPORARY(clob_var) = 1) THEN
    DBMS_OUTPUT.PUT_LINE('clob_var is temporary');
  END IF;

  DBMS_LOB.READ(
    clob_var, amount_var, offset_var, char_buffer_var
  );
  DBMS_OUTPUT.PUT_LINE('char_buffer_var = ' || char_buffer_var);

  DBMS_LOB.FREETEMPORARY(clob_var);
END temporary_lob_example;
/
```

The following example calls temporary_lob_example():

```
CALL temporary_lob_example();
clob_var is temporary
char_buffer_var = Juliet is the sun
```

ERASE()

You use ERASE() to remove all or part of a LOB.

```
DBMS_LOB.ERASE(
   lob    IN OUT NOCOPY BLOB,
   amount IN OUT NOCOPY INTEGER,
   offset IN            INTEGER := 1
);

DBMS_LOB.ERASE(
   lob    IN OUT NOCOPY CLOB CHARACTER SET ANY_CS,
   amount IN OUT NOCOPY INTEGER,
   offset IN            INTEGER := 1
);
```

where

■ *lob* is the LOB to erase.

■ *amount* is the number of characters when reading from a CLOB, and the number of bytes when reading from a BLOB or BFILE.

■ *offset* is the offset in characters or bytes in *lob* to start the erasure.

Table 14-8 shows the exceptions thrown by ERASE().
The following erase_example() procedure performs the following tasks:

■ Selects clob_column into clob_var from clob_content where id is 1 for update.

■ Calls read_clob_example() to read and display the contents of clob_var.

■ Calls ERASE() to erase part of clob_var.

Exception	Thrown When
VALUE_ERROR	Any of the parameters are null.
INVALID_ARGVAL	Either: ■ *amount* < 1 ■ *amount* > LOBMAXSIZE ■ *offset* < 1 ■ *offset* > LOBMAXSIZE

TABLE 14-8. *Exceptions Thrown by* ERASE()

■ Calls read_clob_example() again to read and display the contents of clob_var.

■ Performs a ROLLBACK to undo the erase.

```
CREATE OR REPLACE PROCEDURE erase_example IS
  clob_var CLOB;
  offset_var INTEGER := 2;
  amount_var INTEGER := 5;
BEGIN
  SELECT clob_column
  INTO clob_var
  FROM clob_content
  WHERE id = 1
  FOR UPDATE;

  read_clob_example(1);
  DBMS_LOB.ERASE(clob_var, amount_var, offset_var);
  read_clob_example(1);

  ROLLBACK;
END erase_example;
/
```

The following example calls erase_example():

```
CALL erase_example();
char_buffer_var = Creeps in this petty pace
amount_var = 25
char_buffer_var = C     in this petty pace
amount_var = 25
```

FILECLOSE()

You use FILECLOSE() to close a BFILE.

```
DBMS_LOB.FILECLOSE(
  bfile IN OUT NOCOPY BFILE
);
```

where

■ *bfile* is the BFILE to close.

Table 14-9 shows the exceptions thrown by FILECLOSE().
You'll see an example of FILECLOSE() later in the section on LOADFROMFILE().

Exception	Thrown When
VALUE_ERROR	The *bfile* parameter is null.
UNOPENED_FILE	The file hasn't been opened yet.
NOEXIST_DIRECTORY	The directory doesn't exist.
NOPRIV_DIRECTORY	You don't have privileges to access the directory.
INVALID_DIRECTORY	The directory is invalid.
INVALID_OPERATION	The file exists, but you don't have privileges to access the file.

TABLE 14-9. *Exceptions Thrown by FILECLOSE()*

FILECLOSEALL()

You use FILECLOSEALL() to close all BFILE objects.

```
DBMS_LOB.FILECLOSEALL;
```

Table 14-10 shows the exception thrown by FILECLOSEALL().

FILEEXISTS()

You use FILEEXISTS() to check if a file exists on the server.

```
DBMS_LOB.FILEEXISTS(
   bfile IN BFILE
) RETURN INTEGER;
```

where

- *bfile* is the pointer to the file to check exists.

   FILEEXISTS() returns

- 0 if the file doesn't exist.
- 1 if the file exists.

Exception	Thrown When
UNOPENED_FILE	No files have been opened in the session.

TABLE 14-10. *Exception Thrown by FILECLOSEALL()*

Exception	Thrown When
VALUE_ERROR	The *bfile* parameter is null.
NOEXIST_DIRECTORY	The directory doesn't exist.
NOPRIV_DIRECTORY	You don't have privileges to access the directory.
INVALID_DIRECTORY	The directory is invalid.

TABLE 14-11.   *Exceptions Thrown by FILEEXISTS()*

Table 14-11 shows the exceptions thrown by FILEEXISTS().
You'll see an example of FILEEXISTS() later in the section on LOADFROMFILE().

FILEGETNAME()

You use FILEGETNAME() to get the directory alias and file name.

```
DBMS_LOB.FILEGETNAME(
    bfile      IN  BFILE,
    dir_alias OUT VARCHAR2,
    filename  OUT VARCHAR2
);
```

where

- *bfile* is the BFILE that points to the file.

- *dir_alias* is the directory alias.

- *filename* is the name of the file.

Table 14-12 shows the exceptions thrown by FILEGETNAME().
You'll see an example of FILEGETNAME() later in the section on LOADFROMFILE().

Exception	Thrown When
VALUE_ERROR	Any of the input parameters are null or invalid.
INVALID_ARGVAL	The *dir_value* or *filename* parameters are null.

TABLE 14-12.   *Exceptions Thrown by FILEGETNAME()*

FILEISOPEN()

You use `FILEISOPEN()` to check if a file is open.

```
DBMS_LOB.FILEISOPEN(
   bfile IN BFILE
) RETURN INTEGER;
```

where

■ *bfile* is the pointer to the file.

`FILEISOPEN()` returns:

■ 0 if the file isn't open.

■ 1 if the file is open.

Table 14-13 shows the exceptions thrown by `FILEISOPEN()`.
You'll see an example of `FILEISOPEN()` later in the section on `LOADFROMFILE()`.

FILEOPEN()

You use `FILEOPEN()` to open a file.

```
DBMS_LOB.FILEOPEN(
   bfile      IN OUT NOCOPY BFILE,
   open_mode IN            BINARY_INTEGER := DBMS_LOB.FILE_READONLY
);
```

where

■ *bfile* is the `BFILE` that points to the file.

■ *open_mode* indicates the open mode. The default (and currently only open mode) is `DBMS_LOB.FILE_READONLY`, which indicates the file may only be read from.

Exception	Thrown When
NOEXIST_DIRECTORY	The directory doesn't exist.
NOPRIV_DIRECTORY	You don't have privileges to access the directory.
INVALID_DIRECTORY	The directory is invalid.
INVALID_OPERATION	The file doesn't exist or you don't have access privileges on the file.

TABLE 14-13. *Exceptions Thrown by* `FILEISOPEN()`

Exception	Thrown When
VALUE_ERROR	Any of the input parameters are null or invalid.
INVALID_ARGVAL	The *open_mode* is not set to FILE_READONLY.
OPEN_TOOMANY	An attempt is made to open more than SESSION_MAX_OPEN_ FILES files. SESSION_MAX_OPEN_FILES is an initialization parameter.
NOEXIST_DIRECTORY	The directory doesn't exist.
INVALID_DIRECTORY	The directory is invalid.
INVALID_OPERATION	The file exists, but you don't have privileges to access the file.

TABLE 14-14.   *Exceptions Thrown by FILEOPEN()*

Table 14-14 shows the exceptions thrown by FILEOPEN().
You'll see an example of FILEOPEN() later in the section on LOADFROMFILE().

FREETEMPORARY()

You use FREETEMPORARY() to free the temporary BLOB or CLOB in the default temporary tablespace of the user.

```
DBMS_LOB.FREETEMPORARY (
    lob IN OUT NOCOPY BLOB
);

DBMS_LOB.FREETEMPORARY (
    lob IN OUT NOCOPY CLOB CHARACTER SET ANY_CS
);
```

where

- *lob* is the lob to be freed.

Table 14-15 shows the exception thrown by FREETEMPORARY().
You saw an example of FREETEMPORARY() earlier in the section on CREATETEMPORARY().

Exception	Thrown When
VALUE_ERROR	Any of the input parameters are null or invalid.

TABLE 14-15.   *Exception Thrown by FREETEMPORARY()*

GETCHUNKSIZE()

You use `GETCHUNKSIZE()` to get the amount of space used in the LOB chunk to store the LOB value.

```
DBMS_LOB.GETCHUNKSIZE(
  lob IN BLOB
) RETURN INTEGER;

DBMS_LOB.GETCHUNKSIZE(
  lob IN CLOB CHARACTER SET ANY_CS
) RETURN INTEGER;
```

where

- `lob` is the LOB to get the chunk size for.

`GETCHUNKSIZE()` returns

- The chunk size in bytes for a `BLOB`.

- The chunk size in characters for a `CLOB`.

Table 14-16 shows the exception thrown by `GETCHUNKSIZE()`.
You'll see an example of `GETCHUNKSIZE()` later in the section on `LOADFROMFILE()`.

GET_STORAGE_LIMIT()

You use `GET_STORAGE_LIMIT()` to get the storage limit of a LOB.

```
DBMS_LOB.GET_STROAGE_LIMIT()
RETURN INTEGER;
```

`GET_STORAGE_LIMIT()` returns

- The maximum allowable size of for a LOB.

GETLENGTH()

You use `GETLENGTH()` to gets the length of the LOB value.

Exception	Thrown When
VALUE_ERROR	The `lob` parameter is null.

TABLE 14-16.   *Exception Thrown by GETCHUNKSIZE()*

```
DBMS_LOB.GETLENGTH(
    lob IN BLOB
) RETURN INTEGER;

DBMS_LOB.GETLENGTH(
    lob IN CLOB CHARACTER SET ANY_CS
) RETURN INTEGER;

DBMS_LOB.GETLENGTH(
    bfile IN BFILE
) RETURN INTEGER;
```

where

- *lob* is the BLOB or CLOB to get the length of.
- *bfile* is the BFILE to get the length of.

GETLENGTH() returns

- The length in bytes for a BLOB or BFILE.
- The length in characters for a CLOB.

Table 14-17 shows the exception thrown by GETLENGTH().
You'll see an example of GETLENGTH() later in the section on LOADFROMFILE().

INSTR()

You use INSTR() to get the matching position of the *n*th occurrence of the pattern in the LOB.

```
DBMS_LOB.INSTR(
    lob       IN BLOB,
    pattern IN RAW,
    offset  IN INTEGER := 1,
    n         IN INTEGER := 1
) RETURN INTEGER;

DBMS_LOB.INSTR(
    lob       IN CLOB      CHARACTER SET ANY_CS,
    pattern IN VARCHAR2 CHARACTER SET lob%CHARSET,
    offset  IN INTEGER := 1,
    n         IN INTEGER := 1
) RETURN INTEGER;

DBMS_LOB.INSTR (
    bfile     IN BFILE,
    pattern IN RAW,
    offset  IN INTEGER := 1,
    n         IN INTEGER := 1
) RETURN INTEGER;
```

Exception	Thrown When
VALUE_ERROR	The *lob* or *bfile* parameter is null.

TABLE 14-17. *Exception Thrown by GETLENGTH()*

where

- *lob* is the BLOB or CLOB to read from.
- *bfile* is the BFILE to read from.
- *pattern* is the pattern to search for. The pattern is a group of RAW bytes for a BLOB or BFILE, and a VARCHAR2 character string for a CLOB. The maximum size of the pattern is 16,383 bytes.
- *offset* is the offset in bytes for a BLOB or BFILE and the characters for a CLOB at which the pattern matching is to start. The first byte or character is numbered as 1.
- *n* is the occurrence of pattern in the LOB content to search for.

INSTR() returns

- The offset of the start of the pattern (if found).
- Zero if the pattern isn't found.
- Null if:
  - Any of the IN parameters are null or invalid
  - *offset* < 1 or *offset* > LOBMAXSIZE
  - *n* < 1 or *n* > LOBMAXSIZE

Table 14-18 shows the exceptions thrown by INSTR().

Exception	Thrown When
VALUE_ERROR	Any of the input parameters are null or invalid.
UNOPENED_FILE	The BFILE isn't open.
NOEXIST_DIRECTORY	The directory doesn't exist.
NOPRIV_DIRECTORY	You don't have privileges on the directory.
INVALID_DIRECTORY	The directory is invalid.
INVALID_OPERATION	The file exists, but you don't have privileges to access the file.

TABLE 14-18. *Exception Thrown by INSTR()*

The following `instr_example()` procedure performs the following tasks:

- Creates a VARCHAR2 variable named `char_buffer_var` containing the string It is the east and Juliet is the sun.

- Calls CREATETEMPORARY() to create a temporary CLOB named `clob_var`.

- Calls WRITE() to write the contents of a VARCHAR2 variable named `char_buffer_var` to `clob_var`.

- Calls READ() to read the contents of `clob_var` into `char_buffer_var`.

- Calls INSTR() to search `clob_var` for the second occurrence of is, which returns 29.

- Calls INSTR() to search `clob_var` for the first occurrence of Moon, which returns 0 because Moon doesn't appear in `clob_var`.

- Calls FREETEMPORARY() to free `clob_var`.

```
CREATE OR REPLACE PROCEDURE instr_example IS
  clob_var CLOB;
  char_buffer_var VARCHAR2(50) :=
    'It is the east and Juliet is the sun';
  pattern_var VARCHAR2(5);
  offset_var INTEGER := 1;
  amount_var INTEGER := 38;
  occurrence_var INTEGER;
  return_var INTEGER;
BEGIN
  DBMS_LOB.CREATETEMPORARY(clob_var, TRUE);
  DBMS_LOB.WRITE(clob_var, amount_var, offset_var, char_buffer_var);

  DBMS_LOB.READ(
    clob_var, amount_var, offset_var, char_buffer_var
  );
  DBMS_OUTPUT.PUT_LINE('char_buffer_var = ' || char_buffer_var);

  DBMS_OUTPUT.PUT_LINE('Searching second ''is''');
  pattern_var := 'is';
  occurrence_var := 2;
  return_var := DBMS_LOB.INSTR(
    clob_var, pattern_var, offset_var, occurrence_var
  );
  DBMS_OUTPUT.PUT_LINE('return_var = ' || return_var);

  DBMS_OUTPUT.PUT_LINE('Searching for ''Moon''');
  pattern_var := 'Moon';
  occurrence_var := 1;
  return_var := DBMS_LOB.INSTR(
    clob_var, pattern_var, offset_var, occurrence_var
  );
```

```
      DBMS_OUTPUT.PUT_LINE('return_var = ' || return_var);

      DBMS_LOB.FREETEMPORARY(clob_var);
   END instr_example;
   /
```

The following example calls `instr_example()`:

```
CALL instr_example();
char_buffer_var = It is the east and Juliet is the sun
Searching second 'is'
return_var = 29
Searching for 'Moon'
return_var = 0
```

ISOPEN()

You use `ISOPEN()` to check if the LOB was already opened using the input locator.

```
DBMS_LOB.ISOPEN(
   lob IN BLOB
) RETURN INTEGER;

DBMS_LOB.ISOPEN(
   lob IN CLOB CHARACTER SET ANY_CS
) RETURN INTEGER;

DBMS_LOB.ISOPEN(
   bfile IN BFILE
) RETURN INTEGER;
```

where

- `lob` is the BLOB or CLOB to check.
- `bfile` is the BFILE to check.

`ISOPEN()` returns

- 0 if the LOB isn't open.
- 1 if the LOB is open.

Table 14-19 shows the exception thrown by `ISOPEN()`.

Exception	Thrown When
VALUE_ERROR	The `lob` or `bfile` parameter is null or invalid.

TABLE 14-19. *Exception Thrown by* `ISOPEN()`

ISTEMPORARY()

You use `ISTEMPORARY()` to check if the locator is pointing to a temporary LOB.

```
DBMS_LOB.ISTEMPORARY(
   lob IN BLOB
) RETURN INTEGER;

DBMS_LOB.ISTEMPORARY (
   lob IN CLOB CHARACTER SET ANY_CS
) RETURN INTEGER;
```

where

■   *lob* is the BLOB or CLOB to check.

`ISTEMPORARY()` returns

■   0 if the LOB isn't temporary.

■   1 if the LOB is temporary.

Table 14-20 shows the exception thrown by `ISTEMPORARY()`.
You saw an example of `ISTEMPORARY()` earlier in the section on `CREATETEMPORARY()`.

LOADFROMFILE()

You use `LOADFROMFILE()` to load BFILE data into an internal LOB.

```
DBMS_LOB.LOADFROMFILE(
   dest_lob    IN OUT NOCOPY BLOB,
   src_bfile   IN           BFILE,
   amount      IN           INTEGER,
   dest_offset IN           INTEGER  := 1,
   src_offset  IN           INTEGER  := 1
);

DBMS_LOB.LOADFROMFILE(
   dest_lob    IN OUT NOCOPY CLOB CHARACTER SET ANY_CS,
   src_bfile   IN           BFILE,
   amount      IN           INTEGER,
   dest_offset IN           INTEGER := 1,
   src_offset  IN           INTEGER := 1
);
```

where

■   *dest_lob* is the target LOB into which the data is to be loaded.

Exception	Thrown When
VALUE_ERROR	The `lob` parameter is null or invalid.

TABLE 14-20.   *Exception Thrown by* `ISTEMPORARY()`

- `src_bfile` is the source BFILE from which the data is to be read.
- `amount` is the number of bytes to load from `src_bfile`.
- `dest_offset` is the offset in bytes or characters in `dest_lob` to start the load (offset starts at 1).
- `src_offset` is the offset in bytes in `src_bfile` to start reading (offset starts at 1).

Table 14-21 shows the exceptions thrown by `LOADFROMFILE()`.
The following `file_example()` procedure performs the following tasks:

- Creates a temporary lob named `dest_clob_var`.
- Calls `FILEEXISTS()` to check if the file exits.
- If the file exists, calls `FILEISOPEN()` to check if the file is open.
- If the file is not open, calls `FILEOPEN()` to open the BFILE, storing the locator in `src_bfile_var`.
- Calls `FILEGETNAME()` to get the name of the file and the directory alias.
- Calls `GETCHUNKSIZE()` to get the chunk size from `dest_clob_var`.

Exception	Thrown When
VALUE_ERROR	Any of the input parameters are null or invalid.
INVALID_ARGVAL	Either: ■ `src_offset` < 1 ■ `dest_offset` < 1 ■ `src_offset` > LOBMAXSIZE ■ `dest_offset` > LOBMAXSIZE ■ `amount` < 1 ■ `amount` > LOBMAXSIZE

TABLE 14-21.   *Exceptions Thrown by* `LOADFROMFILE()`

- Calls GETLENGTH() to get the length from src_bfile_var and stores it in length_var.
- While the number of characters read (stored in chars_read_var) is less than length_var:
  - If length_var minus chars_read is less than amount_var (amount_var is initially set to 20), sets amount_var to length_var minus chars_read_var. This is done because LOADFROMFILE() expects amount_var to be less than or equal to the content read from src_bfile_var.
  - Loads amount_var characters from clob_var using LOADFROMFILE().
  - Calls READ() to read the contents of dest_clob_var into char_buffer_var.
  - Calls PUT_LINE() to display the contents of char_buffer_var.
  - Adds amount_var to chars_read_var.
- Calls FILECLOSE() to close src_bfile_var.
- Calls FREETEMPORARY() to free dest_clob_var.

```
CREATE OR REPLACE PROCEDURE file_example IS
  src_bfile_var BFILE;
  dir_alias_var VARCHAR2(50);
  filename_var VARCHAR2(50);
  chunk_size_var INTEGER;
  length_var INTEGER;
  chars_read_var INTEGER;
  dest_clob_var CLOB;
  amount_var INTEGER := 20;
  dest_offset_var INTEGER := 1;
  src_offset_var INTEGER := 1;
  char_buffer_var VARCHAR2(20);
BEGIN
  SELECT bfile_column
  INTO src_bfile_var
  FROM bfile_content
  WHERE id = 1;

  DBMS_LOB.CREATETEMPORARY(dest_clob_var, TRUE);

  IF (DBMS_LOB.FILEEXISTS(src_bfile_var) = 1) THEN
    IF (DBMS_LOB.FILEISOPEN(src_bfile_var) = 0) THEN
      DBMS_LOB.FILEOPEN(src_bfile_var);
      DBMS_LOB.FILEGETNAME(
        src_bfile_var, dir_alias_var, filename_var
      );
      DBMS_OUTPUT.PUT_LINE(
        'Directory alias = ' || dir_alias_var
      );
```

```
            DBMS_OUTPUT.PUT_LINE('Filename = ' || filename_var);

            chunk_size_var := DBMS_LOB.GETCHUNKSIZE(dest_clob_var);
            DBMS_OUTPUT.PUT_LINE('Chunk size = ' || chunk_size_var);

            length_var := DBMS_LOB.GETLENGTH(src_bfile_var);
            DBMS_OUTPUT.PUT_LINE('Length = ' || length_var);

            chars_read_var := 0;
            WHILE (chars_read_var < length_var) LOOP
              IF (length_var - chars_read_var < amount_var) THEN
                amount_var := length_var - chars_read_var;
              END IF;
              DBMS_LOB.LOADFROMFILE(
                dest_clob_var, src_bfile_var,
                amount_var, dest_offset_var,
                src_offset_var + chars_read_var
              );
              DBMS_LOB.READ(
                dest_clob_var, amount_var, src_offset_var, char_buffer_var
              );
              DBMS_OUTPUT.PUT_LINE(
                'char_buffer_var = ' || char_buffer_var
              );
              chars_read_var := chars_read_var + amount_var;
            END LOOP;
          END IF;
        END IF;
        DBMS_LOB.FILECLOSE(src_bfile_var);
        DBMS_LOB.FREETEMPORARY(dest_clob_var);
      END file_example;
      /
```

The following example calls `file_example()`:

```
CALL file_example();
Directory alias = SAMPLE_FILES_DIR
Filename = textContent.txt
Chunk size = 4036
Length = 416
char_buffer_var = To-morrow, and to-mo
char_buffer_var = rrow, and to-morrow,
char_buffer_var =
Creeps in this pet
char_buffer_var = ty pace from day to
char_buffer_var = day,
To the last sy
char_buffer_var = llable of recorded t
```

```
char_buffer_var = ime;
And all our ye
char_buffer_var = sterdays have lighte
char_buffer_var = d fools
The way to
char_buffer_var = a dusty death. Out,
char_buffer_var = out, brief candle!
char_buffer_var = Life's but a walking
char_buffer_var =  shadow; a poor play
char_buffer_var = er,
That struts and
char_buffer_var =  frets his hour upon
char_buffer_var =  the stage,
And the
char_buffer_var = n is heard no more:
char_buffer_var = it is a tale
Told b
char_buffer_var = y an idiot, full of
char_buffer_var = sound and fury,
Sig
char_buffer_var = nifying nothing.
```

LOADBLOBFROMFILE()

You use LOADBLOBFROMFILE() to load BFILE data into an internal BLOB.

```
DBMS_LOB.LOADBLOBFROMFILE(
    dest_blob   IN OUT NOCOPY BLOB,
    src_bfile   IN            BFILE,
    amount      IN            INTEGER,
    dest_offset IN OUT        INTEGER := 1,
    src_offset  IN OUT        INTEGER := 1
);
```

where

- *dest_blob* is the target BLOB into which the data is to be loaded.

- *src_bfile* is the source BFILE from which the data is to be read.

- *amount* is the number of bytes to load from *src_bfile*.

- *dest_offset* is the offset in bytes or characters in *dest_lob* to start the load (offset starts at 1).

- *src_offset* is the offset in bytes in *src_bfile* to start reading (offset starts at 1).

Table 14-22 shows the exceptions thrown by LOADBLOBFROMFILE().

LOADCLOBFROMFILE()

You use LOADCLOBFROMFILE() to load BFILE data into an internal CLOB.

Exception	Thrown When
VALUE_ERROR	Any of the input parameters are null or invalid.
INVALID_ARGVAL	Either: ■ *src_offset* < 1 ■ *dest_offset* < 1 ■ *src_offset* > LOBMAXSIZE ■ *dest_offset* > LOBMAXSIZE ■ *amount* < 1 ■ *amount* > LOBMAXSIZE

TABLE 14-22.   *Exceptions Thrown by LOADBLOBFROMFILE()*

```
DBMS_LOB.LOADCLOBFROMFILE(
   dest_clob    IN OUT NOCOPY CLOB,
   src_bfile    IN            BFILE,
   amount       IN            INTEGER,
   dest_offset  IN OUT        INTEGER,
   src_offset   IN OUT        INTEGER,
   src_csid     IN            NUMBER,
   lang_context IN OUT        INTEGER,
   warning      OUT           INTEGER
);
```

where

- *dest_blob* is the target BLOB into which the data is to be loaded.

- *src_bfile* is the source BFILE from which the data is to be read.

- *amount* is the number of bytes to load from *src_bfile*.

- *dest_offset* is the offset in bytes or characters in *dest_lob* to start the load (offset starts at 1).

- *src_offset* is the offset in bytes in *src_bfile* to start reading (offset starts at 1).

- *src_csid* is the character set of *src_bfile*.

- *lang_context* is the language context of the load (the default is 0, which means the default language context is used).

- *warning* is a warning message that contains information if there was a problem with the load. An example problem is a character in *src_bfile* cannot be converted to a character in *dest_lob*.

Table 14-23 shows the exceptions thrown by LOADCLOBFROMFILE().

Exception	Thrown When
VALUE_ERROR	Any of the input parameters are null or invalid.
INVALID_ARGVAL	Either: ■ *src_offset* < 1 ■ *dest_offset* < 1 ■ *src_offset* > LOBMAXSIZE ■ *dest_offset* > LOBMAXSIZE ■ *amount* < 1 ■ *amount* > LOBMAXSIZE

TABLE 14-23.   *Exceptions Thrown by LOADCLOBFROMFILE()*

OPEN()

You use OPEN() to open a LOB (internal, external, or temporary) in the indicated mode.

```
DBMS_LOB.OPEN(
   lob        IN OUT NOCOPY BLOB,
   open_mode IN             BINARY_INTEGER
);

DBMS_LOB.OPEN(
   lob        IN OUT NOCOPY CLOB CHARACTER SET ANY_CS,
   open_mode IN             BINARY_INTEGER
);

DBMS_LOB.OPEN(
   bfile      IN OUT NOCOPY BFILE,
   open_mode IN             BINARY_INTEGER := DBMS_LOB.FILE_READONLY
);
```

where

■   *lob* is the BLOB or CLOB to open.

■   *bfile* is the BFILE to open.

■   *open_mode* indicates the open mode. The default is DBMS_LOB.FILE_READONLY which indicates the LOB may only be read from. DBMS_LOB.FILE_READWRITE indicates the LOB may read from and written to.

Table 14-24 shows the exception thrown by OPEN().

Exception	Thrown When
VALUE_ERROR	Any of the input parameters are null or invalid.

TABLE 14-24. *Exception Thrown by OPEN ()*

SUBSTR()

You use SUBSTR() to read part of the LOB value starting at the specified offset.

```
DBMS_LOB.SUBSTR(
  lob    IN BLOB,
  amount IN INTEGER := 32767,
  offset IN INTEGER := 1
) RETURN RAW;

DBMS_LOB.SUBSTR (
  lob    IN CLOB CHARACTER SET ANY_CS,
  amount IN INTEGER := 32767,
  offset IN INTEGER := 1
) RETURN VARCHAR2 CHARACTER SET lob%CHARSET;

DBMS_LOB.SUBSTR (
  bfile  IN BFILE,
  amount IN INTEGER := 32767,
  offset IN INTEGER := 1
) RETURN RAW;
```

where

- *lob* is the CLOB or BLOB to read from.

- *bfile* is the BFILE to read from.

- *amount* is the number of characters to read from the CLOB or the number of bytes to read from the BLOB or BFILE.

- *offset* is the offset in characters to read from the CLOB or the number of bytes to read from the BLOB or BFILE (offset starts at 1).

SUBSTR() returns

- RAW data when reading from a BLOB or BFILE.

- VARCHAR2 data when reading from a CLOB.

- Null if:

  - Any of the IN parameters are null

- *amount* < 1
- *amount* > 32767
- *offset* < 1
- *offset* > LOBMAXSIZE

Table 14-25 shows the exceptions thrown by SUBSTR().

TRIM()

You use TRIM() to cut off the LOB value to the specified shorter length.

```
DBMS_LOB.TRIM(
    lob     IN OUT NOCOPY BLOB,
    newlen IN             INTEGER
);

DBMS_LOB.TRIM(
    lob     IN OUT NOCOPY CLOB CHARACTER SET ANY_CS,
    newlen IN             INTEGER
);
```

where

- *lob* is the BLOB or CLOB to open.
- *newlen* is the new length of the BLOB in bytes or characters of the CLOB.

Table 14-26 shows the exceptions thrown by TRIM().

Exception	Thrown When
VALUE_ERROR	Any of the input parameters are null or invalid.
UNOPENED_FILE	The BFILE isn't open.
NOEXIST_DIRECTORY	The directory doesn't exist.
NOPRIV_DIRECTORY	You don't have privileges on the directory.
INVALID_DIRECTORY	The directory is invalid.
INVALID_OPERATION	The file exists, but you don't have privileges to access the file.

TABLE 14-25. *Exceptions Thrown by SUBSTR ()*

Exception	Thrown When
VALUE_ERROR	The lob parameter is null.
INVALID_ARGVAL	Either: ■ *newlen* < 0 ■ *newlen* > LOBMAXSIZE

TABLE 14-26. *Exceptions Thrown by* TRIM()

WRITEAPPEND()

You use WRITEAPPEND() to write data from the buffer to the end of a LOB.

```
DBMS_LOB.WRITEAPPEND(
   lob      IN OUT NOCOPY BLOB,
   amount IN              BINARY_INTEGER,
   buffer IN              RAW
);

DBMS_LOB.WRITEAPPEND(
   lob      IN OUT NOCOPY CLOB CHARACTER SET ANY_CS,
   amount IN              BINARY_INTEGER,
   buffer IN              VARCHAR2 CHARACTER SET lob%CHARSET
);
```

where

■ *lob* is the CLOB or BLOB to write to.

■ *amount* is the number of characters to write to the CLOB or the number of bytes to write to the BLOB.

■ *buffer* is the storage variable where the input to the write is to be read from.

Table 14-27 shows the exceptions thrown by WRITEAPPEND().

Exception	Thrown When
VALUE_ERROR	Any of the input parameters are null or invalid.
INVALID_ARGVAL	Either: ■ *amount* < 1 ■ *amount* > MAXBUFSIZE

TABLE 14-27. *Exceptions Thrown by* WRITEAPPEND()

Understanding the LONG and LONG RAW Types

I mentioned at the start of this chapter that LOBs are now the preferred storage type for large blocks of data, but you may encounter older databases that still use the following types:

- **LONG**   Used to store up to 2 gigabytes of character data
- **LONG RAW**   Used to store up to 2 gigabytes of binary data
- **RAW**   Used to store up to 4 kilobytes of binary data

In this section, you'll learn how to use LONG and LONG RAW types in SQL and PL/SQL. RAW may be used in the same manner as a LONG RAW, so I've omitted coverage of RAW.

The Example Tables

In this section, I'll use two new tables in the examples (created by the lob_schema.sql script):

- **long_content**   Contains a LONG column named long_column
- **long_raw_content**   Contains a LONG RAW column named long_raw_column

In addition, both of these tables also contain a column to store the name of the file from which the content was originally read. These two tables are defined as follows:

```
CREATE TABLE long_content (
    id          INTEGER PRIMARY KEY,
    long_column LONG NOT NULL
);

CREATE TABLE long_raw_content (
    id              INTEGER PRIMARY KEY,
    long_raw_column LONG RAW NOT NULL
);
```

Using LONG and LONG RAW Columns

In this section, you'll learn how to use LONG and LONG RAW columns from within SQL. The following INSERT statements add rows to the long_content table:

```
INSERT INTO long_content (
    id,
    long_column
) VALUES (
    1,
    'Creeps in this petty pace'
);

INSERT INTO long_content (
    id,
```

```
  long_column
) VALUES (
  2,
  ' from day to day'
);
```

The next INSERT adds a row to the long_raw_content table:

```
INSERT INTO long_raw_content (
  id,
  long_raw_column
) VALUES (
  1,
  '1001110101010111111'
);
```

The following query retrieves the row from long_content:

```
SELECT *
FROM long_content;
ID
----------
LONG_COLUMN
-----------------------
         1
Creeps in this petty pace

         2
 from day to day
```

Oracle Database 10*g* Enhancements to Large Objects

In this section, you'll learn about the following enhancements made to large objects in Oracle Database 10*g*:

- Implicit conversion between CLOB and NCLOB objects
- Use of the :new attribute when using LOBs in a trigger

NOTE
The various DDL statements that create the items shown in this section are contained in the lob_schema_10g.sql script. The script connects as lob_user with a password of lob_password, so if you're using a different password (or you're using a service name), you'll need to edit the script first. Also, you must have already run lob_schema.sql before you attempt to run lob_schema_10g.sql.

Implicit Conversion Between CLOB and NCLOB Objects

With the advent of global business, you might have to convert between Unicode and a national language character set. In versions of the database beneath Oracle Database 10*g*, you can explicitly convert between Unicode and a national character set using the TO_CLOB() and TO_NCLOB() functions (conversion functions were covered in Chapter 3).

Oracle Database 10*g* allows implicit conversion between CLOB and NCLOB objects, which saves you from using TO_CLOB() and TO_NCLOB(). You can use this implicit conversion for IN and OUT variables in queries and DML statements, as well as for PL/SQL method parameters and variable assignments.

Let's take a look at an example. The following statement creates a table named nclob_content that contains an NCLOB column named nclob_column:

```
CREATE TABLE nclob_content (
  id INTEGER PRIMARY KEY,
  nclob_column NCLOB
);
```

The following nclob_example() procedure performs the following tasks:

- Creates a CLOB named clob_var. and sets its content to the string It is the east and Juliet is the sun.

- Creates an NCLOB named nclob_var.

- Inserts clob_var into nclob_column, thus demonstrating that an implicit conversion between a CLOB and an NCLOB is performed.

- Selects nclob_column into clob_var, thus demonstrating that an implicit conversion between an NCLOB and a CLOB is performed.

```
CREATE OR REPLACE PROCEDURE nclob_example
AS
  clob_var CLOB := 'It is the east and Juliet is the sun';
  nclob_var NCLOB;
BEGIN
  -- insert clob_var into nclob_column
  INSERT INTO nclob_content (
    id, nclob_column
  ) VALUES (
    1, clob_var
  );

  -- select nclob_column into clob_var
  SELECT nclob_column
  INTO clob_var
```

```
        FROM nclob_content
        WHERE id = 1;

        -- display the CLOB
        DBMS_OUTPUT.PUT_LINE('clob_var = ' || clob_var);
    END nclob_example;
    /
```

The following example connects as `lob_user`, turns server output on, and calls `nclob_example()`:

```
CONNECT lob_user/lob_password
SET SERVEROUTPUT ON
CALL nclob_example();
clob_var = It is the east and Juliet is the sun
```

Use of the :new Attribute When Using LOBs in a Trigger

You can use the `:new` attribute when using LOBs in a `BEFORE UPDATE` or `BEFORE INSERT` row level trigger. The following example creates a trigger named `before_clob_content_update` that displays the length of `clob_column` when the `clob_content` table is updated. Notice that `:new` is used when accessing `clob_column`:

```
CREATE OR REPLACE TRIGGER before_clob_content_update
BEFORE UPDATE
ON clob_content
FOR EACH ROW
BEGIN
  DBMS_OUTPUT.PUT_LINE('clob_content changed');
  DBMS_OUTPUT.PUT_LINE(
    'Length = ' || DBMS_LOB.GETLENGTH(:new.clob_column)
  );
END before_clob_content_update;
/
```

The following example connects as `lob_user` and updates the `clob_content` table (which causes the trigger to be fired):

```
CONNECT lob_user/lob_password
SET SERVEROUTPUT ON
UPDATE clob_content
SET clob_column = 'Creeps in this petty pace'
WHERE id = 1;
clob_content changed
Length = 25
```

Summary

In this chapter, you learned that

- LOBs may be used to store binary data, character data, and references to external files. LOBs can store up to 128 terabytes of data.

- There are four LOB types: CLOB, NCLOB, BLOB, and BFILE.

- A CLOB is used to store character data.

- An NCLOB is used to store multiple byte character data.

- A BLOB is used to store binary data.

- A BFILE is used to store pointers to files located in the file system.

- A LOB consists of two parts: a locator that specifies the location of the LOB content, and the content.

- A table may contain LOB columns and you can add content to those columns.

- The DBMS_LOB PL/SQL package contains methods to manipulate LOBs.

In the next chapter you'll learn how to run SQL statements from a Java program.

CHAPTER
15

Running SQL
Using Java

In this chapter, you will

- Learn the basics of running SQL using Java through the Java Database Connectivity (JDBC) Application Programming Interface (API); JDBC enables a Java program to access a database

- Examine the various Oracle JDBC drivers that may be used to connect to an Oracle database

- Perform SQL DML statements to retrieve, add, modify, and delete rows from database tables using Java

- Learn how to use the various Java types to get and set column values in the database, including how to handle numbers and database NULL values using Java

- Examine how to perform transaction control statements and SQL DDL statements

- Handle database exceptions that may occur when your Java programs are run

- Gain access to all of the data types supported by an Oracle database using Oracle's extensions to JDBC

NOTE
This chapter gives an introduction to JDBC. For full details of using JDBC with an Oracle database, you should read my book Oracle9i JDBC Programming *(McGraw-Hill/Osborne, 2002).*

Getting Started

Prior to running the examples in this chapter, you'll need to install a version of the Sun Microsystems Java Software Development Kit (SDK). You can download the SDK and view full installation instructions from Sun's Java web site at java.sun.com. This site also contains all the reference materials for Java and JDBC.

The directory where you installed the Oracle client software on your machine is called the ORACLE_HOME directory. This directory contains various subdirectories, one of which is the BIN directory, which contains the Oracle executable programs; another is the jdbc directory, which contains the following:

- A text file named Readme.txt. You should open and read this file; it contains important information such as the latest installation requirements, which may have changed since this book was written.

- A directory named doc, which has a Zip file that contains the Oracle JDBC API reference documentation.

- A directory named demo, which has a Zip file that contains sample Java programs from Oracle.

- A directory named lib, which contains a number of Zip and Java Archive (JAR) files.

Configuring Your Computer

Once you've downloaded and installed the required software, your next step is to configure your computer to develop and run Java programs containing JDBC statements. You must set four environment variables on your machine:

- ORACLE_HOME

- JAVA_HOME (and J2EE_HOME if you're using Java 2 Enterprise Edition)

- PATH

- CLASSPATH (and J2EE_CLASSPATH if you're using Java 2 Enterprise Edition)

If you're using Unix or Linux, you'll also need to set the additional LD_LIBRARY_PATH environment variable. You'll learn how to set these environment variables in the following sections.

Setting the ORACLE_HOME Environment Variable

The ORACLE_HOME directory is where you installed the Oracle software, and you'll need to set an environment variable named ORACLE_HOME on your machine that specifies this directory.

Setting an Environment Variable with Windows

To set an environment variable in Windows, you use the Environment Variables dialog box. To do this on Windows 2000, you perform the following steps:

1. Open the Control Panel.

2. Double-click System. This displays the System Properties dialog box.

3. Select the Advanced tab.

4. Click Environment Variables. This displays the Environment Variables dialog box.

Check if there's currently an ORACLE_HOME system variable defined, and if so, check that it's set to the directory where you installed the Oracle software. If there's no ORACLE_HOME defined, go ahead and create one by clicking New in the System Variables area. On my computer, ORACLE_HOME is set to E:\oracle\Ora10.

Setting an Environment Variable with Unix or Linux

To set an environment variable in Unix or Linux, you'll need to add additional lines to a special file, and the file you need to modify depends on which shell you're using. If you're using the Bourne or Korn shell, you add the following lines to your .profile file using the following syntax:

```
ORACLE_HOME=install_directory
export ORACLE_HOME
```

You replace *install_directory* with the directory where you installed the Oracle software. If you're using the Bash shell with Linux, you use the same syntax but add the lines to your .bash_ profile file. For example:

```
ORACLE_HOME=/usr/local/oracle
export ORACLE_HOME
```

If you're using the C shell, you add the environment variable to your .login file using the following syntax:

```
setenv ORACLE_HOME install_directory
```

For example:

```
setenv ORACLE_HOME /usr/local/oracle
```

Setting the JAVA_HOME Environment Variable

The JAVA_HOME environment variable specifies the directory where you installed your Java SDK. For example, if you installed the SDK in the E:\sdk directory, you need to set your JAVA_HOME variable to that directory using the steps I showed you in the previous section.

NOTE
If you're using Java 2 Enterprise Edition, you need to also set J2EE_HOME to the directory where you installed J2EE. Refer to Sun's documentation for further installation details.

Setting the PATH Environment Variable

The PATH environment variable contains a list of directories. When you enter a command using your operating system command line, the command searches the directories in your PATH for the executable specified. You'll probably already have a PATH set to some directories on your computer, and you need to add the following two directories to your existing PATH:

- The bin subdirectory of the directory where you installed the Java SDK
- The BIN subdirectory of the directory where you installed the Oracle software

For example, if you installed the SDK in the E:\sdk directory, and you installed the Oracle software in E:\oracle\Ora10, you would add E:\sdk\bin;E:\oracle\Ora10\BIN to your PATH. Notice the semicolon (;) that separates the two directories. To set the PATH in Windows 2000, use the same steps I showed you earlier.

To add to an existing PATH in Unix or Linux, you need to modify the appropriate file for your shell. For example, if you're using the Bash shell with Linux, add lines to your .bash_profile file that are similar to the following:

```
PATH=$PATH:$JAVA_HOME/bin:$ORACLE_HOME/BIN
export PATH
```

Notice the colon (:) that separates the directories.

Setting the CLASSPATH Environment Variable

The CLASSPATH environment variable contains a list of locations where Java class packages are found. A location can be a directory name or the name of a Zip file or JAR file containing classes. The ORACLE_HOME\jdbc\lib directory contains a number of Zip files; which ones you add to your CLASSPATH depends on what Java SDK you're using and what features you need.

NOTE
You must consult the Readme.txt file located in the ORACLE_HOME\ jdbc directory for exact details on which Zip files to add to your CLASSPATH.

At time of writing, the following was correct for setting a CLASSPATH:

- If you're using JDK 1.2.*x* (or higher), add classes12.zip to your CLASSPATH. If you need National Language support, also add nls_charset12.zip to your CLASSPATH.

- If you're using JDK 1.1.*x*, add classes111.zip to your CLASSPATH. If you need National Language support, also add nls_charset11.zip to your CLASSPATH.

NOTE
You also need to add the current directory to your CLASSPATH. You do this by adding a period (.) to your CLASSPATH. That way, the classes in your current directory will be found by Java when you run your programs.

A typical CLASSPATH for Windows 2000 might be:

```
.;E:\oracle\Ora10\jdbc\lib\classes12.zip;E:\oracle\
Ora10\jdbc\lib\nls_charset12.zip
```

If you're using Windows 2000, use the steps described earlier to set your CLASSPATH. If you're using Linux, you should add lines to your .bash_profile file similar to the following:

```
CLASSPATH=$CLASSPATH:.:$ORACLE_HOME/jdbc/lib/classes12.zip:
$ORACLE_HOME/jdbc/lib/nls_charset12.zip
export CLASSPATH
```

NOTE
If you're using Java 2 Enterprise Edition, you'll also need to set J2EE_CLASSPATH. Refer to Sun's documentation for further installation details.

Setting the LD_LIBRARY_PATH Environment Variable

If you're using Unix or Linux, you'll also need to set the `LD_LIBRARAY_PATH` environment variable to $ORACLE_HOME/lib. This directory contains shared libraries that are used by the JDBC OCI driver.

That concludes configuring your computer; you'll learn about the Oracle JDBC drivers next.

The Oracle JDBC Drivers

In this section, you'll learn about the various Oracle JDBC drivers that enable the JDBC statements in a Java program to access an Oracle database. It is through a JDBC driver that your JDBC statements access a database. There are four Oracle JDBC drivers:

- Thin driver
- OCI driver
- Server-side internal driver
- Server-side Thin driver

The following sections describe each of these drivers in detail.

The Thin Driver

The Thin driver has the smallest footprint of all the drivers, meaning that it requires the least amount of system resources to run, and it is written entirely in Java. If you are writing a Java applet, you should use the Thin driver. The Thin driver may also be used in stand-alone Java applications and may be used to access all versions of the Oracle database. The Thin driver only works with TCP/IP and requires that Oracle Net be up and running. For details on Oracle Net, speak with your DBA or consult the Oracle Net documentation.

NOTE
You don't have to install anything on the client computer to use the Thin driver and therefore you can use it for applets.

The OCI Driver

The OCI driver requires more resources than the Thin driver, but generally has better performance. The OCI driver is suitable for programs deployed on the middle tier—a web server, for example.

NOTE
The OCI driver requires that you install it on the client computer and is therefore not suitable for applets.

The OCI driver has a number of performance enhancing features, including the ability to pool database connections and prefetch rows from the database. The OCI driver works with all versions of the database and all of the supported Oracle Net protocols.

The Server-Side Internal Driver

The server-side internal driver provides direct access to the database, and is used by the Oracle JVM to communicate with that database The Oracle JVM is a Java Virtual Machine that is integrated with the database—you can load a Java class into the database, then publish and run methods contained in that class using the Oracle JVM.

The Server-Side Thin Driver

The server-side Thin driver is also used by the Oracle JVM, and provides access to remote databases. Like the Thin driver, this driver is also written entirely in Java.

Importing the JDBC Packages

In order for your programs to use JDBC, you must import the required JDBC packages into your Java programs. There are two sets of JDBC packages: the standard JDBC packages from Sun Microsystems and Oracle's extension packages. The standard JDBC packages enable your Java programs to access the basic features of most databases, including the Oracle database, SQL Server, DB2, and MySQL. The Oracle extensions to JDBC enable your programs to access all of the Oracle-specific features, as well as the Oracle-specific performance extensions. You'll learn about some of the Oracle-specific features later in this chapter.

To use JDBC in your programs you should import the `java.sql.*` packages, as shown in the following `import` statement:

```
import java.sql.*;
```

Of course, importing `java.sql.*` imports *all* of the standard JDBC packages. As you become proficient in JDBC, you'll find that you don't always need to import all the classes: you can just import those packages that your program actually uses.

Registering the Oracle JDBC Drivers

Before you can open a database connection, you must first register the Oracle JDBC drivers with your Java program. As mentioned earlier, the JDBC drivers enable your JDBC statements to access the database.

There are two ways to register the Oracle JDBC drivers: the first is to use the `forName()` method of the class `java.lang.Class`, and the second is to use the `registerDriver()` method of the JDBC `DriverManager` class. The following example illustrates the use of the `forName()` method:

```
Class.forName("oracle.jdbc.OracleDriver");
```

The second way to register the Oracle JDBC drivers is to use the `registerDriver()` method of the `java.sql.DriverManager` class, as shown in the following example:

```
DriverManager.registerDriver(new oracle.jdbc.OracleDriver());
```

Once you have registered the Oracle JDBC drivers, you can open a connection to a database.

Opening a Database Connection

Before you can issue SQL statements in your Java programs, you must open a database connection. There are two main ways to open a database connection. The first way is to use the `getConnection()` method of the `DriverManager` class. The second way uses an Oracle data source object, which must first be created and then connected to. This method uses a standardized way of setting database connection details, and an Oracle data source object may be used with the *Java Naming and Directory Interface* (JNDI).

I'll describe both of these ways to open a database connection in the following sections, starting with the first way—which uses the `getConnection()` method of the `DriverManager` class.

Connecting to the Database Using the getConnection() Method of the DriverManager Class

The `getConnection()` method accepts three parameters: a database username, a password, and a database URL. The `getConnection()` method returns a JDBC `Connection` object, which should be stored in your program so it may be referenced later. The syntax of a call to the `getConnection()` method is as follows:

```
DriverManager.getConnection(URL, username, password);
```

where

- *URL* is the database that your program connects to, along with the JDBC driver you want to use. See the following section, "The Database URL," for details on the URL.

- *username* is the name of the database user that your program connects as.

- *password* is the password for the username.

The following example shows the `getConnection()` method being used to connect to a database:

```
Connection myConnection = DriverManager.getConnection(
    "jdbc:oracle:thin:@localhost:1521:ORCL",
    "store",
    "store_password"
);
```

In this example, the connection is made to a database running on the machine identified as `localhost` with an Oracle System Identifier (SID) of `ORCL`, using the Oracle JDBC Thin driver. The connection is made with the username `store` and the password `store_password`. The `Connection` object returned by the call to `getConnection()` is stored in `myConnection`. I'll use the Oracle JDBC Thin driver for the program examples in this chapter. The connection to a database is made through Oracle Net, which should be up and running.

The Database URL

The database URL specifies where the database your program connects to is located. The structure of the database URL is dependent on the vendor who provides the JDBC drivers. In the case of Oracle's JDBC drivers, the database URL structure is as follows:

```
driver_name:@driver_information
```

where

- *driver_name* is the name of the Oracle JDBC driver that your program uses. This may be set to one of the following:

  - **jdbc:oracle:thin**   The Oracle JDBC Thin driver

  - **jdbc:oracle:oci**   The Oracle JDBC OCI driver

- *driver_information*   The driver-specific information required to connect to the database. This is dependent on the driver being used. In the case of the Oracle JDBC Thin driver, the driver-specific information may be specified in the following format:

  - **host_name:port:database_SID**   For the Oracle JDBC Thin driver

For all the Oracle JDBC drivers, including the Thin driver and the various OCI drivers, the driver-specific information may also be specified using Oracle Net keyword-value pairs, which may be specified in the following format:

```
(description=(address=(host=host_name)(protocol=tcp)(port=port))
(connect_data=(sid=database_SID)))
```

where

- *host_name* is the name of the machine on which the database is running.

- *port* is the port number on which the Oracle Net database listener waits for requests; 1521 is the default port number. Your DBA can provide the port number.

- *database_SID* is the Oracle SID of the database instance to which you want to connect. Your DBA can provide the database SID.

For the Oracle OCI driver, you may also use an Oracle Net TNSNAMES string (for more information on this, speak with your DBA or consult the Oracle documentation that describes Oracle Net).

The following example shows the getConnection() method being used to connect to a database using the Oracle OCI driver, with the driver-specific information specified using Oracle Net keyword-value pairs:

```
Connection myConnection = DriverManager.getConnection(
  "jdbc:oracle:oci:@(description=(address=(host=localhost)" +
   "(protocol=tcp)(port=1521))(connect_data=(sid=ORCL)))",
  "store",
  "store_password"
);
```

As you can see, in this example a connection is made to a database running on the machine identified as localhost, with an Oracle SID of ORCL, using the Oracle OCI driver. The connection to the database is made with the username store, with a password of store_password. The Connection object returned by the call to getConnection() is stored in myConnection.

Connecting to the Database Using an Oracle Data Source

You can also use an Oracle *data source* to connect to a database. An Oracle data source uses a more standardized way of supplying the various parameters to connect to a database than the previous method that used the `DriverManager.getConnection()` method. In addition, an Oracle data source may also be registered with JNDI. Using JNDI with JDBC is very useful because it allows you to register, or *bind*, data sources, and then *look up* those data sources in your program without having to provide the exact database connection details. Thus, if the database connection details change, only the JNDI object must be changed.

NOTE
You can learn about JNDI in my book Oracle9*i* JDBC Programming *(McGraw-Hill/Osborne, 2002).*

There are three steps that must be performed to use an Oracle data source:

1. Create an Oracle data source object of the `oracle.jdbc.poo.OracleDataSource` class.

2. Set the Oracle data source object attributes using the set methods, which are defined in the class.

3. Connect to the database via the Oracle data source object using the `getConnection()` method.

The following sections describe these three steps.

Step 1: Create an Oracle Data Source Object   The first step is to create an Oracle data source object of the `oracle.jdbc.pool.OracleDataSource` class. The following example creates an `OracleDataSource` object named `myDataSource` (you may assume that the `oracle.jdbc.pool.OracleDataSource` class has been imported):

```
OracleDataSource myDataSource = new OracleDataSource();
```

Once you have your `OracleDataSource` object, the second step is to set that object's attributes using the set methods.

Step 2: Set the Oracle Data Source Object Attributes   Before you can use your `OracleDataSource` object to connect to a database, you must set a number of attributes in that object to indicate the connection details using various set methods defined in the class. These details include items like the database name, the JDBC driver to use, and so on; each of these details has a corresponding attribute in an `OracleDataSource` object.

The `oracle.jdbc.pool.OracleDataSource` class actually implements the `javax.sql.DataSource` interface provided with JDBC. The `javax.sql.DataSource` interface defines a number of attributes, which are listed in Table 15-1. This table shows the name, description, and type of each attribute.

The `oracle.jdbc.pool.OracleDataSource` class provides an additional set of attributes, which are listed in Table 15-2.

Attribute Name	Attribute Description	Attribute Type
databaseName	The database name (Oracle SID).	String
dataSourceName	The name of the underlying data source class.	String
description	Description of the data source.	String
networkProtocol	The network protocol to use to communicate with the database. This only applies to the Oracle JDBC OCI drivers, and defaults to tcp. For further details, see the Oracle Net documentation provided by Oracle Corporation.	String
password	The password for the supplied username.	String
portNumber	The port on which the Oracle Net listener waits for database connection requests. The default is 1521. For further details, see the Oracle Net documentation.	int
serverName	The database server machine name (TCP/IP address or DNS alias).	String
user	The database username.	String

TABLE 15-1.   *DataSource Attributes*

You may use a number of methods to read from and write to each of the attributes listed in Tables 15-1 and 15-2. The methods that read from the attributes are known as *get* methods, and the methods that write to the attributes are known as *set* methods.

Attribute Name	Attribute Description	Attribute Type
driverType	The JDBC driver to use. If you are using the server-side internal driver, this is set to kprb, and the other settings for the attributes are ignored.	String
url	May be used to specify an Oracle database URL, which can be used as an alternative to setting the database location. See the section earlier on database URLs for details.	String
tnsEntryName	May be used to specify an Oracle Net TNSNAMES string, which can also be used to specify the database location when using the OCI drivers.	String

TABLE 15-2.   *OracleDataSource Attributes*

The set and get method names are easy to remember: take the attribute name, convert the first letter to uppercase, and add the word "set" or "get" to the beginning. For example, to set the database name (stored in the `databaseName` attribute), you use the `setDatabaseName()` method; to get the name of the database currently set, you use the `getDatabaseName()` method. There is one exception to this: there is no `getPassword()` method that you can call. This is for security reasons—you don't want someone to be able to get your password programmatically!

Most of the attributes are Java `String` objects, so most of the set methods accept a single `String` parameter, and most of the get methods return a `String`. The exception to this is the `portNumber` attribute, which is an `int`. Therefore, its set method `setPortNumber()` accepts an `int`, and its get method `getPortNumber()` returns an `int`.

The following examples illustrate the use of the set methods to write to the attributes of the `OracleDataSource` object `myDataSource` that was created earlier in Step 1:

```
myDataSource.setServerName("localhost");
myDataSource.setDatabaseName("ORCL");
myDataSource.setDriverType("oci");
myDataSource.setNetworkProtocol("tcp");
myDataSource.setPortNumber(1521);
myDataSource.setUser("scott");
myDataSource.setPassword("tiger");
```

The next examples illustrate the use of some of the get methods to read the attributes previously set in `myDataSource`:

```
String serverName = myDataSource.getServerName();
String databaseName = myDataSource.getDatabaseName();
String driverType = myDataSource.getDriverType();
String networkProtocol = myDataSource.getNetworkProtocol();
int portNumber = myDataSource.getPortNumber();
```

Once you've set your `OracleDataSource` object attributes, you can use it to connect to the database.

Step 3: Connect to the Database via the Oracle Data Source Object   The third step is to connect to the database via the `OracleDataSource` object. You do this by calling the `getConnection()` method using your `OracleDataSource` object. The `getConnection()` method returns a JDBC `Connection` object, which must be stored.

The following example shows how to call the `getConnection()` method using the `myDataSource` object populated in the previous step:

```
Connection myConnection = myDataSource.getConnection();
```

The `Connection` object returned by `getConnection()` is stored in `myConnection`. You can also pass a username and password as parameters to the `getConnection()` method, as shown in the following example:

```
Connection myConnection = myDataSource.getConnection(
  "store", "store_password"
);
```

In this case, the username and password will override the username and password previously set in myDataSource. Therefore, the connection to the database will be made using the username of store with a password of store_password, rather than scott and tiger, which were set in myDataSource in the previous section.

Once you have your Connection object, you can use it to create a JDBC Statement object.

Creating a JDBC Statement Object

Before you can issue SQL statements using JDBC, you need to create a JDBC Statement object of the class java.sql.Statement. A Statement object is used to represent a SQL statement, such as a DML statement (SELECT, INSERT, UPDATE, or DELETE) or a DDL statement (such as CREATE TABLE). You'll learn how to issue both DML and DDL statements later in this chapter.

To create a Statement object, you use the createStatement() method of a Connection object. In the following example, a Statement object named myStatement is created using the createStatement() method of the myConnection object that was created in the previous section:

```
Statement myStatement = myConnection.createStatement();
```

Depending on the SQL statement you want to perform, you use a different method in the Statement class to run the SQL statement. If you want to perform a SELECT statement, you use the executeQuery() method. If you want to perform an INSERT, UPDATE, or DELETE statement, you use the executeUpdate() method. If you don't know ahead of time which type of SQL statement is to be performed, you can use the execute() method, which may be used to perform SELECT, INSERT, UPDATE, or DELETE statements. You may also use the execute() method to perform DDL statements, as you'll learn later in this chapter.

There is another JDBC class that may be used to represent a SQL statement: the PreparedStatement class. This offers more advanced functionality than the Statement class; I will defer discussion of the PreparedStatement class until after I have discussed the use of the Statement class.

Once you have a Statement object, you're ready to issue SQL statements using JDBC.

Retrieving Rows from the Database

To perform a SELECT statement using JDBC, you use the executeQuery() method of the Statement object, which accepts a Java String containing the text for the SELECT statement.

Now, because a SELECT statement may return more than one row, the executeQuery() method returns an object that stores the row(s) returned by your SELECT statement. This object is known as a JDBC *result set* and is of the java.sql.ResultSet class. When using a ResultSet object to read rows from the database, there are three steps you follow:

1. Create a ResultSet object and populate it using a SELECT statement.

2. Read the column values from the ResultSet object using get methods.

3. Close the ResultSet object.

I will now walk you through an example that uses a `ResultSet` object to retrieve the rows from the `customers` table. This example will illustrate the use of these three steps.

Step 1: Create and Populate a ResultSet Object

You must first create a `ResultSet` object and populate it using a `SELECT` statement that retrieves the required rows from the database. The `SELECT` statement in the example is run using the `Statement` object named `myStatement` that was created earlier. The following example creates a `ResultSet` object named `customerResultSet` and populates it using a `SELECT` statement that retrieves the `customer_id`, `first_name`, `last_name`, `dob`, and `phone` columns for each row in the `customers` table:

```
ResultSet customerResultSet = myStatement.executeQuery(
    "SELECT customer_id, first_name, last_name, dob, phone " +
    "FROM customers"
);
```

After this statement has been run, the `ResultSet` object will contain the column values for the rows retrieved by the `SELECT` statement. The `ResultSet` object may then be used to access the column values for the retrieved rows. In this example, `customerResultSet` will contain the five rows retrieved from the `customers` table. Of course, a `ResultSet` object may also be used to store one row when only one row is returned by your `SELECT` statement.

Because the `execute()` method accepts a Java `String`, you can build up your SQL statements when your program actually runs. This means that you can do some fairly powerful things in JDBC. For example, you could have the user of your program type in a string containing a `WHERE` clause for a `SELECT` statement when they run your program, or even enter the whole `SELECT` statement. The following example shows a `WHERE` clause being set and added to the query executed by another `ResultSet` object:

```
String whereClause = "WHERE customer_id = 1";
ResultSet customerResultSet2 = myStatement.executeQuery(
    "SELECT customer_id, first_name, last_name, dob, phone " +
    "FROM customers " +
    whereClause
);
```

You're not limited to building up `SELECT` statements dynamically: you can build up other SQL statements in a similar manner.

Step 2: Read the Column Values from the ResultSet Object

To read the column values for the rows stored in a `ResultSet` object, the `ResultSet` class provides a series of get methods. Before I get into the details of these get methods, you need to understand how the data types used to represent values in Oracle may be mapped to compatible Java data types.

Oracle and Java Types

A Java program uses a different set of types from the Oracle types to represent values. Fortunately, the types used by Oracle are compatible with certain Java types. This allows Java and Oracle to interchange data stored in their respective types. Table 15-3 shows one set of compatible type mappings.

Oracle Type	Java Type
CHAR	String
VARCHAR2	String
DATE	java.sql.Date java.sql.Time java.sql.Timestamp
INTEGER	short int long
NUMBER	float double java.math.BigDecimal

TABLE 15-3. *Compatible Type Mappings*

From this table, you can see that an Oracle INTEGER is compatible with a Java int. (I'll talk about the other numeric types later in this chapter in the section "Handling Numbers.") This means that the customer_id column of the customers table (which is defined as an Oracle INTEGER) may be stored in a Java int variable. Similarly, the first_name, last_name, and phone column values may be stored in Java String variables.

The Oracle DATE type stores a year, month, day, hour, minute, and second. You may use a java.sql.Date object to store the date part of the dob column value and a java.sql.Time variable to store the time part. You may also use a java.sql.Timestamp object to store both the date and time parts of the dob column. Later in this chapter, I'll discuss the oracle.sql.DATE type, which is an Oracle extension to the JDBC standard and provides an alternative to storing dates and times.

The customer_id, first_name, last_name, dob, and phone columns are retrieved by the SELECT statement in the previous section, and the following examples declare Java variables and objects that are compatible with those columns:

```
int customerId = 0;
String firstName = null;
String lastName = null;
java.sql.Date dob = null;
String phone = null;
```

The int and String types are part of the core Java language, while java.sql.Date is part of JDBC and is an extension of the core Java language. JDBC provides a number of such types that allow Java and a relational database to exchange data. However, JDBC doesn't cover types that handle all of the types used by Oracle, one example of which is the ROWID type—you must use the oracle.sql.ROWID type to store an Oracle ROWID.

To handle all of the Oracle types, Oracle provides a number of additional types, which are defined in the oracle.sql package. Also, Oracle has a number of types that may be used as an alternative to the core Java and JDBC types, and in some cases these alternatives offer more functionality and better performance than the core Java and JDBC types. I'll talk more about the Oracle types defined in the `oracle.sql` package later in this chapter.

Now that you understand a little bit about compatible Java and Oracle types, let's continue with the discussion on using the get methods to read column values.

Using the Get Methods to Read Column Values

As mentioned earlier, the get methods are used to read values stored in a `ResultSet` object. The name of each get method is simple to understand: take the name of the Java type you want the column value to be retuned as and add the word "get" to the beginning. For example, use `getInt()` to read a column value as a Java `int`, and use `getString()` to read a column value as a Java `String`. To read the value as a `java.sql.Date`, you would use `getDate()`. Each get method accepts one parameter: an `int` representing the position of the column in the original `SELECT` statement, or a `String` containing the name of the column. Let's examine some examples based on the earlier example that retrieved the columns from the `customers` table in the `customerResultSet` object.

To get the value of the `customer_id` column, which was the first column specified in the earlier `SELECT` statement, you use `getInt(1)`. You can also use the name of the column in the get method, so you could also use `getInt("customer_id")` to get the same value.

TIP
*Using the column name rather than the column position number
in a get method makes your code easier to read.*

To get the value of the `first_name` column, which was the second column specified in the earlier `SELECT` statement, you use `getString(2)` or `getString("first_name")`. You use similar method calls to get the `last_name` and `phone` column values because those columns are also text strings. To get the value of the `dob` column, you could use `getDate(4)` or `getDate("dob")`. To actually read the values stored in a `ResultSet` object, you must call the get methods using that `ResultSet` object.

Because a `ResultSet` object may contain more than one row, JDBC provides a method named `next()` that allows you to step through each row stored in a `ResultSet` object. You must call the `next()` method to access the first row in the `ResultSet` object, and each successive call to `next()` steps to the next row. When there are no more rows in the `ResultSet` object to read, the `next()` method returns the Boolean `false` value.

Okay, let's get back to our example: we have a `ResultSet` object named `customerResultSet` that has five rows containing the column values retrieved from the `customer_id`, `first_name`, `last_name`, `dob`, and `phone` columns in the `customers` table. The following example shows a `while` loop that reads the column values from `customerResultSet` into the `customerId`, `firstName`, `lastName`, `dob`, and `phone` objects created earlier, the contents of which are displayed:

```
while (customerResultSet.next()) {
    customerId = customerResultSet.getInt("customer_id");
    firstName = customerResultSet.getString("first_name");
    lastName = customerResultSet.getString("last_name");
    dob = customerResultSet.getDate("dob");
```

```
    phone = customerResultSet.getString("phone");

    System.out.println("customerId = " + customerId);
    System.out.println("firstName = " + firstName);
    System.out.println("lastName = " + lastName);
    System.out.println("dob = " + dob);
    System.out.println("phone = " + phone);
} // end of while loop
```

When there are no more rows to read from `customerResultSet`, the `next()` method returns `false` and the loop terminates. You'll notice that the example passes the name of the column to be read to the get methods, rather than numeric positions. Also, I've copied the column values into Java variables and objects; for example, the value returned from `customerResultSet` `.getInt("customer_id")` is copied to `customerId`. You don't have to do that copy: you could simply use the get method call whenever you need the value. However, it is generally better if you copy it to a Java variable or object because it will save time if you use that value more than once, and it makes your code more readable.

Step 3: Close the ResultSet Object

Once you've finished with your `ResultSet` object, you must close that `ResultSet` object using the `close()` method. The following example closes `customerResultSet`:

```
customerResultSet.close();
```

NOTE
It is important that you remember to close your `ResultSet` object once you've finished with it. This ensures that it is scheduled for garbage collection.

Now that you've seen how to retrieve rows, I will show you how to add rows to a database table using JDBC.

Adding Rows to the Database

You use the SQL `INSERT` statement to add rows to a table. There are two main ways you can perform an `INSERT` statement using JDBC:

- Use the `executeUpdate()` method defined in the `Statement` class.

- Use the `execute()` method defined in the `PreparedStatement` class. (I will discuss this class later in this chapter.)

The examples in this section illustrate how to add a row to the `customers` table. The `customer_id`, `first_name`, `last_name`, `dob`, and `phone` columns for this new row will be set to 6; Jason; Price; February 22, 1969; and 800-555-1216, respectively.

To add this new row, I'll use the same `Statement` object declared earlier (`myStatement`), along with the same variables and objects that were used to retrieve the rows from the `customers` table in the previous section. First off, I'll set those variables and objects to the values that I want to set the database columns to in the customers table:

```
customerId = 6;
firstName = "Jason";
lastName = "Red";
dob = java.sql.Date.valueOf("1969-02-22");
phone = "800-555-1216";
```

> **NOTE**
> *The java.sql.Date class stores dates using the format YYYY-MM-DD, where YYYY is the year, MM is the month number, and DD is the day number. You can also use the java.sql.Time and java.sql.Timestamp classes to represent times and dates containing times, respectively.*

When you attempt to specify a date in a SQL statement, you first convert it to a format that the database can understand using the TO_DATE() built-in database function. TO_DATE() accepts a string containing a date, along with the format for that date. You'll see the use of the TO_DATE() function shortly in the INSERT statement example. Later in this chapter, I'll discuss the Oracle JDBC extensions, and you'll see an additional—and superior—way of representing Oracle specific dates using the oracle.sql.DATE type.

Okay, we're ready to perform an INSERT to add the new row to the customers table. The myStatement object is used to perform the INSERT statement, setting the customer_id, first_name, last_name, dob, and phone column values equal to the values previously set in the customerId, firstName, lastName, dob, and phone variables.

```
myStatement.executeUpdate(
  "INSERT INTO customers " +
  "(customer_id, first_name, last_name, dob, phone) VALUES (" +
    customerId + ", '" + firstName + "', '" + lastName + "', " +
  "TO_DATE('" + dob + "', 'YYYY, MM, DD'), '" + phone + "')"
);
```

Notice the use of the TO_DATE() function to convert the contents of the dob object to an acceptable Oracle database date. Once this statement has completed, the customers table will contain the new row.

Modifying Rows in the Database

You use the SQL UPDATE statement to modify existing rows in a table. Just as with performing an INSERT statement with JDBC, you can use the executeUpdate() method defined in the Statement class or the execute() method defined in the PreparedStatement class. Use of the PreparedStatement class is covered later in this chapter.

The following example illustrates how to modify the row where the customer_id column is equal to 1:

```
first_name = "Jean";
myStatement.executeUpdate(
```

```
  "UPDATE customers " +
  "SET first_name = '" + firstName + "' " +
  "WHERE customer_id = 1"
);
```

Once this statement has completed, customer #1's first name will be set to "Jean".

Deleting Rows from the Database

You use the SQL DELETE statement to delete existing rows from a table. You can use the executeUpdate() method defined in the Statement class or the execute() method defined in the PreparedStatement class.

The following example illustrates how to delete customer #5 from the customers table:

```
myStatement.executeUpdate(
  "DELETE FROM customers " +
  "WHERE customer_id = 5"
);
```

Once this statement has completed, the row for customer #5 will have been removed from the customers table.

Handling Numbers

This section describes the issues associated with storing numbers in your Java programs. An Oracle database is capable of storing numbers with a precision of up to 38 digits. In the context of number representation, precision refers to the accuracy with which a floating-point number may be represented in a digital computer's memory. The 38 digits of precision offered by the database allows you to store very large numbers.

That's fine when working with numbers in the database, but as you have seen, Java uses its own set of types to represent numbers, so you must be careful when selecting the Java type that will be used to represent numbers in your programs, especially if those numbers are going to be stored in a database.

To store integers in your Java program, you can use the short, int, long, or java.math .BigInteger types, depending on how big the integer you want to store is and how much memory space you want to use. Table 15-4 shows the number of bits used to store short, int, and long types, along with the low and high values supported by each type:

Type	Bits	Low Value	High Value
short	16	–32768	32767
int	32	–2147483648	2147483647
long	64	–9223372036854775808	9223372036854775807

TABLE 15-4. *short, int, and long Types*

To store floating-point numbers in your Java programs, you can use the `float`, `double`, or `java.math.BigDecimal` types. Table 15-5 shows the same columns as Table 15-4 for the `float` and `double` types, along with the precision supported by each of these types:

As you can see, a `float` may be used to store floating-point numbers with a precision of up to 6 digits, and a `double` may used for floating-point numbers with a precision of up to 15 digits. If you have a floating-point number that requires more than 15 digits of precision for storage in your Java program, you can use the `java.math.BigDecimal` type, which can store an arbitrarily long floating-point number.

In addition to these types, you can also use one of the Oracle JDBC extension types to store your integer or floating-point numbers. This type is `oracle.sql.NUMBER`, and allows you to store numbers with up to 38 digits of precision. You'll learn more about the `oracle.sql.NUMBER` type later in this chapter.

NOTE
For Oracle10g, you can use the `oracle.sql.BINARY_FLOAT` and `oracle.sql.BINARY_DOUBLE` types. These types allow you to store the new Oracle10g BINARY_FLOAT and BINARY_DOUBLE numbers.

Let's take a look at some examples of using these integer and floating-point types to store the `product_id` and `price` column values for a row retrieved from the `products` table. Assume that a `ResultSet` object named `productResultSet` has been populated with the `product_id` and `price` columns for a row from the `products` table. The `product_id` column is defined as a database `INTEGER`, and the price column is defined as a database `NUMBER`. The following example creates variables of the various integer and floating-point types and retrieves the `product_id` and `price` column values into those variables:

```
short productIdShort = productResultSet.getShort("product_id");
int productIdInt = productResultSet.getInt("product_id");
long productIdLong = productResultSet.getLong("product_id");
float priceFloat = productResultSet.getFloat("price");
double priceDouble = productResultSet.getDouble("price");
java.math.BigDecimal priceBigDec = productResultSet.getBigDecimal("price");
```

Notice the use of the different get methods to retrieve the column values as the different types, the output of which is then stored in a Java variable of the appropriate type.

Type	Bits	Low Value	High Value	Precision
float	32	−3.4E+38	3.4E+38	6 digits
double	64	−1.7E+308	1.7E+308	15 digits

TABLE 15-5.   *float and double Types*

Handling Database Null Values

A column in a database table may be defined as being NULL or NOT NULL. NULL indicates that the column may store a NULL value; NOT NULL indicates that the column may not contain a NULL value. A NULL value means that the value is unknown. When a table is created in the database and you don't specify that a column is NULL or NOT NULL, the database assumes you mean NULL.

The Java object types, such as String, may be used to store database NULL values. When a SELECT statement is used to retrieve a column that contains a NULL value into a Java String, that String will contain a Java null value. For example, the phone column (defined as a VARCHAR2) for customer #5 is NULL, and the following statement uses the getString() method to read that value into a String named phone:

```
phone = customerResultSet.getString("phone");
```

Once the statement is run, the phone Java String will contain the Java null value.

That's fine for NULL values being stored in Java objects, but what about the Java numeric, logical, and bit type types? If you retrieve a NULL value into a Java numeric, logical, or bit variable— int, float, boolean, and byte, for example—that variable will contain the value zero. To the database, zero and NULL are different values: zero is a definite value, NULL means the value is unknown. This causes a problem if you want to differentiate between zero and NULL in your Java program.

There are two ways to get around this problem:

■ You can use the wasNull() method in the ResultSet. The wasNull() method returns true if the value retrieved from the database was NULL; otherwise, the method returns false.

■ You can use a Java *wrapper class*. A wrapper class is a Java class that allows you to define a *wrapper object*, which can then be used to store the column value returned from the database. A wrapper object stores database NULL values as Java null values, and non-NULL values are stored as regular values.

Let's take a look at an example that illustrates the use of first technique, using product #12 from the products table. This row has a NULL value in the product_type_id column, and this column is defined as a database INTEGER. Also, assume that a ResultSet object named productResultSet has been populated with the product_id and product_type_id columns for product #12 from the products table. The following example uses the wasNull() method to check if the value read for the product_type_id column was NULL:

```
System.out.println("product_type_id = " +
  productResultSet.getInt("product_type_id"));
if (productResultSet.wasNull()) {
  System.out.println("Last value read was NULL");
}
```

Because the product_type_id column contains a NULL value, wasNull() will return true, so the string "Last value read was NULL" would be displayed.

Before you see an example of the second method that uses the Java wrapper classes, I need to explain what these wrapper classes actually are. The wrapper classes are defined in the `java.lang` package, with the following seven wrapper classes being defined in that package:

- `java.lang.Short`
- `java.lang.Integer`
- `java.lang.Long`
- `java.lang.Float`
- `java.lang.Double`
- `java.lang.Boolean`
- `java.lang.Byte`

Objects declared using these wrapper classes can be used to represent database NULL values for the various types of numbers, as well as for the `Boolean` type. When a database NULL is retrieved into such an object, it will contain the Java `null` value. The following example declares a `java.lang.Integer` named `productTypeId`:

```
java.lang.Integer productTypeId;
```

A database NULL may then be stored in `productTypeId` using a call to the `getObject()` method, as shown in the following example:

```
productTypeId =
    (java.lang.Integer) productResultSet.getObject("product_type_id");
```

The `getObject()` method returns an instance of the `java.lang.Object` class and must be cast into an appropriate type, in this case, to a `java.lang.Integer`. Assuming this example reads the same row from `productResultSet` as the previous example, `getObject()` will return a Java `null` value, and this value will be copied into `productTypeId`. Of course, if the value retrieved from the database had a value other than NULL, `productTypeId` would contain that value. For example, if the value retrieved from the database was 1, `productTypeId` would contain the value 1.

You can also use a wrapper object in a JDBC statement that performs an INSERT or UPDATE to set a column to a regular value or a NULL value. If you want to set a column value to NULL using a wrapper object, you would set that wrapper object to `null` and use it in an INSERT or UPDATE statement to set the database column to NULL. The following example sets the `price` column for product #12 to NULL using a `java.lang.Double` object that is set to `null`:

```
java.lang.Double price = null;
myStatement.executeUpdate(
    "UPDATE products " +
    "SET price = " + price + " " +
    "WHERE product_id = 12"
);
```

Controlling Database Transactions

In Chapter 8 you learned about database transactions and how to use the SQL COMMIT statement to permanently record changes you make to the contents of tables. You also saw how to use the ROLLBACK statement to undo changes in a database transaction. The same concepts apply to SQL statements executed using JDBC statements within your Java programs.

By default, the results of your INSERT, UPDATE, and DELETE statements executed using JDBC are immediately committed. This is known as *auto-commit* mode.

NOTE
Generally, using auto-commit mode is not the preferred way of committing changes because it is counter to the idea of considering transactions as logical units of work. With auto-commit mode, all statements are considered as individual transactions, and this is usually an incorrect assumption. Also, auto-commit mode may cause your SQL statements to take longer to complete, due to the fact that each statement is always committed.

Fortunately, you can enable or disable auto-commit mode using the setAutoCommit() method of the Connection class, passing it a Boolean true or false value. The following example disables auto-commit mode for the Connection object named myConnection:

```
myConnection.setAutoCommit(false);
```

NOTE
You can also enable auto-commit mode using
setAutoCommit(true).

Once auto-commit has been disabled, you can commit your transaction changes using the commit() method of the Connection class, or you can roll back your changes using the rollback() method. In the following example, the commit() method is used to commit changes made to the database using the myConnection object:

```
myConnection.commit();
```

In the next example, the rollback() method is used to roll back changes made to the database:

```
myConnection.rollback();
```

If auto-commit has been disabled and you close your Connection object, an implicit commit is performed. Therefore, any DML statements you have performed up to that point and haven't already committed will be committed automatically.

Performing Data Definition Language Statements

The SQL Data Definition Language (DDL) statements are used to create database users, tables, and many other types of database structures that make up a database. DDL consists of statements such as CREATE, ALTER, DROP, TRUNCATE, and RENAME. DDL statements may be performed in JDBC using the execute() method of the Statement class. In the following example, the CREATE TABLE statement is used to create a table named addresses, which may be used to store customer addresses:

```
myStatement.execute(
    "CREATE TABLE addresses (" +
    "  address_id INTEGER CONSTRAINT addresses_pk PRIMARY KEY," +
    "  customer_id INTEGER CONSTRAINT addresses_fk_customers " +
    "    REFERENCES customers(customer_id)," +
    "  street VARCHAR2(20) NOT NULL," +
    "  city VARCHAR2(20) NOT NULL," +
    "  state CHAR(2) NOT NULL" +
    ")"
);
```

NOTE
Performing a DDL statement results in an implicit commit being issued. Therefore, if you've performed uncommitted DML statements prior to issuing a DDL statement, those DML statements will also be committed.

Handling Exceptions

When an error occurs in either the database or the JDBC driver, a java.sql.SQLException will be raised. The java.sql.SQLException class is a subclass of the java.lang.Exception class. For this reason, you must either place all your JDBC statements within a try/catch statement, or your code must throw a java.sql.SQLException. When such an exception occurs, Java attempts to locate the appropriate handler to process the exception.

If you include a handler for a java.sql.SQLException in a catch clause, when an error occurs in either the database or the JDBC driver, Java will move to that handler and run the appropriate code that you've included in that catch clause. In this code, you can do things like display the error code and error message, which will help you determine what happened.

The following try/catch statement contains a handler for exceptions of type java.sql .SQLException that may occur in the try statement:

```
try {
    ...
} catch (SQLException e) {
    ...
}
```

NOTE
I'm assuming java.sql. has been imported so I can simply
use SQLException in the catch, rather than having to reference
java.sql.SQLException.*

The try statement will contain your JDBC statements that may cause a SQLException to
be thrown, and the catch clause will contain your error handling code.

The SQLException class defines four methods that are useful for finding out what caused
the exception to occur:

- **getErrorCode()**   In the case of errors that occur in the database or the JDBC driver,
  this method returns the Oracle error code, which is a five-digit number.

- **getMessage()**   In the case of errors that occur in the database, this method returns
  the error message, along with the five-digit Oracle error code. In the case of errors that
  occur in the JDBC driver, this method returns just the error message.

- **getSQLState()**   In the case of errors that occur in the database, this method returns
  a five-digit code containing the SQL state. In the case of errors that occur in the JDBC
  driver, this method doesn't return anything of interest.

- **printStackTrace()**   This method displays the contents of the stack when the exception
  occurred. This information may further assist you in finding out what went wrong.

The following try/catch statement illustrates the use of these four methods:

```
try {
  ...
} catch (SQLException e) {
  System.out.println("Error code = " + e.getErrorCode());
  System.out.println("Error message = " + e.getMessage());
  System.out.println("SQL state = " + e.getSQLState());
  e.printStackTrace();
}
```

If your code throws a SQLException rather than handling it locally as just shown, Java will
search for an appropriate handler in the calling procedure or function until one is found. If none
are found, the exception will be handled by the default exception handler, which displays the
Oracle error code, the error message, and the stack trace.

Closing Your JDBC Objects

In the examples shown in this chapter, I've created a number of JDBC objects: a Connection
object named myConnection, a Statement object named myStatement, and two ResultSet
objects named customerResultSet and productResultSet. As mentioned earlier in the
section on result sets, ResultSet objects should be closed when they are no longer needed

using the close() method. Similarly, you should also close the Statement and Connection objects when those objects are no longer needed.

In the following example, the myStatement and myConnection objects are closed using the close() method:

```
myStatement.close();
myConnection.close();
```

You should typically close your Statement and Connection objects in a finally clause. Any code contained in a finally clause is guaranteed to be run, no matter how control leaves the try statement. If you want to add a finally clause to close your Statement and Connection objects, those objects should be declared before the first try/catch statement used to trap exceptions. The following example shows how to structure the main() method so that the Statement and Connection objects may be closed in a finally clause:

```
public static void main (String args []) {
  // declare Connection and Statement objects
  Connection myConnection = null;
  Statement myStatement = null;

  try {
    // register the Oracle JDBC drivers
    DriverManager.registerDriver(
      new oracle.jdbc.driver.OracleDriver()
    );

    // connect to the database as store
    // using the Oracle JDBC Thin driver
    myConnection = DriverManager.getConnection(
      "jdbc:oracle:thin:@localhost:1521:ORCL",
      "store",
      "store_password"
    );

    // create a Statement object
    myStatement = myConnection.createStatement();

    // more of your code goes here
    ...
  } catch (SQLException e) {
    e.printStackTrace();
  } finally {
    try {
      // close the Statement object using the close() method
      if (myStatement != null) {
        myStatement.close();
      }

      // close the Connection object using the close() method
      if (myConnection != null) {
```

```
      myConnection.close();
    }
  } catch (SQLException e) {
    e.printStackTrace();
  }
}
} // end of main()
```

Notice that the code in the `finally` clause checks to see if the `Statement` and `Connection` objects are not equal to `null` before closing them using the `close()` method. If they are equal to `null`, there is no need to close them. Because the code in the `finally` clause is the last thing to be run and is guaranteed to be run, the `Statement` and `Connection` objects are always closed if required, regardless of what else happens in your program. For the sake of brevity, only the first program featured in this chapter uses a `finally` clause to close the `Statement` and `Connection` objects.

You have now seen how to write JDBC statements that connect to a database, run DML and DDL statements, control transactions, handle exceptions, and close JDBC objects. The following section contains a complete program that illustrates the use of JDBC.

Example Program: BasicExample1.java

The program `BasicExample1.java` shown in the following listing is a complete Java program that uses JDBC to access the database tables owned by `store`. This program and the other programs featured in this chapter may be found in the `Java` folder where you extracted this book's Zip file. The program performs the following tasks:

1. Imports the JDBC packages

2. Registers the Oracle JDBC drivers

3. Creates `Connection` and `Statement` objects

4. Connects to the database as the `store` database user using the Oracle JDBC Thin driver

5. Adds a new row to the `customers` table using an `INSERT` statement

6. Updates customer #1's first name using an `UPDATE` statement

7. Deletes customer #5 using a `DELETE` statement

8. Creates and populates a `ResultSet` object using a `SELECT` statement that retrieves the column values for all the rows from the `customers` table

9. Reads the values from the `ResultSet` object using the get methods and stores those values for subsequent display

10. Closes that `ResultSet` object

11. Performs a rollback to undo the changes made to the `customers` table

12. Creates and populates another `ResultSet` object with the `product_id, product_type_id,` and `price` columns for product #12 (which has a database `NULL` value in the `product_type_id` column) retrieved from the `products` table

13. Reads and displays the column values for product #12 using the get methods, checks the `product_type_id` column using the `wasNull()` method, stores the value for the `product_type_id` column in a `java.lang.Integer` wrapper object (wrapper objects store database NULL values as Java `null` values), and uses various numeric variables to retrieve and display the `product_id` and `price` column values

14. Closes the `ResultSet` object

15. Creates a new table named `addresses` using the SQL DDL `CREATE TABLE` statement

16. Drops the `addresses` table using the `DROP TABLE` statement

17. Closes the `Statement` and `Connection` objects in a `finally` clause

```
/*
  BasicExample1.java shows how to:
  - import the JDBC packages
  - load the Oracle JDBC drivers
  - connect to a database
  - perform DML statements
  - control transactions
  - use ResultSet objects to retrieve rows
  - use the get methods
  - perform DDL statements
*/

// import the JDBC packages
import java.sql.*;

public class BasicExample1 {
  public static void main (String args []) {
    // declare Connection and Statement objects
    Connection myConnection = null;
    Statement myStatement = null;

    try {
      // register the Oracle JDBC drivers
      DriverManager.registerDriver(
        new oracle.jdbc.OracleDriver()
      );

      // EDIT IF NECESSARY
      // create a Connection object, and connect to the database
      // as store using the Oracle JDBC Thin driver
      myConnection = DriverManager.getConnection(
        "jdbc:oracle:thin:@localhost:1521:ORCL",
        "store",
        "store_password"
      );
```

```java
// disable auto-commit mode
myConnection.setAutoCommit(false);

// create a Statement object
myStatement = myConnection.createStatement();

// create variables and objects used to represent
// column values
int customerId = 6;
String firstName = "Jason";
String lastName = "Red";
java.sql.Date dob = java.sql.Date.valueOf("1969-02-22");
java.sql.Time dobTime;
java.sql.Timestamp dobTimestamp;
String phone = "800-555-1216";

// perform SQL INSERT statement to add a new row to the
// customers table using the values set in the previous
// step - the executeUpdate() method of the Statement
// object is used to perform the INSERT
myStatement.executeUpdate(
  "INSERT INTO customers " +
  "(customer_id, first_name, last_name, dob, phone) VALUES (" +
    customerId + ", '" + firstName + "', '" + lastName + "', " +
  "TO_DATE('" + dob + "', 'YYYY, MM, DD'), '" + phone + "')"
);
System.out.println("Added row to customers table");

// perform SQL UPDATE statement to modify the first_name
// column of customer #1
firstName = "Jean";
myStatement.executeUpdate(
  "UPDATE customers " +
  "SET first_name = '" + firstName + "' " +
  "WHERE customer_id = 1"
);
System.out.println("Updated row in customers table");

// perform SQL DELETE statement to remove customer #5
myStatement.executeUpdate(
  "DELETE FROM customers " +
  "WHERE customer_id = 5"
);
System.out.println("Deleted row from customers table");

// create a ResultSet object, and populate it with the
// result of a SELECT statement that retrieves the
// customer_id, first_name, last_name, dob, and phone columns
```

```
// for all the rows from the customers table  - the
// executeQuery() method of the Statement object is used
// to perform the SELECT
ResultSet customerResultSet = myStatement.executeQuery(
  "SELECT customer_id, first_name, last_name, dob, phone " +
  "FROM customers"
);
System.out.println("Retrieved rows from customers table");

// loop through the rows in the ResultSet object using the
// next() method, and use the get methods to read the values
// retrieved from the database columns
while (customerResultSet.next()) {
  customerId = customerResultSet.getInt("customer_id");
  firstName = customerResultSet.getString("first_name");
  lastName = customerResultSet.getString("last_name");
  dob = customerResultSet.getDate("dob");
  dobTime = customerResultSet.getTime("dob");
  dobTimestamp = customerResultSet.getTimestamp("dob");
  phone = customerResultSet.getString("phone");

  System.out.println("customerId = " + customerId);
  System.out.println("firstName = " + firstName);
  System.out.println("lastName = " + lastName);
  System.out.println("dob = " + dob);
  System.out.println("dobTime = " + dobTime);
  System.out.println("dobTimestamp = " + dobTimestamp);
  System.out.println("phone = " + phone);
} // end of while loop

// close the ResultSet object using the close() method
customerResultSet.close();

// rollback the changes made to the database
myConnection.rollback();

// create numeric variables to store the product_id and price columns
short productIdShort;
int productIdInt;
long productIdLong;
float priceFloat;
double priceDouble;
java.math.BigDecimal priceBigDec;

// create another ResultSet object and retrieve the
// product_id, product_type_id, and price columns for product #12
// (this row has a NULL value in the product_type_id column)
```

```
ResultSet productResultSet = myStatement.executeQuery(
  "SELECT product_id, product_type_id, price " +
  "FROM products " +
  "WHERE product_id = 12"
);
System.out.println("Retrieved row from products table");

while (productResultSet.next()) {
  System.out.println("product_id = " +
    productResultSet.getInt("product_id"));
  System.out.println("product_type_id = " +
    productResultSet.getInt("product_type_id"));

  // check if the value just read by the get method was NULL
  if (productResultSet.wasNull()) {
    System.out.println("Last value read was NULL");
  }

  // use the getObject() method to read the value, and convert it
  // to a wrapper object - this converts a database NULL value to a
  // Java null value
  java.lang.Integer productTypeId =
    (java.lang.Integer) productResultSet.getObject("product_type_id");
  System.out.println("productTypeId = " + productTypeId);

  // retrieve the product_id and price column values into
  // the various numeric variables created earlier
  productIdShort = productResultSet.getShort("product_id");
  productIdInt = productResultSet.getInt("product_id");
  productIdLong = productResultSet.getLong("product_id");
  priceFloat = productResultSet.getFloat("price");
  priceDouble = productResultSet.getDouble("price");
  priceBigDec = productResultSet.getBigDecimal("price");
  System.out.println("productIdShort = " + productIdShort);
  System.out.println("productIdInt = " + productIdInt);
  System.out.println("productIdLong = " + productIdLong);
  System.out.println("priceFloat = " + priceFloat);
  System.out.println("priceDouble = " + priceDouble);
  System.out.println("priceBigDec = " + priceBigDec);
} // end of while loop

// close the ResultSet object
productResultSet.close();

// perform a SQL DDL CREATE TABLE statement to create a new table
// that may be used to store customer addresses
```

```
myStatement.execute(
  "CREATE TABLE addresses (" +
  "  address_id INTEGER CONSTRAINT addresses_pk PRIMARY KEY," +
  "  customer_id INTEGER CONSTRAINT addresses_fk_customers " +
  "    REFERENCES customers(customer_id)," +
  "  street VARCHAR2(20) NOT NULL," +
  "  city VARCHAR2(20) NOT NULL," +
  "  state CHAR(2) NOT NULL" +
  ")"
);
System.out.println("Created addresses table");

// drop this table using the SQL DDL DROP TABLE statement
myStatement.execute("DROP TABLE addresses");
System.out.println("Dropped addresses table");
} catch (SQLException e) {
System.out.println("Error code = " + e.getErrorCode());
System.out.println("Error message = " + e.getMessage());
System.out.println("SQL state = " + e.getSQLState());
e.printStackTrace();
} finally {
try {
  // close the Statement object using the close() method
  if (myStatement != null) {
    myStatement.close();
  }

  // close the Connection object using the close() method
  if (myConnection != null) {
    myConnection.close();
  }
} catch (SQLException e) {
  e.printStackTrace();
}
}
} // end of main()
}
```

NOTE
*You may need to edit the line labeled with the text "EDIT IF
NECESSARY" with the correct settings to access your database. Speak
with your DBA if necessary. Also, if your DBA changes the connection
information for the database, you'll need to edit and recompile the
program before running it.*

Compile BasicExample1

To compile `BasicExample1.java`, type the following command at your operating system command prompt:

```
javac BasicExample1.java
```

If you haven't set the CLASSPATH environment variable properly, you'll get the following error message when trying to compile the `FirstExample.java` program:

```
FirstExample.java:22: cannot resolve symbol
symbol   : class OracleDriver
location: package jdbc
        new oracle.jdbc.OracleDriver()
                   ^
1 error
```

You should check the setting for your CLASSPATH environment variable—it's likely your CLASSPATH is missing the Oracle JDBC classes Zip file (`classes12.zip`, for example). Refer to the earlier section "Setting the CLASSPATH Environment Variable." Alternatively, you can simply include the full directory path to the front of `BasicExample1.java` where you saved this file. For example, if you saved the file in `E:\sql_book\java` on Windows, the command would be:

```
javac E:\sql_book\java\BasicExample1.java
```

You'll also need the operating system write permission to write the `.class` file into the directory where you perform the compilation, but that won't be a problem if you're using Windows. If you're using Unix or Linux, speak with your system administrator about directory permissions.

TIP
You can enter `javac -help` *to get help on the Java compiler.*

Run BasicExample1

Once `BasicExample1.java` is compiled, you can run the resulting executable class file named `BasicExample1.class` by first changing to the directory where that file is stored and then entering the following command:

```
java BasicExample1
```

CAUTION
Java is case-sensitive so make sure you enter `BasicExample1` *with uppercase B and E characters.*

If the program fails with the following error code and message, it means the `store` user with a password of `store_password` doesn't exist in your database:

```
Error code = 1017
Error message = ORA-01017: invalid username/password; logon denied
```

If you get this error, ask your DBA for the correct username and password.

The program may also be unable to find your database, in which case you'll get the following error:

```
Error code = 17002
Error message = Io exception: The Network Adapter could not establish
 the connection
```

Typically, there are two reasons why you might get this error:

- There is no database running on your `localhost` machine with the Oracle SID of `ORCL`.

- Oracle Net is not running, or is not listening for connections on port 1521.

You should once again check with the DBA to resolve this issue.

Assuming the program runs you should get the following output:

```
Added row to customers table
Updated row in customers table
Deleted row from customers table
Retrieved rows from customers table
customerId = 1
firstName = Jean
lastName = Brown
dob = 1965-01-01
dobTime = 00:00:00
dobTimestamp = 1965-01-01 00:00:00.0
phone = 800-555-1211
customerId = 2
firstName = Cynthia
lastName = Green
dob = 1968-02-05
dobTime = 00:00:00
dobTimestamp = 1968-02-05 00:00:00.0
phone = 800-555-1212
customerId = 3
firstName = Steve
lastName = White
dob = 1971-03-16
dobTime = 00:00:00
dobTimestamp = 1971-03-16 00:00:00.0
phone = 800-555-1213
```

```
customerId = 4
firstName = Gail
lastName = Black
dob = null
dobTime = null
dobTimestamp = null
phone = 800-555-1214
customerId = 6
firstName = Jason
lastName = Red
dob = 1969-02-22
dobTime = 00:00:00
dobTimestamp = 1969-02-22 00:00:00.0
phone = 800-555-1216
Retrieved row from products table
product_id = 12
product_type_id = 0
Last value read was NULL
productTypeId = null
productIdShort = 12
productIdInt = 12
productIdLong = 12
priceFloat = 13.49
priceDouble = 13.49
priceBigDec = 13.49
Created addresses table
Dropped addresses table
```

Prepared SQL Statements

When you send a SQL statement to the database, the database software reads the SQL statement and verifies that it is correct. This is known as *parsing* the SQL statement. The database software then builds a plan, known as the *execution plan*, to actually run the statement. So far, all the SQL statements sent to the database through JDBC have required a new execution plan to be built. This is because each SQL statement sent to the database has been different.

Suppose you had a Java application that was performing the same INSERT statement repeatedly—an example might be loading many new products to our example store, a process that would require adding lots of rows to the products table using INSERT statements. Let's consider an example that would actually do this. Assume that a class named Product has been defined as follows:

```
class Product {
   int productId;
   int productTypeId;
   String name;
   String description;
   double price;
}
```

The following code creates an array of five `Product` objects. Because the `products` table already contains rows with `product_id` values from 1 to 12, the `productId` attributes for the new `Product` objects start at 13:

```
Product [] productArray = new Product[5];
for (int counter = 0; counter < productArray.length; counter ++) {
  productArray[counter] = new Product();
  productArray[counter].productId = counter + 13;
  productArray[counter].productTypeId = 1;
  productArray[counter].name = "Test product";
  productArray[counter].description = "Test product";
  productArray[counter].price = 19.95;
} // end of for loop
```

To add the rows to the `products` table, we'll use a `for` loop that contains a JDBC statement to perform an `INSERT` statement, and the column values will come from `productArray`:

```
Statement myStatement = myConnection.createStatement();
for (int counter = 0; counter < productArray.length; counter ++) {
  myStatement.executeUpdate(
    "INSERT INTO products " +
    "(product_id, product_type_id, name, description, price) VALUES (" +
    productArray[counter]. productId + ", " +
    productArray[counter]. productTypeId + ", '" +
    productArray[counter].name + "', '" +
    productArray[counter].description + "', " +
    productArray[counter].price + ")"
  );
} // end of for loop
```

Each iteration through the loop results in an `INSERT` statement being sent to the database. Because the string representing each `INSERT` statement contains different values, the actual `INSERT` sent to the database is slightly different each time. This means that the database creates a different execution plan for every `INSERT` statement—very inefficient.

You'll be glad to know that JDBC provides a better way to run such SQL statements. Instead of using a JDBC `Statement` object to run your SQL statements, you can use a JDBC `PreparedStatement` object. A `PreparedStatement` object allows you to perform the same SQL statement but supply different values for actual execution of that statement. This is more efficient because the same execution plan is used by the database when the SQL statement is run. The following example creates a `PreparedStatement` object containing an `INSERT` statement similar to the one used in the previous loop:

```
PreparedStatement myPrepStatement = myConnection.prepareStatement(
  "INSERT INTO products " +
  "(product_id, product_type_id, name, description, price) VALUES (" +
  "?, ?, ?, ?, ?"
  ")"
);
```

There are two things you should notice about this example:

- The prepareStatement() method is used to specify the SQL statement.

- Question mark characters (?) are used to indicate the positions where you will later provide variables to be used when the SQL statement is actually run.

The positions of the question marks are important: they are referenced according to their position, with the first question mark being referenced using number 1, the second as number 2, and so forth.

The process of supplying Java variables to a prepared statement is known as *binding* the variables to the statement, and the variables themselves are known as *bind variables*. To actually supply variables to the prepared SQL statement, you must use *set* methods. These methods are similar to the get methods that I've already discussed in the section on result sets, except that set methods are used to supply variable values, rather than read them.

For example, to bind a Java int variable named intVar to the product_id column in the PreparedStatement object previously created, you use setInt(1, intVar). The first parameter indicates the numeric position of the question mark (?) in the string previously specified in the prepareStatement() method call. For this example, the value 1 corresponds to the first question mark, which supplies a value to the product_id column in the INSERT statement. Similarly, to bind a Java String variable named stringVar to the name column, you use setString(3, stringVar), because the third question mark corresponds to the name column. Other methods you can call in a PreparedStatement object include setFloat() and setDouble() for setting single-precision floating point and double-precision floating point numbers.

The following example features a loop that shows the use of set methods to bind the attributes of the Product objects in productArray to the PreparedStatement object. Notice that the execute() method is used to actually run the SQL statement:

```
for (int counter = 0; counter < productArray.length; counter ++) {
  myPrepStatement.setInt(1, productArray[counter]. productId);
  myPrepStatement.setInt(2, productArray[counter]. productTypeId);
  myPrepStatement.setString(3, productArray[counter].name);
  myPrepStatement.setString(4, productArray[counter].description);
  myPrepStatement.setDouble(5, productArray[counter].price);
  myPrepStatement.execute();
} // end of for loop
```

Once this code has completed, the products table will contain five new rows.

To set a database column to NULL using a PreparedStatement object, you may use the setNull() method. For example, the following statement sets the description column to NULL:

```
myPrepStatement.setNull(4, java.sql.Types.VARCHAR);
```

The first parameter in the call to setNull() is the numeric position of the column you want to set to NULL. The second parameter is an int that corresponds to the database type of the column that is to be set to NULL. This second parameter should be specified using one of the constants defined in the java.sql.Types class. For a VARCHAR2 column (the description column is defined as a VARCHAR2), you should use java.sql.Types.VARCHAR.

Example Program: BasicExample2.java

The program BasicExample2.java shown in the following listing contains the statements shown in the previous section.

```java
/*
  BasicExample2.java shows how to use prepared SQL statements
*/

// import the JDBC packages
import java.sql.*;

class Product {
  int productId;
  int productTypeId;
  String name;
  String description;
  double price;
}

public class BasicExample2 {
  public static void main (String args []) {
    try {
      // register the Oracle JDBC drivers
      DriverManager.registerDriver(
        new oracle.jdbc.OracleDriver()
      );

      // EDIT IF NECESSARY
      // create a Connection object, and connect to the database
      // as store using the Oracle JDBC Thin driver
      Connection myConnection = DriverManager.getConnection(
        "jdbc:oracle:thin:@localhost:1521:ORCL",
        "store",
        "store_password"
      );

      // disable auto-commit mode
      myConnection.setAutoCommit(false);

      Product [] productArray = new Product[5];
      for (int counter = 0; counter < productArray.length; counter ++) {
        productArray[counter] = new Product();
        productArray[counter].productId = counter + 13;
        productArray[counter].productTypeId = 1;
        productArray[counter].name = "Test product";
        productArray[counter].description = "Test product";
        productArray[counter].price = 19.95;
      } // end of for loop

      // create a PreparedStatement object
```

```java
PreparedStatement myPrepStatement = myConnection.prepareStatement(
  "INSERT INTO products " +
  "(product_id, product_type_id, name, description, price) VALUES (" +
  "?, ?, ?, ?, ?" +
  ")"
);

// initialize the values for the new rows using the
// appropriate set methods
for (int counter = 0; counter < productArray.length; counter ++) {
  myPrepStatement.setInt(1, productArray[counter].productId);
  myPrepStatement.setInt(2, productArray[counter].productTypeId);
  myPrepStatement.setString(3, productArray[counter].name);
  myPrepStatement.setString(4, productArray[counter].description);
  myPrepStatement.setDouble(5, productArray[counter].price);
  myPrepStatement.execute();
} // end of for loop

// close the PreparedStatement object
myPrepStatement.close();

// retrieve the product_id, product_type_id, name, description, and
// price columns for these new rows using a ResultSet object
Statement myStatement = myConnection.createStatement();
ResultSet productResultSet = myStatement.executeQuery(
  "SELECT product_id, product_type_id, " +
  "  name, description, price " +
  "FROM products " +
  "WHERE product_id > 12"
);

// display the column values
while (productResultSet.next()) {
  System.out.println("product_id = " +
    productResultSet.getInt("product_id"));
  System.out.println("product_type_id = " +
    productResultSet.getInt("product_type_id"));
  System.out.println("name = " +
    productResultSet.getString("name"));
  System.out.println("description = " +
    productResultSet.getString("description"));
  System.out.println("price = " +
    productResultSet.getDouble("price"));
} // end of while loop

// close the ResultSet object using the close() method
productResultSet.close();

// rollback the changes made to the database
myConnection.rollback();
```

```
        // close the other JDBC objects
        myStatement.close();
        myConnection.close();

    } catch (SQLException e) {
      System.out.println("Error code = " + e.getErrorCode());
      System.out.println("Error message = " + e.getMessage());
      System.out.println("SQL state = " + e.getSQLState());
      e.printStackTrace();
    }
  } // end of main()
}
```

The output from this program is as follows:

```
product_id = 13
product_type_id = 1
name = Test product
description = Test product
price = 19.95
product_id = 14
product_type_id = 1
name = Test product
description = Test product
price = 19.95
product_id = 15
product_type_id = 1
name = Test product
description = Test product
price = 19.95
product_id = 16
product_type_id = 1
name = Test product
description = Test product
price = 19.95
product_id = 17
product_type_id = 1
name = Test product
description = Test product
price = 19.95
```

The Oracle JDBC Extensions

As mentioned earlier, the Oracle extensions to JDBC contain packages and interfaces that enable you to access all of the data types provided by Oracle, along with Oracle-specific performance extensions. This section introduces you to the classes and interfaces in the Oracle JDBC packages and covers how to access some of the Oracle-specific types using the Oracle JDBC extensions. This section doesn't cover all of the Oracle types; you may read my book *Oracle9i JDBC Programming* for all Oracle types and performance enhancements. You'll learn about handling of strings, numbers, dates, and row identifiers in this section.

There are two JDBC extension packages supplied by Oracle:

- **oracle.sql** Contains the classes that support all the Oracle types
- **oracle.jdbc** Contains the interfaces that support access to an Oracle database

To import the Oracle JDBC packages into your Java programs, you may add the following `import` statements to your program:

```
import oracle.sql.*;
import oracle.jdbc.*;
```

Of course, you don't have to import all the packages: you could just import the classes and interfaces you actually use in your program. In addition, you should still import the `java.sql` packages you reference in your program. In the following sections, you'll learn the key features of the `oracle.sql` and `oracle.jdbc` packages.

The oracle.sql Package

The `oracle.sql` package contains the classes that support all of the Oracle types. Using objects of the classes defined in this package to access database columns is more efficient than using regular Java objects. This is because the database column values don't need to be converted to an appropriate base Java type first. Also, using a Java `float` or `double` to represent a floating-point number may result in a loss of precision for that number. If you use an `oracle.sql.NUMBER` object, your numbers never lose precision.

TIP
If you are writing a program that moves a lot of data around in the database, you should use the oracle.sql. classes.*

All of the `oracle.sql.*` type classes extend the `oracle.sql.Datum` class, which contains the functionality that is common to all the classes. Table 15-6 shows a subset of the `oracle.sql` classes, along with the mapping to the compatible Oracle database types.

From Table 15-6, you can see that an `oracle.sql.NUMBER` object is compatible with a database column defined using the `INTEGER` or `NUMBER` type, and a `VARCHAR2` column is compatible with an `oracle.sql.CHAR` object. Notice that an `oracle.sql.CHAR` object is also compatible with the `NCHAR` and `NVARCHAR2` database types. These types allow you to store multi-byte character sets in the database (for full details on how Oracle may be used with such types, refer to the *Globalization Support Guide* published by Oracle Corporation). The `ROWID` pseudo-column contains the physical address of a table row in the database. You can use an `oracle.sql.ROWID` object to store that.

Objects declared using the `oracle.sql.*` classes store the data as byte arrays—also known as *SQL format*—and don't reformat the data retrieved from the database. This means that no information is ever lost due to conversion into a core Java type. Each of the classes provides a `getBytes()` method that returns the binary data stored in an `oracle.sql` object as a byte array, and a `toJdbc()` method that returns the binary data as a compatible Java type. The only exception to this is the `oracle.sql.ROWID`, `toJdbc()`, which returns only an `oracle.sql.ROWID`.

Class	Compatible Database Type
oracle.sql.NUMBER	INTEGER NUMBER
oracle.sql.BINARY_FLOAT	BINARY_FLOAT (new for Oracle10g)
oracle.sql.BINARY_DOUBLE	BINARY_DOUBLE (new for Oracle10g)
oracle.sql.CHAR	CHAR VARCHAR2 NCHAR NVARCHAR2
oracle.sql.DATE	DATE
oracle.sql.ROWID	ROWID

TABLE 15-6.   *Classes and Compatible Oracle Database Types*

Each class also provides methods to convert their SQL format data to a core Java type. For example, stringValue() returns the value as Java String, intValue() returns a Java int, floatValue() returns a float, doubleValue() returns a double, bigDecimalValue() returns a java.math.BigDecimal, dateValue() returns a java.sql.Date, and so forth. You use these methods when you want to store the SQL format data in a core Java type or output the SQL data on the screen.

As you will learn shortly, the OraclePreparedStatement class, which is defined in the oracle.jdbc package, contains a number of set methods that may be used to specify column values using oracle.sql.* objects. The OracleResultSet class defines a number of get methods that may be used to read column values as oracle.sql.* objects.

Each of the oracle.sql.* classes contains a constructor that may take a byte array as input, or, as you will more frequently use, a Java variable or object. The following sections describe the details of using some of the oracle.sql classes shown in Table 15-6 in your Java programs.

The oracle.sql.NUMBER Class

The oracle.sql.NUMBER class is compatible with the database INTEGER and NUMBER types and may be used to represent a number with up to 38 digits of precision. The following example creates an oracle.sql.NUMBER object named customerId, which is set to the value 6 using the constructor:

```
oracle.sql.NUMBER customerId = new oracle.sql.NUMBER(6);
```

You can read the value stored in customerId using the intValue() method, which returns the value as a Java int. For example:

```
int customerIdInt = customerId.intValue();
```

You can also set an oracle.sql.NUMBER object to a floating-point number. The next example passes the value 19.95 to the constructor of an oracle.sql.NUMBER object named price:

```
oracle.sql.NUMBER price = new oracle.sql.NUMBER(19.95);
```

You can read the floating-point number stored in `price` using the `floatValue()`, `doubleValue()`, and `bigDecimalValue()` methods, which return a Java `float`, `double`, or `bigDecimal` respectively. You can also get the value truncated to an `int` using `intValue()`, so `19.95` would be returned as `19`. The following examples show the use of these methods:

```
float priceFloat = price.floatValue();
double priceDouble = price.doubleValue();
java.math.BigDecimal priceBigDec = price.bigDecimalValue();
int priceInt = price.intValue();
```

The `stringValue()` method returns the value as a Java `String`:

```
String priceString = price.stringValue();
```

The oracle.sql.CHAR Class

The `oracle.sql.CHAR` class is compatible with the database `CHAR`, `VARCHAR2`, `NCHAR`, and `NVARCHAR2` types. Both the Oracle database and the `oracle.sql.CHAR` class contain globalization support for many different languages. For full details of the various languages supported by Oracle, see the *Globalization Support Guide* published by Oracle Corporation.

When you retrieve character data from the database into an `oracle.sql.CHAR` object, the Oracle JDBC driver constructs and returns that object using either the database character set, WE8ISO8859P1 (ISO 8859-1 West European), or UTF8 (Unicode 3.0 UTF-8 Universal).

If you are creating your own `oracle.sql.CHAR` object for storage in the database, there are restrictions on which character set you may use, depending on the database column type that the object will be stored in. If you are storing your `oracle.sql.CHAR` object in a `CHAR` or `VARCHAR2` column, you must use US7ASCII (ASCII 7-bit American), WE8ISO8859P1 (ISO 8859-1 West European), or UTF8 (Unicode 3.0 UTF-8 Universal). If you are storing your `oracle.sql.CHAR` object in an `NCHAR` or `NVARCHAR2` column, you must use the character set used by the database.

When creating your own `oracle.sql.CHAR` object, there are two steps you must follow:

1. Create an `oracle.sql.CharacterSet` object containing the character set you wish to use.

2. Create an `oracle.sql.CHAR` object using the `oracle.sql.CharacterSet` object to specify the character set.

The following sections describe the details of these steps.

Step 1: Create an oracle.sql.CharacterSet Object   The following example creates an `oracle.sql.CharacterSet` object named `myCharSet`:

```
oracle.sql.CharacterSet myCharSet =
  CharacterSet.make(CharacterSet.US7ASCII_CHARSET);
```

The `make()` method accepts an `int` that specifies the character set to use. In this case, the constant `US7ASCII_CHARSET` (defined in the `oracle.sql.CharacterSet` class) is used to specify that the US7ASCII character set is to be used. Other values include `UTF8_CHARSET` (for UTF8), and `DEFAULT_CHARSET` (for the character set used by the database).

Step 2: Create an oracle.sql.CHAR Object   The following example creates an `oracle.sql`
`.CHAR` object named `firstName`, using the `myCharSet` object created in the previous step:

```
oracle.sql.CHAR firstName = new oracle.sql.CHAR("Jason", myCharSet);
```

The `firstName` object is populated with the string `Jason`. You can read the value stored in
`firstName` using the `stringValue()` method, which returns the value as a Java `String`. For
example:

```
String firstNameString = firstName.stringValue();
System.out.println("firstNameString = " + firstNameString);
```

This will display `firstNameString = Jason`.
Similarly, the following example creates another `oracle.sql.CHAR` object named `lastName`:

```
oracle.sql.CHAR lastName = new oracle.sql.CHAR("Price", myCharSet);
```

You can also display the value in an `oracle.sql.CHAR` object directly, as shown in the
following example:

```
System.out.println("lastName = " + lastName);
```

This statement will display the following:

```
lastName = Price
```

The oracle.sql.DATE Class
The `oracle.sql.DATE` class is compatible with the database `DATE` type. The following example
creates an `oracle.sql.DATE` object named `dob`:

```
oracle.sql.DATE dob = new oracle.sql.DATE("1969-02-22 13:54:12");
```

Notice that the constructor may accept a string in the format YYYY-MM-DD HH:MI:SS, where
YYYY is the year, MM is the month, DD is the day, HH is the hour, MI is the minute, and SS is the
second. You can read the value stored in `dob` as a Java `String` using the `stringValue()`
method, as shown in the following example:

```
String dobString = dob.stringValue();
```

In this case, `dobString` will contain `2/22/1969 13:54:12`—notice the change in format
to MM/DD/YYYY HH:MI:SS.
You can also pass a `java.sql.Date` object into the `oracle.sql.DATE` constructor, as
shown in the following example:

```
oracle.sql.DATE anotherDob =
    new oracle.sql.DATE(java.sql.Date.valueOf("1969-02-22"));
```

So, `anotherDob` will contain the `oracle.sql.DATE 1969-02-22 00:00:00`.

The oracle.sql.ROWID Class

The oracle.sql.ROWID class is compatible with the database ROWID type. The following example creates an oracle.sql.ROWID object named rowid:

```
oracle.sql.ROWID rowid;
```

Because the ROWID pseudo-column in the database contains the internal address of a row and is set by Oracle, you should only retrieve values from the database into an oracle.sql.ROWID object. I'll show you how to do that shortly.

The oracle.jdbc Package

The classes and interfaces of the oracle.jdbc package allow you to read and write column values in the database using objects declared using the oracle.sql.* classes. The oracle.jdbc package also contains a number of performance enhancements specifically for use with an Oracle database. In this section, you'll learn about the contents of the oracle.sql package and how to create a row in the customers table. Then you'll learn how to read that row using the oracle.sql.* objects created in the previous section.

The Classes and Interfaces of the oracle.jdbc Package

Table 15-7 outlines the classes and interfaces of the oracle.jdbc package.

Name	Class or Interface	Description
OracleDriver	Class	Implements java.sql.Driver. You input an object of this class when registering the Oracle JDBC drivers in your programs using the registerDriver() method of the java.sql.DriverManager class.
OracleConnection	Interface	Implements java.sql.Connection. This interface extends the standard JDBC connection functionality to use OracleStatement objects, plus Oracle performance extensions.
OracleStatement	Interface	Implements java.sql.Statement and is the superclass of the OraclePreparedStatement and OracleCallableStatement classes. This interface supports Oracle performance extensions on a per-statement basis.

TABLE 15-7. *Classes and Interfaces of the oracle.jdbc Package*

Name	Class or Interface	Description
`OraclePreparedStatement`	Interface	Implements `java.sql.PreparedStatement`, and is the superclass of `OracleCallableStatement`. This interface supports Oracle performance extensions on a per-statement basis, plus various set methods for binding `oracle.sql.*` objects.
`OracleCallableStatement`	Interface	Implements `java.sql.CallableStatement`. This interface contains various get and set methods for binding `oracle.sql.*` objects.
`OracleResultSet`	Interface	Implements `java.sql.ResultSet`. This interface contains various get methods for binding `oracle.sql.*` objects.
`OracleResultSetMetaData`	Interface	Implements `java.sql.ResultSetMetaData`. This interface contains methods for retrieving meta data about Oracle result sets, like the column names and types.
`OracleDatabaseMetaData`	Class	Implements `java.sql.DatabaseMetaData`. This class contains methods for retrieving meta data about the Oracle database, like the software version.
`OracleTypes`	Class	Defines integer constants that are used by JDBC to identify database types. This class duplicates the standard `java.sql.Types` class, along with the new constants for the Oracle types.

TABLE 15-7. *Classes and Interfaces of the* `oracle.jdbc` *Package* (continued)

In the following sections, you'll learn how to use an `OraclePreparedStatement` object, add a row to the `customers` table, and use an `OracleResultSet` object to read that row.

Using an OraclePreparedStatement Object

The `OraclePreparedStatement` interface implements `java.sql.PreparedStatement`. I described the use of a `java.sql.PreparedStatement` object to add a row to a table earlier in the section "Prepared SQL Statements." If you need a refresher on this use of such objects, I suggest you take a look at that section before proceeding.

In the previous section, you saw how to create the following four objects using the classes in the `oracle.sql` package:

- An `oracle.sql.NUMBER` object named `customerId`, which was set to 6

- An `oracle.sql.CHAR` object named `firstName`, which was set to `Jason`

- Another `oracle.sql.CHAR` object named `lastName`, which was set to `Price`

- An `oracle.sql.DATE` object named `dob`, which was set to `1969-02-22 13:54:12`

To use these objects directly in a SQL DML statement, you must use an `OraclePrepared Statement` object, which contains set methods that are capable of handling `oracle.sql.*` objects. The following example creates an `OraclePreparedStatement` named `myPrepStatement`, which will be used to add a row to the `customers` table using the `customerId`, `firstName`, `lastName`, and `dob` objects:

```
OraclePreparedStatement myPrepStatement =
  (OraclePreparedStatement) myConnection.prepareStatement(
    "INSERT INTO customers " +
    "(customer_id, first_name, last_name, dob, phone) VALUES (" +
    "?, ?, ?, ?, ?" +
    ")"
  );
```

Notice that I've used the JDBC `Connection` object created earlier named `myConnection`, and I've cast the JDBC `PreparedStatement` object returned by the `prepareStatement()` method to an `OraclePreparedStatement` object, which is stored in `myPrepStatement`. Also, I want to specify a value for the `phone` column using the fifth `?` character, even though I haven't created a corresponding `oracle.sql.*` object. I'm going to specify a database `NULL` value for this column shortly.

The next step is to bind the `oracle.sql.*` objects to `myPrepStatement` using the set methods. This involves assigning values to the placeholders marked by `?` characters in `myPrepStatement`. Just as you use set methods like `setInt()`, `setFloat()`, `setString()`, and `setDate()` to bind Java variables to a `PreparedStatement` object, you also use set methods to bind `oracle.sql.*` objects to an `OraclePreparedStatement` object, such as `setNUMBER()`, `setCHAR()`, and `setDATE()`.

The following examples illustrate how to bind the `customerId`, `firstName`, `lastName`, and `dob` objects to `myPrepStatement` using the appropriate set methods:

```
myPrepStatement.setNUMBER(1, customerId);
myPrepStatement.setCHAR(2, firstName);
myPrepStatement.setCHAR(3, lastName);
myPrepStatement.setDATE(4, dob);
```

To specify a database `NULL` value for the `phone` column (which corresponds to the fifth `?` in `myPrepStatement`), I will use the `setNull()` method:

```
myPrepStatement.setNull(5, OracleTypes.CHAR);
```

The int constant OracleTypes.CHAR is used to specify that the database column type is compatible with the oracle.sql.CHAR type. The phone column is defined as a database VARCHAR2, which is compatible with oracle.sql.CHAR.

The only thing left to do now is to run the INSERT statement using the execute() method:

```
myPrepStatement.execute();
```

This adds the row to the customers table.

Using an OracleResultSet Object

The OracleResultSet interface implements java.sql.ResultSet and contains get methods that are capable of handling oracle.sql.* objects. In this section, you'll see how to use an OracleResultSet object to retrieve the row previously added to the customers table.

The first thing needed is a JDBC Statement object through which a SQL statement may be run:

```
Statement myStatement = myConnection.createStatement();
```

Next, the following example creates an OracleResultSet object named customerResultSet, which is populated with the ROWID, customer_id, first_name, last_dob, and phone columns for customer #6:

```
OracleResultSet customerResultSet =
    (OracleResultSet) myStatement.executeQuery(
       "SELECT ROWID, customer_id, first_name, last_name, dob, phone " +
       "FROM customers " +
       "WHERE customer_id = 6"
    );
```

I defined five oracle.sql.* objects earlier: rowid, customerId, firstName, lastName, and dob. These may be used to hold the first five column values. In order to store the phone column, which contains a database NULL value. I'll create another oracle.sql.CHAR object using the myCharSet CharacterSet object created earlier:

```
oracle.sql.CHAR phone = new oracle.sql.CHAR("", myCharSet);
```

An OracleResultSet object contains a number of get methods to return the various oracle.sql.* objects. You use getCHAR() to get an oracle.sql.CHAR, getNUMBER() to get an oracle.sql.NUMBER, getDATE() to get an oracle.sql.DATE, and so forth.

The following example uses a while loop, which uses the appropriate get methods to copy the column values into the rowid, customerId, firstName, lastName, dob, and phone objects. To display the values, the example uses calls to the stringValue() method to convert the rowid, customerId, and dob objects to Java String values. For the firstName, lastName, and phone objects, the example simply uses these objects directly in the System.out.println() calls:

```
while (customerResultSet.next()) {
    rowid = customerResultSet.getROWID("ROWID");
    customerId = customerResultSet.getNUMBER("customer_id");
    firstName = customerResultSet.getCHAR("first_name");
    lastName = customerResultSet.getCHAR("last_name");
```

```
dob = customerResultSet.getDATE("dob");
phone = customerResultSet.getCHAR("phone");

System.out.println("rowid = " + rowid.stringValue());
System.out.println("customerId = " + customerId.stringValue());
System.out.println("firstName = " + firstName);
System.out.println("lastName = " + lastName);
System.out.println("dob = " + dob.stringValue());
System.out.println("phone = " + phone);
} // end of while loop
```

You have seen how to use the Oracle JDBC extension packages to add and retrieve a database row. The following section contains a complete program that illustrates the use of the Oracle JDBC extensions.

Example Program: BasicExample3.java

The program BasicExample3.java, shown in the following listing, is a complete Java program that uses the Oracle JDBC extensions to add a row to the customers table and retrieve and display that row's column values. The program performs the following tasks:

1. Imports the Oracle JDBC extension packages

2. Creates an oracle.sql.NUMBER object named customerId and sets it to 6

3. Creates two oracle.sql.CHAR objects named firstName and lastName and sets them to Jason and Price

4. Creates an oracle.sql.DATE object named dob and sets it to 1969-02-22 13:54:12

5. Creates an OraclePreparedStatement object named myPrepStatement, which contains an INSERT statement to add a row to the customers table

6. Binds the customerId, firstName, lastName, and dob objects to myPrepStatement, and sets the phone column to NULL using the setNull() method

7. Executes myPrepStatement, which adds the row to the customers table

8. Creates and populates an OracleResultSet object named customerResultSet with the ROWID, customer_id, first_name, last_name, dob, and phone columns for the new row retrieved from the customers table

9. Uses a while loop to retrieve the column values into the oracle.sql.* objects and displays their values

10. Closes the various JDBC objects

```
/*
  BasicExample3.java shows how to use the Oracle JDBC extensions
  to add a row to the customers table, and then retrieve that row
*/
```

```
// import the JDBC packages
import java.sql.*;

// import the Oracle JDBC extension packages
import oracle.sql.*;
import oracle.jdbc.*;

public class BasicExample3 {
  public static void main (String args []) {
    try {
      // register the Oracle JDBC drivers
      DriverManager.registerDriver(
        new oracle.jdbc.OracleDriver()
      );

      // EDIT IF NECESSARY
      // create a Connection object, and connect to the database
      // as store using the Oracle JDBC Thin driver
      Connection myConnection = DriverManager.getConnection(
        "jdbc:oracle:thin:@localhost:1521:ORCL",
        "store",
        "store_password"
      );

      // disable auto-commit mode
      myConnection.setAutoCommit(false);

      // create an oracle.sql.NUMBER object
      oracle.sql.NUMBER customerId = new oracle.sql.NUMBER(6);
      int customerIdInt = customerId.intValue();
      System.out.println("customerIdInt = " + customerIdInt);

      // create two oracle.sql.CHAR objects
      oracle.sql.CharacterSet myCharSet =
        CharacterSet.make(CharacterSet.US7ASCII_CHARSET);
      oracle.sql.CHAR firstName = new oracle.sql.CHAR("Jason", myCharSet);
      String firstNameString = firstName.stringValue();
      System.out.println("firstNameString = " + firstNameString);
      oracle.sql.CHAR lastName = new oracle.sql.CHAR("Price", myCharSet);
      System.out.println("lastName = " + lastName);

      // create an oracle.sql.DATE object
      oracle.sql.DATE dob = new oracle.sql.DATE("1969-02-22 13:54:12");
      String dobString = dob.stringValue();
      System.out.println("dobString = " + dobString);
```

```java
// create an OraclePreparedStatement object
OraclePreparedStatement myPrepStatement =
  (OraclePreparedStatement) myConnection.prepareStatement(
    "INSERT INTO customers " +
    "(customer_id, first_name, last_name, dob, phone) VALUES (" +
    "?, ?, ?, ?, ?" +
    ")"
  );

// bind the objects to the OraclePreparedStatement using the
// appropriate set methods
myPrepStatement.setNUMBER(1, customerId);
myPrepStatement.setCHAR(2, firstName);
myPrepStatement.setCHAR(3, lastName);
myPrepStatement.setDATE(4, dob);

// set the phone column to NULL
myPrepStatement.setNull(5, OracleTypes.CHAR);

// run the PreparedStatement
myPrepStatement.execute();
System.out.println("Added row to customers table");

// retrieve the ROWID, customer_id, first_name, last_name, dob, and
// phone columns for this new row using an OracleResultSet
// object
Statement myStatement = myConnection.createStatement();
OracleResultSet customerResultSet =
  (OracleResultSet) myStatement.executeQuery(
    "SELECT ROWID, customer_id, first_name, last_name, dob, phone " +
    "FROM customers " +
    "WHERE customer_id = 6"
  );
System.out.println("Retrieved row from customers table");

// declare an oracle.sql.ROWID object to store the ROWID, and
// an oracle.sql.CHAR object to store the phone column
oracle.sql.ROWID rowid;
oracle.sql.CHAR phone = new oracle.sql.CHAR("", myCharSet);

// display the column values for row using the
// get methods to read the values
while (customerResultSet.next()) {
  rowid = customerResultSet.getROWID("ROWID");
  customerId = customerResultSet.getNUMBER("customer_id");
```

```
      firstName = customerResultSet.getCHAR("first_name");
      lastName = customerResultSet.getCHAR("last_name");
      dob = customerResultSet.getDATE("dob");
      phone = customerResultSet.getCHAR("phone");

      System.out.println("rowid = " + rowid.stringValue());
      System.out.println("customerId = " + customerId.stringValue());
      System.out.println("firstName = " + firstName);
      System.out.println("lastName = " + lastName);
      System.out.println("dob = " + dob.stringValue());
      System.out.println("phone = " + phone);
    } // end of while loop

    // close the OracleResultSet object using the close() method
    customerResultSet.close();

    // rollback the changes made to the database
    myConnection.rollback();

    // close the other JDBC objects
    myPrepStatement.close();
    myConnection.close();

  } catch (SQLException e) {
    System.out.println("Error code = " + e.getErrorCode());
    System.out.println("Error message = " + e.getMessage());
    System.out.println("SQL state = " + e.getSQLState());
    e.printStackTrace();
  }
  } // end of main()
}
```

The output from this program is as follows:

```
customerIdInt = 6
firstNameString = Jason
lastName = Price
dobString = 2/22/1969 13:54:12
Added row to customers table
Retrieved row from customers table
rowid = 41414149465441414241414150414A70414146
customerId = 6
firstName = Jason
lastName = Price
dob = 2/22/1969 13:54:12
phone = null
dobString2 = 2/22/1969 0:0:0
```

Summary

In this chapter, you learned that

- The JDBC API enables Java to access a database.
- The Oracle JDBC drivers are used to connect to an Oracle database.
- SQL statements may be executed using JDBC.
- Oracle has developed a number of extensions to standard JDBC that allow you to gain access to all of the data types supported by an Oracle database.

In the next chapter, you'll learn how to tune your SQL statements for maximum performance.

CHAPTER
16

High Performance
SQL Tuning

In this chapter, you will

- Be introduced to SQL tuning
- See SQL tuning tips that you can use to shorten the length of time your queries take to execute
- Learn about the Oracle optimizer
- See how to compare the cost of performing queries
- Examine how to pass hints to the optimizer
- Learn about some additional tuning tools

Introducing SQL Tuning

One of the main strengths of SQL is that you don't have to tell the database exactly how to obtain the data requested. You simply issue a query specifying the information you want, and the database software figures out the best way to get it. Sometimes, you can improve the performance of your SQL statements by tuning them. In the following sections, you'll see tuning tips that can make your queries run faster; later, you'll see more advanced tuning techniques.

Use a WHERE Clause to Filter Rows

Many novices retrieve all the rows from a table when they only want one row (or a few rows). This is very wasteful. A better approach is to use a WHERE clause in a SELECT statement. That way, you restrict the rows retrieved to just those actually needed.

For example, lets say you want the details for customer #1 and #2. The following query retrieves all the rows from the customers table in the store schema (wasteful):

```
-- BAD (retrieves all rows from the customers table)
SELECT *
FROM customers;

CUSTOMER_ID FIRST_NAME LAST_NAME  DOB        PHONE
----------- ---------- ---------- ---------  ------------
          1 John       Brown      01-JAN-65  800-555-1211
          2 Cynthia    Green      05-FEB-68  800-555-1212
          3 Steve      White      16-MAR-71  800-555-1213
          4 Gail       Black                 800-555-1214
          5 Doreen     Blue       20-MAY-70
```

The next query adds a WHERE clause to the previous example to limit the rows to just those whose customer_id is 1 or 2:

```
-- GOOD (uses a WHERE clause to limit rows retrieved)
SELECT *
FROM customers
```

```
WHERE customer_id IN (1, 2);

CUSTOMER_ID FIRST_NAME LAST_NAME  DOB       PHONE
----------- ---------- ---------- --------- ------------
          1 John       Brown      01-JAN-65 800-555-1211
          2 Cynthia    Green      05-FEB-68 800-555-1212
```

You should avoid using functions in the WHERE clause as that increases execution time.

Use Table Joins Rather than Multiple Queries

It is generally more efficient to perform table joins rather than using multiple queries when retrieving data from multiple related tables. In the following example, two queries are used to get the product name and the product type name for product #1 (using two queries is wasteful). The first query gets the name and product_type_id column values from the products table for product #1. The second query then uses that product_type_id to get the name column from the product_types table.

```
-- BAD (two separate queries when one would work)
SELECT name, product_type_id
FROM products
WHERE product_id = 1;

NAME                            PRODUCT_TYPE_ID
------------------------------ ---------------
Modern Science                               1

SELECT name
FROM product_types
WHERE product_type_id = 1;

NAME
----------
Book
```

Rather than using the two queries just shown, you should write one query that uses a join between the products and product_types tables in order to retrieve the same information. The following query uses a join between the products and product_types tables using the product_type_id column:

```
-- GOOD (one query with join rather than two queries)
SELECT p.name, pt.name
FROM products p, product_types pt
WHERE p.product_type_id = pt.product_type_id
AND p.product_id = 1;

NAME                           NAME
------------------------------ ----------
Modern Science                 Book
```

This query results in the same product name and product type name being retrieved as in the first example, but the results are obtained using one query. Executing one query is generally more efficient than executing two.

You should choose the join order in your query so that you join fewer rows to tables later in the join order. For example, say you were joining three related tables named `tab1`, `tab2`, and `tab3`. Also assume `tab1` contains 1,000 rows, `tab2` 100 rows, and `tab3` 10 rows. You should join `tab1` with `tab2` first, followed by `tab2` and `tab3`.

Avoid joining complex views in your queries, because this results in the queries for the views being run first, followed by your actual query. Instead, write your query using the tables rather than the views.

Use Fully Qualified Column References When Performing Joins

Always include table aliases in your queries and explicitly indicate the appropriate alias for each column referenced in your query (this is known as fully qualifying your column references). That way, the database doesn't have to search for each column in the tables used in your query.

The following example uses the aliases p and pt for the `products` and `product_types` tables respectively, but the query doesn't fully qualify the `description` and `price` columns (bad):

```
-- BAD (description and price columns not fully qualified)
SELECT p.name, pt.name, description, price
FROM products p, product_types pt
WHERE p.product_type_id = pt.product_type_id
AND p.product_id = 1;
```

```
NAME                                   NAME
------------------------------  ----------
DESCRIPTION                                                PRICE
--------------------------------------------------  ----------
Modern Science                  Book
A description of modern science                           19.95
```

This example works, of course, but the database has to search both the `products` and `product_types` tables for the `description` and `price` columns; that's because there's no alias that tells the database which table those columns are in. The time spent by the database having to do the search is time wasted.

The next example includes the table alias p to fully qualify the `description` and `price` columns:

```
-- GOOD (fully qualified columns)
SELECT p.name, pt.name, p.description, p.price
FROM products p, product_types pt
WHERE p.product_type_id = pt.product_type_id
AND p.product_id = 1;
```

```
NAME                                NAME
----------------------------- ----------
DESCRIPTION                                          PRICE
-------------------------------------------------- ----------
Modern Science                      Book
A description of modern science                      19.95
```

Because all references to columns include a table alias, the database doesn't have to waste time searching the tables for the columns and execution time is reduced.

Use CASE Expressions Rather than Multiple Queries

Use CASE expressions rather than multiple queries when you need to perform many calculations on the same rows in a table. The following example uses multiple queries to count the number of products within various price ranges (bad):

```
-- BAD (three separate queries when one CASE statement would work)
SELECT COUNT(*)
FROM products
WHERE price < 13;

  COUNT(*)
----------
         2

SELECT COUNT(*)
FROM products
WHERE price BETWEEN 13 AND 15;

  COUNT(*)
----------
         5

SELECT COUNT(*)
FROM products
WHERE price > 15;

  COUNT(*)
----------
         5
```

Rather than using the three queries just shown, you should write one query that uses CASE expressions. For example:

```
-- GOOD (one query with a CASE expression rather than three queries)
SELECT
 COUNT(CASE WHEN price < 13 THEN 1 ELSE null END) low,
```

```
COUNT(CASE WHEN price BETWEEN 13 AND 15 THEN 1 ELSE null END) med,
COUNT(CASE WHEN price > 15 THEN 1 ELSE null END) high
FROM products;
```

```
       LOW        MED       HIGH
---------- ---------- ----------
         2          5          5
```

Notice the counts of the products with prices below $13 are labeled as `low`, products between $13 and $15 are labeled `med`, and products greater than $15 are labeled `high`.

NOTE
You can, of course, use overlapping ranges and different functions in your CASE expressions.

Add Indexes to Tables

When looking for a particular topic in a book, you can either scan the whole book looking for your topic, or you can use the book's index to find the exact location of the topic directly. An index for a database table is similar in concept to a book index, except that database indexes are used to find specific rows in a table. The downside of indexes is that when a row is added to the table, additional time is required to update the index for the new row.

Generally, you should only create an index on a column when you are retrieving a small number of rows from a table containing many rows. A good rule of thumb is that an index is useful when you expect a single query to retrieve 10 percent or less of the total rows in a table. This means that the candidate column for an index should be used to store a wide range of values. A good candidate for indexing would be a column containing a unique number for each record, while a poor candidate for indexing would be a column that only contains a small range of numeric codes, such as 1, 2, 3, or 4. This consideration applies to all database types, not just numbers. An Oracle database automatically creates an index for the primary key of a table and for columns included in a unique constraint.

Also, when you perform a hierarchical query (i.e., a query containing a CONNECT BY) you should add indexes to the columns referenced in the START WITH and CONNECT BY clauses (see Chapter 7 for details on hierarchical queries).

Normally, the DBA is responsible for creating indexes, but as an application developer, you'll be able to provide the DBA with feedback on which columns are good candidates for indexing. This is because you may know more about the application than the DBA. Chapter 10 covers indexes in depth; in that chapter you'll see how to add indexes.

Use WHERE Rather than HAVING

You use the WHERE clause to filter rows; you use the HAVING clause to filter groups of rows. Because HAVING filters groups of rows *after* they have been grouped together (which takes some time to do), you should filter rows using a WHERE clause whenever possible. That way, you avoid the time taken to group the filtered rows in the first place.

The following query retrieves the product_type_id and average price for products whose product_type_id is 1 or 2. To do this, the query performs the following:

- It uses the GROUP BY clause to group rows into blocks with the same product_type_id.

- It uses the HAVING clause to limit the returned results to those groups that have a product_type_id in 1 or 2 (bad since a WHERE clause would work).

```
-- BAD (uses HAVING rather than WHERE)
SELECT product_type_id, AVG(price)
FROM products
GROUP BY product_type_id
HAVING product_type_id IN (1, 2);

PRODUCT_TYPE_ID AVG(PRICE)
--------------- ----------
              1     24.975
              2      26.22
```

The next query rewrites the previous example to use WHERE rather than HAVING to first limit the rows whose product_type_id is 1 or 2:

```
-- GOOD (uses WHERE rather than HAVING)
SELECT product_type_id, AVG(price)
FROM products
WHERE product_type_id IN (1, 2)
GROUP BY product_type_id;

PRODUCT_TYPE_ID AVG(PRICE)
--------------- ----------
              1     24.975
              2      26.22
```

Use UNION ALL Rather than UNION

You use UNION ALL to get all the rows retrieved by two queries, including duplicate rows; you use UNION to get all non-duplicate rows retrieved by the queries. Because UNION removes duplicate rows (which takes some time to do), use UNION ALL whenever possible.

The following query uses UNION (bad since UNION ALL would work) to get the rows from the products and more_products tables; notice all non-duplicate rows from products and more_products are retrieved:

```
-- BAD (uses UNION rather than UNION ALL)
SELECT product_id, product_type_id, name
FROM products
```

```
UNION
SELECT prd_id, prd_type_id, name
FROM more_products;

PRODUCT_ID PRODUCT_TYPE_ID NAME
---------- --------------- -------------------
         1               1 Modern Science
         2               1 Chemistry
         3               2 Supernova
         3                 Supernova
         4               2 Lunar Landing
         4               2 Tank War
         5               2 Submarine
         5               2 Z Files
         6               2 2412: The Return
         7               3 Space Force 9
         8               3 From Another Planet
         9               4 Classical Music
        10               4 Pop 3
        11               4 Creative Yell
        12                 My Front Line
```

The next query rewrites the previous example to use UNION ALL. Notice all the rows from products and more_products are retrieved, including duplicates:

```
-- GOOD (uses UNION ALL rather than UNION)
SELECT product_id, product_type_id, name
FROM products
UNION ALL
SELECT prd_id, prd_type_id, name
FROM more_products;

PRODUCT_ID PRODUCT_TYPE_ID NAME
---------- --------------- -----------------------------
         1               1 Modern Science
         2               1 Chemistry
         3               2 Supernova
         4               2 Tank War
         5               2 Z Files
         6               2 2412: The Return
         7               3 Space Force 9
         8               3 From Another Planet
         9               4 Classical Music
        10               4 Pop 3
        11               4 Creative Yell
        12                 My Front Line
         1               1 Modern Science
         2               1 Chemistry
         3                 Supernova
         4               2 Lunar Landing
         5               2 Submarine
```

Use EXISTS Rather than IN

Use IN to check if a value is contained in a list. EXISTS is different from IN: EXISTS just checks for the existence of rows, whereas IN checks actual values. EXISTS typically offers better performance than IN with subqueries. Therefore you should use EXISTS rather than IN whenever possible.

The following query uses IN (bad since EXISTS would work) to retrieve products that have been purchased:

```
-- BAD (uses IN rather than EXISTS)
SELECT product_id, name
FROM products
WHERE product_id IN
  (SELECT product_id
   FROM purchases);


PRODUCT_ID NAME
---------- ----------------------------
         1 Modern Science
         2 Chemistry
         3 Supernova
```

The next query rewrites the previous example to use EXISTS:

```
-- GOOD (uses EXISTS rather than IN)
SELECT product_id, name
FROM products outer
WHERE EXISTS
  (SELECT 1
   FROM purchases inner
   WHERE inner.product_id = outer.product_id);


PRODUCT_ID NAME
---------- ----------------------------
         1 Modern Science
         2 Chemistry
         3 Supernova
```

Use EXISTS Rather than DISTINCT

You can suppress the display of duplicate rows using DISTINCT; you use EXISTS to check for the existence of rows returned by a subquery. Whenever possible, you should use EXISTS rather than DISTINCT because DISTINCT sorts the retrieved rows before suppressing the duplicate rows.

The following query uses DISTINCT (bad since EXISTS would work) to retrieve products that have been purchased:

```
-- BAD (uses DISTINCT when EXISTS would work)
SELECT DISTINCT pr.product_id, pr.name
FROM products pr, purchases pu
WHERE pr.product_id = pu.product_id;
```

```
PRODUCT_ID NAME
---------- ------------------------------
         1 Modern Science
         2 Chemistry
         3 Supernova
```

The next query rewrites the previous example to use EXISTS rather than DISTINCT:

```
-- GOOD (uses EXISTS rather than DISTINCT)
SELECT product_id, name
FROM products outer
WHERE EXISTS
  (SELECT 1
   FROM purchases inner
   WHERE inner.product_id = outer.product_id);
```

```
PRODUCT_ID NAME
---------- ------------------------------
         1 Modern Science
         2 Chemistry
         3 Supernova
```

Use Bind Variables

The Oracle database software caches SQL statements issued; the cached statement is then reused if an identical statement is issued later. When a statement is reused the execution time is reduced. There's a catch, however: the SQL statement must be *absolutely identical* in order for the cached statement to be reused. This means that

■ All characters must be the same.

■ All letters must be of the same case.

■ The use of spaces in the statement must be the same.

If you need to supply different column values in a statement then you can use bind variables instead of literal column values. You'll see examples that clarify these ideas next.

Non-Identical SQL Statements

In this section, you'll see some non-identical SQL statements. The following examples retrieve products #1 and #2 using separate non-identical SELECT statements:

```
SELECT * FROM products WHERE product_id = 1;
SELECT * FROM products WHERE product_id = 2;
```

These statements are not identical, because the value 1 is used in the first statement but the value 2 is used in the second.

The following non-identical statements have spaces in different positions:

```
SELECT * FROM  products  WHERE  product_id = 1;
SELECT * FROM products WHERE product_id = 1;
```

The following non-identical statements use a different case for some characters:

```
select * from products where product_id = 1;
SELECT * FROM products WHERE product_id = 1;
```

Now that you've seen some non-identical statements, let's take a look at defining an identical statement using a bind variable.

Defining Identical SQL Statements Using a Bind Variable

You can ensure a statement is identical by using bind variables to represent column values. You create a bind variable using the VARIABLE command. For example, the following command creates a variable named product_id_bv of type NUMBER:

```
VARIABLE product_id_bv NUMBER
```

> **NOTE**
> *You can use the types shown in Table A-1 of Appendix A to define the type of a bind variable.*

You can reference a bind variable in a SQL or PL/SQL statement by specifying a colon followed by the variable name. The following example shows an anonymous PL/SQL block that sets product_id_bv to 1:

```
BEGIN
  :product_id_bv := 1;
END;
/
```

The following query uses product_id_bv to specify the product_id column value in the WHERE clause. Because product_id_bv was set to 1 earlier, the query retrieves the details of product #1:

```
SELECT * FROM products WHERE product_id = :product_id_bv;

PRODUCT_ID PRODUCT_TYPE_ID NAME
---------- --------------- ------------------------------
DESCRIPTION                                                PRICE
-------------------------------------------------- ----------
         1               1 Modern Science
A description of modern science                           19.95
```

The next example sets product_id_bv to 2 and repeats the query:

```
BEGIN
  :product_id_bv := 2;
END;
/
SELECT * FROM products WHERE product_id = :product_id_bv;
```

```
PRODUCT_ID PRODUCT_TYPE_ID NAME
---------- --------------- -----------------------------
DESCRIPTION                                              PRICE
-------------------------------------------------- ----------
         2               1 Chemistry
Introduction to Chemistry                                  30
```

Because the query used in this example is identical to the previous query, the cached query is reused and there's an improvement in performance.

TIP
You should typically use bind variables if you're performing the same query many times. Also, in the example the bind variables are session specific and need to be reset if the session is lost.

Listing and Printing Bind Variables

You list bind variables in SQL*Plus using the VARIABLE command. For example:

```
VARIABLE
variable   product_id_bv
datatype   NUMBER
```

You display the value of a bind variable in SQL*Plus using the PRINT command. For example:

```
PRINT product_id_bv
PRODUCT_ID_BV
-------------
            2
```

Using a Bind Variable to Store a Value Returned by a PL/SQL Function

You can also use a bind variable to store returned values from a PL/SQL function. The following example creates a bind variable named average_product_price_bv and stores the result returned by the function average_product_price() (this function was described in Chapter 11 and calculates the average product price for the supplied product_type_id):

```
VARIABLE average_product_price_bv NUMBER
BEGIN
  :average_product_price_bv := average_product_price(1);
END;
/
PRINT average_product_price_bv

AVERAGE_PRODUCT_PRICE_BV
------------------------
                  24.975
```

Using a Bind Variable to Store Rows from a REFCURSOR

You can also use a bind variable to store returned values from a REFCURSOR, which can contain a list of rows. The following example creates a bind variable named products_refcursor_bv and stores the result returned by the function product_package.get_products_ref_cursor() (described in Chapter 11 and returns rows from the products table in a REFCURSOR):

```
VARIABLE products_refcursor_bv REFCURSOR
BEGIN
  :products_refcursor_bv := product_package.get_products_ref_cursor();
END;
/
PRINT products_refcursor_bv
```

```
PRODUCT_ID NAME                           PRICE
---------- ------------------------------ ----------
         1 Modern Science                 19.95
         2 Chemistry                         30
         3 Supernova                      25.99
         4 Tank War                       13.95
         5 Z Files                        49.99
         6 2412: The Return               14.95
         7 Space Force 9                  13.49
         8 From Another Planet            12.99
         9 Classical Music                10.99
        10 Pop 3                          15.99
        11 Creative Yell                  14.99

PRODUCT_ID NAME                           PRICE
---------- ------------------------------ ----------
        12 My Front Line                  13.49
```

Comparing the Cost of Performing Queries

The Oracle database software uses a subsystem known as the optimizer to generate the most efficient path to access the data stored in the tables. This path that the optimizer generates to access the data for each query is known as the execution plan. Oracle10g automatically gathers statistics about the data in your tables and indexes in order to generate the most optimal execution plan; this is known as cost-based optimization.

Comparing the execution plans generated by the optimizer will allow you to judge the relative cost of one SQL statement versus another. You can use the results to make your statements optimal. In this section, you'll learn how to view and interpret a couple of example execution plans.

NOTE
Database versions prior to Oracle10g don't automatically gather statistics, and the optimizer automatically defaults to rule-based optimization. Rule-based optimization uses syntactic rules to generate the execution plan. Cost-based optimization is typically better than rule-based optimization since the former uses actual information gathered from the data in the tables and indexes. If you're using Oracle9i or below, you can gather statistics yourself and you'll learn how to do that later in the section, "Gathering Table Statistics."

Examining Execution Plans

The optimizer generates an execution plan for a SQL statement. You can examine the execution plan using the SQL*Plus EXPLAIN PLAN command. The EXPLAIN PLAN command populates a table named plan_table with the SQL statement's execution plan; plan_table is often referred to as the plan table. You may then examine that execution plan by querying the plan table. The first thing you must do is to create the plan table.

Creating the Plan Table

To create the plan table you must run the SQL*Plus script utlxplan.sql contained in the directory ORACLE_HOME\rdbms\admin. ORACLE_HOME is the directory where the Oracle database software is installed. The following example shows the command to run the utlxplan.sql script:

```
SQL> @ e:\oracle\ora10\rdbms\admin\utlxplan.sql
```

NOTE
You'll need to replace the directory path with the path for your environment.

Creating a Central Plan Table
Your DBA could create one central plan table. That way, individual users wouldn't have to create their own plan tables. To do this, your DBA must perform the following steps:

1. Create the plan table in a schema of their choice by running the utlxplan.sql script.

2. Create a public synonym for the plan table.

3. Grant access on the plan table to the public.

For example:

```
@ e:\oracle\ora10\rdbms\admin\utlxplan.sql
CREATE PUBLIC SYNONYM plan_table FOR plan_table;
GRANT SELECT, INSERT, UPDATE, DELETE ON plan_table TO PUBLIC;
```

The `utlxplan.sql` script contains the following statement that creates the plan table:

```
create table PLAN_TABLE (
    statement_id        varchar2(30),
    timestamp           date,
    remarks             varchar2(80),
    operation           varchar2(30),
    options             varchar2(255),
    object_node         varchar2(128),
    object_owner        varchar2(30),
    object_name         varchar2(30),
    object_instance     numeric,
    object_type         varchar2(30),
    optimizer           varchar2(255),
    search_columns      number,
    id                  numeric,
    parent_id           numeric,
    position            numeric,
    cost                numeric,
    cardinality         numeric,
    bytes               numeric,
    other_tag           varchar2(255),
    partition_start     varchar2(255),
    partition_stop      varchar2(255),
    partition_id        numeric,
    other               long,
    distribution        varchar2(30),
    cpu_cost            numeric,
    io_cost             numeric,
    temp_space          numeric,
    access_predicates   varchar2(4000),
    filter_predicates   varchar2(4000),
    projection          varchar2(4000),
    time                numeric);
```

The most important columns in the plan table are shown in Table 16-1.

Generating an Execution Plan

Once you've created the plan table, you can use the EXPLAIN PLAN command to generate an execution plan for a SQL statement. The syntax for the EXPLAIN PLAN command is as follows:

```
EXPLAIN PLAN SET STATEMENT_ID = statement_id FOR sql_statement;
```

where

- *statement_id* specifies the name that you assign to the execution plan. This can be alphanumeric text.

- *sql_statement* specifies the SQL statement for which the execution plan is to be generated.

Column	Description
statement_id	Name you assign to the execution plan.
operation	Database operation performed, which can be • scanning a table • scanning an index • accessing rows from a table by using an index • joining two tables together • sorting a row set For example, the operation for accessing a table is TABLE ACCESS.
options	Name of the option used in the operation. For example, the option for a complete scan is FULL.
object_name	Name of the database object referenced in the operation.
object_type	Attribute of object. For example, a unique index has the attribute of UNIQUE.
id	Number assigned to this operation in the execution plan.
parent_id	Parent number for the current step in the execution plan. The parent_id value relates to an id value from a parent step.
position	Processing order for steps that have the same parent_id.
cost	Estimate of units of work for operation. Cost-based optimization uses disk I/O, CPU usage, and memory usage as units of work. So, the cost is an estimate of the number of disk I/Os and the amount of CPU and memory used in performing an operation.

TABLE 16-1. *Plan Table Columns*

The EXPLAIN PLAN command in the following example populates the plan table with the execution plan for a query that retrieves all rows from the customers table (notice the statement_id is CUSTOMERS):

```
EXPLAIN PLAN SET STATEMENT_ID = 'CUSTOMERS' FOR
SELECT customer_id, first_name, last_name FROM customers;
```

Once you've run this command, you may examine the execution plan stored in the plan table.

NOTE
The SELECT in the EXPLAIN PLAN statement doesn't actually return rows retrieved from the customers table. The EXPLAIN PLAN statement simply generates the execution plan that would be used if the SELECT were to be performed.

Querying the Plan Table

For querying the plan table, I have provided a SQL*Plus script named `explain_plan.sql` in the SQL directory where you extracted this book's Zip file. The script will prompt you for the `statement_id` and will then display the execution plan for the associated statement.

The `explain_plan.sql` script is as follows:

```
-- The explain_plan.sql script displays the
-- execution plan for the specified statement_id

UNDEFINE v_statement_id;

SELECT
  id ||
  DECODE(id, 0, '', LPAD(' ', 2*(level - 1))) || ' ' ||
  operation || ' ' ||
  options || ' ' ||
  object_name || ' ' ||
  object_type || ' ' ||
  DECODE(cost, NULL, '', 'Cost = ' || position)
AS execution_plan
FROM plan_table
CONNECT BY PRIOR id = parent_id
AND statement_id = '&&v_statement_id'
START WITH id = 0
AND statement_id = '&v_statement_id';
```

An execution plan stored in the plan table is organized into a hierarchy of operations similar to a tree. The operation with the `id` column value of 0 is the root of the hierarchy, and all the other operations in the plan stem from this operation. The SELECT statement in the `explain_plan.sql` script shows the operations performed in the execution plan, starting with the operation having an `id` value of 0, and navigating downward through the hierarchy of relationships between each of the operations.

The following example shows how to run the `explain_plan.sql` script to retrieve the plan created earlier for the query on the `customers` table (that plan had a `statement_id` of CUSTOMERS):

```
SQL> @ e:\sql_book\sql\explain_plan.sql
Enter value for v_statement_id: CUSTOMERS
old  12:     statement_id = '&&v_statement_id'
new  12:     statement_id = 'CUSTOMERS'
old  14:     statement_id = '&v_statement_id'
new  14:     statement_id = 'CUSTOMERS'

EXECUTION_PLAN
-----------------------------------------------
0 SELECT STATEMENT      Cost = 4
1    TABLE ACCESS FULL CUSTOMERS TABLE Cost = 1
```

Operations are executed in the following order: from inside out, and from top to bottom. Each operation feeds its results back up the chain to its immediate parent operation; the parent is then executed. In the output from the explain_plan.sql script, the operation ID is shown on the far left.

In the example execution plan, operation 1 is run first, with the results of that operation being passed to operation 0. Operation 1 involves a full table scan—indicated by the string TABLE ACCESS FULL—on the customers table. A full table scan is performed because the original SELECT statement specified that all rows be retrieved from the table (i.e., no WHERE clause is used to restrict the rows). The total cost of the entire SELECT statement is four work units, as indicated in the cost part of operation 0 in the execution plan. A work unit is the amount of processing the software has to do to perform a given operation.

NOTE
If you're using a version of the database prior to Oracle10g, then the output for the overall statement cost may be blank. That's because earlier database versions don't automatically collect table statistics. In order to gather statistics, you have to use the ANALYZE command. You'll learn how to do that later in the section, "Gathering Table Statistics."

Execution Plans Involving Table Joins

Execution plans for table joins are more complex. The following example generates the execution plan for a query that joins the products and product_types tables:

```
EXPLAIN PLAN SET STATEMENT_ID = 'PRODUCTS' FOR
SELECT p.name, pt.name
FROM products p, product_types pt
WHERE p.product_type_id = pt.product_type_id;
```

The execution plan for this query is as follows:

```
0 SELECT STATEMENT      Cost = 7
1   MERGE JOIN     Cost = 1
2     TABLE ACCESS BY INDEX ROWID PRODUCT_TYPES TABLE Cost = 1
3       INDEX FULL SCAN PRODUCT_TYPES_PK INDEX (UNIQUE) Cost = 1
4     SORT JOIN    Cost = 2
5       TABLE ACCESS FULL PRODUCTS TABLE Cost = 1
```

NOTE
If you run the example, you may get a slightly different execution plan depending on the version of the database you are using and the settings of the parameters in the database's init.ora configuration file.

This time the execution plan is more complex, and you can see the hierarchical relationships between the various operations. As mentioned, operations are executed from inside out and from top to bottom. The order in which the operations are executed in the example is 3, 2, 5, 4, 1, and 0. Table 16-2 describes each operation in the order in which they are performed.

Operation ID	Description
3	Full scan of the index `product_types_pk` (which is a unique index) to obtain the addresses of the rows in the `product_types` table. The addresses are in the form of `ROWID` values, which are passed to operation 2.
2	Accesses rows in the `product_types` table using the list of `ROWID` values passed from operation 3. The rows are passed to operation 1.
5	Accesses rows in the `products` table, which are passed to operation 4.
4	Sorts the rows passed from operation 5, which are passed to operation 1.
1	Merges the rows passed from operations 2 and 5. The merged rows are passed to operation 0.
0	Returns the rows from operation 1 to the user. Total cost of the `SELECT` is 7 work units.

TABLE 16-2. *Execution Plan Operations*

Gathering Table Statistics

If you're using a version of the database prior to Oracle10*g* (such as Oracle9*i*), then you'll have to gather table statistics yourself using the `ANALYZE` command. By default, if no statistics are available then rule-based optimization is used. Rule-based optimization isn't usually as good as cost-based optimization.

The following examples use the `ANALYZE` command to gather statistics for the `products` and `product_types` tables:

```
ANALYZE TABLE products COMPUTE STATISTICS;
ANALYZE TABLE product_types COMPUTE STATISTICS;
```

Once the statistics have been gathered, cost-based optimization will be used rather than rule-based optimization.

Comparing Execution Plans

By comparing the total cost shown in the execution plan for different SQL statements, you can determine the value of tuning your SQL. In this section, you'll compare two execution plans to see the benefit of using `EXISTS` rather than `DISTINCT` (a tip I gave earlier). The following query uses `EXISTS`:

```
-- GOOD (uses EXISTS rather than DISTINCT)
SELECT product_id, name
FROM products outer
WHERE EXISTS
  (SELECT 1
   FROM purchases inner
   WHERE inner.product_id = outer.product_id);
```

The execution plan for this query is as follows:

```
0 SELECT STATEMENT Cost = 5
1    MERGE JOIN SEMI Cost = 1
2       TABLE ACCESS BY INDEX ROWID PRODUCTS TABLE Cost = 1
3          INDEX FULL SCAN PRODUCTS_PK INDEX (UNIQUE) Cost = 1
4       SORT UNIQUE Cost = 2
5          INDEX FULL SCAN PURCHASES_PK INDEX (UNIQUE) Cost = 1
```

As you can see, the total cost of the query is 5 work units. The next query uses DISTINCT:

```
-- BAD (uses DISTINCT when EXISTS would work)
SELECT DISTINCT pr.product_id, pr.name
FROM products pr, purchases pu
WHERE pr.product_id = pu.product_id;
```

The execution plan for this query is as follows:

```
0 SELECT STATEMENT Cost = 6
1    SORT UNIQUE Cost = 1
2       MERGE JOIN Cost = 1
3          TABLE ACCESS BY INDEX ROWID PRODUCTS TABLE Cost = 1
4             INDEX FULL SCAN PRODUCTS_PK INDEX (UNIQUE) Cost = 1
5          SORT JOIN    Cost = 2
6             INDEX FULL SCAN PURCHASES_PK INDEX (UNIQUE) Cost = 1
```

The cost for the query is 6 work units. This query is more costly than the first, which only had a cost of 5 work units. If the purchases table contained more rows, then the cost difference would be even higher.

Passing Hints to the Optimizer

You can pass hints to the optimizer. A hint is an optimizer directive that influences the optimizer's choice of execution plan. The correct hint may improve the performance of a SQL statement. You can check the effectiveness of a hint by comparing the cost in the execution plan of a SQL statement with and without the hint.

NOTE
*The optimizer will typically pick the best execution plan for you without the use of hints. With the introduction of Oracle10*g *and the automatic gathering of statistics, my opinion is that the use of hints will diminish. I've included this section to show you one useful hint, and to give you a basic introduction to the subject of hints.*

In this section, you'll see an example query that uses one of the more useful hints: the FIRST_ROWS(*n*) hint. The FIRST_ROWS(*n*) hint tells the optimizer to generate an execution plan that will minimize the time taken to return the first *n* rows in a query. This hint can be useful when you don't want to wait around too long before getting *some* rows back from your query, but you still want to see all the rows.

For example, the following statement uses `FIRST_ROWS(2)` in a query that retrieves rows from the `customer` table; 2 indicates the first two rows are to be returned as soon as possible. Notice that the hint is placed within the strings `/*+` and `*/`:

```
EXPLAIN PLAN SET STATEMENT_ID = 'HINT' FOR
SELECT /*+ FIRST_ROWS(2) */ p.name, pt.name
FROM products p, product_types pt
WHERE p.product_type_id = pt. product_type_id;
```

CAUTION
Your hint must use the exact syntax shown—otherwise, the hint will be ignored. The syntax is: /*+ followed by one space, the hint, followed by one space, and */.

There are many hints that you can use, and this section has merely given you a taste of the subject. For a comprehensive list of hints, you can read the *Oracle10g Database Performance Tuning Guide* (Oracle Corporation).

Additional Tuning Tools

In this final section, I'll mention some other tools you may use for tuning, but whose use is beyond the scope of this book. Again, you can read the *Oracle10g Database Performance Tuning Guide* for full details.

Statspack Package

The Statspack package is a set of SQL, PL/SQL, and SQL*Plus scripts that allow you to collect and view performance data, such as high-resource SQL statements and database load. The most current instructions and information on installing and using the Statspack package are contained in the file `spdoc.txt` installed with the database. You'll find this file in the `ORACLE_HOME\rdbms\doc` directory.

Oracle Enterprise Manager Diagnostics Pack

The Oracle Enterprise Manager Diagnostics Pack captures operating-system, middle-tier, and application-performance data, as well as database-performance data. The Diagnostics Pack analyzes this performance data and displays the results graphically. You can also configure the Diagnostics Pack to alert you immediately to performance problems via e-mail or page. Oracle Enterprise Manager also includes software guides to help you resolve performance problems.

Automatic Database Diagnostic Monitoring

Automatic database diagnostic monitoring allows you to monitor the database for performance problems by analyzing system performance over a long period of time. You can view the performance information in Oracle Enterprise Manager. When you find performance problems, you can use the Oracle Advisors feature to further analyze and correct the problems. You'll learn about the SQL Tuning Advisor and SQLAccess Advisor next.

SQL Tuning Advisor

The SQL Tuning Advisor allows you to tune a SQL statement using the following items:

- The text of the statement
- The SQL identifier of the statement (obtained from the V$SQL_PLAN view, which is one of the views available to the DBA)
- The range of snapshot identifiers
- The SQL Tuning Set name

A SQL Tuning Set is a set of SQL statements with their associated execution plan and execution statistics. SQL Tuning Sets are analyzed to generate SQL Profiles that help the optimizer to choose the optimal execution plan. SQL Profiles contain collections of information that enable optimization of the execution plan.

SQLAccess Advisor

The SQLAccess Advisor provides you with performance advice on materialized views, indexes, and materialized view logs. The SQLAccess Advisor examines space usage and query performance and recommends the most cost-effective configuration of new and existing materialized views and indexes.

Summary

In this chapter, you learned that

- Tuning is the process of making your SQL statements run faster.
- There are a number of tips you can use to tune your SQL statements.
- The optimizer is a subsystem of the Oracle database software that generates an execution plan.
- An execution plan is a set of operations used to perform a particular SQL statement.
- Hints may be passed to the optimizer to influence the generated execution plan.
- There are a number of additional software tools you can use to tune SQL statements. One tool is the Statspack package, which is a set of SQL, PL/SQL, and SQL*Plus scripts that allow you to collect and view performance data.

Apart from the final appendix, that's the end of this book. I hope you've found the book informative and useful, and I hope I've held your interest! As you've seen, SQL is a very large subject. But armed with this book, I have every confidence you will master the subject.

APPENDIX

Oracle Data Types

This appendix contains two tables that document the data types available in Oracle SQL and may be used to define columns in a table, along with the additional types supported by Oracle PL/SQL.

Oracle SQL Types

Table A-1 shows the Oracle SQL types.

Type	Description
CHAR[(length [BYTE | CHAR])][1]	Fixed-length character data of *length* bytes or characters and padded with trailing spaces. Maximum length is 2,000 bytes.
VARCHAR2(length [BYTE | CHAR])[1]	Variable-length character data of up to *length* bytes or characters. Maximum length is 4,000 bytes.
NCHAR[(length)]	Fixed-length Unicode character data of *length* characters. Number of bytes stored is 2 * *length* for AL16UTF16 encoding and 3 * *length* for UTF8. Maximum length is 2,000 bytes.
NVARCHAR2(length)	Variable-length Unicode character data of *length* characters. Number of bytes stored is 2 * *length* for AL16UTF16 encoding and 3 * *length* for UTF8 encoding. Maximum length is 4,000 bytes.
BINARY_FLOAT	New for Oracle Database 10*g*. Stores a single precision 32-bit floating-point number. Operations involving BINARY_FLOAT are typically performed faster than on NUMBERs. BINARY_FLOAT requires 5 bytes of storage space.
BINARY_DOUBLE	New for Oracle Database 10*g*. Stores a double precision 64-bit floating-point number. Operations involving BINARY_ DOUBLE are typically performed faster than on NUMBERs. BINARY_DOUBLE requires 9 bytes of storage space.

[1]The BYTE and CHAR keywords only work with Oracle9*i* and above. If neither BYTE nor CHAR is specified, the default is BYTE.

TABLE A-1. *Oracle SQL Types*

Type	Description
NUMBER(*precision, scale*) and NUMERIC(*precision, scale*)	Variable-length number; *precision* is the maximum number of digits (in front of and behind a decimal point, if used) that may be used for the number. The maximum precision supported is 38; *scale* is the maximum number of digits to the right of a decimal point (if used). If neither *precision* nor *scale* is specified, then a number with up to a precision and scale of 38 digits may be supplied (meaning you can supply a number with up to 38 digits, and any of those 38 digits may be in front of or behind the decimal point).
DEC and DECIMAL	Subtype of NUMBER. A fixed-point decimal number with up to 38 digits of decimal precision.
DOUBLE PRECISION and FLOAT	Subtype of NUMBER. A floating-point number with up to 38 digits of precision.
REAL	Subtype of NUMBER. A floating-point number with up to 18 digits of precision.
INT, INTEGER, and SMALLINT	Subtype of NUMBER. An integer with up to 38 digits of decimal precision.
DATE	Date and time with the century, all four digits of year, month, day, hour (in 24-hour format), minute, and second. May be used to store a date and time between January 1, 4712 B.C. and December 31, 4712 A.D. Default format is specified by the NLS_DATE_FORMAT parameter (for example: DD-MON-RR).
INTERVAL YEAR[(*years_precision*)] TO MONTH	Time interval measured in years and months; *years_precision* specifies the precision for the years, which may be an integer from 0 to 9 (default is 2). Can be used to represent a positive or negative time interval.
INTERVAL DAY[(*days_precision*)] TO SECOND[(*seconds_precision*)]	Time interval measured in days and seconds; *days_precision* specifies the precision for the days, which is an integer from 0 to 9 (default is 2); *seconds_precision* specifies the precision for the fractional part of the seconds, which is an integer from 0 to 9 (default is 6). Can be used to represent a positive or negative time interval.

TABLE A-1. *Oracle SQL Types* (continued)

Type	Description
TIMESTAMP[(*seconds_precision*)]	Date and time with the century, all four digits of year, month, day, hour (in 24-hour format), minute, and second; *seconds_precision* specifies the number of digits for the fractional part of the seconds, which can be an integer from 0 to 9 (default is 6). Default format is specified by the NLS_TIMESTAMP_FORMAT parameter.
TIMESTAMP[(*seconds_precision*)] WITH TIME ZONE	Extends TIMESTAMP to store a time zone. The time zone can be an offset from UTC, such as '-5:0', or a region name, such as 'US/Pacific'. Default format is specified by the NLS_TIMESTAMP_TZ_FORMAT parameter.
TIMESTAMP[(*seconds_precision*)] WITH LOCAL TIME ZONE	Extends TIMESTAMP to convert a supplied datetime to the local time zone set for the database. The process of conversion is known as *normalizing* the datetime. Default format is specified by the NLS_TIMESTAMP_FORMAT parameter.
CLOB	Variable length single-byte character data of up to 128 terabytes.
NCLOB	Variable length Unicode national character set data of up to 128 terabytes.
BLOB	Variable length binary data of up to 128 terabytes.
BFILE	Pointer to an external file.
LONG	Variable length character data of up to 2 gigabytes. Superceded by CLOB and NCLOB types, but supported for backwards compatibility.
RAW(*length*)	Variable length binary data of up to *length* bytes. Maximum length is 2,000 bytes. Superceded by BLOB type, but supported for backwards compatibility.
LONG RAW	Variable length binary data of up to 2 gigabytes. Superceded by BLOB type but supported for backwards compatibility.

TABLE A-1. *Oracle SQL Types* (continued)

Type	Description
ROWID	Hexadecimal string used to represent a row address.
UROWID[(*length*)]	Hexadecimal string representing the logical address of a row of an index-organized table; *length* specifies the number of bytes. Maximum length is 4,000 bytes (also default).
REF *object_type*	Reference to an object type. Similar to a pointer in C.
VARRAY	Variable length array. This is a composite type and stores an ordered set of elements.
NESTED TABLE	Nested table. This is a composite type and stores an unordered set of elements.
XMLType	Stores XML data.
User defined object type	You can define your own object type and create objects of that type.

TABLE A-1. *Oracle SQL Types* (continued)

Oracle PL/SQL Types

Oracle PL/SQL supports all the types previously shown in Table A-1, plus the following additional Oracle PL/SQL specific types shown in Table A-2.

Type	Description
BOOLEAN	Boolean value (TRUE, FALSE, or NULL).
BINARY_INTEGER	Integer between -2^{31} ($-2,147,483,648$) and 2^{31} ($2,147,483,648$).

TABLE A-2. *Oracle PL/SQL Types*

Type	Description
NATURAL	Subtype of BINARY_INTEGER. A non-negative integer.
NATURALN	Subtype of BINARY_INTEGER. A non-negative integer (and cannot be NULL).
POSITIVE	Subtype of BINARY_INTEGER. A positive integer.
POSITIVEN	Subtype of BINARY_INTEGER. A positive integer (and cannot be NULL).
SIGNTYPE	Subtype of BINARY_INTEGER. An integer of –1, 0, or 1.
PLS_INTEGER	Integer between -2^{31} (–2,147,483,648) and 2^{31} (2,147,483,648). Similar to BINARY_INTEGER, but computations involving PLS_INTEGER values are faster.
STRING	Same as VARCHAR2.
RECORD	Composite of a group of other types. Similar to a structure in C.
REF CURSOR	Pointer to a set of rows.

TABLE A-2. *Oracle PL/SQL Types* (continued)

Index

O

INTERNATIONAL CONTACT INFORMATION

AUSTRALIA
McGraw-Hill Book Company
Australia Pty. Ltd.
TEL +61-2-9900-1800
FAX +61-2-9878-8881
http://www.mcgraw-hill.com.au
books-it_sydney@mcgraw-hill.com

CANADA
McGraw-Hill Ryerson Ltd.
TEL +905-430-5000
FAX +905-430-5020
http://www.mcgraw-hill.ca

**GREECE, MIDDLE EAST, & AFRICA
(Excluding South Africa)**
McGraw-Hill Hellas
TEL +30-210-6560-990
TEL +30-210-6560-993
TEL +30-210-6560-994
FAX +30-210-6545-525

MEXICO (Also serving Latin America)
McGraw-Hill Interamericana Editores
S.A. de C.V.
TEL +525-1500-5108
FAX +525-117-1589
http://www.mcgraw-hill.com.mx
carlos_ruiz@mcgraw-hill.com

SINGAPORE (Serving Asia)
McGraw-Hill Book Company
TEL +65-6863-1580
FAX +65-6862-3354
http://www.mcgraw-hill.com.sg
mghasia@mcgraw-hill.com

SOUTH AFRICA
McGraw-Hill South Africa
TEL +27-11-622-7512
FAX +27-11-622-9045
robyn_swanepoel@mcgraw-hill.com

SPAIN
McGraw-Hill/
Interamericana de España, S.A.U.
TEL +34-91-180-3000
FAX +34-91-372-8513
http://www.mcgraw-hill.es
professional@mcgraw-hill.es

**UNITED KINGDOM, NORTHERN,
EASTERN, & CENTRAL EUROPE**
McGraw-Hill Education Europe
TEL +44-1-628-502500
FAX +44-1-628-770224
http://www.mcgraw-hill.co.uk
emea_queries@mcgraw-hill.com

ALL OTHER INQUIRIES Contact:
McGraw-Hill/Osborne
TEL +1-510-420-7700
FAX +1-510-420-7703
http://www.osborne.com
omg_international@mcgraw-hill.com

Sound Off!

Visit us at **www.osborne.com/bookregistration** and let us know what you thought of this book. While you're online you'll have the opportunity to register for newsletters and special offers from McGraw-Hill/Osborne.

We want to hear from you!

Sneak Peek

Visit us today at **www.betabooks.com** and see what's coming from McGraw-Hill/Osborne tomorrow!

Based on the successful software paradigm, Bet@Books™ allows computing professionals to view partial and sometimes complete text versions of selected titles online. Bet@Books™ viewing is free, invites comments and feedback, and allows you to "test drive" books in progress on the subjects that interest you the most.

GET YOUR FREE SUBSCRIPTION
TO ORACLE MAGAZINE

Oracle Magazine is essential gear for today's information technology professionals. Stay informed and increase your productivity with every issue of *Oracle Magazine*. Inside each free bimonthly issue you'll get:

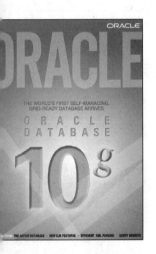

- Up-to-date information on Oracle Database, Oracle Application Server, Web development, enterprise grid computing, database technology, and business trends
- Third-party vendor news and announcements
- Technical articles on Oracle and partner products, technologies, and operating environments
- Development and administration tips
- Real-world customer stories

IF THERE ARE OTHER ORACLE USERS AT YOUR LOCATION WHO WOULD LIKE TO RECEIVE THEIR OWN SUBRIPTION TO ORACLE MAGAZINE, PLEASE PHOTOCOPY THIS FORM AND PASS IT ALONG.

Three easy ways to subscribe:

① Web
Visit our Web site at otn.oracle.com/oraclemagazine. You'll find a subscription form there, plus much more!

② Fax
Complete the questionnaire on the back of this card and fax the questionnaire side only to +1.847.763.9638.

③ Mail
Complete the questionnaire on the back of this card and mail it to P.O. Box 1263, Skokie, IL 60076-8263

YOU MUST ANSWER ALL TEN QUESTIONS BELOW.

① WHAT IS THE PRIMARY BUSINESS ACTIVITY OF YOUR FIRM AT THIS LOCATION? (check one only)
- ☐ 01 Aerospace and Defense Manufacturing
- ☐ 02 Application Service Provider
- ☐ 03 Automotive Manufacturing
- ☐ 04 Chemicals, Oil and Gas
- ☐ 05 Communications and Media
- ☐ 06 Construction/Engineering
- ☐ 07 Consumer Sector/Consumer Packaged Goods
- ☐ 08 Education
- ☐ 09 Financial Services/Insurance
- ☐ 10 Government (civil)
- ☐ 11 Government (military)
- ☐ 12 Healthcare
- ☐ 13 High Technology Manufacturing, OEM
- ☐ 14 Integrated Software Vendor
- ☐ 15 Life Sciences (Biotech, Pharmaceuticals)
- ☐ 16 Mining
- ☐ 17 Retail/Wholesale/Distribution
- ☐ 18 Systems Integrator, VAR/VAD
- ☐ 19 Telecommunications
- ☐ 20 Travel and Transportation
- ☐ 21 Utilities (electric, gas, sanitation, water)
- ☐ 98 Other Business and Services

② WHICH OF THE FOLLOWING BEST DESCRIBES YOUR PRIMARY JOB FUNCTION? (check one only)
Corporate Management/Staff
- ☐ 01 Executive Management (President, Chair, CEO, CFO, Owner, Partner, Principal)
- ☐ 02 Finance/Administrative Management (VP/Director/ Manager/Controller, Purchasing, Administration)
- ☐ 03 Sales/Marketing Management (VP/Director/Manager)
- ☐ 04 Computer Systems/Operations Management (CIO/VP/Director/ Manager MIS, Operations)
IS/IT Staff
- ☐ 05 Systems Development/ Programming Management
- ☐ 06 Systems Development/ Programming Staff
- ☐ 07 Consulting
- ☐ 08 DBA/Systems Administrator
- ☐ 09 Education/Training
- ☐ 10 Technical Support Director/Manager
- ☐ 11 Other Technical Management/Staff
- ☐ 98 Other

③ WHAT IS YOUR CURRENT PRIMARY OPERATING PLATFORM? (select all that apply)
- ☐ 01 Digital Equipment UNIX
- ☐ 02 Digital Equipment VAX VMS
- ☐ 03 HP UNIX
- ☐ 04 IBM AIX
- ☐ 05 IBM UNIX
- ☐ 06 Java
- ☐ 07 Linux
- ☐ 08 Macintosh
- ☐ 09 MS-DOS
- ☐ 10 MVS
- ☐ 11 NetWare
- ☐ 12 Network Computing
- ☐ 13 OpenVMS
- ☐ 14 SCO UNIX
- ☐ 15 Sequent DYNIX/ptx
- ☐ 16 Sun Solaris/SunOS
- ☐ 17 SVR4
- ☐ 18 UnixWare
- ☐ 19 Windows
- ☐ 20 Windows NT
- ☐ 21 Other UNIX
- ☐ 98 Other
- 99 ☐ None of the above

④ DO YOU EVALUATE, SPECIFY, RECOMMEND, OR AUTHORIZE THE PURCHASE OF ANY OF THE FOLLOWING? (check all that apply)
- ☐ 01 Hardware
- ☐ 02 Software
- ☐ 03 Application Development Tools
- ☐ 04 Database Products
- ☐ 05 Internet or Intranet Products
- 99 ☐ None of the above

⑤ IN YOUR JOB, DO YOU USE OR PLAN TO PURCHASE ANY OF THE FOLLOWING PRODUCTS? (check all that apply)
Software
- ☐ 01 Business Graphics
- ☐ 02 CAD/CAE/CAM
- ☐ 03 CASE
- ☐ 04 Communications
- ☐ 05 Database Management
- ☐ 06 File Management
- ☐ 07 Finance
- ☐ 08 Java
- ☐ 09 Materials Resource Planning
- ☐ 10 Multimedia Authoring
- ☐ 11 Networking
- ☐ 12 Office Automation
- ☐ 13 Order Entry/Inventory Control
- ☐ 14 Programming
- ☐ 15 Project Management
- ☐ 16 Scientific and Engineering
- ☐ 17 Spreadsheets
- ☐ 18 Systems Management
- ☐ 19 Workflow

Hardware
- ☐ 20 Macintosh
- ☐ 21 Mainframe
- ☐ 22 Massively Parallel Processing
- ☐ 23 Minicomputer
- ☐ 24 PC
- ☐ 25 Network Computer
- ☐ 26 Symmetric Multiprocessing
- ☐ 27 Workstation
Peripherals
- ☐ 28 Bridges/Routers/Hubs/Gateways
- ☐ 29 CD-ROM Drives
- ☐ 30 Disk Drives/Subsystems
- ☐ 31 Modems
- ☐ 32 Tape Drives/Subsystems
- ☐ 33 Video Boards/Multimedia
Services
- ☐ 34 Application Service Provider
- ☐ 35 Consulting
- ☐ 36 Education/Training
- ☐ 37 Maintenance
- ☐ 38 Online Database Services
- ☐ 39 Support
- ☐ 40 Technology-Based Training
- ☐ 98 Other
- 99 ☐ None of the above

⑥ WHAT ORACLE PRODUCTS ARE IN USE AT YOUR SITE? (check all that apply)
Oracle E-Business Suite
- ☐ 01 Oracle Marketing
- ☐ 02 Oracle Sales
- ☐ 03 Oracle Order Fulfillment
- ☐ 04 Oracle Supply Chain Management
- ☐ 05 Oracle Procurement
- ☐ 06 Oracle Manufacturing
- ☐ 07 Oracle Maintenance Management
- ☐ 08 Oracle Service
- ☐ 09 Oracle Contracts
- ☐ 10 Oracle Projects
- ☐ 11 Oracle Financials
- ☐ 12 Oracle Human Resources
- ☐ 13 Oracle Interaction Center
- ☐ 14 Oracle Communications/Utilities (modules)
- ☐ 15 Oracle Public Sector/University (modules)
- ☐ 16 Oracle Financial Services (modules)
Server/Software
- ☐ 17 Oracle9i
- ☐ 18 Oracle9i Lite
- ☐ 19 Oracle8i
- ☐ 20 Other Oracle database
- ☐ 21 Oracle9i Application Server
- ☐ 22 Oracle9i Application Server Wireless
- ☐ 23 Oracle Small Business Suite

Tools
- ☐ 24 Oracle Developer Suite
- ☐ 25 Oracle Discoverer
- ☐ 26 Oracle JDeveloper
- ☐ 27 Oracle Migration Workbench
- ☐ 28 Oracle9i/AS Portal
- ☐ 29 Oracle Warehouse Builder
Oracle Services
- ☐ 30 Oracle Outsourcing
- ☐ 31 Oracle Consulting
- ☐ 32 Oracle Education
- ☐ 33 Oracle Support
- ☐ 98 Other
- 99 ☐ None of the above

⑦ WHAT OTHER DATABASE PRODU IN USE AT YOUR SITE? (check all
- ☐ 01 Access
- ☐ 02 Baan
- ☐ 03 dbase
- ☐ 04 Gupta
- ☐ 05 IBM DB2
- ☐ 06 Informix
- ☐ 07 Ingres
- ☐ 98 Other
- ☐ 08 Microsoft
- ☐ 09 Microsoft
- ☐ 10 PeopleSo
- ☐ 11 Progress
- ☐ 12 SAP
- ☐ 13 Sybase
- ☐ 14 VSAM
- 99 ☐ None of the above

⑧ WHAT OTHER APPLICATION SER PRODUCTS ARE IN USE AT YOUR (check all that apply)
- ☐ 01 BEA
- ☐ 02 IBM
- ☐ 03 Sybase
- ☐ 04 Sun
- ☐ 05 Other

⑨ DURING THE NEXT 12 MONTHS, MUCH DO YOU ANTICIPATE YOU ORGANIZATION WILL SPEND ON COMPUTER HARDWARE, SOFTW PERIPHERALS, AND SERVICES FOR YOUR LOCATION? (check only
- ☐ 01 Less than $10,000
- ☐ 02 $10,000 to $49,999
- ☐ 03 $50,000 to $99,999
- ☐ 04 $100,000 to $499,999
- ☐ 05 $500,000 to $999,999
- ☐ 06 $1,000,000 and over

⑩ WHAT IS YOUR COMPANY'S YEA SALES REVENUE? (please choose on
- ☐ 01 $500, 000, 000 and above
- ☐ 02 $100, 000, 000 to $500, 000, 0
- ☐ 03 $50, 000, 000 to $100, 000, 0
- ☐ 04 $5, 000, 000 to $50, 000, 000
- ☐ 05 $1, 000, 000 to $5, 000, 000